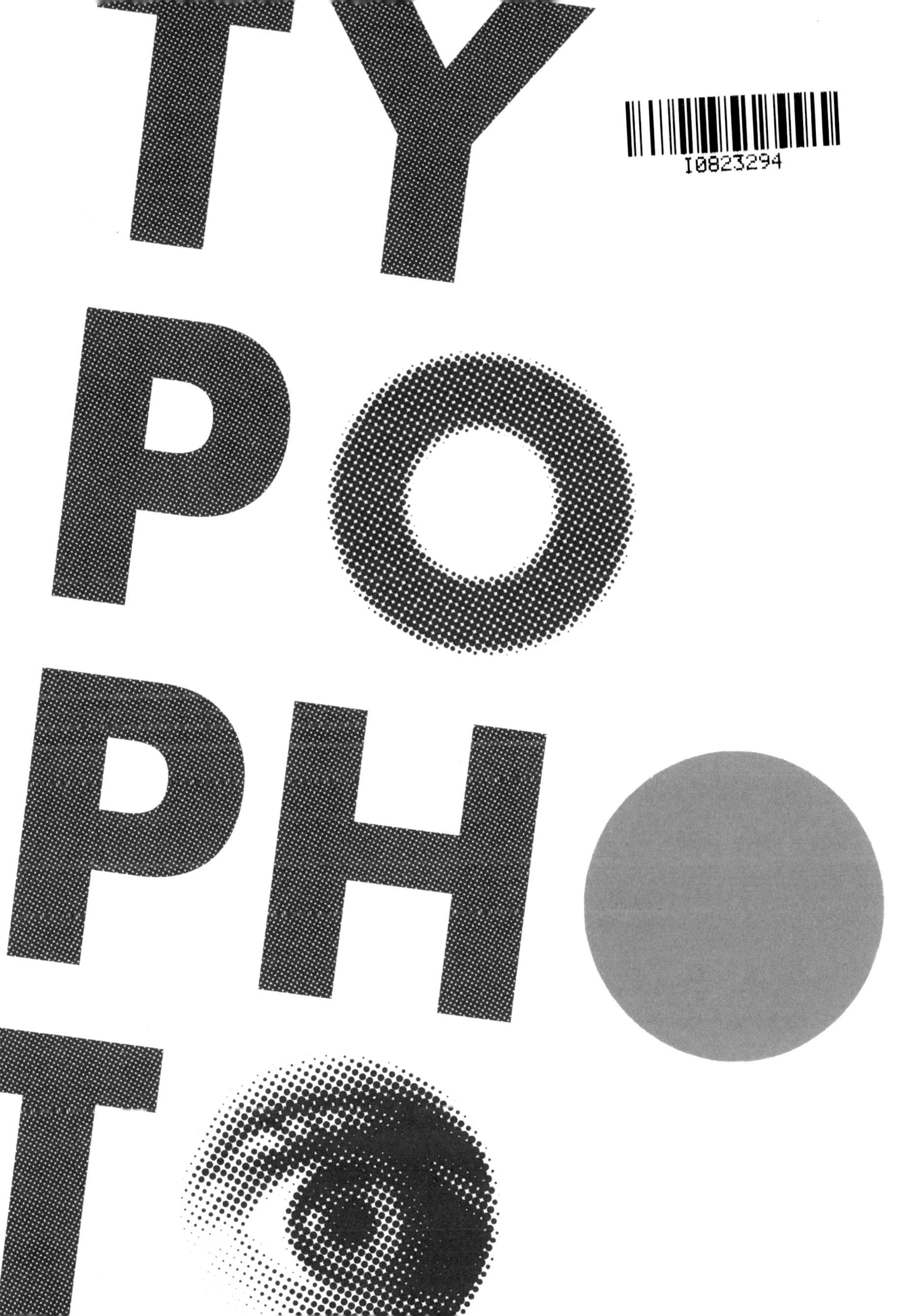
TY
PO
PH
TO
I0823294

TYPOPHOTO

NEW TYPOGRAPHY AND THE REINVENTION OF PHOTOGRAPHY

JESSICA D. BRIER

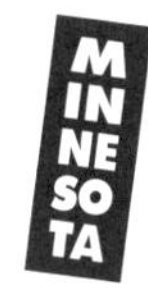

University of Minnesota Press
Minneapolis
London

The University of Minnesota Press gratefully acknowledges the generous assistance provided for the publication of this book by Vassar College.

Published by the University of Minnesota Press
111 Third Avenue South, Suite 290
Minneapolis, MN 55401-2520
http://www.upress.umn.edu

ISBN 978-1-5179-1822-4 (hc)
ISBN 978-1-5179-1823-1 (pb)

A Cataloging-in-Publication record for this book is available from the Library of Congress.

Printed in Canada on acid-free paper

34 33 32 31 30 29 28 27 26 25   10 9 8 7 6 5 4 3 2 1

For my girl, Beth

CONTENTS

INTRODUCTION

The Photo-Typographer

Between the World Wars, the young field of graphic design incubated quickly. German periodicals dedicated to typography, printing, and bookmaking were hothouses for sharing and debating what graphic design could and should be. At stake was the legitimacy of a burgeoning communication industry still finding its footing in a time of profound cultural, economic, and political upheaval. Practitioners in the nascent field translated collective dilemmas into the particulars of their trade. Would new printing technologies and economic motivations supersede the value of centuries-old traditions? Could they coexist? Between the wars, ideas about meaning, truth, and the ethics of persuasion, both deeply held and rapidly changing, informed newly articulated principles for combining word and image. Graphic designers fixated on how readers read, as a direct extension of design itself. They understood production and consumption as mutually interdependent under modern capitalism, especially in the context of Germany's post–World War I economic rehabilitation.

Photography played a central role in defining modern graphic design. In January 1932, the editors of *Typographic*

Newsletter (*Typographische Mitteilungen*)[1]—one of Germany's most important and widely read trade journals on typography and book printing—announced a new monthly supplement: "The Photo-Typographer" ("Der Phototypograph") was dedicated to "photo-design and the use of photography in modern commercial typesetting."[2] Curiously, by the time of this announcement, "photo-design" was nothing new; photographic images had appeared in print for over half a century, since the commercialization of photogravure in the 1870s and the halftone process in the 1880s. What, then, compelled these editors to promote the "necessity" of a supplement dedicated to the photo-typographer as late as 1932?[3] What was still novel, they suggested, was thinking of photography not just as a technology for producing or reproducing illustrations, but rather as a conceptual technique that belonged to and embodied the ambitions of modern graphic design: "Photo-design in the typographic sense is still uncharted territory, which is only now being tilled."[4] The launch of "The Photo-Typographer" marked the apogee of an intensive decade of experimenting with and articulating photo-design. Between the World Wars, designers in Europe and the United States vehemently took up the controversial question of photography's place in graphic design—with varying degrees of excitement, trepidation, and everything in between.

The pivotal and complex role of photography in graphic design during the 1920s and 1930s is encapsulated by an invented term: *Typophoto.* Coined by Hungarian American artist, designer, and Bauhaus pedagogue László Moholy-Nagy (1895–1946), *Typophoto* named the synthesis of typography and photography.[5] For Moholy-Nagy, *Typophoto* was predictive of a future in which visual literacy would be dominant: in his view, this synthesis portended the inevitable replacement of text, as a primary device of communication, with images—namely photography—and eventually with the moving images of cinema. The term *Typophoto* first appeared in 1925 in two publications: Moholy-Nagy's book *Painting Photography Film* (*Malerei Photographie Film*), published in the Bauhausbücher series, as well as in his contribution to a special supplement of *Typographische Mitteilungen* edited by German typographer Jan Tschichold (1902–1974).[6] Tschichold's supplement adopted *Typophoto* as a central principle of New Typography, which he deemed an international graphic design movement and introduced to the journal's vast readership of German printers, typesetters, designers, and bookmakers.[7]

Tschichold reoriented *Typophoto* toward design in the present. In 1928, he codified the tenets of New Typography in his first book and modernist treatise, *The New Typography* (*Die Neue Typographie*). Citing examples of graphics by an array of avant-garde European designers, the book promoted the asymmetrical arrangement of type according to the invisible grid; the use of white space as a compositional device; the rejection of typographic ornament; and the exclusive use of sans serif typefaces and photographic illustration as suitable for all graphics, from books to advertisements.[8] In various writings published between 1925 and 1933, Tschichold promoted strict adherence to these principles to optimize the function of all graphics as universally legible, efficient, objective, and clear. Tschichold and his associates advocated "functional" graphic design as the synthesis of rationalism and aesthetic harmony.[9] Unpacking *Typophoto* as a central tenet of New Typography is essential to understanding how the movement's enduring legacy as a source of "functionalism" has eclipsed the conditions in which it emerged.[10] The postwar assimilation of New Typography into the teaching and practice of graphic design in the United States and Europe has made its claims seem timeless and self-evident.[11] However, New Typography's notions of legibility and objectivity were determined by the circumstances and economic imperatives of interwar German culture and industry. New Typography amalgamated elements of advertising theory, applied psychology, social science, and photography theory in the 1920s. Importantly, the movement's most successful practical application was in commercial design for the German industrial sector, which capitalized on the novelty of avant-garde styles in an effort to rehabilitate chemical manufacturing and heavy industry between the Wars.

The New Typography is widely regarded as the movement's foundational text. Yet it was one among many attempts to define New Typography as a set of ideas about visual communication, and to articulate its relationship to contemporaneous art practices. Tschichold's book was the first comprehensive effort to bring together the heterogeneous practices of a far-flung network of graphic designers, and to identify key affinities between trends in contemporary art, graphic design, and the printing trade. Between 1923 and 1933, the parameters of the movement changed continuously and developed largely through advertising design. Though New Typography sought to contrast itself with mainstream commercial design, its rhetoric of objectivity, efficiency, and legibility was borrowed, in part, from an international professional discourse. In the pages of journals dedicated to typography, printing, and advertising, designers discussed methods of optimizing the effectiveness of mass-produced graphics as tools of persuasion. These discussions often centered on how to control perception, and photography was a key tool, medium, and idea that designers reached for.

While New Typography's embrace of sans serif type is well-known, Tschichold was equally insistent on photography as graphic design's sole means of image production. This insistence underscores the charged and contested meanings of "photography" to interwar designers. Both as a technology and as an idea, photography was regarded as a product—and therefore, a symbol—of modern invention. The medium was associated with precision, clarity, and efficiency—all qualities articulated as "functional" in New Typography, betraying the movement as an implicitly capitalist ideology of communication. Yet these associations were loose and unreliable; photography also holds the inverse possibilities of vagueness and ambiguity—qualities that also proved useful to New Typographers, especially in commercial design. Photography was particularly malleable in relation to type, where verbal and visual modes of expression and reception intermingle, overlap, and sometimes clash. Ultimately, "photography" served New Typography as an ideology of communication and perception—expressed as the conceptual technique *Typophoto.*

Not intended as a comprehensive treatment of New Typography, this book offers a focused study of *Typophoto* as one of its central ideas and, by extension, as a key term for expanded histories of graphic design. Moholy-Nagy's invented term has been repeated so often that its ambiguity, and manifold implications for the graphic design profession, have become obscured. *Typophoto* deserves closer scrutiny for all the ways it stands for New Typography's ambitions: to mechanize ocular perception; to transform reading from a process of idle contemplation to one of active consumption; and to embrace technology as an antidote to the crises of modernity. It encapsulates the singular and complex importance of photography to New Typography and to broader practices of graphic design.

Tschichold championed photographs as objective visual information—an assertion that thoroughly papered over the technical and conceptual complexities involved in actually combining photography and type. These complexities begin with the photographic halftone. Tschichold characterized the halftone as the material embodiment of photography's compatibility with type, calling for the replacement of hand-drawn illustrations with photographs.[12] The halftone process translated photographic images into dots of ink printed from the same matrix as type. This process atomized photographic images into irregular, abstract grids, which required both optical and psychological translation on the part of a reader: halftones cohere as recognizable images through optical illusion. The halftone's integration into graphics also required montage and "retouching"—an umbrella term for an array of manual and mechanized techniques for the manipulation of images. Despite the simplifying rhetoric of New Typography, designers knew full well the complexity that *Typophoto* implied.

They exploited the material hybridity of the halftone to complicate the relationship between word and image and the perception of color and space, and to create tension between representational and abstract forms. These material and visual transformations of photography in print, and its use as a technique of design, amounted to a reinvention of the medium in graphic design.

Photography was subsumed into graphics through the halftone process, retouching, photomontage, and methods of perceptual psychology. When Tschichold claimed *Typophoto* as a principle of New Typography, the term already connoted a utopian ideology of capitalist, technologically driven progress, and a desire to merge international constructivism with the traditions of German printing. This utopianism was specifically expressed through *Typophoto* as an idea of hybridity—not only the integration of photography and graphics, but the creation of a new medium of communication. It flagged the techniques and logic of montage as fundamental to graphic design and advertising, facilitating semiotic play, unfixed meaning, and active consumer–reader participation.

Graphic designers, especially those associated with New Typography, were prolific theorists of the medium of photography. Its history has been shaped not only by those who used cameras and worked in darkrooms, but equally by those who used and manipulated the medium through design, printing, reproduction, and circulation. Like many of Moholy-Nagy's ideas, *Typophoto* is both an object worthy of study and an enduring theoretical framework. Like "design" and "halftone," *Typophoto* connotes both process and product. The New Typographers recognized how photography translated through the halftone process could transform the practice of design—and, in turn, how its use as a design tool could transform the nature of photography. Beyond the ambitions of the avant-garde, *Typophoto* is a useful term for the broader integration of histories of photography and graphic design and for understanding the rootedness of present-day media studies in the interwar period. In the pages that follow, *Typophoto* is a paradigm for the myriad ways that photography has been reinvented in commercial graphics, namely through the practices of applied psychology and retouching, and through the layered discourses of the nascent field of commercial graphic design.

THE HALFTONE: PHOTOGRAPHY TRANSLATED AS PRINT

Typophoto was materialized by the photographic halftone. New Typography's discussions of *Typophoto* alluded to photography in printed matter as a medium between text and image—and correspondingly, to beholding *Typophoto* as a mode between reading text and viewing images. The photographic halftone materializes this hybrid state. Critical to understanding photography as a mass medium is the fact that, to circulate, photographic images had to be translated as print. Halftone reproduction was a two-part process: First, a photographic print was rephotographed and developed through a screen, with light penetrating only the apertures in the screen. The resulting exposure consisted of an uneven matrix of dots—concentrated densely to articulate forms and sparsely where there was negative space—rather than continuous tones. A printing plate or cylinder was then etched using the dot pattern, which could be used to make multiple prints, each with a single ink color.[13] As a multistep process of material translation, the halftone simulated the continuous tones of the photographic print through printed dots distributed in varied concentration, meant to appear as shades of gray. The halftone grid was intended to be invisible to the naked eye.

Typophoto signified the conceptual and material translation of photography into graphic form. Graphic designers' desire to reinvent photography was expressed through their interest in the halftone: as a technology, as an experimental form, and as a hybrid medium that belongs as much to the printed page as it does to photographic practice. Interwar graphic designers including Willi Baumeister (1889–1955), Max Burchartz (1887–1961), Johannes Canis (1895–1977), Walter Dexel (1890–1973), Piet Zwart (1885–1977), and Georg Trump (1896–1985) used the halftone to convert photography into the visual language of industrial printing. Rather than adhere to codified "rules" of halftone printing by trying to hide the halftone grid, they used it as a visual motif that called attention to the composite medium of *Typophoto*. Recognizing *Typophoto* as the material, visual, and conceptual translation of photography goes beyond a consideration of typography as merely context for photographic reproductions. In 1953, William Ivins praised the photographic halftone as "a cheap and easy means of symbolic communication without syntax," which yielded "exactly repeatable pictorial statements."[14] This notorious claim is thoroughly complicated by critical study of the halftone process as one of translation rather than of reproduction. Photomechanical reproduction is more accurately understood as a thorough transmutation of images through techniques of engraving, stereotyping, electrotyping, casting, inking, printing, painting, drawing, carving, and airbrushing, as well as through the optical and psychological mechanisms of perception.[15]

The halftone process was developed and perfected to circulate photographic images in print quickly and cheaply, shoring up photography's currency as information. Experiments with halftone printing began around

1850, when William Henry Fox Talbot began using screens, patenting a gauze mesh screen in 1852. The process was introduced commercially in 1881 in the United States by Frederic Ives, followed by another version in Germany by Georg Meisenbach in 1882, and the subsequent release of a crossline screen by Max Levy in 1893.[16] By the mid-1920s, the halftone was ubiquitous in newspapers and magazines, yet it was debated continuously, especially by designers who feared that mechanized image-making would threaten the artistry of advertising design or even the existence of the individual designer.

Writing on photography for the *Frankfurter Illustrierte Zeitung* in 1927, German cultural critic Siegfried Kracauer noted the visual disjuncture between the abstracted dot matrix, which constitutes a halftone image, and the photographic referent: "This is what the film diva looks like. She is twenty-four years old, featured on the cover of an illustrated magazine, standing in front of the Hotel Excelsior on the Lido. The date is September. If one were to look through a magnifying glass one could make out the grain, the millions of little dots that constitute the diva, the waves and the hotel. The picture, however, does not refer to the dot matrix but to the living diva on the Lido."[17] Kracauer observed that halftones forced readers to subconsciously and instantaneously navigate between seeing and reading. The photographic halftone presents itself as both an abstract grid and as a representational image; readers suspend recognition of one to see the other. Reading the image as a coherent whole, and in relation to text and other graphic marks on a page, necessitates a willful disregard for the dot matrix that, in isolation, might be read as an abstract pattern.

Kracauer's perceptual encounter with a magazine cover in 1927 evokes the capacity of technology to bring us closer to the world even as it distances us from it—a phenomenon so relevant to our present moment, as we navigate the digital world, that it is often difficult to articulate. Yet in looking back at the persistent strangeness of the halftone—still remarkable half a century after its invention—we might grapple anew with our own ongoing alienation from a world mediated many times over by technology. Like images constituted by digital pixels, the halftone facilitated the mass circulation of photography while simultaneously calling attention to the stark difference between image and referent. In Kracauer's observations, the halftone revealed the extent to which "photography" is an imagined category that had to be preserved in the minds of readers as they rely on optical illusion to see dot matrices as coherent images, and to understand those images as meaningfully connected to their referents.[18] For New Typography, the ambiguity of the halftone was an opportunity rather than a liability. The New Typographers used it not simply as a tool for multiplying the presence of photographs in the world, but as a unique medium of communication.

Photographic halftones belong to a category of images that German artist Hito Steyerl has called "poor images."[19] She uses this term to describe how digital images undergo visual and material corrosion when copied and circulated: "The poor image is a copy in motion. Its quality is bad, its resolution substandard. As it accelerates, it deteriorates. It is a ghost of an image, a preview, a thumbnail, an errant idea, an itinerant image distributed for free, squeezed through slow digital connections, compressed, reproduced, ripped, remixed, as well as copied and pasted into other channels of distribution."[20] In the process of information loss through endless reproduction and circulation, "poor images" accrue connotative value as vague signifiers that stand in for shared ideologies, beliefs, and aspirations. Like pictograms, poor images masquerade as iconic signs while trading on the symbolic. They insinuate, promote, and endorse more than they represent. In the vagueness of their form, they can signify much more than a faithfully mimetic representation. Steyerl continues: "The poor image . . . builds alliances as it travels, provokes translation or mistranslation, and creates new publics and debates. By losing its visual substance it recovers some of its political punch and creates a new aura around it. This aura is no longer based on the permanence of the 'original,' but on the transience of the copy."[21] It is not despite the deterioration of the poor image, but rather *because* of it, that this "new aura" develops. As a "poor" image, a vague signifier premised on material corrosion, the halftone has been enormously useful to graphic design as an image type that retains a link to the "real" world while requiring the reader's interpretation to truly make sense of it.

Photography is situated in this book as a "conceptual framework" of graphic design.[22] I borrow this phrase from Steffen Siegel who has posited that, in the mid-nineteenth century, "photography" was constituted as much as an *idea* as it was by tangible objects, technologies, practices, or processes. This remained as true in the 1920s and 1930s as it had been almost a century earlier, intensified by collective anticipation of the centennial of photography's first public announcements, which culminated in some of the first published histories of the medium.[23] More recently, Japanese graphic designer and curator Kenya Hara observed that "verbalizing design is another act of design."[24] The theoretical writings of interwar graphic designers are inseparable from their approach to material and form, and theirs are among the most prolific and consequential theories of photography in the medium's history.[25]

Most critical attention to the halftone has focused on its early commercial development and initial receptions in the 1880s and 1890s, when it began to dominate newspaper illustration.[26] Yet the halftone continued to be an object of conceptual and visual interest—and fervent debate—well into the twentieth century, particularly among graphic designers.[27] As a complement to understanding the technology of the halftone process, its cultural significance inheres in the connotations of formal and theoretical experiments in graphic design. This study centers the halftone as both an element of graphic design and as a form of photography worthy of study in its own right. Despite its vast literature, the history of photography is still too hamstrung by medium specificity by privileging what Sally Stein called "the photograph as an autonomous artifact."[28] This preoccupation tends to obscure the impact of photographic images on modern life. In the dominant practices of collecting and exhibiting photography in museums, darkroom prints are almost always favored to the exclusion of "reproductions" in books, periodicals, and printed ephemera, which are typically found in library collections and archives. This practice fetishizes the "vintage" print, a term invented by the art market, which denotes the rarity and authenticity of a lifetime print made by a photographer or their assistant, which therefore confers cultural and monetary value.[29] The staying power of the vintage print in museum collecting endorses a narrow definition of photography that is, ironically, borrowed from other mediums: the scarcity model of valuing vintage prints in small, limited editions imposes the value logic of rare, unique objects like paintings and sculptures onto a reproducible medium like photography.[30] The consequence of this practice is the sidelining of photography as it is typically circulated and experienced in everyday life. While relatively few people encounter darkroom prints made by photographers, everyone encounters photography mediated by halftone printing and by digital pixels on screens.

Although Moholy-Nagy's *Painting Photography Film* is considered among the most important theories of photography ever published, the concept of *Typophoto* itself—and its powerful currency among contemporaneous designers—has curiously received little attention. In studying *Typophoto,* I follow interwar graphic designers who took up the idea, whether as inspiration or provocation. Geoffrey Batchen has asserted, in the digital era, the need for "a history [of photography] freed from the tyranny of the photograph," a history that would "trace, not the production of singular photographs, but the dissemination of photographic images."[31] This history dates back at least as far as the first commercial uses of the halftone process in the 1880s—but perhaps to the very first attempts to fix images through the action of light.

LEGACIES OF NEW TYPOGRAPHY AND THE CULT OF THE GRID

Tschichold was not the first to articulate New Typography as a design ethos. Rather, his first book was an attempt to translate the shared ideological affinities and formal approaches of international constructivism into the professional context of German typography and printing.[32] Paul Stirton has observed that Tschichold's primary role in New Typography was as a voracious collector of designs clipped from periodicals and printed ephemera sent to him by far-flung practitioners across Europe.[33] The present study reconstitutes now-dispersed materials that were once contained in the vast personal archive that Tschichold amassed between the Wars, now divided among collections in Switzerland, Germany, and the United States.[34] By virtually reconstituting this archive, New Typography can be properly understood as a heterogeneous, international network of ideas and practices by designers from Germany, Russia, Czechoslovakia, Hungary, Austria, Switzerland, and the Netherlands. Some of their names are known today; others remain yet unidentified. While some explicitly identified with New Typography, others were labeled externally by Tschichold. This study includes teachings of some of New Typography's proponents at the Meisterschule für Deutschlands Buchdrucker in Munich, namely Paul Renner and Georg Trump, and unattributed student work that pushed *Typophoto* in new directions.

The enduring legacy of New Typography in the teaching and practice of graphic design in Europe and the United States is steeped in irony. In the late 1930s, after immigrating to Switzerland, Tschichold began to disavow the dogma of New Typography both in his writing and through his own design practice, a shift that culminated in an infamous public dispute with Swiss designer Max Bill in 1946.[35] In the 1940s, Bill continued to adhere to New Typography and—along with fellow designers Theo Ballmer, Armin Hofmann, Josef Müller-Brockmann, Richard Lohse, Hans Neuberg, Ernst Keller, and Carlo Vivarelli—promoted Swiss Style graphic design, also known as International Style.[36] This approach was in essence an assimilation of New Typography, championing sans serif type, asymmetrical layout, photographic illustration, and the typographic grid.[37] In Müller-Brockmann's 1961 book *Grid Systems in Graphic Design,* he emulated the rhetoric of New Typography even more closely than its style, writing, "The use of the grid as an ordering system is the expression of a certain mental attitude inasmuch as it shows that the designer conceives his work in terms that are constructive and oriented toward the future."[38] His language was infused with the utopian dream of universal standardization and internationalism that had motivated Tschichold to write

The New Typography over thirty years earlier—and which ultimately found lasting currency in the Western dominance of International Style design.

Tschichold's postwar disavowal of New Typography—as exemplary of what, in 1946, he called "the German bent for the absolute, and its military will to order and claim to sole domination"—was an attempt to make sense of Nazi appropriation of modernist techniques in building a fascist culture.[39] While he defended the New Typographers as "vehement enemies of Nazism," he rejected modernist dogma. In retrospect, he recognized a dangerous intolerance to heterogeneity that had undergirded avant-garde utopianism. He even went as far as comparing his own position, in retrospect, to "a 'Führer' role, signifying, as it did, an intellectual guardianship of 'followers' typical of dictator states."[40] This comparison implied that madness had been lurking within interwar modernist functionalism. His comments stopped just short of calling New Typography fascist or suggesting a causal link between modernism and fascism.

Tschichold's reversal in exile bespeaks the paradoxical nature of Weimar-era functionalism, which we might understand as embodied by the relentless regularity of the typographic grid. Adherence to the logic of the grid, perhaps the most important artifact of New Typography in Swiss Style graphics, makes visible the modernist dream of universal standardization that, by the end of World War II, Tschichold had come to see as dangerous. Decades later, writing in 1985, art historian Rosalind Krauss puzzled over what she regarded as a modernist obsession with the grid: "I do not think it is an exaggeration to say that behind every twentieth-century grid there lies—like a trauma that must be repressed—a symbolist window parading in the guise of a treatise on optics."[41] Krauss recognized the relentless rationality of the grid not as the antithesis of the irrational, but rather as a sign of trauma or madness. This idea is rendered visually in the raster pattern, a form that distorts as much as it regularizes. Such distortion is most blatant in the photographic halftone and digital photographic image, which imitate the tonality of a photographic print through pixilation. The halftone explodes an image into a mass of dots that must be pieced back together in the mind's eye. It reveals the rational, functionalist ambitions of modernist design to be a fantasy, reliant on the beholder's subconscious to create meaning as representation. The utility of interwar advertising design, especially in its use of photography, depended on the subconscious processes of perception, cognition, and mental association.

The context of the emerging, international field of advertising is indispensable for understanding photography as a tool of design and, equally, as a potent metaphor for modern designers' ambitions to control reader–consumer perception and attention.[42] Applied psychologists emphasized how line, color, and form could be used in graphic design to control memory and reading. This was a key framework for the modernist concept of New Vision, especially as an ideology for using photography to transform perception and reading.[43] Advertising designers relied on montage and formal abstraction to create evocative symbols and text–image composites. They used photomontage to create images that were read simultaneously as real and constructed, evoking the emotions, memories, desires, and fantasies of consumers. Many designers used photographic metaphors in writing about advertising, invoking the idea of visual memory as a set of latent images that lived in the sensitive substrate of the human mind. Fueled by theories of psychology, designers conjectured that, although seen only momentarily, advertisements could be imprinted on the minds of consumers. They believed that, through repeated viewing and mnemonic stimulation, the best advertisements could be transferred from the pages of newspapers or magazines, or from posters pasted on the sides of buildings, into the mind's eye.[44] In 1928, one commentator wrote, "When novelty of form and colour have struck forcibly, the visual memory is impressed; and when it occurs again, the conscious mind gradually becomes aware of this repeated significance of form and colour."[45]

From its earliest days, advertising was a medium that "thrived on a certain kind of instability," as Frederic Schwartz has written.[46] Just as advertisers sought to technologize perception by applying scientific principles, they also recognized that meaning was mutable and subjective. Psychologists and designers in the 1920s described their ambitions to reinvent reading as a protracted process that occurred not only within the time it took to apprehend an advertisement, but which continued to unfold in the mind. In fact, the most important stage of perception, as described by advertisers, was thought to occur long after an initial encounter with an advertisement. Even as consumers tried to ignore advertising, images were designed to imprint themselves on the human memory, recalled and interpreted subconsciously. This delayed process would ideally stimulate the consumer's own mental associations, emotions, and, ultimately, purchasing decisions. Repetition was regarded as key to effective advertising. Consumers recognized and remembered brands and products through frequent and repeated encounters with advertisements, which consequently accrued "memory-value," "attention-value," and "suggestion-value."[47]

In Germany, advertising discourse of the Wilhelmine and Weimar eras set the stage for the ethos of New Typography. Before the First World War, advertising agents, designers, social scientists, and psychologists debated how commodities might embody and shape German identity, whether advertising could serve aesthetic interests and act as a vehicle for persuasion and agitation, and to what extent German advertising should adopt American techniques of applied psychology and market research.[48] Indeed, many wondered whether advertising was ethical at all.[49] These debates were indicative of existential dilemmas about the nature of modernity: what it meant to be German in an era of internationalism, and how ordinary Germans could participate in society both as consumers and as parts of a spiritually healthy society. Designers struggled to express enduring cultural values while responding to technological, political, and economic change, a task that inspired experimentation in Weimar-era advertising.[50] That "functionalist" design emerged during this tumultuous period of German history is precisely why the complexities masked by its aesthetic merit closer scrutiny.

In 1926, Kracauer described the "cult of distraction" that seemed to pervade daily life in Weimar Germany.[51] Following Kracauer's appraisal, Janet Ward has described Weimar-era, urban advertising as a medium that "radically reshaped the experience of idle *flânerie* into distraction with an applied purpose."[52] Paradoxically, the distractibility of modern life was facilitated by advertising designers who were thoroughly preoccupied by the desire to harness consumer attention. Frederic Schwartz has identified a shared preoccupation with "attention" at the intersection of art and design, intellectual currents of the Frankfurt School, and experimental psychology in Weimar Germany.[53] The very people at whose feet Kracauer laid blame for fracturing public attention were fiercely committed to doing precisely the opposite. Advertising designers sought to capture attention through visual and verbal play by creating "striking" advertisements that could not be missed or soon forgotten.[54]

The emergence of New Typography corresponded with the professionalization of graphic design in Germany. "Design," in the modern sense, is typically defined by the separation of concept from production, bracketing the conceptual work of graphic design from the labor of printing.[55] However, the professionalization of graphic design was also a process of consolidating a heterogeneous set of techniques, terms, traditions, and disciplines into a single field.[56] In response to a growing demand for mass-circulated commercial graphics in Weimar Germany, the practices of typography, book design, advertising design, printing, art directing, commercial photography, and layout were subsumed into the field that became known as *Gebrauchsgraphik.* The closest German equivalent to "graphic design," this term came into common use by the end of World War I. By the mid-1920s, it had mostly collapsed a variety of terms applied to specific print mediums, including *Schriftkunst, Buchkunst, Plakatkunst,* and *Reklamekunst.*[57] The modern *Gebrauchsgraphiker* was expected to have expertise in calligraphy, book art, poster art, and advertising design—a set of skills that connected the centuries-long history of fine book printing to the burgeoning practices of modern advertising. Importantly, in the 1920s *Gebrauchsgraphik* was also frequently translated in English as "commercial art," which became indistinguishable from "graphic design" as the field matured under Western capitalism.[58]

Shortly before World War I, German type foundries including Bauer, Klingspor, Stempel, Berthold, Ludwig and Mayer, Weber, and Brüder Butter began commissioning individual typographers, such as Peter Behrens, Fritz Ehmcke, Otto Eckmann, Rudolf Koch, and Paul Renner, to create new typeface designs.[59] These foundries capitalized on the accelerated industrialization of the Wilhelmine era as an opportunity to revitalize Germany's legacy as home to two of the most important inventions in the history of printing: Johannes Gutenberg's movable-type printing press in the 1450s and the technique of lithography, invented by Aloïs Senefelder in 1798.[60] Modern visual communication was facilitated, in large part, by the transformation of modern printing technology that had taken place in the nineteenth century: between 1820 and 1850, various mechanized rotary printing presses were invented and patented, and the commercial halftone was introduced in the early 1880s, followed closely by the advent of mechanized typesetting and offset printing.[61]

The consolidation of *Gebrauchsgraphik* as a professional field went hand in hand with the rise of the German advertising industry. In 1908, the Verein Deutscher Reklamefachleute (VDR), the first German association of advertising professionals, was founded.[62] In 1919, the newsletter of the VDR became the widely circulated journal *Die Reklame,* which covered all aspects of advertising.[63] By 1929, fifteen professional advertising and marketing associations had been established in Germany alone.[64] The advertising industry's initial claim to cultural legitimacy was the artistic contribution of designers to German culture, exemplified by the advertising poster.[65] Arguably the most important early milestone in the professionalization of German graphic design was the founding of the Bund Deutscher Gebrauchsgraphiker (BDG) in 1919 by Max

Hertwig, Jupp Wiertz, and Hans Meyer.[66] The graphic arts journal *Das Plakat*, begun in 1921, was renamed *Gebrauchsgraphik* in 1924, and became the official organ of the BDG by 1928, edited by graphic designer Hermann K. Frenzel.[67] This transition signified far more than a name change. Under Frenzel and the BDG, *Gebrauchsgraphik* pivoted away from *Das Plakat*'s focus on graphic arts, adopting an explicit orientation toward commercial design. By the late 1920s, *Gebrauchsgraphik* was recognized internationally as one of the graphic design profession's most influential trade publications, and in 1927, it became a bilingual platform for discourse among European and American professionals.[68] The nascent "science" of advertising in the 1920s was popularized through *Gebrauchsgraphik* as well as more established publications dedicated to graphic arts and typography, namely *Das Kunstblatt* and *Typographische Mitteilungen*.

Beyond Germany, graphic design was formed professionally in large part through the international circulation of trade journals published in the United States (*Advertising Arts, Printers' Ink*), Britain (*Commercial Art*), and France (*Arts et métiers graphiques*). These publications dedicated significant space to synthesizing advertising theory and debates around standards for commercial printed matter. This book pays significant attention to this international field of publications, because they were crucially important to establishing "graphic design" as a modern profession. Key to the formation of the young profession's identity was international exchange; while of course there were localized debates and ideas specific to the German context, graphic designers understood the stakes and practices of their field to transcend national borders or concerns.

LEGIBILITY AND THE LABOR OF LOOKING

Teal Triggs once argued that graphic design is a field "still searching for its past."[69] To some extent, this is still true. A relatively new field, graphic design history in the West was largely founded by practicing designers who had been trained in the mid-twentieth century according to the modernist principles first codified as New Typography and assimilated as International Style after World War II. Early English-language surveys of graphic design history portrayed design as the creative prerogative of heroic individuals progressing toward ever-increasing clarity.[70] Consequently, the field has historically taken for granted what determines the parameters of "legibility," and how those parameters intersect with aesthetic tastes, styles, and the needs of clients.[71] As Julia Meer has shown, New Typography emerged from an array of ideas rooted in the Wilhelmine era and the social and economic contexts of

Weimar Germany.[72] These contexts are crucial to the assumptions and values embedded in New Typography's definition of legibility. Graphic design does not represent a static or universal notion of "legible communication," as Tschichold once argued, but is rather a framework for endlessly redefining the terms of legibility.

This book treats legibility as an object of study through analysis of both theory and graphic form. I apply linguist E. A. Levenston's method of paragraphemic analysis, which attends to type and layout as material and visual form, a practice still strikingly uncommon in graphic design histories.[73] This method is particularly important given the prevalence of nonrepresentational forms in the New Typographers' designs (such as circles, rules, arrows, and solid planes of color), which I refer to here as "abstract graphic elements" in the absence of a proper term. This absence indicates that the terminology of the graphic design profession itself is insufficient for the critical analysis of graphic form. The field lacks a name for nonrepresentational, compositional forms that are intended as both nonsymbolic and nondecorative—that is, marks that are understood to perform the function of directing or stopping the reader's eye (the role often played by abstract raster patterns).[74] The closest term that exists in contemporary graphic design is "dingbat," but this refers specifically to an ornamental, abstract graphic mark. This gap suggests the extent to which the field of graphic design was built on an ethos inherited from New Typography, which insisted (in theory) on the mutual exclusivity of ornament and function.

Fragmented images like halftones call our attention to labor that is meant to go undetected: the labor of looking. By interrupting a passive sense of continuity in what we see, they serve as jolting reminders that we, as consumers, perform necessary, material labor—even as consumption is presented as an effortless reflex—just by looking at advertising. The raster pattern—which simultaneously atomizes halftones and coheres them—disrupts the ideology of legibility on which commercial design depends. This is the paradox embedded in *Typophoto:* the very tool that designers praised for its efficiency as visual communication was embedded with the potential to resist participating in the endless cycle of productivity demanded by consumer capitalism. In the designs of New Typography, we might actually see a stark contradiction between stated aims of legibility and the actual experiences of it.

The lessons of *Typophoto* extend far beyond the brief period in which New Typography took hold. This book stakes a claim for the expanded study of the raster pattern as a motif of twentieth- and twenty-first-century art and design. In American and European art made after World War II, raster patterns served explicitly as signs of resistance to the scopic complacency both ingrained and required by Western consumer culture. The 1960s and 1970s saw a fascination in the form of the raster among artists working between screen printing and painting. Pop artists subverted the expectations of mechanized regularity associated with print media by adopting the visual language of print in painting, blurring the distinction between machine- and handmade images. Richard Hamilton, Roy Lichtenstein, Sigmar Polke, Robert Rauschenberg, J. C. J. Vanderheyden, Andy Warhol all used the raster grid in their work—whether in reference to comic strip Ben Day dots or newspaper halftones (Plate 1, Plate 2). By appropriating fragmented dots as a motif of mass culture, they called attention to the connotations of the raster as cheap, fast, objective, and throwaway. By rendering Ben Day and halftone dots in paint, Pop artists upended such expectations to thumb their noses at the highbrow art world. Their works compromised the coherence of representation in exchange for monumentalizing crude dot patterns usually intended to be ignored, turning them instead into objects of visual contemplation. David Hopkins has described how simulated halftone dots in Sigmar Polke's *Rasterbilder* paintings "achieved a distracting autonomy" in their visual irregularity.[75] Though the halftone was invented to force the infinitely variable tones of the photographic print to conform to the rigid mechanization of industrial printing, dots appear in Polke's paintings as unruly and inconsistent.[76]

Photography's presumed objectivity has, in large part, been supported by the prevalence of the halftone in newspapers. While the halftone process enabled the mass circulation of photography as news, it has paradoxically kept us from seeing the world coherently. The halftone embodies both the lofty promises and dismal failures of modernity—especially industrial capitalism—to create an efficient, egalitarian, informed, and virtuous world. Many contemporary artists subvert and reclaim the halftone as a visual metaphor for the ultimate failures of technology to convey truth or uphold justice. They use the halftones and pixelation as visual motifs for the rejection of photography's assumed authority, and to center ethical concerns that underlie our reliance on photographs as conveyors of truth. Filipino American artist Stephanie Syjuco has used the raster pattern as a visual metaphor for the erasure of human agency in colonial traditions of ethnographic photography made by white Westerners (Figure 1). In the series *Cargo Cults* (2013–16), Syjuco uses patterns as disorienting "dazzle camouflage," borrowed from the World War I practice of painting battleships with abstract patterns. The raster visually disrupts the authority of her fictional ethnographic portrait, making its

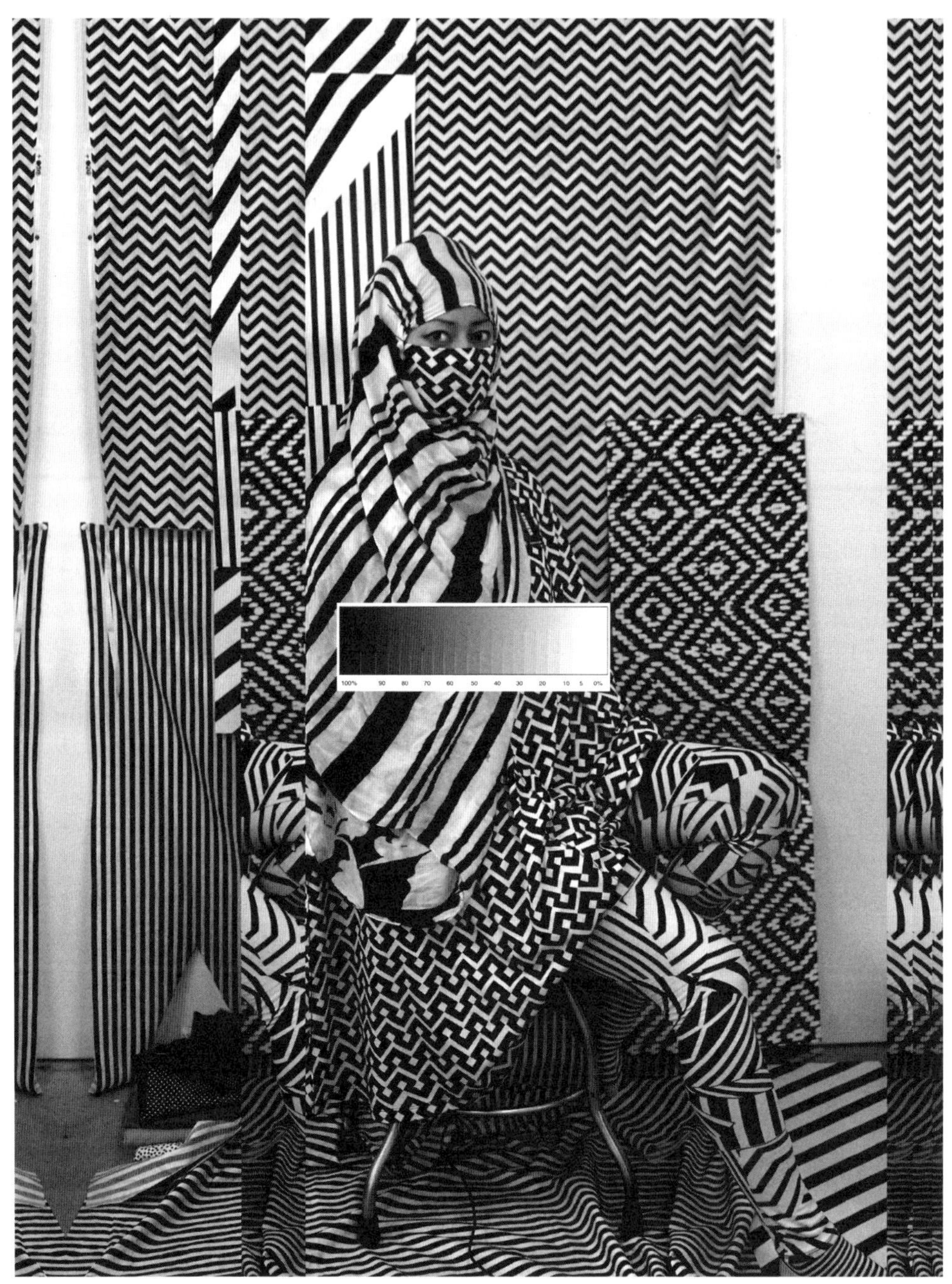

FIGURE 1 Stephanie Syjuco, *Cargo Cults (Cover-Up)*, 2018, archival pigment print. Copyright Stephanie Syjuco; courtesy of the artist and RYAN LEE Gallery, New York.

"false subject"—performed by the artist herself—hard to see and therefore impossible to find.[77] The dazzling patterns of "ethnic" fabrics ubiquitous in American retailers clash with that of a grayscale color bar placed in the center of the image. Like the halftone or pixel grid, this artifact of Adobe Photoshop is usually meant to be invisible, and its presence here challenges the supposed neutrality of photographic technologies. Rather than looking past evidence of technological and manual manipulation to see a legible portrait, we recognize in it a resistance to the legibility of racist objectification—and to the "neutral" technology that disguised its insidiousness.

OVERVIEW OF CHAPTERS

The aim of this book is to illuminate the layered meanings of *Typophoto,* both to recover a deeper understanding of New Typography's designs and to better understand the place of photography in the broader professionalization of graphic design in Germany and across Europe and the United States between the World Wars. Its chapters alternate between a focused, chronological account of *Typophoto* as a dynamic, ever-changing conceptual technique of New Typography—tracing debates, practices, and events between 1923 and 1933—and two interspersed studies of how typography and photography were effectively hybridized in European and American graphic design, through practices of applied psychology and photographic retouching respectively. These broader practices suggest a meaning of *Typophoto* beyond New Typography: as a paradigm for understanding myriad ways that graphic design and photography are intertwined. New Typography is a focal point of this larger project but also a case study among many potential case studies. It is situated here within international discourse to recover the rich theoretical landscape of the graphic design, advertising, and printing industries, which have too often been overlooked as sources of avant-garde experimentation.

Chapter 1, "Photographic Language: A Genealogy of *Typophoto,* 1923–1928," parses the meanings and uses of *Typophoto* in the writing of László Moholy-Nagy, Jan Tschichold, Johannes Molzahn (1892–1965), and Max Burchartz. For these modernists, the term conveyed an ideology of modern visual communication: the amalgamation of verbal and visual representation to engender the hyperefficiency of reading. In its early articulations, *Typophoto* connoted the hybridization of word and image through the abstraction of typographic form and the transmutation of photography into graphic material through the halftone process. The New Typographers regarded photographic halftones as graphic material native to the printed page and shared the goal of transforming reading from a laborious pastime into an instantaneous and effortless reflex.

Chapter 2, "The Motivation of Form: Defining Legibility in Perceptual Psychology," surveys early experiments in perceptual psychology primarily in the United States and Germany, popularized in synthetic books on advertising theory published in the 1920s and 1930s. The concept of legibility in the graphic design profession was borrowed from psychologists' methods of measuring and describing perception, memory, and visual attention. Graphic design established its professional legitimacy, in large part, by assimilating psychological principles in articles on advertising design written for trade journals. In the experimental context of perceptual psychology, *Typophoto* connotes the mechanization of perception in experiments designed to study reading, in which psychologists used graphic forms as optical devices and photography as visual data. Experimental psychology is positioned here not as a direct influence on New Typography, but rather as a context for recovering both the complexity of "legibility" as a key term in graphic design and the enduring efficacy of *Typophoto.*

Chapter 3, "*Typophoto* and the New Photomontage, 1928–1933," considers how Tschichold's initial understanding of *Typophoto* became more nuanced and complex after the publication of *The New Typography.* This shift reflected how New Typographers often used experimental photography to destabilize—rather than clarify—relationships between word and image, especially in advertising. Their designs implicated readers as coproducers of graphics. By 1930, *Typophoto* came to signify not the pure functionality of visual communication that Tschichold had proposed in his first book, but rather the formal experiment, semiotic play, and persuasive power associated with photomontage. Tschichold's typescript for a never-published book, *Fotomontage* (ca. 1930–31), offered photomontage as a paradigm for the layering of media in advertising design and the construction of meaning through reading. This chapter situates the book *The Captured Glance* (*Gefesselter Blick*), edited by architects and designers Heinz Rasch (1902–1996) and Bodo Rasch (1903–1995) in 1930, and the contemporaneous theoretical writings of Franz Roh (1890–1965), as critical frameworks for understanding New Typography's uses of experimental photography.

Chapter 4, "Too Much and Too Little: Photographic Halftones, Bare and Retouched," proposes that practices of halftone retouching—and the surrounding debates among designers and advertisers—established *Typophoto* as a hybridized alternative to medium-specific understandings of photography and typography. Retouching was practiced and discussed by designers as an amalgamation of manual and mechanized production, yielding a new kind of image that was neither drawing nor pure photography, but rather a "photographic" image made for print advertising. International debates on retouching, which were published in German, American, and British trade magazines, reveal a remarkable lack of consensus among graphic designers about the efficacy of photography as a commercial tool. They suggest that "photography" was most valuable in design as an elusive idea above all else. Despite Tschichold's insistence on the "pure" photographic halftone, New Typography's designs did not dispense with the practice of retouching, but rather reframed it rhetorically as photomontage.

The fifth and final chapter, "*Typophoto* and the Professionalization of Graphic Design: Munich Meisterschule für Deutschlands Buchdrucker, 1927–1932," revisits the founding and early years of this vocational school for training printing house proprietors—an unexpected site of experimentation with *Typophoto*. A key example of the pedagogical approaches that shaped the German graphic design profession, the Meisterschule was founded by Paul Renner (1878–1956), and the faculty in its early years included Jan Tschichold and Georg Trump (1896–1985). Evident in student and faculty designs, as well as both published and unpublished pedagogical statements, the halftone was an object of formal, material, and theoretical experiment at the Meisterschule. They explored *Typophoto* by combining established typographic traditions, contemporary theories of business management, and new printing technologies. This case study is but one example of how photography—as circulated and experienced in popular media—is made as much by printers and designers as it is by photographers.

1

PHOTOGRAPHIC LANGUAGE

A Genealogy of *Typophoto*, 1923–1928

The New Typography, by virtue of its methods of design, embraces the whole domain of printing and not merely the narrow field of pure type. Thus in photography we possess an objective means of reproducing objectivity . . . which is comprehensible to all. Photography because it is another method of visual speech is also regarded as type.

—JAN TSCHICHOLD, "NEW LIFE IN PRINT" (1930)

The photo is the pacesetter for the tempo of time and development; the multitude and arrangement of visual sensations forces the uninterrupted work on the eye and the psyche.

—JOHANNES MOLZAHN, "STOP READING! LOOK!" (1928)

In 1931, Berlin-based publisher Eugen Gutnoff penned an ambitious book review for the *Archiv für Buchgewerbe und Gebrauchsgraphik*.[1] Much more than a critical summary, Gutnoff's review theorized that the medium of photography had been reinvented through its integration with type on the printed page. To establish this claim, he compared two recent books on photography: Helmuth

Bossert and Heinrich Guttmann's *Aus der Frühzeit der Photographie, 1840–70* (1930) and Franz Roh's *foto-auge: 76 fotos der zeit* (1929), a collaboration with Jan Tschichold.[2] Bossert and Guttmann's book was one of a spate of photography histories published around 1930, anticipating the centennial of the first public announcements of the medium's "invention" in 1839.[3] Like the exhibition *Film und Foto,* Tschichold and Roh's book was a touchstone for New Vision photography.[4] The two publications under review by Gutnoff each made their own claims to photography's past and future, respectively, disseminated to a mass audience through the centuries-old German book trade.

Gutnoff selected a pair of photographs, one reproduced in each book, to show how photography had radically changed between its first public announcements and the present day. He compared a high-contrast photograph by Charles-Victor Hugo—made between 1853 and 1855, depicting the hand of the photographer's father, Victor Hugo, isolated against a dark monochrome background—with El Lissitzky's 1924 composite photograph of his own hand (Figure 2).[5] Lissitzky's appeared with the caption "Hand of an architect or engineer, with compass. Composition by El Lissitzky."[6] On the surface, these images feature identical subject matter, but Gutnoff paired them to underscore their inherent difference: whereas Lissitzky intended to represent an anonymous type, Hugo depicted the hand of a specific, well-known individual, using dramatic lighting to imbue each detail with the expressiveness of early photographic portraiture.[7] Gutnoff described the contemporary reinvention of photography in terms of class consciousness; this pairing demonstrated how the medium transformed from one utilized by the bourgeoisie to display status and fame during the nineteenth century to one embraced by the masses in the twentieth century.[8]

In Gutnoff's view, these photographs evidenced how thoroughly the medium of photography had been reinvented since the turn of the twentieth century. Key to this reinvention was the uneasy marriage of photography and type. Printed from multiple exposures, Lissitzky's composite photograph dramatized the encroachment of photographic representation into the planar space of typography. A hand and compass hover, casting shadows across a ruled surface that appears to be the page itself, obdurately flat.[9] The beholder is challenged to read the curved line drawn with the compass as a mark that belongs to both the space of the photograph and the space of the page. It ultimately illustrates the fusion of typography and photography into a single medium, photo-typography, which the publisher regarded as key to photography's future use: "Today, photography is a big thing. It has benefitted from both New Vision

Vergleichende Photobildbetrachtung 93

Vergleichende Photobildbetrachtung

Comparer, ce n'est pas juger — Vergleichen, das heißt noch nicht urteilen. Das ist richtig; aber durch vergleichende Betrachtung der Dinge vermag man zu Urteilen und zu Beurteilungen zu kommen, die auf keine andre Weise zu erreichen sind. Heute ist die Photographie eine große Sache. Sie hat vom neuen Sehen und von der neuen Sachlichkeit profitiert. Es genügt ihr schon nicht mehr Bild oder Bildausschnitt zu sein, sie will konstruieren, läßt sich in Elemente zerlegen, die montiert, photomontiert werden: Photomontage, Photokombination. Sie drängt weiter und dringt in das typographische Satzbild ein, verdrängt gestalteten Satz, will mit der Typographie verschmelzen und erscheint als Phototypographie auf dem Plan.

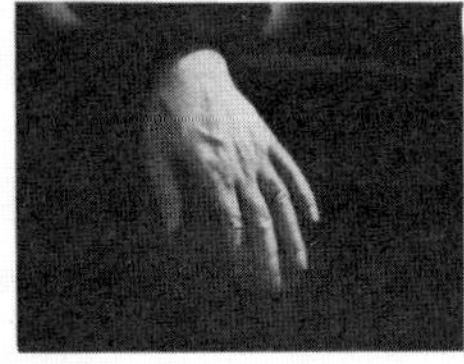

Etwa **1850**
Hand eines Dichters: Victor Hugos Hand, photographiert von Ch.-V. Hugo. Aus: Bossert und Guttmann, Aus der Frühzeit der Photographie. Societäts-Verlag, Frankfurt a. M. 1930

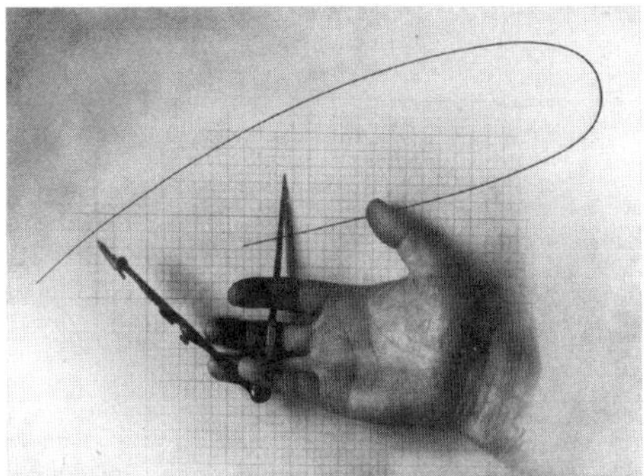

1930
Hand mit Zirkel eines Architekten oder Ingenieurs. Komposition von el lissitzky.
Aus: foto-auge von roh und tschichold. akademischer verlag dr. fritz wedekind, stuttgart 1930

FIGURE 2 Eugen Gutnoff, "Vergleichende Photobildbetrachtung," *Archiv für Buchgewerbe und Gebrauchsgraphik* 68, no. 3 (1931): 93. General Research Division, The New York Public Library. Copyright 2024 Artists Rights Society (ARS), New York.

and New Objectivity. It is no longer enough for photography to be a picture or a detail; rather, it wants to construct, to allow itself to be moved and photomontaged among assembled elements: photomontage, photo-combination. It pushes further and penetrates the typographic sentence-picture, replacing a structured sentence, and wants to merge with typography to appear in the graphic schema as photo-typography [*Phototypographie*]."[10]

More than simply the sum of photographic and typographic parts, Gutnoff described photo-typography as a hybrid übermedium that could transcend the constraints of image and text as discrete categories of representation, replaced by a new visual–verbal syntax rife with unprecedented formal and communicative possibilities. Importantly, he saw the merging of photo-typography to be rooted in the photographic medium. As a book publisher, Gutnoff had a particular interest in portraying photo-typography not as a manipulation of photography by typographers and printers, but rather as a logical extension of the modern medium. This implicated the printed halftone—which had enabled photographic reproduction on an unprecedented scale—as innately photographic.

Most commonly, the idea of photo-typography materialized in images that circulated not in photography books or as fine art, but rather as advertisements reproduced in newspapers, magazines, and promotional brochures. The basic composition of Lissitzky's 1924 photograph, for example, appeared in an advertisement for Pelikan drawing ink (Figure 3). Reproduced in a variety of sizes, it shows how commonplace the merging of photography and typography had become in commercial graphic design.[11] The disembodied hand of the "architect or engineer" in Lissitzky's original photograph now belongs to a different everyman: the consumer, who is identified only by the addition of the smart cuff of a shirt and jacket. The original, gridded surface has been wiped clean. A hand reaches for a compass and ink jar that seem to float in space, projecting toward the beholder against a planar, monochrome background. The curved line that appeared to be drawn with the compass now traces a perfect circle, circumscribing the words "Drawing Ink," rendered as a logo. This design combines the rationality of centripetal composition with implausible spatial relationships to sell jars of ink. It has been heavily retouched to smooth out the tonal variation of the original photographic image, especially the hand, areas of color applied evenly with an airbrush. Materially, this design retains little of Lissitzky's composite photograph—and yet it is undeniably a result of his photographic experiments. His disembodied hand, repurposed to sell a product, suggests advertising as a surreal endgame for the hybridization of photography and type.

Gutnoff's comment on photo-typography is one of many attempts by interwar printers and graphic designers to articulate their interest in the medium of photography. His remarks betrayed an urgency among designers and printers to understand what it meant to transform photographic images into graphic material, and how photographic images should be used on the printed page. These questions became particularly pressing as graphic designers attempted to define their profession—and the roles of technology, handcraft, and commerce within it—after the First World War. The network of designers known as the New Typographers articulated this set of dilemmas about the efficacy of photography in graphic design as *Typophoto*.

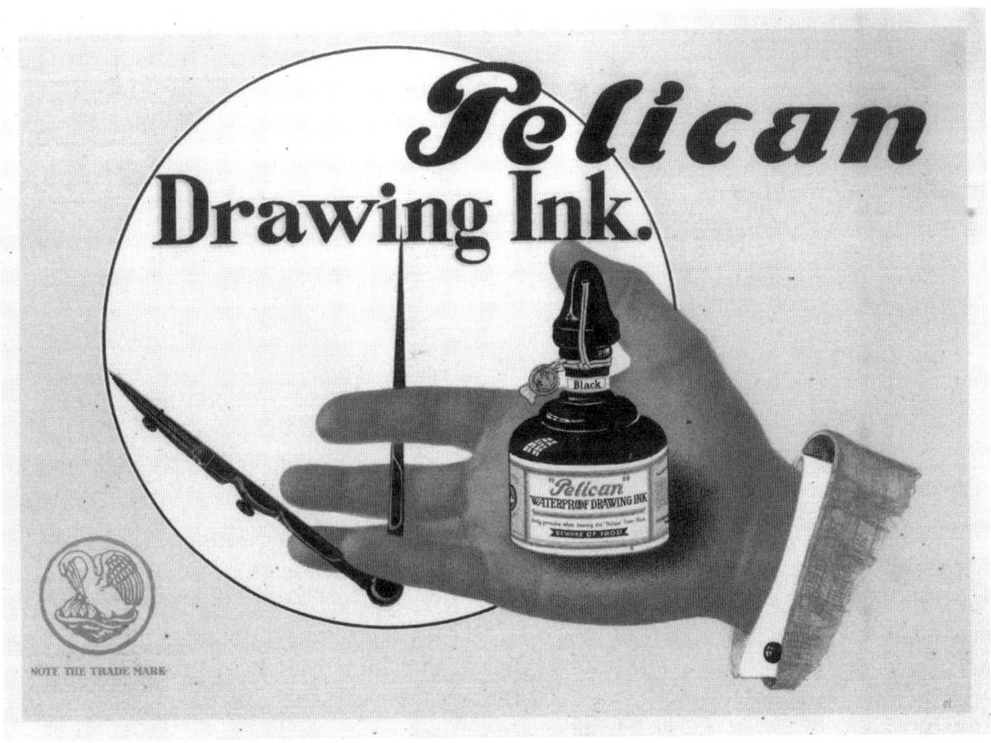

FIGURE 3 El Lissitzky, *Advertisement for Pelikan Drawing Ink*, 1924, offset lithograph. HIP / Art Resource, NY. Copyright 2024 Artists Rights Society (ARS), New York.

Typophoto was a multivalent idea and practice of graphic design, connoting the hybridization of word and image through the transmutation of photography into graphic material—chiefly through the halftone process. The New Typographers aspired to integrate type and photographic halftones with the goal of transforming the process of reading from a laborious practice into an instantaneous, effortless reflex. Whereas most discussions of *Typophoto* begin and end with Moholy-Nagy's *Painting Photography Film* (*Malerei Photographie Film*), the life of this concept began before this book's publication and remained integral to the aspirations of New Typography. Examples of typographic design—as both process and product—offer visual arguments about New Typography's investment in combining photography and typography. This extends to looking at nonphotographic forms to understand how designers understood photography, identifying "photographic" strategies in the design of type and handmade illustrations.

Beginning in the early 1920s, Moholy-Nagy treated type as abstract form in his own typographic work.[12] Rather than clinging to conventional type design, he advocated for the construction of letterforms and arrangement of graphic elements to stimulate the eye and mind through visual relationships between line, form, and color. This approach to typography accompanied his belief in photography not merely as a signifier of information, but as visual information in and of itself—that is, as a medium that could instantiate a subject on the printed page. His experiments with *Typophoto* were consistent with his prediction that photography and film would eventually replace written language as primary forms of communication.[13] However, as Pepper Stetler has argued, Moholy-Nagy did not imagine this as the "assimilation of photography to traditionally textual ways of making meaning."[14] Rather, he believed that photographic images introduced new kinds of temporality to printed matter, thereby necessarily transforming the modern practice of reading. A single photograph could be read instantly, while a sequence of images invited readers' own interpretations and associations, protracting reading through cognition and memory.

In *The New Typography,* Tschichold wrote, "We today have recognized photography as an essential typographic tool of the present."[15] While he did not advocate for visual media to replace written language, he borrowed the idea of *Typophoto* to promote the visual and material merging of photography and typography through offset printing and the halftone process. Like Moholy-Nagy, he experimented with the abstraction of type in productive contrast to what he described as the precision of photography.[16] He embraced *Typophoto* as a distinctly modern medium that would radically transform typography and book printing.

INVENTING *TYPOPHOTO* AND NEW TYPOGRAPHY

The seeds of New Typography as a doctrine for graphic design that would center ideas about photography were sown in Jan Tschichold's first encounter with the work of Moholy-Nagy at the first public exhibition of the Bauhaus in the summer of 1923.[17] Shortly after visiting the exhibition, Tschichold began corresponding with Moholy-Nagy directly, and it was likely through him that Tschichold also learned more about the work of El Lissitzky, with whom he began to correspond in 1925.[18] Though he would not verbalize the term *Typophoto* until 1925, Moholy-Nagy introduced the idea in 1923 through his design and writing for the first Bauhaus exhibition catalog, *Staatliches Bauhaus, Weimar, 1919–1923*.[19]

This book proposed the interconnectedness of photography and typography in three important and contradictory ways, thereby gesturing toward the layered meanings of *Typophoto* from the start. First, the catalog demonstrated—both verbally and visually—that photographic illustrations could complement typography as what Moholy-Nagy would later call "primary visual facts."[20] He believed that photography's capacity to render texture and the visual effects of light through contrast—thereby visually instantiating the materiality of an object on the page—could effectively free typography from its signifying function.[21] Second, Moholy-Nagy established the idea that photography fortifies typography with clarity, legibility, and efficiency.[22] And third, Moholy-Nagy's visual experiments with letterforms made reference to the raster pattern of the photographic halftone—a ubiquitous example of photography's influence on a new and experimental approach to graphic form.

Moholy-Nagy's essay "The New Typography" ("Die Neue Typographie") appeared in *Staatliches Bauhaus, Weimar, 1919–1923* and provided the moniker that Tschichold would soon adopt.[23] In the space of a page, Moholy-Nagy described "the new typography" as a paradigm for communication in which the optical effects of formal abstraction could be effectively combined with the "objectivity" (*Objektivität*) of photographic illustration. The essay began with a simple assertion that "typography is an instrument of communication."[24] This statement introduced the idea that effectiveness of visual communication depended on an understanding of the basic elements of typographic form—that is, the size, color, scale, and arrangement of letterforms, illustrations, and abstract graphic elements. He made the rather radical case that the clarity (*Klarheit*) and legibility (*Lesbarkeit*) of printed communication depended on principles of formal abstraction, rather than on the familiarity of the reader with conventional typographic styles. He proposed that "optical and physical laws" could mobilize "the unrestrained use of all line directions (not only horizontal arrangement), all types, letterform sizes, geometric forms, colors, et cetera," to ensure that the form of printed communication was a clear expression of its contents.[25] Through experiment with the "elasticity, variability, and freshness of typesetting materials," he proposed "a new typographic language" with myriad applications.[26]

Moholy-Nagy's design of the catalog's interior pages was as important for Tschichold's doctrine of New Typography, if not more so, than Moholy-Nagy's written commentary on typographic form.[27] The title page suggests another use of photography in graphic design apart from the "objectivity" described in Moholy-Nagy's writing or suggested by the photographic illustrations found in the book. In what would seem to be the artless task of typesetting the book's title and publisher name, Moholy-Nagy presented this information as a visually dynamic construction using sans serif type, contrasting color and scale, asymmetrical layout, variable line weight, and abstract form.[28] Text is staggered and printed at disparate sizes. Two lines are turned sideways, prompting the reader to understand the orientation of the page in two directions, and perhaps to physically turn the book (or cock their head) sideways. The decentered arrangement of type mirrors the form of the upper left corner of the page. Syncopated lines interrupt the regularity of the typographic grid, nested together like the corners of a set of concentric squares. The layout's asymmetry is emphasized by the square format of the book, which measures approximately ten by ten inches.[29]

The corner composition of the title page layout is emphasized graphically by the treatment of the word "BAUHAUS," its magnitude amplified by bold red ink and exaggerated scale. Due to the disparity in size between the *B* and the rest of the word, the first letter is made to look like a logo, which is simultaneously read separate from, and in relation to, the subsequent red letters. Though the page is only printed in black and red ink, a detail shows that a third color is created by screened patterns of parallel lines that spell out the school's name. The patterned text treatment gives these words a relative weightlessness in contrast to the heaviness of the letters printed in opaque black and red ink. They appear to float on the page, an effect enhanced by the overprinting of *S* and *T*, and by the overall layout of the page. As when looking at a halftone, the eye blends the screened pattern—to clearly read the words "Staatliches" and "Weimar"—such that they appear translucent and gray.

If not a direct reference to the photographic halftone, this treatment of text demonstrates how the raster pattern produced by halftone printing was useful to designers like Moholy-Nagy as a typographic, formal, and optical device.[30] The overall effect of this typographic treatment is much more than an efficient presentation of information, as Moholy-Nagy described in "Die Neue Typographie," and as Tschichold would later reiterate. Rather, this design implicated the printed page as a physical and psychological space for experimenting with the optical effects of form between the modes of verbal and visual communication. Moholy-Nagy played with the raster pattern as a photographic trope that would be repeated and elaborated by designers including Walter Dexel, Georg Trump, and Piet Zwart (Figure 4, Plate 3). Each used the halftone grid and the positive–negative quality of photography to play with typographic form and suggest the verbal–visual hybridity of *Typophoto.*

Reading the typographic treatment of the catalog's title page as an indirect homage to photography also situates this design among Moholy-Nagy's many experiments with painting, printmaking, and photography in the early 1920s. In their interconnectedness, we see his interest in the manipulation of light as not only fundamental to photography, but as something he explored with paint on a canvas or with ink on a page. The 1923 postcard Moholy-Nagy designed for the first Bauhaus exhibition, for example, reproduces one of many abstract "constructions" (Plate 4). This four-color lithograph is among many variations in which planes of primary color are arranged against a black background. Stippled dots of ink mix where the forms overlap. They mimic photography by simulating both the way light and shadow fall across or penetrate variously translucent or opaque surfaces, and the reproduction of halftones in patterns of dots that cohere optically. Illusions of the action of light, the forms appear to glow as though they are projected in darkness, or like negative images etched into the emulsion of a photogram.[31]

Apparent across Moholy-Nagy's design of the catalog *Staatliches Bauhaus, Weimar, 1919–1923* is a stark disjuncture between theory and practice. This book demonstrates how the rhetoric of clarity and legibility in his writing contradicts the playful use of abstract forms, scale, color, and layout in his typographic work. Throughout, he used sans serif type for titles and subject headings, enlarged to establish a visual hierarchy of information.[32] Yet, abstract graphic elements, including vertical and horizontal rules and circles, also call attention to the book's asymmetrical layout and muddle the boundary between abstract and representational form.[33] While most of the book was printed in black ink, Moholy-Nagy used the color red judiciously, yet playfully. On the title page of each subsection, he emphasized black text with red overlines.[34] On pages where essays are printed, he arranged author names perpendicular to the body text and printed them in red. Moholy-Nagy also created enlarged, elongated roman numerals using thick vertical rules that operate as optical devices, leading the eye across the page, while remaining recognizable as letterforms.

Inspired by his encounter with the first Bauhaus exhibition, especially the graphics by Moholy-Nagy, Tschichold began experimenting with what he called "elemental forms" and incorporating the visual language of constructivism into his own designs. While still living in Leipzig, where the designer had received a traditional education as a lettering artist (*Schriftzeichner*), he began

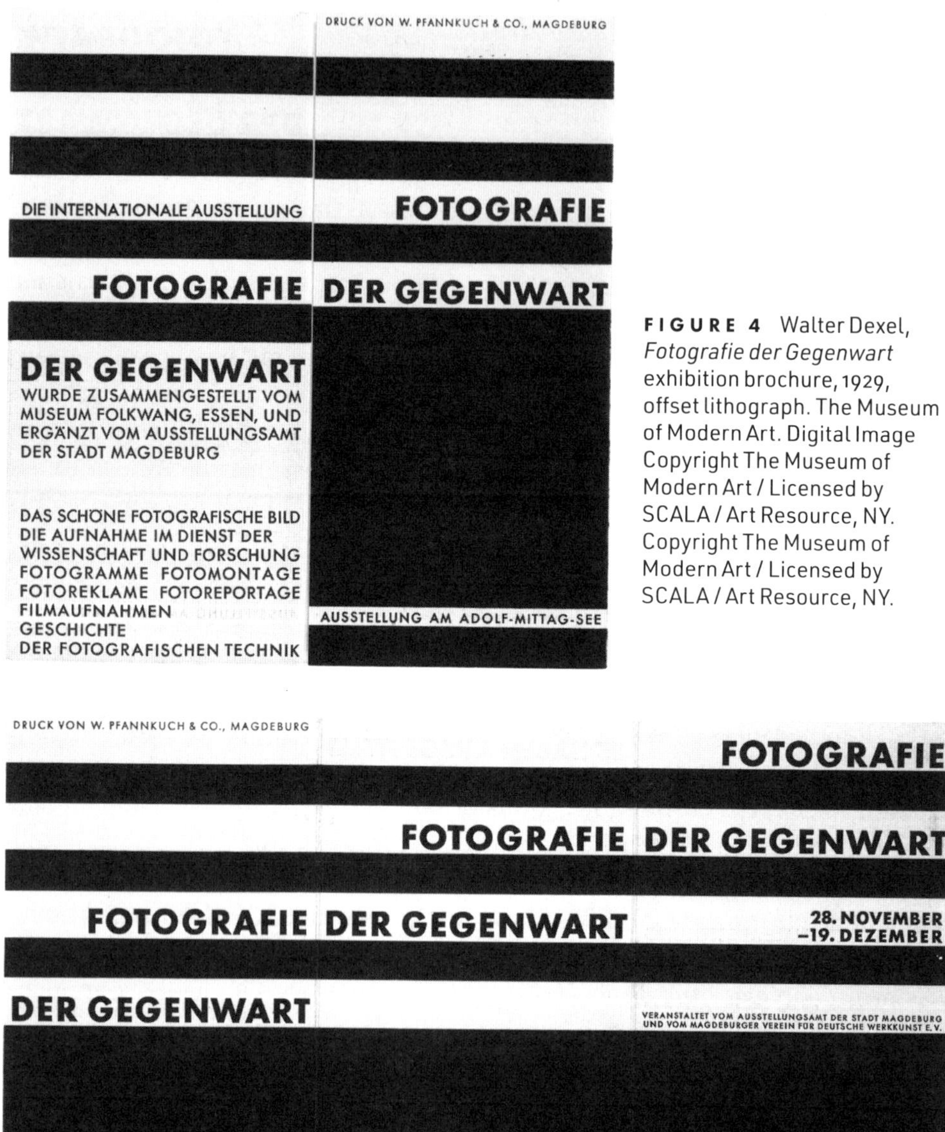

FIGURE 4 Walter Dexel, *Fotografie der Gegenwart* exhibition brochure, 1929, offset lithograph. The Museum of Modern Art. Digital Image Copyright The Museum of Modern Art / Licensed by SCALA / Art Resource, NY. Copyright The Museum of Modern Art / Licensed by SCALA / Art Resource, NY.

to explore the boundaries between abstract and typographic form by playing with form and color (Plate 5).[35] Moholy-Nagy's early typographic designs provided visual guidelines that Tschichold would, between 1923 and 1928, codify as a set of principles for using abstract graphic elements intended as optical devices to train the reader's attention and memory. What also emerged in Tschichold's first attempts to apply constructivist ideas to type design and layout was an interest in creating forms that toggled between representation and abstraction, in effect blurring the distinction between verbal and visual modes of communication. As in Moholy-Nagy's typographic work, theory and practice were evidently at odds in New Typography.

The same year that Tschichold traveled to Weimar to attend the first Bauhaus exhibition, Russian critic and formalist poet Viktor Schlovskii dismissed "nonobjective art" as a monolithic category. He proposed instead that "there is only motivated art and unmotivated art."[36] Schlovskii underlined the fact that abstract form could sometimes also be representational or perform a signifying function, as was the case with abstract elements used as compositional devices in graphic design. In 1930, Tschichold similarly articulated the relationship between abstract forms in contemporary painting and in typography, which he called a "genetic connection." Whereas "abstract painting is the 'unpurposing' . . . of pure colour and form," he wrote that "typography signifies the visual (or aesthetic) ordering of given elements (practical requirements, type, pictures, colour, etc.) on a plane surface. The difference between painting and typography exists only inasmuch as in the former there is a free choice of elements and the resulting design has no practical purpose."[37]

In Tschichold's earliest experiments with constructivism, we already see his keen interest in deciphering the differences between what Schlovskii called "motivated" and "unmotivated" forms. In 1923, he began to understand the "purpose" of typographic form in an expanded way, as more than a linguistic signifier. New Typography's eventual call for the banishment of typographic ornament meant that all forms incorporated into typesetting would have to be "motivated," or purposeful, even those that lacked a clear semiotic function. If all formal choices were "motivated," then any form could be read as simultaneously representational and abstract. Indeed, all form would draw its motivation from serving as an optical device that guided the eye deliberately around the page.

In the summer of 1924, Tschichold began compiling material for a special issue of *Typographische Mitteilungen*.[38] In an early version of his cover design for this issue, Tschichold arranged the title—"Konstruktive Typographie" in this prototype—around the tilted axis of a large red rule (Plate 6). In it, we can see what he described as "elemental typography": the red rule reads as a nonrepresentational form and, at the same time, as the stem of the letter *T*. Likewise, an unattached, black rule arranged perpendicular to the red rule forms the top bar of the letter *T*. Its orientation on the page is echoed by the arrangement of the letters "YPO / GRAPHIE" that cut into the red rule below.[39] Tschichold used color, asymmetrical layout, and deconstructed words and letterforms to test the limits of legibility. These choices render the design like a logo—a constructed image that relies on the interrelation of color and form to direct the movement of a reader's eye, rather than the familiarity of conventional typefaces.

The fusion of text and image in this design was achieved in large part through the process by which it was created: it began as a pencil sketch, in which Tschichold began to map out the formal relationships of the design's composition. He then created a collage of paper strips, using gridded paper to create uniform letterforms arranged irregularly, adding paint to heighten the contrast between red and black ink on white paper. The design retained its basic orientation, but rotated to the right, at a roughly forty-five-degree angle. The move from sketch to collage allowed Tschichold to arrange deconstructed letterforms and parts of each word as autonomous elements that could be overlapped to create different compositional effects.[40]

The medium of collage facilitated the "construction" of design, which Tschichold described as an iterative process of layering abstract elements such that they would cohere into a unified design while remaining visually distinct as parts of a whole.[41] In the final version of the cover design, Tschichold pulled the stem and arm further apart, making them function more like Moholy-Nagy's overlines—to emphasize the title—than like a distinctly legible letterform. Without the collaged mock-up for comparison, the *T* shape of the horizontal and vertical rules is all but undetectable in the final, printed cover design. Operating more as ground than figure, the vertical and horizontal rules allude to the underlying structure of the typographic grid. On one level, this process of abstracting and constructing letterforms using collage techniques was a far cry from Tschichold's formal training in calligraphy. Yet, hand-lettering was also a process of building the anatomy of type with elemental, abstract forms, as is evident in his early designs that combined the conventional style of calligraphic lettering with colorful elements that might function either as typographic ornament or as optical devices, using the primary color palette that would soon become emblematic of New Typography.

Tschichold's special edition of *Typographische Mitteilungen* was not published until October 1925.[42] Meanwhile, his much shorter manifesto "Die Neue Typographie" appeared in the pages of the journal *Kulturschau* in the spring of that year, borrowing the title and design tropes of Moholy-Nagy's essay in *Staatliches Bauhaus, Weimar, 1919–1923*.[43] Tschichold laid out a succinct list of sixteen principles, printed alongside typographic samples by Lissitzky and Moholy-Nagy. He dedicated one principle to what he regarded as the visual eloquence and cost-effectiveness of photography, claiming the superiority of photographic illustrations over reproductions of drawings: "Photography is more persuasive than drawing. With increasing usage and the corresponding reduction in cost of the new reproduction technologies, there is no further obstruction to the exclusive and expanded application of photography as a means of illustration, which we fundamentally aspire to."[44]

Tschichold's praise of photography underlined New Typography as a system of communication born of the urgent need to persuade as wide a readership as possible. Tschichold invoked photography as both a means of illustration and reproduction, functions that were mutually reinforcing. He recognized photography's usefulness to graphic design as a medium for creating new images and for generating faithful reproductions. In doing so, he acknowledged the limitless flexibility of the photographic medium as a tool for visual communication.

In 1925, the special issue of *Typographische Mitteilungen*, which Tschichold titled "elementare typographie" ("elemental typography"), was published as a much-expanded manifesto for New Typography with many authors.[45] The movement was presented as truly international and collective, defined verbally and visually. The issue brought together short texts and designs by practitioners scattered across Central and Eastern Europe, most of whom had traveled through or immigrated permanently to Germany after World War I.[46] Included was Moholy-Nagy's essay "Typographie-Photographie / TYPO-PHOTO," in which he reiterated photography and typography as the "basic elements of the new typography."[47] Also included were several short essays by Tschichold, presenting New Typography as international and decisive for the revolutionary potential of visual communication.[48]

Tschichold's texts for "elementare typographie" reframed the paradox that lay at the heart of New Typography that Moholy-Nagy had already articulated in the first Bauhaus exhibition catalog. Both emphasized New Typography as purely functional while also implicating this new mode of design as experimental and persuasive, especially regarding the interplay between linguistic representation and formal abstraction. One of Tschichold's short essays in "elementare typographie," which shares the issue's title, focused on how the spirit and aesthetic of constructivism could be applied to the practice of typography.[49] It began with a numbered list of four aphorisms, starting with the ostensibly simple declaration that "the new typography is functional [*zweckbetont*]."[50] Each principle builds on the last; the second clarifies that "the purpose of any typography is communication," which "must appear in the shortest, simplest, and strongest form."[51] The third principle emphasizes the importance of the relationship between typographic form and the content it represents.

The fourth and final principle announced photography as fundamental to modern visual communication:

> 4. *Internal organization* is restriction to the basic elements of typography: letters, figures, signs, lines of type set by hand and by machine.
>
> The basic elements of the new typography also include, in the optically organized world, the exact image: photography.
>
> Elemental type form is sans serif in all its variations: thin—medium—**fat**—narrow to wide.[52]

Like Moholy-Nagy, Tschichold characterized photographic illustration as an "exact picture" (*exakte Bild*) that should be combined with sans serif type, which he described as the "elemental form of writing" (*elementare Schriftform*). Despite the prominence of photography in this short outline, Tschichold gave no explanation for why he regarded photography as a superior means of illustration. Rather, the inherent precision of photographic images is taken to be self-evident.

The idea of photographic images as visual facts was not only intended to promote photographic illustration, but also to fortify the efficacy of New Typography. Perhaps the most important hallmark of New Typography was promotion of sans serif typefaces at a time when they were still relatively scarce in mass media. By insisting on the compatibility of the photographic halftone and simplified form of sans serif type, Tschichold attempted to establish the superiority of sans serif (*Grotesk*) type based on its association with photography—not because the two were similar, but because of their productive contrast. As a means of three-dimensional representation, photography forced a new concept of graphic space: "The introduction of the photographic block has enabled us to use the dynamics of three dimensions. It is precisely the contrast between the apparent three dimensions of photography and the plane form of type that gives our typography its strength."[53] He reiterated this productive contrast as key to legibility. By corroborating the superior legibility of *Grotesk,* the presence of photographic illustration could help combat the dominance of *Fraktur,* which in the mid-1920s was the dominant typeface in German newspapers.[54] Given its ubiquity in the popular press, *Fraktur* was likely the most legible typeface for the average German reader in the 1920s.[55] What is more, deep-seated associations of *Fraktur* with the history of German printing infused these typefaces with strong connotations of nationalism and ethnic identity.[56] True to its constructivist origins, New Typography's advocacy of *Grotesk* over *Fraktur* was explicitly internationalist. Thus, making a strong case for the superiority of sans serif type was a defining and radical stance for New Typography.

Despite its strict functionalist rhetoric, New Typography's principles—especially the association of sans serif type with photography—proved far more malleable in practice than Tschichold initially proposed. *Typophoto* was, explicitly, a declaration of the superiority of photographic illustration over drawing and of photomechanical reproduction enabled by the halftone process. However, on an implicit level, *Typophoto* was indicative of the pervasiveness of rationalization, scientific management, and romanticization of technology in Weimar German culture. As in Russian constructivist graphics, the presence of photographic images in New Typography's designs signaled a belief in technology as the coproducer of a utopian future. In the context of Central Europe, and especially the rehabilitation of German industry between the Wars, these beliefs were strongly underpinned by capitalist ideology.

Typophoto served as a guiding ideology for New Typography, which acted as a stand in for capitalist interest. The movement's stated aims as an unequivocally objective and efficient system of communication were visualized through the ubiquity of photographic illustration. Importantly, the ideological function of *Typophoto* could not be separated from its practical efficacy; photographic halftones in the designs of New Typography were not merely the most "efficient" means of illustration. Rather, their presence signified the importance of industrial-scale printing for the future of visual communication. They acted as symbols of healthy industry and economic prosperity—critical aspirations of interwar European culture and politics. Thus, the conflation of "photography" as both means of illustration and reproductive technology was key to the symbolic value of *Typophoto* for New Typography.

PRINTING *TYPOPHOTO*: PHOTOGRAPHIC MATERIAL AND TYPOGRAPHIC FORM

The early writings of Tschichold and Moholy-Nagy on *Typophoto* suggest that one of its most important, explicit meanings was the material instantiation of photographic facts on the printed page. This betrays the deep influence of the Russian avant-garde on their thinking about the usefulness of photography in graphic design. Their matter-of-fact appeals to the exactitude of photographic representation echoed similar declarations by photographer–designers and theorists Aleksandr Rodchenko, Osip Brik, and El Lissitzky. In the mid-1920s, Russian constructivists began to champion photographs as unmediated traces of reality—rather than pictorial representations of the world—which they called "factography."[57] By reproducing photographic images in journals such as *Left (Lef)* and *New Left (Novyi Lef)*, they fused a belief in the indexical quality of the photograph—as a material trace of its referent—with their use of printed matter as a space for active reader participation, rather than passive reception. "Elemental typography" enhanced the reader's sense of the printed page as a constructed space, in productive contrast to the immediacy of photographic images as visual facts.

The term *Typophoto* first appeared in László Moholy-Nagy's 1925 book *Painting Photography Film,* the eighth volume in the Bauhausbücher series. In a section dedicated to *Typophoto,* he boldly declared, "The printer's work is part of the foundation on which the *new world* will be built."[58] He framed *Typophoto* as part of a belief in printing as utopian—and the printing press as a cornerstone of future society.[59] He identified artists, scientists, and, above all, printers as revolutionaries of modern communication, and thus visionaries of a progressive future. Moreover, he implicated printers as creators of *Typophoto.* In describing the wide reach of the printer in shaping society, he insisted that photography had revolutionized printing through processes of photomechanical reproduction. He therefore called for "every printing press [to] possess its own block-making plant" to facilitate photomechanical reproduction in all printing.[60]

Moholy-Nagy presented *Typophoto* as a hybrid medium, predicated on the material connection between photography and typography, that would engender mass photographic literacy. This was an idea that Tschichold, as a typographer, found particularly compelling. Between 1923 and 1928,

Moholy-Nagy and Tschichold developed parallel theories that, when studied together, amount to a collective understanding of photography as an inherently graphic medium. Both men considered photography's material transmutation through the halftone process into a medium of communication that delivered pure information. This freed typographic form to function in other ways—namely, to direct and control a reader's attention and memory. For the New Typographers, the interrelation of type as pure form and photographic images as materialized information—rendered tangible by the halftone—established a way of thinking about how *Typophoto* could transform the everyday practice of reading in the modern era.

When Tschichold first recapitulated Moholy-Nagy's concept of *Typophoto,* he used it to elaborate photography's importance to industrial-scale printing, and thus to graphic design:

> The invention [of photographic blocks] has introduced a new epoch in graphic design, in whose beginning we now first find ourselves. Nearly everything formerly achieved by drawings, whether engraved, cut, or etched, can now be done better, faster, and usually more cheaply by photos and blocks. . . . Photographs, like letters, are a means of communication. The faster and simpler the means of communication the better. The development of our type from pictures to writing was intended to increase, as much as possible, understanding between people. Today there is much that we can "say" more simply with photographs than with words.[61]

He lauded the efficiency of photographic illustrations, both in terms of the speed of their production and consumption, and as visual forms that could be instantaneously apprehended and therefore speed up the process of reading. On a technological level, the photographic block had created a material equivalence between photographic halftone and type. The halftone process had not only made reproductions of photographs faster, cheaper, and thus more ubiquitous, but in fact had fundamentally altered the materiality of photographic images printed in the pages of newspapers, magazines, and books.

Introduced commercially in 1880, the halftone process translated the continuous-tone photographic print into a matrix of dots of ink that could be printed from the same matrix as type.[62] Together, they could be impressed onto paper with printing plates or cylinders, which ultimately enabled the cheap, industrial-scale reproduction of photographic images. This process effectively turned photography into a medium of mass communication. Yet the photographic halftone did not replace other forms of illustration altogether, nor was it easily assimilated into daily reading habits. When photographic halftones first appeared in the illustrated press, readers struggled to see coherent, photographic images through the graphic matrix of the halftone. They learned to interpret the halftone over time through increasingly frequent encounters with photographic reproductions, ultimately understanding to read abstract patterns of printed dots as photographic images. Moreover, the halftones they encountered in newspapers and magazines were heavily retouched by typographers, engravers, and printers. These practices often made drawn illustration and photography visually indistinguishable, as in the advertisement by Lissitzky described at the top of this chapter.[63]

When Moholy-Nagy announced the halftone as complementary to typography in 1925, *Typophoto* was, in a sense, already nearly a half century old. Still, New Typography's attempt to reinvent photography in print was radical in several ways. Although photographic halftones were already commonplace in periodicals, this was still a practice widely regarded as suitable only for disposable media, and their use was not yet routine in book printing.[64] *Typophoto* also indicated a campaign not only for the inclusion of photographic illustrations in all printed matter, but the wholesale replacement of drawn illustration with photographic images.[65] Moreover, for many of the New Typographers, *Typophoto* indicated a collective interest in the visibility of the halftone as such—not disguised through extensive retouching or airbrushing. The halftone's visibility on the page served as an important reminder that printing—the technological foundation of graphic design—enabled the mass dissemination of photography as information to be read.

Over half of Moholy-Nagy's 1923 essay "Die Neue Typographie," included in *Staatliches Bauhaus, Weimar, 1919–1923*, was dedicated to a discussion of photography as a visual medium and as modern technology. He regarded it as crucial to the "New Typography" in two ways: as a technology that enabled photomechanical reproduction, and as a direct means of image production. Embedded in this discussion of photography as a typographic tool was the idea of the medium as both reproductive and productive—today considered one of Moholy-Nagy's most important contributions to theories of photography.[66] He foregrounded the preeminence of photomechanical technology in facilitating visual communication: "Of utmost importance to typography today is the use of zincographic techniques, the mechanical production of photographic reproductions in all formats."[67]

This assertion points to the multiple meanings of *Typophoto*. It referred simultaneously to the combined verbal-visual language of typography and photographic illustration, as well as to how photographic technology facilitated the mass circulation of typographic form and material. This accounts for a notable slippage in Tschichold's discussions of photography. He often referred to the precision of "photography" without distinguishing between the photographic image and photomechanical reproduction. Noting this imprecision in the designer's writing, Robin Kinross has argued that Tschichold was primarily advocating the presence of photographic images in printed matter, rather than photomechanical reproduction.[68] Yet, for Tschichold as for Moholy-Nagy, it seems that these connotations could not be pulled apart: the capaciousness of "photography"—and the dual status of the halftone as both a means of image production and a technology of reproduction—was precisely what fortified it as a cornerstone of New Typography. Any given usage of the word could connote photography as a means of image production, a technology of reproduction, or a symbol of mechanized utopia. *Typophoto* preserved all these meanings simultaneously.

Moholy-Nagy believed that reproductive technologies had turned photography into "typographical material," thereby producing a new, superior medium of communication. As "typographical material," photographic images could be used as communicative devices integrated with type, or as "**Fototext**" that could replace written language altogether as unmediated information, which could be immediately understood.[69] This idea was initially interpreted and restated by Tschichold as a claim to the objectivity of photography as a communicative device. Yet, in *Painting Photography Film*, Moholy-Nagy added, "The form, the rendering is constructed out of the optical and associative relationships: into a visual, associative, conceptual, synthetic continuity: into the Typophoto as an unambiguous rendering in an *optically* valid form."[70] He implied that reading *Typophoto* could also be an act of visual construction on the part of the reader: seeing and interpreting relationships between forms, and perhaps producing new meaning through cognitive association. Already in its earliest iteration, *Typophoto* connoted both objective communication and open interpretation. From its inception, the term held contradiction and ambiguity, even in the most direct attempts to define it.

Tschichold adopted *Typophoto* as a pillar of modernist graphic design in his first book, *Die Neue Typographie* (1928), which translated the theoretical claims first articulated by Moholy-Nagy in 1923 into a universal handbook for graphic design and printing. The book was published three years after "elementare typographie," elaborating the ideas of its dispersed contributors in Tschichold's own words. He had continued to solicit and compile designs from fellow designers to help visually articulate the principles of New Typography between

1925 and 1928, and much of this material was reproduced in the book as illustrations.[71] Intended for a readership of typographers and printers, *Die Neue Typographie* offered a little history of typography and a fully codified guide to the standardized design and production of all printed matter.[72] Equally, the layouts and typographic treatments of both "elementare typographie" and *Painting Photography Film,* like the 1923 Bauhaus exhibition catalog, served as visual precedents for the principles of New Typography as Tschichold outlined them in 1928.

For both its style and content, Tschichold's book is best described as a design handbook and a theoretical manifesto, a format that was as novel as its contents. He borrowed the conversational, emphatic tone typical of avant-garde manifestos, combined with the didacticism of a practical handbook. One section, "Photographie und Typographie," dedicated to a lengthy defense of the relationship between photography and typography, begins by firmly dismissing the objections of unnamed "book craftsmen" to combining photography with type. This rhetorical strategy permeates much of Tschichold's writing: he frequently referred to antiquated positions of unnamed naysayers as straw man arguments, anticipating critiques and emphasizing his own position as modern and future facing.

Indeed, the publication of *Die Neue Typographie* was met with criticism, especially from the printing world. Leipzig Typographical Society chair Rudolf Engel-Hardt praised the "guiding idea of new typography . . . [as] the expression of the spirit of the present" and "an enrichment of typographic design."[73] However, he sharply rejected Tschichold's promotion of a standardized formula for all printed matter. Rather, he maintained that "typographic form and content" must be reconciled with "the affirmation of a new will to form-production" such that typographic form "corresponds to the character of the printed matter."[74] At issue for Engel-Hardt, as for many printers and typographers, was how to preserve the craft of bookmaking and the agency of the typographer even with the increasing standardization of industrialized printing. Engel-Hardt portrayed New Typography's emphasis on the pure functionality as essentially soulless, a threat to typographic skill, and a dangerous harbinger of "'Neue Sachlichkeit' at any price."[75] Tschichold's claims to New Typography as an expression of the Zeitgeist are best understood as a defense against such critiques. He insisted that the agency of the individual artist or craftsman could be replaced by the collective agency and power of the consolidated field of graphic design.

As a mechanical means of image production, photography was emblematic of the spirit of what Walter Porstmann called the "age of steel" (*Stahlzeit*) that defined the nineteenth and twentieth centuries.[76] A German engineer and theoretician who had also worked as a typesetter, Porstmann was a founding member of the Deutsche Institut für Normung, whose promotion of script suited to the modern age was deeply influential for Tschichold.[77] *Die Neue Typographie* was Tschichold's boldest attempt to bring Porstmann's theoretical and practical proposals to bear on the field of printing. He envisioned a "graphic culture of the future" in which "photography will be as expressive of our age as the woodcut was of the Middle Ages."[78] He made clear reference to Porstmann's historical categories, building on his claim to photography as "pictorial writing" (*bilderschrift*) apposite to modernity.[79]

Tschichold's promotion of *Typophoto* in bookmaking centered on materiality: "The halftone block is composed of many little raised dots, to which type is in fact related."[80] Like Moholy-Nagy, he recognized that the halftone process effectively transformed photographic images into typographic elements. Moreover, the translation of continuous-tone photographic images into patterns of printed dots forced photography to conform to the logic of the typographic grid. Tschichold also regarded the reproduction of photographic halftones in the pages of magazines and newspapers, which had become common by the 1920s, as a paradigm for the future of bookmaking.[81] The conventions of book design and printing, he insisted, had become outmoded. In his defense of photography's material compatibility with type, he condemned not only the lingering preference among book designers for etchings and drawings in book illustration, but also, implicitly, the practice of tipping in photographic prints rather than directly printing images in book pages as halftones. Photomechanical reproduction had the potential to level the hierarchy of printing if applied to both the traditionally "high" form of bookmaking and "low" form of the popular press. For Tschichold, the economy and material suitability of the halftone process were inextricable and mutually reinforcing, proving that photography was suitable for New Typography and thus for all forms of modern communication.

THE SPEED OF *TYPOPHOTO* AND THE FUTURE METROPOLIS

The ubiquity of photography in the popular press was at the center of a collective reckoning in Weimar Germany with the opportunities and costs of modernity. Shared ambivalence about the marriage of these inventions—and how they would continue to shape modern life—was an important backdrop for the New Typographers' idea of *Typophoto*. In 1925, cultural critic Edlef Köppen chided the illustrated magazine as a "dubious sign" of the times.[82] He regarded the disposability of magazines, and the cursory engagement of readers with their contents, as symptomatic of a nefarious cultural shift that threatened to replace substance with artifice and deliberation with speed: "The mark of our age is haste, hurry, nervousness. People have no time, indeed they flee the calm of contemplation; they reel recklessly through the streets with no intention of catching hold. The rhythm of life pounds short and hard: further—further! The consequence in many respects is superficiality."[83] Siegfried Kracauer similarly wrote about photography as a poor surrogate for memory and lived experience, facilitated in large part by its circulation in the illustrated press. He described the medium—especially reproduced in newspapers and magazines—as one that reduces "the world" to merely "a photographable present," even while promising greater access to it.[84]

Such critiques challenged the New Typographers to make a case for *Typophoto,* and their profession, as the key to a utopian vision for the future. In attempting to do so, they called on photography's common association with speed as proof that the inherent efficiency of *Typophoto* was commercially viable and could therefore aid in Germany's postwar economic recovery. In a promotional brochure for his design studio in Magdeburg, Johannes Molzahn described *Typophoto* as a necessary antidote to the deficit of time in the modern world: "Pictorial representation—*Typophoto* combined with the industrial trademark—will govern the future of advertising and the street, as well as in offices and other economic sites. The fantastic wear of energy in our time will force the most economical means of organization and transportation."[85]

In a related writing for *Das Kunstblatt,* Molzahn characterized *Typophoto* as a modern tool on par with the modern trademark, railroad, or telephone. Invoking *Typophoto,* for Molzahn, meant equating photography with economic efficiency: "The eye of the draftsman is replaced by the eye of the camera . . . because it is the more economical and therefore the only way."[86] The laboriousness of drawing, like the more traditional mode of reading, must necessarily be replaced by the efficiency of making and looking at photographic images: "One-hundredth of a second through the highly sensitive eye of your camera and the picture of the object there on the table is captured on the thin coating of emulsion on the film."[87] Contrary to the critiques of Köppen and Kracauer, Molzahn described photography as not only fast, but also materially linked to an object, apt to produce images more firmly tethered to "the world" than drawings made by hand. Accordingly, he imagined an ideal modern reader who would apprehend information more quickly and more viscerally.

An avid collector of printed matter designed by his contemporaries, Tschichold's earliest articulations of New Typography were particularly informed by the writings of Molzahn as well as Max Burchartz, both of whom contributed to "elementare typographie" in 1925 and to the meaning of *Typophoto.* Burchartz and Molzahn each established commercial design studios in the early 1920s, building their reputations and livelihoods primarily through corporate commissions.[88] As part of their recovery from the devastating economic impact of the First World War, steel and chemical manufacturers relied especially on new graphic identities to help rebuild their businesses and public reputations. In promoting their services as graphic designers, both Burchartz and Molzahn created materials that named photography as key to effective commercial design.

In June 1924, a year before the publication of "elementare typographie" and Moholy-Nagy's *Painting Photography Film,* Burchartz released a self-published leaflet, *Form-Production of Advertising* (*Gestaltung der Reklame*). Printed in red and black ink, Burchartz's four-page prospectus announced itself as the first in an ongoing series.[89] *Form-Production of Advertising* was a promotional tool for the designer's services that doubled as a didactic manual, a trope that by the mid-1920s had become common among German graphic designers. To establish oneself as legitimate in the field, a designer must stake their own claim to the nature and scope of the field itself.

Burchartz claimed the importance of graphic clarity and concision on account of the average consumer's short attention span. He insisted that "the modern person is stingy with time," unable to read, look, or listen for very long, a condition that he deemed an inevitable consequence of modern life.[90] He thus framed the need for economy of form in advertising design as a matter of respect for the modern reader: "Good advertising takes consideration of the public's time." In doing so, advertising need only spark the reader's interest rather than tell a whole story. Burchartz proposed the need for formal "clarity" and "economy" in design, primarily as a necessary adaptation to the inevitable changes in the apprehension of information already wrought by modern life.

Unlike Köppen, Burchartz regarded the "haste" of modernity as an opportunity rather than a threat. He claimed that, to keep pace with modern life, good advertising must use "new tools of communication," both technological and scientific. These included "projection and film, gramophone and radiotelegraphy," as well as photography.[91] Modern technologies of image production were deemed appropriate for mass communication on the basis of their speed, especially compared to drawing: "Within typography, new possibilities . . . arise through the novel use of photographic techniques, for example by retouching the peculiarity of the shots and by putting together various shots at different ratios of size and perspective. In the presentation, photography is superior to obsolete hand-drawing. It is more objective, more economical. Speed of production avoids the overemphasis of the individual hand, avoiding the expression of idiosyncrasy, but still leaving enough room to play in the arrangement."[92]

Though the term *Typophoto* did not yet exist as he wrote about the superiority of photographic illustration in 1924, Burchartz described the sophisticated fusion of typography and photography—especially through techniques like retouching and photomontage—into a medium that could be playful without recourse to the individualized expression of drawing. He implied instead that photography, like type, was a means of collective expression. Both had the potential to convey a shared vision of the future, rather than merely a singular point of view.

Importantly, the New Typographers regarded the usefulness of photography not merely in reaction to the pace of modernity, but also as a means of engendering mass perception. Molzahn predicted that "the shift to the photographic principle in production processes will inaugurate the final revolution. Only once the 'phototype' has matured into a reliable instrument can the whole of book printing be integrated into the economy of contemporary production."[93] Despite their emphasis on *Typophoto* as a medium of collectivist expression and revolution, both Burchartz and Molzahn were necessarily vague, avoiding any particular description of a politics that might challenge the worldviews of their prospective clients—industrial capitalists on whom they relied for work as designers.

READING *TYPOPHOTO*: OPTICAL WORDS, TALKING IMAGES, PHOTOGRAPHIC TYPE

By the end of the 1920s, advertising and commercial design had become the most ubiquitous and public uses of New Typography. Because of commercial design's imperative to sell products, the function of New Typography was increasingly discussed in terms of optimizing the visual impact and memorability of graphics. Tschichold turned his attention increasingly to this subject, notably in the article "Good and Bad Advertising Typography" ("Gute und schlechte Reklametypographie"), which was published several times in 1929 and 1930.[94] He referred to photographic images in commercial design as "optical words," key to a new kind of reading facilitated by effective advertising. In an undated, handwritten note, the designer suggested the hybridization of *Typophoto* in yet another way: "Photography not only as [an image] alongside

[text], but rather as a talking image, as image-type [*Bildtype*]."[95] Both of these descriptions implied the uniqueness of photography in print as a medium that merged written, spoken, and visual communication.

In Tschichold's later writings after his first book, he increasingly associated *Typophoto* with commercial and advertising design. As an "image type" that could operate as an "optical word" and "talking image," the photographic halftone engendered instant comprehension. According to the ethos of advertising, the mental impression of a design and its instantaneous recognition relied on mnemonic stimulation. If words and letterforms could be arranged in an advertisement in such a way that they made a strong, immediate impression on the mind of a reader, they could be just as easily recalled in the absence of that advertisement, ideally prompting the reader–consumer to purchase a product. *Typophoto* connoted an ambition to train readers to recognize and recall unique combinations of image and text—effectively teaching them to read abstract forms as symbols imbued with meaning, thereby triggering desire.

A closer look at the text and layout of *Painting Photography Film* illuminates New Typography's idea of photographic images as optical words and the kind of reading experience they hoped to enable with *Typophoto*. Most of Moholy-Nagy's essay "Typophoto" is dedicated not to the technical or formal aspects of combining typography and photography, but instead to the broader social implications of this newly announced hybrid medium. He described how technology had revolutionized communication, facilitating a new understanding of the world that was shared by the masses. Moholy-Nagy identified "deep human interest," rather than mere "curiosity" or economic drive, as the impetus for the modern advent and expansion of the news mediated by film, radio, electricity, telegraphy, and typography (especially in newspapers and magazines). He insisted that these modern technologies had and would continue to facilitate the "simultaneity of sensorially perceptible events."[96] The effect was, in Moholy-Nagy's view, social transformation forged by technological revolution—a process that he presciently predicted would be ongoing—which had already enabled "all classes" to access "truth" through a multitude of media platforms and thus to attain "international understanding" of a shared world.[97] *Typophoto* was thus a crucial link between advances in technological and social progress.

Even as he seemed to present the term as uncomplicated, Moholy-Nagy's discussion of *Typophoto* is characteristic of his theoretical writing: his words are far more evocative than they are didactic. Superficially, the definition of *Typophoto* was stated simply enough:

What is Typophoto?

Typography is communication formed in print.[98]

Photography is the visual presentation of what can optically be apprehended.

Typophoto is the visually most exact rendering of communication.[99]

At face value, this statement is straightforward. Photography is precise and efficient, legible as soon as it is printed on a page. Yet, Moholy-Nagy did not hold an uncomplicated belief in photography as an objective medium of representation. Rather, by repeatedly invoking the "visual" (*visuell*) and "optical" (*optisch*) in this short passage, Moholy-Nagy suggested *Typophoto* as a paradigm for reading. His introduction of the term *Typophoto* invites us to read words and images not as parallel sign systems, but together as one integrated system, starting with the book *Painting Photography Film* itself. The content of its argument was not only expressed through textual and visual essays, but equally—and perhaps even more importantly—in Moholy-Nagy's treatment of his own words as pliable graphic material. An examination of the book as a physical object—including the formal aspects of its typography and layout—situates the complexity and importance of *Typophoto* in Moholy-Nagy's worldview.[100]

The brief definition of *Typophoto* quoted above appears at the top of the second page of the "Typophoto" essay. This interlude reads like the aphorisms of an avant-garde manifesto—a style also adopted by Tschichold, as noted above. These short lines are wedged into the middle of a longer piece of prose. This narrative interruption is emphasized by its arrangement on the page: these lines are nestled between two circular graphic elements that punctuate the text, above and below, emphasizing its rhetorical dissonance from the narrative style of the surrounding paragraphs. The final line in this set is perhaps the most succinct, and most frequently repeated, definition of the term: "**Typophoto is the visually most exact rendering of communication.**" This line is set in bold and in a contrasting, slightly compressed, sans serif typeface, which Moholy-Nagy uses throughout to punctuate certain phrases and ideas.[101] Like the circles, this dissonant typographic treatment stops the eye, thereby accentuating textual meaning. This typographic play calls attention to narrative interruption. Tschichold would later identify elements like the circles as purely functional, "abstract ornaments" that create optical contrast to lead the eye of the reader and denote a hierarchy of information.[102] The spatial—as well as rhetorical—disjuncture between these short lines of text and the relatively verbose paragraphs preceding and following hint that Moholy-Nagy's succinct definition of *Typophoto* is deceptively simple.

The typographic treatment of the new term's pithy, question-and-answer-style definition does more than just call attention to itself for emphasis. It models an experience that Moholy-Nagy could only describe with words, rendering it viscerally immediate for the reader: bits of information are simultaneously delivered through different modes of communication, competing for the reader's attention. Imagine a reader sitting on a train, reading a newspaper. They look up, their concentration momentarily interrupted by glimpsing an advertisement on the back of the seat in front of them and a billboard outside, each bearing a few lines of text, likely set in different typefaces from the one they've been reading. In the blink of an eye, the billboard passes, and they look back down to the page, returning attention to the newspaper article. In the pages of his book, Moholy-Nagy mimicked this distinctly modern experience of reading: perceptual navigation of the graphic texture of a metropolis, compelled by the endless bombardment of information delivered in different forms and mediated by the inhuman speed of modern transit. Experiences of rupture create the erratic tempo of modernity.

This essay demonstrated *Typophoto* as a crucial component of modern reading as a sensory navigation of visual, spatial, temporal, and somatic experience. The rhetorical style and typographic treatment of the text together require a mode of reading that is an active negotiation of "simultaneity of sensorially perceptible events."[103] If, as he suggested, photography and film would eventually supersede literature as dominant forms of communication, it was because they could be read much faster than written language. As a paradigm for perception, Moholy-Nagy also invoked photography as a new way of seeing typography—a nonphotographic system of representation that nevertheless could be understood as "photographic." That is, modern type—understood "photographically"—could be faster and more efficient than traditional type, implicating syncopated layout and sans serif typefaces as steps toward purely visual communication.

The typographic treatment of Moholy-Nagy's deceptively simple definition of *Typophoto* betrays its implication that montage was a new paradigm for representing, understanding, and navigating the modern world. Rather than explain that *Typophoto* is the process by which word and image fragments are recombined to create new meanings, Moholy-Nagy first demonstrated this typographically. In the book's final section, this idea is elaborated visually through the combination of type, graphic elements, and photographic images in the storyboard for a never-produced film, "Dynamik der Gross-Stadt" (Figure 5).[104] Fourteen pages are given over to "Dynamik der Gross-Stadt," which Moholy-Nagy identified as an example of *Typophoto*.[105] In his introductory remarks, he clarified that this was not intended to be didactic, moralizing, or narrative in any way, but rather he explained that "its effect is meant to be visual, **purely** visual."[106] He continued, "The elements in this film have not an absolute logical connection with one another; their photographic, visual relationships, nevertheless, make them knit together in a vital association of events in space and time and bring the viewer actively into the dynamic of the city."[107] The space of the city finds analogy in the graphic space of the page.

Pepper Stetler has offered an understanding of this book as a whole, and the film sketch in particular, as a training manual for modern perception, which used graphic elements to "guide us through like traffic signs."[108] As Frederic Schwartz has noted, and as its title suggests, Moholy-Nagy's film sketch stressed, above all, the swift pace of visual encounters in the modern metropolis, "perhaps best exemplified by the experience of the railroad."[109] The navigation of disparate and fleeting visual encounters that was only subtly suggested by Moholy-Nagy's treatment of text in the textual essay is here demonstrated unambiguously through a cacophonous amalgamation of photographic images, abstract graphic elements, and text in a variety of sizes and typefaces. The arrangement is an irregular grid, spanning seven consecutive page spreads. However, Schwartz contends that the film sketch not only portrays the urban visual experience as it existed in 1925, but rather "represents and explores the conditions in which perception and therefore visual communication had come to take place," thereby offering a graphic space consonant with "new conditions of attention, perception and thought."[110] We could say, then, that Moholy-Nagy presented graphic space as analogous to the mind space of a modern metropolitan reader, in which perception and cognition are constantly in development.

That *Typophoto* could do more than merely represent the world as it existed—that it could, in fact, be generative of new modes of seeing, thinking, and living—was key to New Typography's ambition to turn photographic images into tools for envisioning and building the future. Likewise, as pliant form, type could be much more than a fixed signifier of language: typographic form could direct and regulate attention, conjure emotional response, and

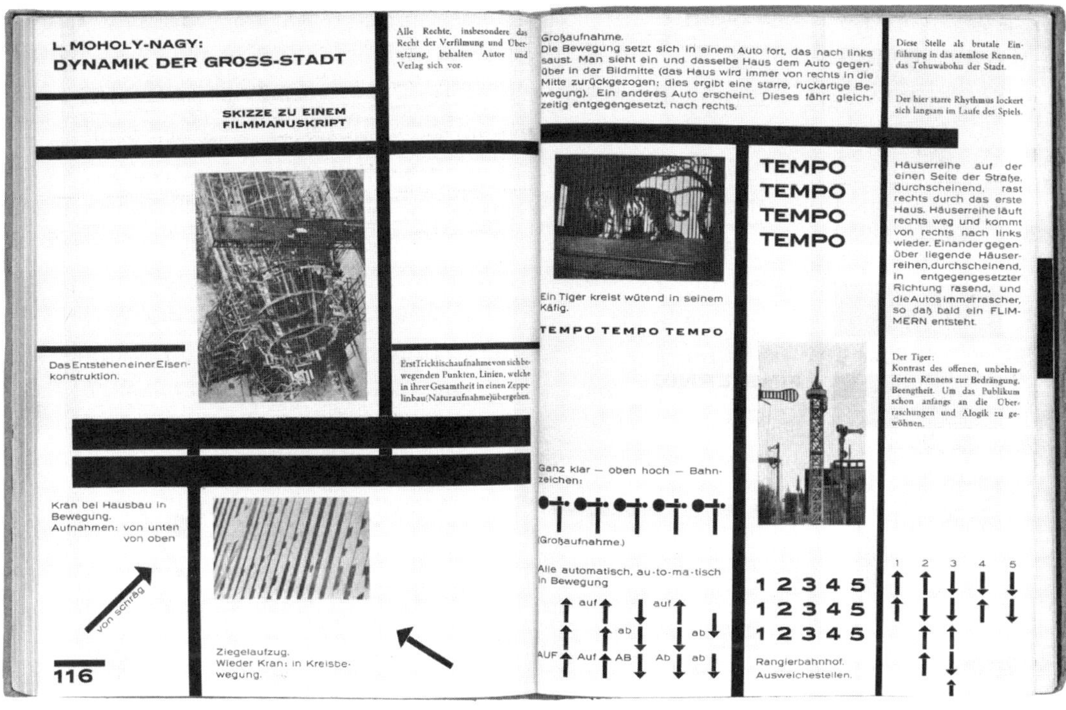

L. MOHOLY-NAGY:
DYNAMIK DER GROSS-STADT

SKIZZE ZU EINEM FILMMANUSKRIPT

Alle Rechte, insbesondere das Recht der Verfilmung und Übersetzung, behalten Autor und Verlag sich vor.

Das Entstehen einer Eisenkonstruktion.

Erst Tricktischaufnahme von sich bewegenden Punkten, Linien, welche in ihrer Gesamtheit in einen Zeppelinbau (Naturaufnahme) übergehen.

Kran bei Hausbau in Bewegung.
Aufnahmen: von unten
von oben

von schräg

Ziegelaufzug.
Wieder Kran: in Kreisbewegung.

116

Großaufnahme.
Die Bewegung setzt sich in einem Auto fort, das nach links saust. Man sieht ein und dasselbe Haus dem Auto gegenüber in der Bildmitte (das Haus wird immer von rechts in die Mitte zurückgezogen: dies ergibt eine starre, ruckartige Bewegung). Ein anderes Auto erscheint. Dieses fährt gleichzeitig entgegengesetzt, nach rechts.

Diese Stelle als brutale Einführung in das atemlose Rennen, das Tohuwabohu der Stadt.

Der hier starre Rhythmus lockert sich langsam im Laufe des Spiels.

Ein Tiger kreist wütend in seinem Käfig.

TEMPO TEMPO TEMPO

TEMPO
TEMPO
TEMPO
TEMPO

Häuserreihe auf der einen Seite der Straße, durchscheinend, rast rechts durch das erste Haus. Häuserreihe läuft rechts weg und kommt von rechts nach links wieder. Einander gegenüber liegende Häuserreihen, durchscheinend, in entgegengesetzter Richtung rasend, und die Autos immer rascher, so daß bald ein FLIMMERN entsteht.

Der Tiger:
Kontrast des offenen, unbehinderten Rennens zur Bedrängung, Beengtheit. Um das Publikum schon anfangs an die Überraschungen und Alogik zu gewöhnen.

Ganz klar — oben hoch — Bahnzeichen:

(Großaufnahme.)

Alle automatisch, au-to-ma-tisch in Bewegung

auf auf auf
ab ab
AUF Auf AB Ab ab

1 2 3 4 5
1 2 3 4 5
1 2 3 4 5

Rangierbahnhof.
Ausweichestellen.

1 2 3 4 5

FIGURE 5 László Moholy-Nagy, "Dynamik der Gross-Stadt," in *Malerei, Photographie, Film* (Munich: Albert Langen Verlag, 1925), 116–17. Digital Image Copyright The Museum of Modern Art / Licensed by SCALA / Art Resource, NY. Copyright 2024 Estate of László Moholy-Nagy / Artists Rights Society (ARS), New York.

imprint itself onto the substrate of a reader's memory. In "elementare typographie," these ideas were embedded in a short statement on advertising, coauthored by El Lissitzky with the Dutch designer, architect, and urban planner Mart Stam. "Advertising," they began, "has become a necessity of contemporary social order, a result of the drive to compete."[111] They framed advertising as distinctly modern, a product of a primal competitiveness that industrial capitalism nurtured.

As a unique form of communication tasked with suggestion, Stam and Lissitzky explained, advertising necessitated a new understanding of the workings of the human memory regarding the arrangement of word and image.

They described briefly how the practice of reading could be rethought to stimulate the instant recognition of a consumer product. Additionally, they encouraged designers to consider their own encounters with advertisements as they approached the problem of commercial design. Stam and Lissitzky distinguished between reading a text and merely recognizing it—describing the superior efficiency of the instantaneous apprehension of a logo over laboriously reading a line of text. Ironically, the desire for instant recognition—as opposed to relying on the procedures of traditional reading—made legibility of utmost importance. Stam and Lissitzky insisted that textual form and color be used only to make text more recognizable, and thus more legible, condemning ornamental graphic elements as useless to the expediency of reading that advertising required.

Stam and Lissitzky offered two clear directives for advertising design that set up the merging of text and image as key to a new way of seeing: "the product must be mentioned," and "the product must be shown."[112] On the subject of the latter, they wrote, "Photographic representation of either the product itself, its function, or both together, should fill the entire surface of the poster."[113] Further, a brand name or logo should also be visible (in keeping with the first directive), and "a photomechanical reproduction, provided with a distinctive signet, is preferable to any more or less skillfully drawn or painted illustration."[114]

As a successful example, Stam and Lissitzky curiously referred to the reproduction of an advertising poster from 1923 by Otto Baumberger, made with graphite, ink, and gouache for the Swiss clothing retailer PKZ, which shares a page with the first half of their essay (Plate 7).[115] Baumberger's design was lauded for its exacting verisimilitude, masquerading as a photographic image.[116] In fact, it is quite possible that Stam and Lissitzky mistook it for a photograph, as evidently did Tschichold.[117] Whether a misunderstanding of its origins or an intentional reading of the image as photographic, Stam and Lissitzky described the advertisement as a successful amalgam of word and image through "photomechanical reproduction." Baumberger's design shows only part of a coat—a close-up that features the lusciously intricate weave of wool fabric and the shine of satin lining—which fills almost the entirety of the poster. As Stam and Lissitzky described, the only text included is the PKZ logo, which is not as text printed over or next to the image, but rather integrated into it, dissolving any meaningful distinction between advertising copy and illustration. One lapel is opened to show the tag, on which the logo appears, sewn into the coat's inner lining below the collar.

The tropes described by Stam and Lissitzky, and exemplified by Baumberger's advertisement for PKZ, marked a reinvention of a form of German advertising design known as the *Sachplakat* (object poster). Fashionable before the First World War and popularized especially by graphic artists Lucian Bernhard, Ludwig Hohlwein, and Julius Klinger, the *Sachplakat* represented mass-manufactured commodities as visually isolated, singular objects.[118] Bernhard's advertising posters featured schematic depictions of commodities in basic outline, rendered with sparing detail against a monochrome background. This style employed a limited, bright color palette that typically had no mimetic relationship to products advertised or their functions. In the interwar period, the *Sachplakat*, like the word *Sachlichkeit*, was reinvented in accordance with the popularity of photography associated with *Neue Sachlichkeit*.[119] In exchange for schematic representations, designers began to mimic the verisimilitude of photography to evoke the material qualities of commodities. Despite the ubiquity of this style of advertising in Weimar Germany, the *Sachplakat* has scarcely been discussed in historical accounts of *Neue Sachlichkeit*, yet it is a crucial link in understanding how *Neue Sachlichkeit* photography informed both photographic and nonphotographic images found in interwar advertising.

The application of *Neue Sachlichkeit* as a mode of picturing and advertising commodities in the late 1920s served to redefine "objectivity" as the material luxury promised by capitalist modernity. It was a style of image-making that was invested in selling a way of seeing the world as much as selling commodities. Though not made with a camera, Baumberger's close-up of the PKZ coat deprives the beholder of a view of the entire object in exchange for sharp surface detail and a more intimate, visceral sense of its textures and haptic qualities. The poster's frame successfully mimics that of a photograph, arbitrarily cutting off the parts of the object that we do not see, and pushing the fabric of the coat against the picture plane, as though pressed against the glass of a storefront window or seen through the magnifying lens of a loupe.

Baumberger's design arguably has more in common with photographs by Albert Renger-Patzsch and Hans Finsler than with the prewar *Sachplakat* advertisements of Bernhard, Hohlwein, or Klinger. Renger-Patzsch and Finsler made close-up, high-contrast photographs, commissioned in the late 1920s by shoe manufacturer Fagus-Werk and lighting manufacturer Osram Licht AG, respectively. Industrially manufactured commodities appear in their photographs as tactile surfaces that fill or float within the photographic frame, rather than as objects with mass, weight, or dimension.[120] Like Baumberger's advertisement for PKZ, these images deprive the beholder of a sense of scale, devoid of human subjects. They emphasize material qualities appreciated through close-up inspection, rather than how these objects might be used or lived with.

Baumberger used graphite and paint to simulate the play of light and shadow on different materials, exploring how the texture of different fabrics affects the appearance of color. Comparison of a sketch of the design and the final color version—itself a chromolithographic reproduction—shows how the image was built up from the gridded surface of the page, ruled in finely drawn pencil lines with the aid of a straightedge (Plate 8). Reproduced through the halftone process, the surface textures rendered in Baumberger's colorful design are retained in black and white, as in "elementare typographie." What is more, the entire design takes on a distinctly "photographic" quality when translated into the monochrome visual language of photography. In reproduction, the poster easily passes for a black-and-white photograph, like those of Renger-Patzsch or Finsler. Printed in black ink, all evidence of Baumberger's handwork is effectively erased by the evenness of photomechanical reproduction.

Baumberger's poster demonstrated that, even without a camera or photochemistry, graphic designers could effectively exploit strategies of photographic imaging to render the page a surface on which commodities could appear to be materially instantiated. For an image to be photographic, it need not necessarily be created with a camera or photochemistry. Instead, it could be imbued with photographic qualities, speed of apprehension chief among them. Likewise, words need not be read, but merely glimpsed in an instant, to be recognized upon repeated viewing. Designers likewise devised ways of rendering words as images, a pervasive strategy across the nascent field of graphic design that transcended stylistic differences and national borders. Through economy of form and text, both images and words could pack a great deal of meaning into a simple design. A close-up view of a man's coat, for example, could signify luxury, style, and quality without the need for a tag line. The New Typographers used the photographic language of *Neue Sachlichkeit* not only to train consumers to become photographically literate, but also to become savvy readers of montage through their everyday encounters with advertising.

2

THE MOTIVATION OF FORM

Defining Legibility in Perceptual Psychology

For does there not in fact exist some graphic means—drawn from aesthetics and psychology—that will, when applied to the fundamental stratum of the individual, allow us to engrave on his mind what image we will, in such a manner that it will not be forgotten?

—JEAN CARLU, "SHOULD A POSTER BE A WORK OF ART?" (1926)

The first thing that must be done is to become familiar with how the psyche records and consumes, using its organs and functions, in order to deduce the effectiveness of the means of propaganda. . . . The type and quality of sensory stimuli have the greatest influence on the function and performance of sensory organs, which in reality are in constant transformation, adapting to changing phenomena and stimuli.

—JOHANNES MOLZAHN, *ÖKONOMIE DER REKLAME-MECHANE* (1926)

Seeing is deceiving.

—MATTHEW LUCKIESH, *VISUAL ILLUSIONS: THEIR CAUSES, CHARACTERISTICS AND APPLICATIONS* (1922)

In a 1927 article for the journal *Photographic Correspondence* (*Photographische Korrespondenz*), László Moholy-Nagy discussed applications of photography in advertising design. Here he recommended photography in combination with a very different kind of graphic tool: experimental psychology. In the fledgling field, he recognized a collective ambition to understand perception on a mass scale: "A beginning exists: there are numerous books about advertising, there are institutes dedicated purely to the psychology of advertising, there are first-rate advertisements—but we do not yet have a clear sense of how advertising in general should adapt to the constantly changing times, how a revolution takes place in the visual and simultaneously in the intellectual sphere without first making itself felt among the masses."[1]

Like photography, Moholy-Nagy regarded experimental psychology as a distinctly modern means of engendering "new vision" in advertising. He called for further "research into the physiological and psychological laws of visual effectiveness."[2] The pairing of photography and psychology was by no means new; by the mid-1920s, photographic technology had long been used by psychologists to measure and study human perception. Applied psychologists in the late nineteenth and early twentieth centuries identified the ability to focus readers' visual attention and memory as key to optimizing the legibility of modern graphics. They used abstract images as both experimental stimuli and visual information to communicate their findings. Their methods were foundational for New Typography and the wider field of graphic design, as their findings were assimilated into and circulated through synthetic books on applied psychology.

A specific and enduring definition of legibility was cultivated in commercial graphic design in the 1920s, which drew from both applied psychology and the typographic traditions and printing technologies that made advertising possible.[3] Commercial designs deemed "legible" were unique and memorable amalgamations of text and image that could be easily replicated—in both print and the mind's eye. Embedded in this formulation was the efficiency of seeing text as form and reading images as information. Moreover, this definition of legibility established *reproducibility*—made possible by offset printing—and *memorability*—as understood by psychologists—as mutually reinforcing, twin pillars of print advertising. New Typography explicitly sought to capture and control readers' attention; imprint photographic images as visual information; and use type and abstract graphic elements as optical devices. These ambitions borrowed from the rhetoric, methods, and findings of applied psychology, a field that developed between Germany and the United States around the turn of the twentieth century and continued to flourish between the World Wars.

Modern psychology originated at the Institut für Experimentelle Psychologie at the Universität Leipzig, the first formal laboratory for psychological research, founded by Wilhelm Wundt in 1879.[4] Wundt's laboratory subjected the human mind to measurable experiments in a controlled environment, effectively establishing psychology as a scientific discipline entirely separate from philosophy and much more akin to physiology.[5] The laboratory was a training ground for some of the most important figures in psychology's early history, including many German émigrés to the United States.[6] Wundt's laboratory, and many modeled after it, established experimental psychology as a field that continued to develop through the exchange of ideas, methods, and individuals between the United States and Germany in the late nineteenth and early twentieth centuries.

The experimental methods pioneered in Leipzig by Wundt and his students had numerous consequences for thinking about the role of images in modern life. Early psychologists understood images to live not only on physical surfaces such as paper or canvas, but in the space of the mind as well. They regarded memory and attention as quantifiable entities that could be studied, measured, and controlled. They devised psychological tests around the turn of the century to study eye movement; the interrelation of visual and haptic perception; the mechanics of optical illusion and after images; and the effects of color, formal symmetry, and bodily movement on human attention and memory. Psychologists also made recommendations for design by assessing the effects of print advertising on modern consumers. They identified the modern fracturing of attention as advertising's major obstacle. Psychologists and designers alike recognized that the fast pace of daily life in urban centers like Berlin, New York, and London meant that advertisements were glimpsed momentarily, if at all. Thus, a designer's first task was to make people see advertisements. However, visibility alone did not guarantee effectiveness. Psychologists identified the need for advertisements to be memorable and devised experiments to test and quantify the memorability of different forms.

In the 1920s, graphic design achieved its professional status, in part, by adopting the rhetoric of applied psychology and loosely applying its principles to the design of print advertising. Graphic design discourse circulated internationally in trade journals, especially those published in Germany (*Gebrauchsgraphik*, *Die Reklame*), the United States (*Advertising Arts*, *Printers' Ink*), Britain (*Commercial Art*), and France (*Arts et métiers graphiques*). The assimilation of experimental psychology by advertising designers yielded a set of deeply held—if vaguely articulated—approaches to visual form. Commercial designers justified their aesthetic choices in terms of utility: they discussed type, illustrations, and layout as optical tools that could be used to capture the attention of consumers, stimulating their memories and affective associations to optimize the likelihood of a future purchase. The New Typographers were among many designers who characterized visual forms as optical–cognitive devices.[7]

In advertising discourse of the 1920s and 1930s, designers in Europe and the United States consistently invoked the importance of harnessing consumer attention and memory to make graphics legible. Disagreements among designers about precisely how advertising should best capture attention and trigger memory reflected the contradictory findings of psychologists. Some argued that advertising should, in one commentator's words, "invite attention" by using visual form to agitate consumers, rather than to "satisfy" them.[8] This assertion was premised on the notion that the best advertising was novel and surprising. However, others believed that advertisements that connoted familiarity, and therefore seemed true and reliable, stimulated attention. American designer Frank H. Young wrote that successful advertising must "hold a reader's attention for a fraction of a second, it must ring true, and do so instantly."[9]

In Germany, the proliferation of print advertising in the late nineteenth century was met with concerns about the ethics of visual persuasion, which persisted into the 1920s. Advertisers and graphic designers defended commercial design as an honest practice with the potential to democratize culture and promote mass economic prosperity. They bolstered these claims by citing the cutting-edge science of applied psychology. In an article published in 1926 in *Gebrauchsgraphik,* for example, German advertising expert Paul Wallfisch-Roulin defended advertising by emphatically comparing it to "*written advice*" that merely encourages the existing desires of consumers.[10] He proposed that "the suggestive advertisement wants to lead, by means of thought association, to a strong development of available inclinations, wishes, and intentions, which finally ends in a *purchasing decision.*"[11] The importance of advertising as "suggestion"—a euphemistic term for "persuasion" or "propaganda" in advertising discourse—was recognized internationally. In the British journal *Commercial Art,* Eric Warne advised businessmen to recognize that effective advertising was defined "not so much by what it depicts as by what it suggests."[12] Yet another (unattributed) contributor to *Commercial Art* echoed this sentiment, writing that product photographs "need for their effective advertisement to be surrounded by an atmosphere of luxury, of refinement, of elegance and charm. The sale is made by suggestion far more than by special concentration of technical talking-points."[13]

The common refrain of advertising as a "suggestive" medium of mass communication among designers borrowed heavily from a vast and growing body of literature that synthesized the findings of applied psychology. A number of books published in the early twentieth century codified "scientific" principles of advertising design based on psychological experiments, including Viktor Mataja's *Die Reklame (Advertising)* (1910), Münsterberg's *Psychology and Industrial Efficiency* (1913), Christoph von Hartungen's *Psychologie der Reklame (Advertising Psychology)* (1921), Theodor König's *Reklame-Psychologie (Advertising-Psychology)* (1924), and Hanns Kropff's *Psychologie in der Reklame als Hilfe zur Bestgestaltung des Entwurfs (Advertising Psychology as an Aid to the Best Design)* (1934).[14] These texts summarized the experimental findings of a growing field that was especially active in Germany and the United States. By the 1920s and early 1930s, their common ideas had filtered into both advertising trade journals and the curricula of trade schools.[15]

Commercial designers who wrote for trade journals shared a common goal of defining the parameters of their profession. This included raising fundamental questions about the nature of advertising: How could text and image be optimized as persuasive tools? Should designers use the same criteria in assessing the efficacy of illustrations for advertising as for journalism? How could designers fortify advertising against the distractions of modern life? Trade journals served as platforms to establish advertising as a unique mode of visual communication with its own rules, referred to colloquially as "laws," invoking the rhetorical certainty of empirical science. Chief among such "laws" were claims about how form, line, and color should be used in illustration, type design, and layout to direct the consumer's eye, imprint on the memory, and evoke affective responses—namely desire.

Due to the influence of psychologists, advertisers and graphic designers regarded print advertising as a technology of perception as much as a means of communication. Photography and printing were tools of psychology, as well as apt metaphors for scientific theories about memory and attention. Daily encounters with images were facilitated by the abundance of print advertising and the ever-increasing accessibility of both handheld cameras and photomechanical image reproductions in books and periodicals.[16] Designers frequently compared the visual attention of consumers to a camera. They likened images "recorded" in the mind or "impressed" on the memory to the physical imprint of images on a page. Hermann Frenzel, publisher of *Gebrauchsgraphik*, described how the advertising poster, for example, should "establish a strong element of optical remembrance, impressing both this and the object itself on the memory."[17] In the context of advertising, "objectivity" connoted the power of images to bring an object—a product for sale—closer to the consumer, especially by imprinting an image on the mind, as Frenzel described.

Given the importance of perception for the consumption of print advertising, the fledgling field of applied psychology focused much of its early experiments on visual attention, memory, and persuasion. Consequently, experimental psychologists produced some of the twentieth century's most influential theories about the perception of line, color, and form. As recent scholarship has shown, Central European modernism was infused with the impetus to apply scientific principles to visual form.[18] Ultimately, experimental psychology supplied designers with a vocabulary for describing modernist graphic design. In turn, the rhetoric and utopian ambitions of New Typography—especially encapsulated by *Typophoto*—illuminate the visual culture of early experimental psychology. This is not to say that New Typography was influenced specifically by the experiments or writings of experimental psychology. Rather, the movement assimilated the ambitions and rhetoric of this growing area of scientific research to bolster their ideas about perception as rational and empirical. These ambitions inhered especially in the concept of *Typophoto*.

As a core value of New Typography, *Typophoto* connoted the collective desire to understand and control perception as an essential aspect of graphic design. This connotation makes the international discourse on experimental psychology—especially as practiced in Germany and the United States, which filtered into the theories of graphic designers—key to defining *Typophoto* for New Typography and the larger field. Perceptual psychologists used photography in myriad ways: as an apparatus of scientific measurement, as a tool to create and record visual data, and as a metaphor to fortify the idea of vision as purely mechanical and therefore governable. In the context of experimental psychology, *Typophoto* takes on several new meanings. First, it connotes the mechanization of perception in psychological experiments designed to study the process of reading. Second, it encompasses the way early psychologists came to understand typography as visual form, and graphic forms as perceptual devices, through their experiments measuring legibility (not unlike Moholy-Nagy's original formulation of *Typophoto*, as discussed in chapter 1). Finally, it captures how applied psychologists used images—especially photographic images reproduced as graphic inscriptions—as information. In doing so, they created a new graphic language with which to describe the elusive complexity of reading.

DEFINING LEGIBILITY: MEASURING MEMORY AND ATTENTION

To study reading in the artificial setting of the laboratory, experimental psychologists in the early twentieth century atomized its components. Doing so allowed them to represent the elusive concept of legibility using numerical data that easily correlated with the monetary value of advertising. They used this data to quantify how memorable, attention-grabbing, and persuasive advertisements were for the average consumer. These characteristics were commonly known as "memory-value," "attention-value," and "suggestion-value," terms popularized by German émigré to the United States Hugo Münsterberg, whose outsized influence on applied psychology is perhaps most apparent in the omnipresence of these concepts across advertising discourse.[19] Together, they defined the legibility of advertising, collapsing criteria for profitability into an ostensibly objective, scientific description of how reading works. In doing so, psychological studies made profit-driven standards for the consumption of advertising seem universal and natural to the efficacy of all graphic form.

In a speech transcribed in the German trade journal *Gebrauchsgraphik* in 1928, W. Buchanan-Taylor, a publicist for the British food manufacturer J. Lyons and Co., emphasized that the field of psychology had proven the scientific basis of effective advertising. He spoke about the application of Taylorist principles to both the production and consumption of commodities through effective commercial propaganda.[20] His speech reached a particularly sympathetic audience in the German readership of *Gebrauchsgraphik*, given the growing popularity of psychotechnics as a branch of applied psychology developed in Germany in direct response to the popularity of Taylorism.[21] As a founding proponent of psychotechnics, Münsterberg advocated the precise regulation of workers' bodily movement and "mental labor" to maximize their productivity.[22] He was instrumental in applying psychotechnical methods to studying the effects of advertising, thereby extending attempts to optimize worker productivity to the production of better consumers. *Psychology and Industrial Efficiency* (1913), arguably Münsterberg's most influential book, is largely dedicated to the selection of ideal industrial workers and strategies for increasing their productivity. He called for the cooperation of "wage-earners, manufacturers and laborers, exporters, importers, storekeepers, salesmen, and customers" in growing an industrial economy, implicating consumerism as civic responsibility.[23]

The book's third and final section, "The Best Possible Effect," concerns practices of buying and selling industrially manufactured goods, including the effects of advertising design and display on consumer behavior. Münsterberg emphasized repeated exposure to advertisements as an indispensable stimulus for recognition, which was therefore key to the "memory-value" of advertising: "The psychologically decisive factor here is not the fact of the mere repetition of the impression, but rather the stimulation of the attention which results from the repetition. . . . The second impression awakes the consciousness of recognition, thus exciting the attention, and through it we now turn actively to the repeated impression which forces itself on our memory with increased vividness on account of this active personal reaction."[24] These comments point to the interrelatedness of attention and memory, described as mutually reinforcing. The visual attention of consumers was required for an advertisement to be remembered. In turn, recognition—visualized rhetorically as the "impression" of advertising on the memory—would trigger "the stimulation of the attention." Thus, memory and attention were often referred to interchangeably in early experimental psychology.

By quantifying and measuring legibility, psychologists—and, by extension, graphic designers—equated ease of reading with efficiency of memory. Most early legibility studies were essentially memory tests that isolated reading in the controlled setting of a laboratory. In his 1914 book *Psychology, General and Applied,* Münsterberg published the results of a set of studies conducted at the Harvard Psychological Laboratory.[25] Under his supervision, subjects were given a book of advertisements, printed at varying sizes and positioned variably on each page, to look at for a finite amount of time. The first experiment tested fifty subjects; each was given ten minutes to look through a one-hundred-page book and asked to record what they remembered afterward. According to Münsterberg, this study showed that full-page advertisements were almost three times more memorable than half-page advertisements and over ten times more memorable than quarter-page advertisements. However, a similar experiment showed that smaller advertisements, when repeated more frequently, were more memorable than full-page advertisements.[26] These experiments also showed that advertisements mixed with other copy were not as memorable as pages solely devoted to advertising.

The idea that legibility was quantified by the speed with which graphics could be read and remembered was central to Tschichold's first attempt to define "New Typography" in his own words in the 1925 issue of *Kulturschau.* In this short manifesto, the designer repeatedly stressed that typographic form should be purposeful and simple. He dismissed the uses of typographic ornament and "national typefaces," namely in the *Fraktur* family, as uneconomical "leftovers from history" that ought to be replaced by sans serif typefaces.[27] His rhetorical emphasis on brevity, efficiency, and simplicity in modern communication betrays a collective urgency around the economic imperatives of advertising in the Weimar era. Against the backdrop of Germany's economic recovery in the aftermath of the First World War, advertising came under the scrutiny of social scientists and economists who sought to coordinate the bodies and minds of consumers through efficient commercial design. Thus, Tschichold stressed the need for formal simplicity in graphic design and the transformation of reading into instant recognition as "economic considerations," rather than stylistic ones.[28] He implicated New Typography not merely as a typographic expression of the Zeitgeist, but as a practical necessity to ensure the cultural and economic well-being of German society. Yet, the economic drives of New Typography were eclipsed in Tschichold's description of its aesthetic in terms of universal clarity and legibility.

Not all psychological experiments designed to test the legibility of printed type attempted to simulate the conditions of encounters with print advertising in newspapers or magazines. In 1938, Dutch typography and legibility scholar Gerrit Ovink aggregated a number of legibility studies, including his own, which compared different typefaces.[29] He described one such experiment that tested the legibility of individual letterforms set in eleven popular display typefaces seen at a distance.[30] Cards printed with one large letterform were inserted one at a time into a box framed with white cardboard and lit with bulbs simulating the lighting in a shop window. The box was hung about a meter and a half above the floor at the end of a long, narrow hallway, which "riveted the subjects' eyes to the lighted area," according to Ovink.[31] Each subject stood at the opposite end of the hallway, approximately fifty meters from the box, and slowly walked toward it, reporting what they saw with each step forward. From their comments, Ovink observed how the design of each typeface affected how quickly and in what way each letterform came into view.

Ovink used this study to make detailed conclusions about how the construction of each letterform—set in eleven different typefaces, in upper and lowercase—affected legibility when seen from various distances. The study was designed to aid in the selection of display typefaces for advertising posters, which were typically seen from afar. Ovink's conclusions included notes about how certain letters—such as *K* and *X*, or *C* and *E*—might be confused when set in a typeface that did not distinguish these letters strongly enough in its design.[32] These conclusions implied that the practice of reading was one of active construction. Similar to how a typeface is constructed out of horizontal and vertical lines, geometric forms, and relationships between positive and negative space, Ovink recognized reading as a process bringing recognizable forms into view, constructed through the perception of abstract fragments that together cohere into meaningful signs.

Even further removed from the daily conditions of reading, psychologists often used abstract images as visual stimuli to test specific aspects of attention-value as it related to legibility, in an attempt to decrease the number of variables (such as typeface, size, type or background color, typographical emphasis, line weight or width) in a given experiment. The attention-value of color was often tested using abstract images. American Harlow Gale was among the first psychologists to conduct experiments on the psychological effects of color.[33] In one study, he used two sets of cards: one set with one-inch, colored squares mounted on white backgrounds and another with one-inch circles on black backgrounds, illuminating the cards in different sequences, for a few seconds at a time, in view of a subject, rotating the cards ninety degrees between each view. Each subject was asked to recall what they had seen. His findings varied along gender lines: while Gale concluded that red on a white background had the greatest attention-value for women, he found that black on white had the greatest attention-value for men.[34] Overall, he concluded that the greatest attention-value belonged to the color red, followed by green, then black. He deduced that black ink printed on a white background was generally more memorable than white printed on black.[35]

Color was tested not only in terms of mnemonic value, but also as a stimulus for affective response, considered relevant to the suggestion-value of advertising. Among Gale's questionnaire-based studies was one on color preference, which found that red was the most commonly preferred color among women, while green was the most commonly disliked among both men and women.[36] However, an article published in *Commercial Art* claimed the universal preference for the color blue among men and women, citing a paper on "Colour Preference" given by Scottish psychologist James Drever to the Psychology Section of the British Association at Liverpool in September 1923.[37] Advertising designers frequently cited such studies as proof that their color choices were not only aesthetically motivated, but also backed by scientific data. These references implicated design as a product of science rather than art, despite the disparate conclusions of psychological studies.

A more complex set of findings on the affective associations of color appeared in American psychologist Albert Poffenberger's influential book *Psychology in Advertising* (1925).[38] Poffenberger summarized a study from 1924 that

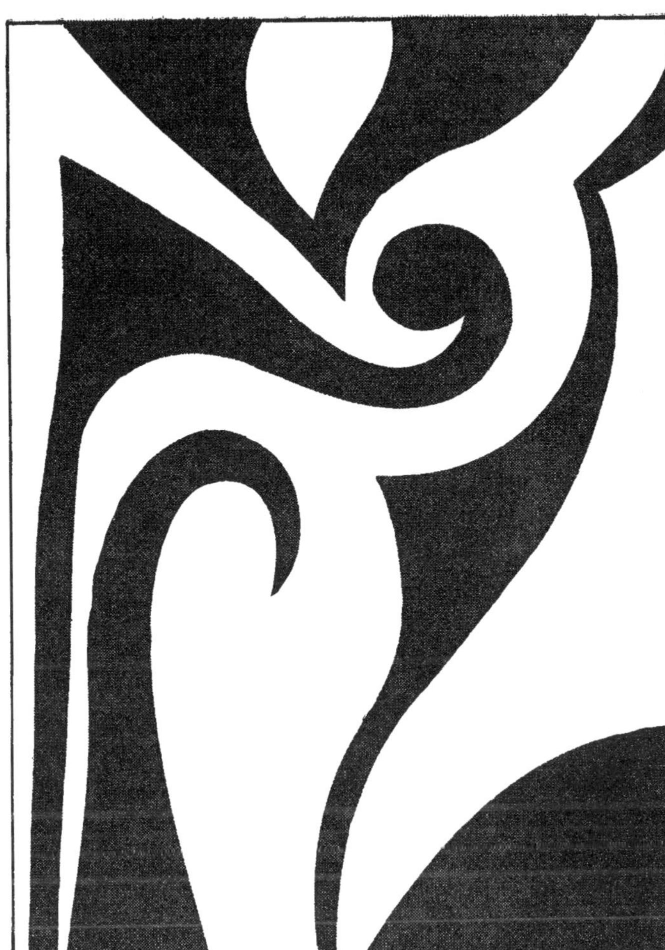

FIGURE 6 Pattern of the color charts used in the study of appropriateness of color combinations, published in Albert T. Poffenberger, *Psychology in Advertising* (New York: McGraw Hill, 1925), 454.

tested the associative qualities of different color combinations using twenty 8½″ × 11″ plates.[39] Each plate featured the same nonrepresentational image, its frame filled with undulating, vegetal forms, each painted in a different pair of color combinations (Figure 6). Along with the plates, one hundred subjects were given a sheet with a list of twenty terms, categorized as "abstract" or "concrete," corresponding to an "abstract quality" or "concrete commodity."[40] The subjects were instructed to match each term to the "meaning or atmosphere" of a given image.[41] Overall, the study found that individual color preferences did not necessarily affect the appropriateness of a given color to represent a commodity.[42] It concluded that colors have "feeling-tone values,"

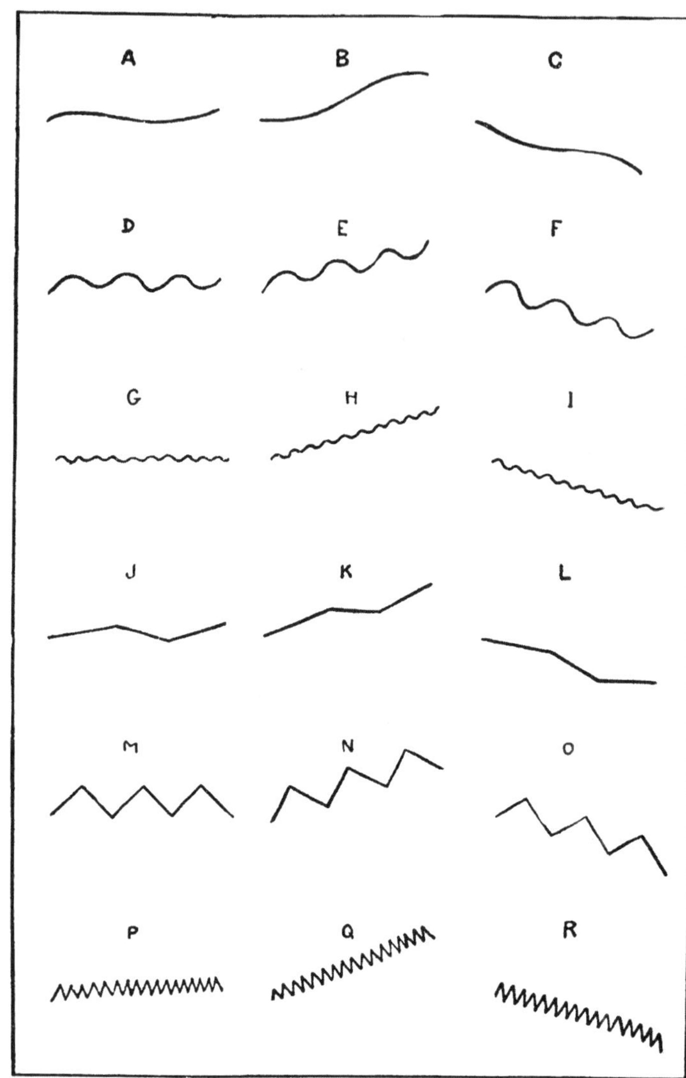

FIGURE 7
Representation of lines used in psychological study, published in Albert T. Poffenberger, *Psychology in Advertising* (New York: McGraw Hill, 1925), 370.

or affective associations, which are "stable and permanent" in the minds of individuals, therefore their "meanings or atmosphere . . . should be utilized wherever possible."[43]

Poffenberger cited another study from the same year that similarly tested the affective associations of different types of line.[44] Five hundred subjects were given eighteen 8½″ × 11″ cyanotypes, each depicting a line in a unique configuration (curved in different directions, zigzagging, randomly oriented), with an instruction sheet listing thirteen sets of adjectives denoting "classes" of emotion (Figure 7). Subjects were asked to match each "class" with one of the images, yielding a set of numerical data showing how the various curvature and orientation of lines corresponded to different emotional responses. Poffenberger suggested that these findings might be useful to advertising designers in selecting ornamental graphic elements, such as borders, to frame advertisements. Such an application implicated the geometric and vegetal motifs of ornamental printed borders—historically used by typographers to signify technical mastery and good taste—as functional, optical devices encoded with affective meaning.

Today, as a century ago, these experiments do not serve as direct explanations for the uses of form, line, and color in interwar graphic design, nor are they evidence of a direct influence on New Typography. The prescriptions of psychologists were useful to designers, in large part, because they so frequently disagreed; there were virtually as many aesthetic choices in design as there were psychological studies to justify them. These experiments instead illuminate how the concept of legibility in graphic design was founded on the shared idea that the memorability of graphics could stimulate attention and, in turn, trigger emotion. More than anything, psychologists gave graphic designers a shared, international language with which to talk about legibility.

Equally illuminating are the methods of experimental psychology. Though their conclusions focused on the clarity, memorability, and legibility of recognizable words and images, psychologists consistently relied on abstract forms in their experiments. The prevalence of abstract images in experiments devised to test legibility suggested the usefulness of text in graphic design not only as a system of linguistic representation, but also as visual form. Psychologists characterized "reading," in the context of advertising, as an instantaneous process that imprinted words and images on the mind and lodged them in the memory. New Typography's appeal to "elemental typography" was, in part, an artifact of how the methods of psychological research had imprinted on the young profession of graphic design.

READING THE EYE READING: OCULOMOTOR RESEARCH AND PATTERNS OF PERCEPTION

Along with attention and legibility, psychologists' understandings of the mechanisms of reading were critically important in establishing graphic design as a profession based in science. Embedded in references to the psychological power of form in advertising were conflicting theories about visual perception.

While some psychologists in the early twentieth century understood perception as a cognitive process, others located it primarily as a function of the eye. The study of perception had been a focus of psychological science since the founding of Wundt's laboratory. Diverging theories of perception as optical or cognitive betrayed the field's diverse origins in the field of physiology and traditions of philosophy.[45] Perception became increasingly important as a subject of psychological research because of its application in advertising design. From experimental psychology, graphic designers inherited theories of perception and reading, as well as a vocabulary for discussing reading in terms of efficiency and control.

Austrian advertising expert Hanns Kropff cited experiments by Poffenberger, among others, in his own volume on advertising psychology published in 1934, which summarized many of the field's findings in the United States and Europe.[46] Much of Kropff's book framed attention-value as a matter of controlling optical perception. A substantial section of his book was dedicated to the subject of "attention and interest," which equated the attention-value of graphics with their visual clarity.[47] Illustrated with examples of advertisements from Germany, Austria, and the United States, Kropff's book deconstructed composition in advertising design to demonstrate how each formal element could be exploited psychologically. He argued that an advertisement as a whole was effectively invisible if its parts did not catch a reader's attention: "When one glances at an advertisement, one sees nothing if the eyes wander over the whole, but rather the eye recognizes and rests only on the individual parts."[48] Kropff therefore advocated an elemental approach to design in direct response to the mechanics of seeing: he suggested that every element of text, image, and layout should be treated as a discrete formal unit, each with its own visual interest.

Kropff described each element of a commercial image as an optical device, or what he called a *Blickführung* (glance-guide); examples included the circle, square, golden section, and black-and-white contrast.[49] He elaborated by offering rules for typographic composition and the construction of text–image combinations.[50] These included reserving the center of a composition for a trademark or an image of a product; using light and the positioning of human figures to direct the gaze; intersecting images with type; exploiting contrast; and arranging type surrounded by ample white space.[51] Similarly, he maintained that a single letter was always easier to read than the same letter printed as part of a word.[52] Among the examples he cited as successful was an unattributed American advertisement for Travelese women's walking shoes

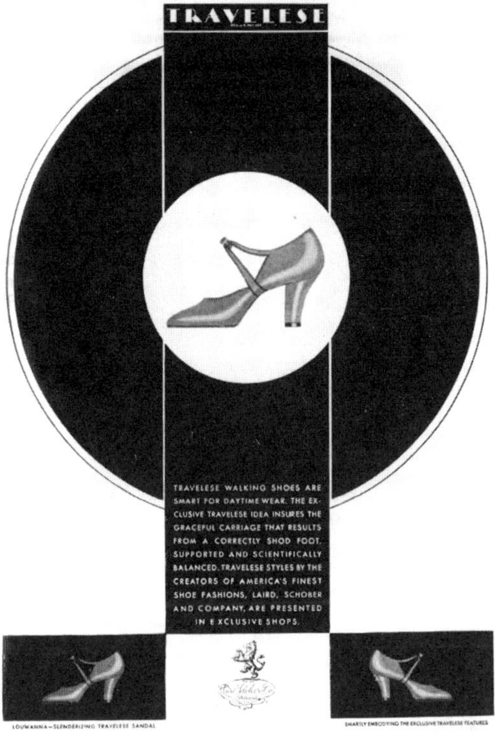

Abb. 36. Einfarbiges Inserat

Kombination von Rechtecken und konzentrischen Kreisen. Die Rechtecke sind entweder mathematische Quadrate, doppelte Quadrate oder nähern sich sehr stark dem goldenen Schnitt. Starke Isolierung durch schwarze Flächen

FIGURE 8 Unattributed advertisement for Travelese women's shoes, reproduced in Hanns Kropff, *Psychologie in der Reklame als Hilfe zur Bestgestaltunq des Entwurfs* (Stuttgart: Poeschel, 1934), n.p.

(Figure 8). His caption described its composition as a construction of abstract forms: "Combination of rectangles and concentric circles. The rectangles are either mathematical squares, doubled squares, or very strongly approaching the golden section. Strong isolation through black planes."[53] He located the strength of this advertisement in its use of formal elements, which each increase its attention-value. His prescriptions for design suggested that the effectiveness of an advertisement depended on the construction of abstract forms, which were as crucial to its overall message as the signification of text and image. Though not all Kropff's principles matched Tschichold's tenets of "elemental typography," his emphasis on optical control, and the efficacy of visual contrast, geometric forms, and ample white space, imbued these elements with scientific validity.[54]

By encouraging the isolation of images and letterforms to optimize the attention-value of graphics, Kropff tacitly urged the replication of laboratory conditions that psychologists created to study reading as an optical phenomenon.[55] Explicitly, he identified the task of focusing visual attention as fundamentally a matter of controlling the reader's eye movement: "The human eyes have a tendency not to be fixated on one point, but to wander around. Each roaming of the eye, however, means the wandering of attention to another point. This roaming, slipping, or wandering of the eye is a sign of the fluctuation of attention. If the eye is in motion, it sees nothing; only at rest does the human eye see something specific, which is then processed by the rest of the mechanism of the body."[56]

These comments implicate the graphic designer as a psychological experimenter who must understand the mechanics of perception to control it. To inhibit the natural, inadvertent "roaming of the eye" was to compel readers to see what they might otherwise ignore. For example, his emphasis on the use of circles was based on the principle that when looking at an advertisement, "one's glance first falls on the center of the page," which he called the "optical center."[57] As evidence, he cited eye-movement studies: "People have photographed people's eyes and found them wandering while reading and looking at images. It has been clearly established how the eyes move, when they rest, and when the attention can take effect."[58]

The study of eye movement began as an observational practice that eventually became mechanized, especially with the use of photography. The earliest studies of eye movement in reading were published by French ophthalmologist Louis Émile Javal in 1878.[59] He devised a study that involved placing a mirror in front of a subject and, standing behind them, counting their eye movements in the reflection as they read. A student and collaborator of German psychologist Benno Erdmann at the University of Halle in the 1890s, American psychologist Raymond Dodge built on Javal's method. Together, Erdmann and Dodge developed a tachistoscope designed specifically for the study of reading.[60] As a result, they posited that words—rather than individual letters—were the fundamental units of recognition in the process of reading.[61] In 1936, American psychologist Miles Tinker noted that Erdmann and Dodge also used a telescope to more accurately observe the eyes of their subjects.[62]

In their early attempts to record eye movement mechanically, psychologists effectively technologized human vision itself. Though intended to objectively represent natural perception, their inventions turned reading into a highly mechanized process fully removed from typical conditions. Moreover, these machines produced images that turned optical and cognitive experiences into abstract images that psychologists interpreted as data, trusted as indexical traces of eye movement. In 1908, American psychologist Edmund Burke Huey published *The Psychology and Pedagogy of Reading*, which summarized his experiments using a complex mechanical apparatus that he developed to record eye movement.[63] He placed a thin plaster cup cut with a small round hole on the eyeball of a subject, who was asked to read a passage of text, their head held steady by a headrest. The cup was attached to a thin lever that activated the movement of an aluminum pointer by horizontal movements of the eye, traced with an electric current onto soot-coated paper mounted on a rotating cylinder.[64]

The resulting images—reproduced as engravings when they were published—condensed perception to the tracking of a single eyeball. They picture the movement of the eye as a continuous line, punctuated by "saccades" caused by pauses of the eye (known as "fixations"), inscribed onto a receptive surface.[65] The use of such images by psychologists was one of many modern practices that trained viewers to understand them, to borrow Lisa Cartwright's terms, as "graphic inscriptions"—or exact corollaries to imperceptible phenomena.[66] Not only were such graphics used as "a disciplinary mode of representation," as Cartwright has argued, but the production of such images around the turn of the twentieth century was one of many scientific conventions of reading abstract graphic forms as coded information.[67] As such, images produced by psychologists essentially functioned as infographics, visual representations of data that became fundamental tools of graphic design in the early twentieth century.[68] Like psychologists, graphic designers created their own visual language of information with the infographic, thereby changing the very nature of information itself. Inscriptions produced through psychological experiments visualized legibility through formal abstraction, and—like charts of numerical data on which psychologists also relied—they became legible and trusted as scientific data over time. Psychologists defined legibility, in part, by creating images that required new modes of reading information for their results to be meaningful.

Around the same time that Huey developed his eye-tracking device, in collaboration with Thomas Cline, Dodge introduced a photochronograph, likely the first camera-based device used to record eye movement.[69] Designed to mechanize the procedures of both reading and observation, this device included a headrest on one end, to restrict a subject's bodily movement, and a camera mounted on the opposite end, which served as a recording device. Printed text was mounted inside the machine, and a beam of light was reflected on the subject's cornea and refracted onto a moving photographic plate in the camera, recording the eye's movement as the subject read.[70] In 1906, Walter Dearborn published photographs that he had produced similarly, using a tachistoscope and photochronograph to record eye movement.[71] A number of experimental psychologists working in the 1920s and 1930s used similar machines and improved on the early photochronographs developed by Dodge and Cline as well as by Dearborn. At the University of Chicago's psychological laboratory, Guy Thomas Buswell and Charles Judd developed a photochronograph loaded with two strips of movable celluloid film, which measured vertical and horizontal eye movement, respectively.[72]

Buswell used photochronography to study the legibility of images in a similar manner, attempting to record and map how people "read" images. He published the findings in his 1935 book *How People Look at Pictures,* which he claimed was the first known study of its kind.[73] The book aggregated the results of different studies in which the eye movement of multiple subjects was recorded while looking at a particular image (Figure 9). Tests used a variety of image reproductions as visual stimuli, including photographs, advertisements, and well-known artworks, such as Katsushika Hokusai's woodblock print *Under the Wave off Kanagawa* (ca. 1830–32); Georges Seurat's oil painting *A Sunday Afternoon on the Island of La Grande Jatte* (1884–86); and Marcel Duchamp's oil painting *The King and Queen Surrounded by Swift Nudes* (1912). The recordings represented the eye in motion with straight lines connecting points scattered across an image, which represented pauses of the eye. Buswell used them as visual proof that the human eye does not move smoothly across images in a single direction, but rather, as with text, moves erratically in fits and starts, pausing in some places and moving past others.

Buswell noted that shorter fixations indicated "the simpler processes of visual perception," while longer fixations likely indicate "a mental process of reflection."[74] He presented this visual data as "the most objective evidence available of the centers of interest within a picture," but stopped short of interpreting "the quality of the mental processes going on," leaving further interpretation to artists.[75] This study reflected an understanding of "attention" counter to that suggested by memory tests. Rather than measuring attention-value as the speed with which an image could be recalled, he instead attributed the highest attention-value to parts of an image on which subjects lingered the longest, effectively using eye tracking to decouple attention and memory.

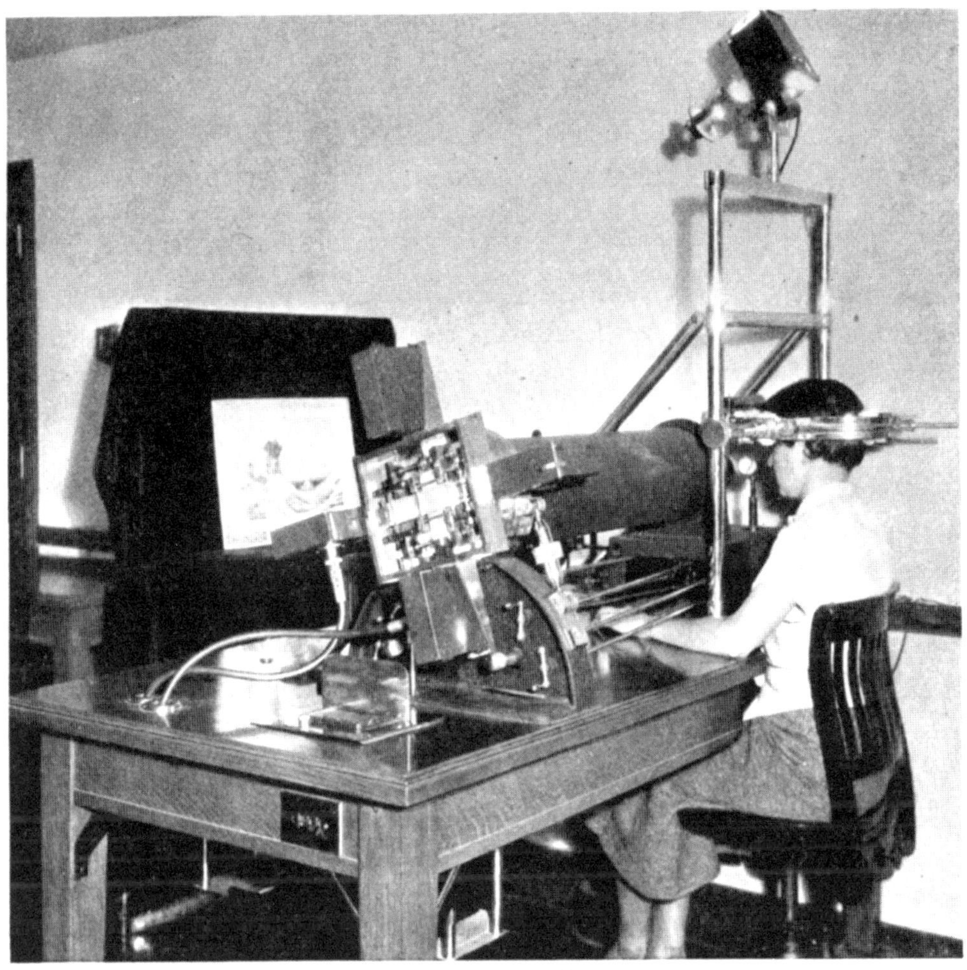

FIGURE 9 Subject being tested with Guy Thomas Buswell's photochronograph (loaded with a reproduction of Katsushika Hokusai, *Under the Wave off Kanagawa*, ca. 1830–32), circa 1930s, reproduced in Guy Thomas Buswell, *How People Look at Pictures; A Study of the Psychology of Perception in Art* (Chicago: University of Chicago Press, 1935), 12. Copyright University of Chicago Press.

Buswell's studies were visualized by several types of abstract images mapped onto muted versions of the reproductions used for each study. Tests of individual subjects were represented by a web of lines connecting fixation points, taken from photochronographic recordings, superimposed onto the image reproduction and accompanied by numerical data (Figure 10). Buswell

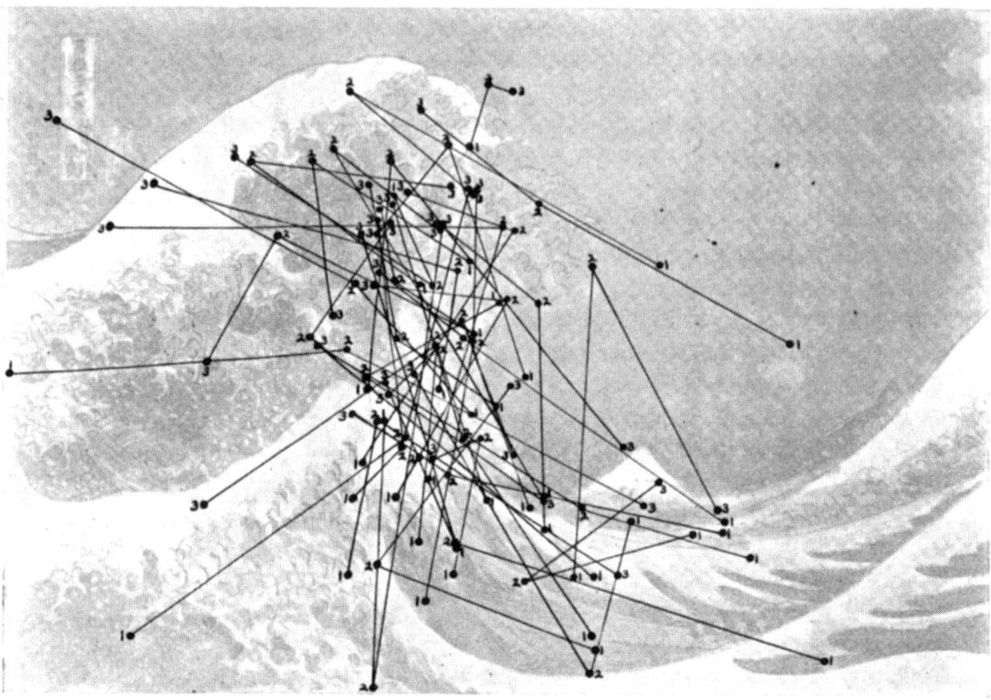

FIGURE 10 Individual subject record (Hokusai, *Under the Wave off Kanagawa*), reproduced in Guy Thomas Buswell, *How People Look at Pictures; A Study of the Psychology of Perception in Art* (Chicago: University of Chicago Press, 1935), Plate 14. Copyright University of Chicago Press.

aggregated multiple photochronographic recordings—usually from at least forty subjects—to create "density plot maps," which represented the "patterns of perception" of a given image (Figure 11).[76] Buswell also produced charts representing the distribution of fixations of a given image, overlaid with a grid to organize numerical data according to the aggregate number of fixations in each part of the image. Like the images produced by Huey and Dearborn, Buswell's represented eye movement using infographics, which condensed information even further by aggregating data collected from multiple subjects to represent the most common perceptual patterns. These charts present the perception of images as abstract visual form. They transform image reproductions used for study into ghostly shadows, overlaid with abstract marks made by the localized movement of the human eyeball recorded photographically, and subsequently printed as scientific illustrations. As true hybrids of photographic imaging

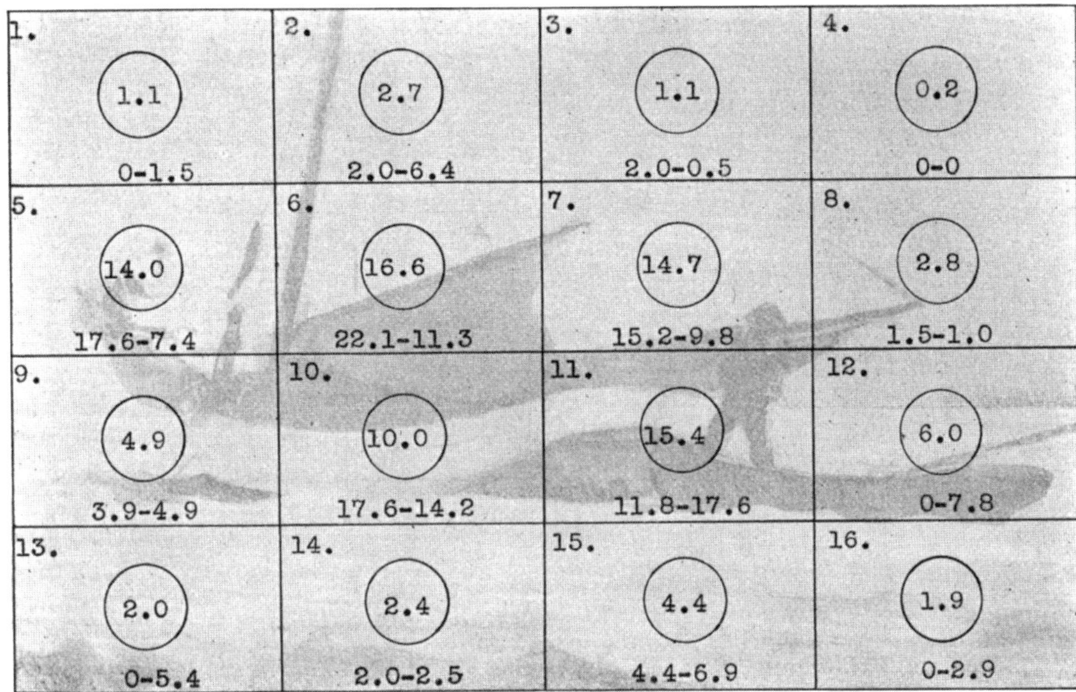

FIGURE 11 Distribution of recorded fixations of forty-two subjects (Hokusai, *Under the Wave off Kanagawa*), reproduced in Guy Thomas Buswell, *How People Look at Pictures; A Study of the Psychology of Perception in Art* (Chicago: University of Chicago Press, 1935), Plate 17. Copyright University of Chicago Press.

and graphic inscription, the images resulting from Buswell's studies suggest a meaning of *Typophoto* latent in perceptual psychology.

Experimental psychologists repeatedly invoked the mutually reinforcing ideas that words operate as formal devices and that images are legible as visual information. Walter Dill Scott advocated for the legibility of "simple" and "heavy" typefaces—such as Block, Futura, and Bodoni—on the premise that they "attract the attention" of the reader.[77] Like Moholy-Nagy, he suggested that legibility could be further optimized by the wholesale replacement of text with images: "The picture which tells the story is more easily comprehended than any possible expression in words."[78] That images could be read efficiently as information was not only made explicit in the writing of early psychologists, it was also embedded in their methods, especially in their uses of photography. Their experiments yielded images that were interpreted as hard scientific data—examples of what Moholy-Nagy called "visual facts."[79] Moreover, the images produced through early research on eye movement, and those used in other psychological studies of legibility, show that formal abstraction was a crucial tool in the nascent field of psychology. Abstract images produced by machines, especially with photographic technology, translated the perception of representational forms—both text and image—into indexical signs understood as raw data.[80] As material traces of scientific experiments, abstract photographic images were presented as data, and therefore seemed to foreclose interpretation. However, like all visual information, people had to be trained to read them as such.

Together, studies of eye movement—commonly known as "oculomotor" research—implicated reading and perception as mechanical processes. Implied in the very term "oculomotor" is the idea of the optical sensorium as an organic machine. Oculomotor experiments suggest that ideas about vision as mechanical not only emerged from social scientific research, but also anticipated it. These experiments began with the assumption that the human eye functions like a machine, and apparatuses were designed to reinforce this assumption. In turn, graphic designers repeatedly referred to reading and perception as the reader's "optical exposure" to a graphic—a rhetorical artifact of the long-standing use of tachistoscopy in laboratory experiments.[81] Despite the artificial conditions in which these machines were used to study reading and legibility, the photographic images they produced nevertheless stood for the mechanics of perception. Perhaps because of this artificiality—and the degree to which psychological research attempted to control vision to study it—graphic designers hoped to optimize reading by treating sites of advertising consumption—such as city streets and the pages of newspapers and magazines—as extensions of the laboratory.[82]

Although designers disagreed about the efficacy of photography in commercial illustration, the idea of photography as a proxy for human vision was reinforced in the writing of psychologists and graphic designers alike. Scott, for example, compared reading to the exposure of the film in a camera, which records light reflected off a subject and refracted through a lens. In doing so, he essentially described photochronographic studies of eye movement as reading itself: "As you look at this page the light is reflected to your eyes from each individual word, so one might say that you receive an impression from each of the words on the page."[83] Several pages later, Scott compared the eye and the camera even more explicitly: "The eye is like a photographer's camera. If it is focused for any particular object, all others appear through it to be blurred and indistinct. If I fix my eyes upon an object directly in front of me, all others are seen but dimly. . . . Objects that fall under the direct gaze of the eyes make stronger visual impressions than those which fall out of the focus."[84]

As in the ideology of New Vision, psychology's idea of vision as photographic implied not just the faithful reproduction of images in the mind, but reinforced perception as something that could be mechanized and optimized. If the eye functioned like a camera, then it could be adjusted and focused to faithfully record particular words and images while cropping out others.[85]

"OPTICAL GEARSHIFTING": SEEING THE WHOLE PICTURE

Eye tracking was not the only method of studying perception in early psychology. Like Hanns Kropff and many others in his field, German psychologist Theodor König named visual contrast as one of the key criteria for increasing the attention-value, memory-value, and suggestion-value of print advertising. However, his emphasis on contrast suggested alternative understandings of perception to those rooted in eye-movement research. Whereas Kropff relied on studies that located perception primarily in the functions of the optical sensorium, König understood perception as a phenomenon of the mind. One section of his 1924 book on advertising psychology was dedicated to "the influence of the form of an object."[86] He categorized visual contrast in advertising and product packaging as two types: simultaneous contrast (*Simultankonstrast*)—how two colors appear to change when viewed together—and successive contrast (*Sukzessivkonstrast*)—how viewing one color affects the appearance of a subsequently viewed color, apart from its material instantiation.[87] These categorizations stressed the impact of color relationships on the appearance of color.[88] Scott likewise named the pairing of complementary colors as a strategy for maximizing the visual impact of advertising: "Contrasts may be so harmoniously formed that the things contrasted are mutually strengthened, just as is the case when red and green are placed in juxtaposition. The red looks redder and the green looks greener."[89]

These observations—and particularly the categories named by König—drew from a vast body of research on optical illusions, which demonstrated that perception begins in the eye but coalesces in the mind.[90] This strain of psychological research recast images not as externally perceived, but as mentally constituted. Though many scientists who studied eye movement also acknowledged perception as a cognitive process, their attempts to precisely measure and quantify the physiology of reading betrayed their belief in the primacy of optical mechanics over cognition. Matthew Luckiesh, an American physicist and lighting engineer at General Electric, synthesized and advanced the study of optical illusions as a subject of psychology in the 1920s through a series of popular books.[91] He pointed to the radical implications of cognitive perception in the introduction to his 1922 book *Visual Illusions:* "Only a part of what is perceived comes through the senses from the object; the remainder always comes from within," which included "past experiences, associations, desires, demands, imaginings."[92] Studies of optical illusions implicated a perceived image as wholly separate, and perhaps even vastly different, from an image printed on a page. Ultimately, they understood readers not as passive consumers of images, but as producers whose perception involved a complex amalgamation of voluntary and involuntary actions including, but not limited to, optical apprehension.

Luckiesh played an important role in popularizing research on visual illusions in the 1920s, especially for graphic designers and advertising commentators. *Visual Illusions* aggregated and summarized over half a century of research, referencing work by numerous German physiologists, physicists, and psychologists, including Hermann Ebbinghaus, Karl Ewald Hering, Ludimar Hermann, Johann Joseph Oppel, Johann Christian Poggendorff, Wilhelm Wundt, and Karl Friedrich Zöllner (Figure 12). Luckiesh summarized their collective findings as proof that visual perception is more cognitive than optical: "The phenomena of binocular vision are far less physical than those of monocular vision. They are much more obscure, illusory, and perplexing because they are completely interwoven with or allied with psychological phenomena."[93] Still, he loosely categorized visual illusions into seven main groups: "geometrical illusions," "equivocal figures," "the influence of angles," "illusions of depth and distance," "irradiation and brightness–contrast," color contrast, and effects of lighting. These categories organized optical illusions into different types of perceptual phenomena, thereby assigning the mostly abstract forms used to illustrate different illusions to groupings that identify their appearance in the "mind's eye." In doing so, Luckiesh not only summed up a massive amount of prior research for a lay audience, but also demonstrated that images could be classified based on perception rather than production.

An unattributed 1925 article in *Commercial Art* cited Luckiesh's *Visual Illusions,* one of many declarations that graphic designers must understand the psychology of perception: "Illusions do not as a rule exist externally, but represent an interpreted judgment of the intellect. Such estimation may be attributed to association, imagination, or simply to the fact that we judge objects not as they are but as they appear related to each other."[94] Still, Luckiesh was a strong advocate for the application of research on optical illusions to various kinds of design. In addition to advertising, he cited the practice of painting war

THE INFLUENCE OF ANGLES

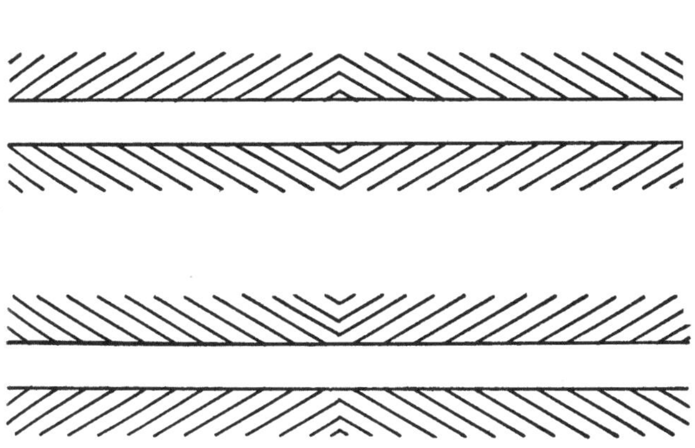

Fig. 38. — Parallel lines which do not appear so.

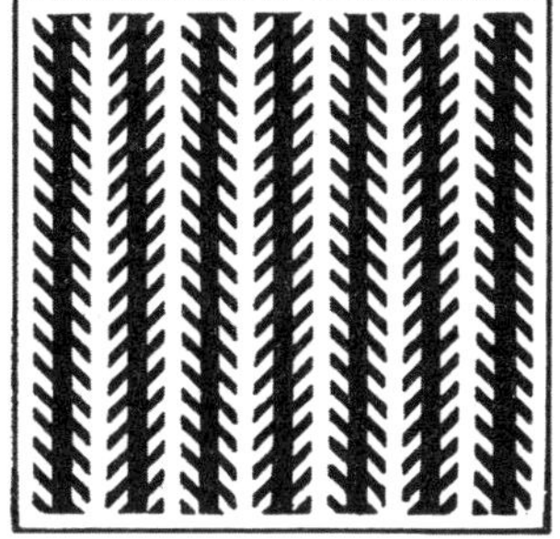

Fig. 37. — Zöllner's illusion of direction.

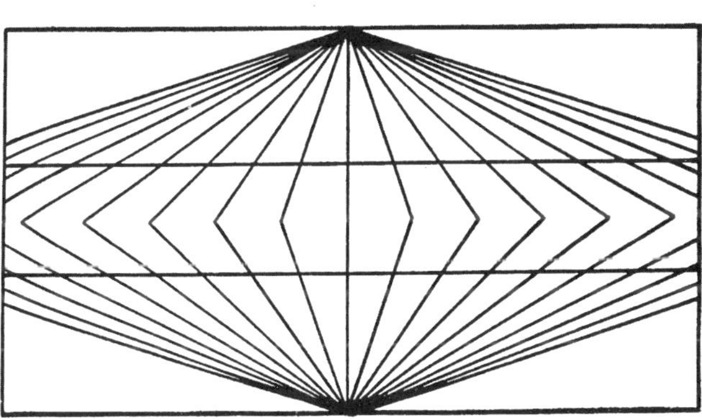

Fig. 39. — Wundt's illusion of direction.

FIGURE 12 Illustrations of illusion by Karl Friedrich Zöllner and Wilwelm Wundt, reproduced in Matthew Luckiesh, *Visual Illusions: Their Causes, Characteristics and Applications* (1922; repr., New York: Dover Publications, 1965), 77, 79. Copyright Dover Publications.

ships in abstract camouflage patterns—or "dazzle patterns"—meant to visually disorient other ships regarding their location or distance (Figure 13).[95] The study of optical illusions suggested an ontological split that is fundamental to image analysis and design practice: it implied that every image exists simultaneously on a physical substrate and in the mind's eye of every beholder who encounters it. Whereas a painted or printed image is relatively static and unchanging, mental images are subject to transformation by the influence of emotion and the degradation of memory. Mental images are available only to

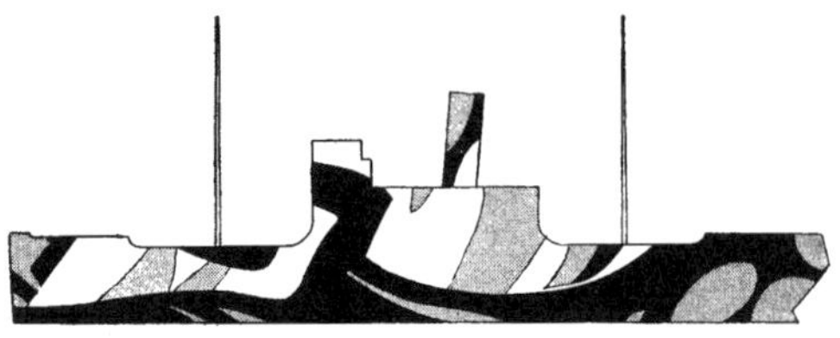

Fig. 92.— A primary stage in the evolution of the use of geometrical-optical illusions on ships.

CAMOUFLAGE

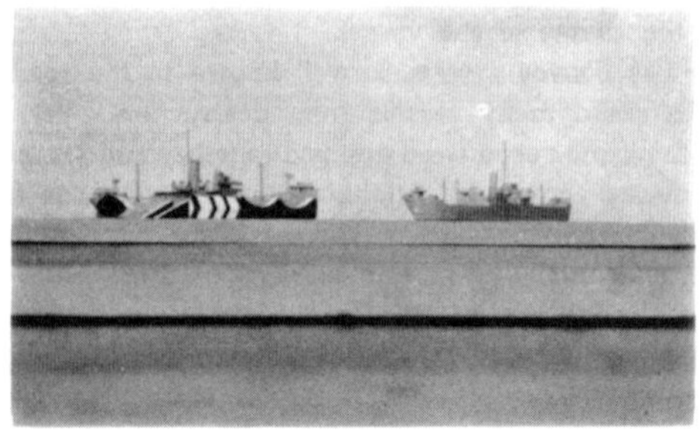

VISUAL ILLUSIONS

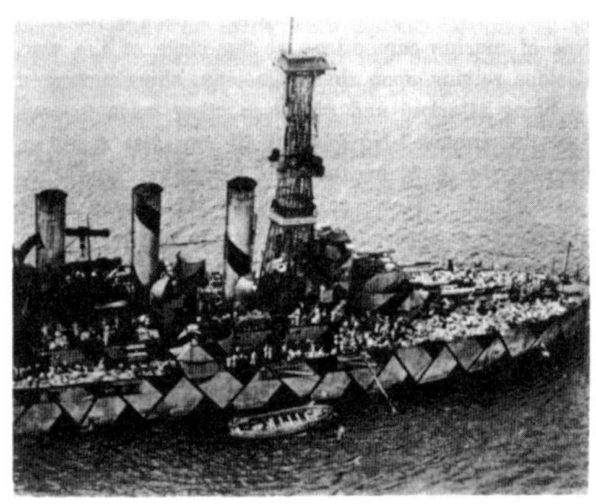

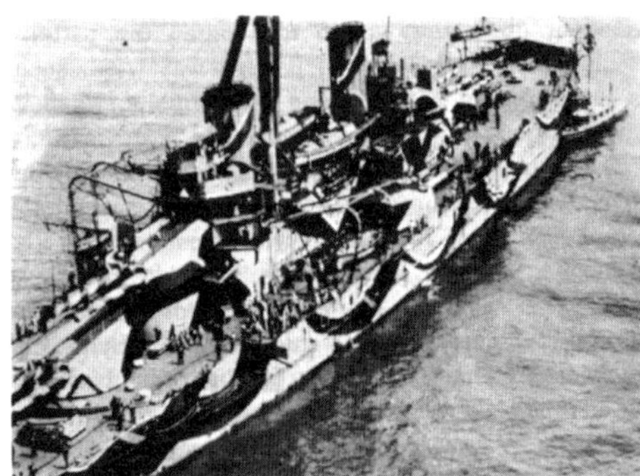

Figs. 93 and 94.— Attempts at distortion of outline which preceded the adoption of geometrical-optical illusions for ships.

Figs. 95 and 96. Illustrating the use of models by the Navy Department in developing the geometrical-illusion for ships.

FIGURE 13 Illustration of applying visual illusions to camouflaging war ships, published in Matthew Luckiesh, *Visual Illusions: Their Causes, Characteristics and Applications* (1922; repr., New York: Dover Publications, 1965), 226, 228–29. Copyright Dover Publications.

an individual beholder, denied to anyone else by the limits of verbal description and visual representation.

Privileging images not simply as they exist physically, but primarily as they are perceived, was foundational to Gestalt psychology, which contended that forms were perceived primarily as wholes made of interrelated parts, rather than as individual elements that constitute the whole. Instead of attempting to isolate visual elements to study perception as an atomized phenomenon, proponents of Gestalt psychology theorized instead fundamental laws of "perceptual organization."[96] As Luckiesh's publications popularized the idea of optical illusions as key for commercial design, Gestalt psychologists codified their own, closely related laws of visual perception, especially in the journal *Psychologische Forschung,* founded in 1922.[97] The movement was founded and shaped primarily by German psychologists Max Wertheimer, Kurt Koffka, and Wolfgang Köhler, especially between the World Wars.[98] Beyond simply a branch of experimental psychology, Gestalt theory reflected a larger worldview that resisted both the elemental approach of nineteenth-century experimental psychology and the notion that cosmopolitanism should subsume categories of individual, cultural, or national identity.[99]

Based on the theory that wholes are fundamental units of perception, the Gestaltists devised experiments to prove the superiority of certain forms based on ease of perception. They advocated the "greater stability of simple forms," in the words of Koffka.[100] Although the image on a page and the image in the mind's eye of any given beholder were inescapably different, Gestalt psychologists contended that simple forms were more "stable" (i.e., more faithfully replicable, or memorable) in the mind's eye. Such an understanding of images undermined the agency of the experimenter and questioned the efficacy of technology designed to record vision as purely mechanical. Moreover, it implicated the agency of the graphic designer who applied its principles. In doing so, Gestaltists gave scientific credence to the idea that simplified forms were inherently more legible, a cornerstone of New Typography.

Gestalt psychology reframed the misperception of images—or optical illusions—as the mind's natural inclination to find order and holistic understanding not only in visual forms, but also in the wider world. While the Gestaltists and Luckiesh agreed that perception was primarily a cognitive phenomenon, the experiments and theories of perception published in *Psychologische Forschung* attempted to rescue perception as a means of making sense of the world, rather than as deception or disorientation. An experiment published by Ernst Lau in 1922, for example, used the phenomenon known as the Zöllner illusion to illustrate the law of similarity, a basic principle of

Gestalt theory positing that the mind organizes images into patterned wholes, grouping together forms perceived as similar.[101]

The basic principles of Gestalt psychology's understanding of image perception have had a deep and lasting impact on graphic design. Gestalt psychology effectively offered a set of rules for the optimization of graphic form. In 1923, Wertheimer introduced the principle of *Prägnanz* (conciseness) as a fundamental aspect of image perception.[102] This was the idea that when looking at objects and images, viewers condense them into simple and distinguishable wholes. Gestaltists further posited that perception entails finding visual patterns; understanding a form through continuity and closure; distinguishing figure from ground; and grouping forms together by size, shape, color, and proximity. Gestaltists frequently illustrated these principles using abstract forms (Figure 14). These illustrations had obvious didactic efficacy, but they also invited graphic designers to understand the perceptual effects of typography in terms of abstract form.[103] Today, conventions of leading, tracking, kerning, and alignment in typography reflect the idea that words are perceived as whole forms.[104] Thus, legibility is also a matter of understanding how words, lines of text, and layouts are perceived as *Gestalten,* or structured wholes.

Divergent theories of perception posited by psychologists were particularly consequential for the efficacy of photographs reproduced as halftones—abstract forms that cohere through optical illusion. One commentator in *Commercial Art,* writing in 1927, described the constant adjustment of the eye during reading, alternating between text and image, as "optical gearshifting."[105] However, they suggested that the use of halftones "introduces a restful midway tone between black and white," thereby facilitating ease of reading.[106] The idea that photographic halftones were akin to type, and thus easier to read—a notion reinforced by New Typography—had a material basis. The reproduction of photographic images with etched plates required photographs to be rephotographed using a camera loaded with a plate and screen. Placed between the lens and plate, the screen (usually fabric) was punctured with a matrix of holes, spaced at a slight distance from the plate. Each hole in the screen acted like a tiny pinhole camera. Photographed through the screen, the new exposure was a noncontinuous translation of the original image, with its many gray tones rendered into a grid of tiny dots of variable sizes. The new plate could then be combined with text on a printing plate or cylinder for reproduction using letterpress, lithography, or rotogravure printing.

However, the dominance of halftones as mass-circulated reproductions of photographs owed as much to optical and psychological translation as it did

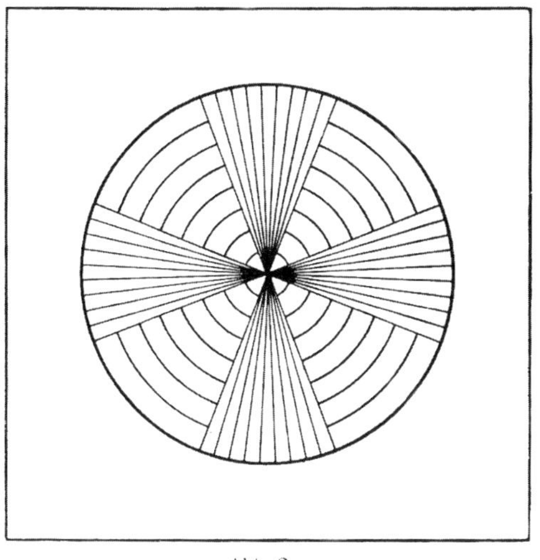

FIGURE 14 Illustration in *Psychologische Forschung* 2 (1922): 187.

to material translation. Halftones cohered as recognizable wholes through perception. The legibility of halftones therefore depended on printing each grid of dots at a small enough size that the eye would interpret them as a single, unbroken image (Figure 15). The modulated concentration of dots of ink, as well as their size and shape, and spaces between them in the grid—such that they would appear under the threshold of human vision—was critically important to printers and designers.[107] Manuals on halftone reproduction were largely dedicated to techniques for rendering the dot matrix invisible, to avoid the disorienting phenomenon known as moiré effect (Figure 16).[108] These manuals offered precise advice about each step of the painstaking halftone process, including the optimal distance between the halftone screen and photographic plate, as well as the ideal shape of apertures in halftone screens, to avoid the visibility of a dot pattern.[109] Because the human eye is far more adept at detecting a pattern when seen as perfectly vertical or horizontal, screens were tilted so that the dot matrix would be printed at a forty-five-degree angle to the frame of the image. For reproductions in color, manuals advised printers to combine multiple halftones in different colors by tilting each at a fifteen-degree angle to ensure that the colors would blend properly in the mind's eye. Manuals also provided guidance about how colors would combine when overprinted, using the principle of complementary colors to offer advice about the most economical uses of multicolor printing.

The prominence of optical illusion as a subject of interest for designers and printers in the early twentieth century underpins the halftone as both a technological and psychological innovation of mass communication. The ongoing, trial-and-error process of perfecting the halftone was indebted not only to technological innovations, but advancements in perceptual psychology as well. By the 1920s, halftones were ubiquitous in newspapers and magazines. Even while graphic designers and printers continued to discuss and fine tune

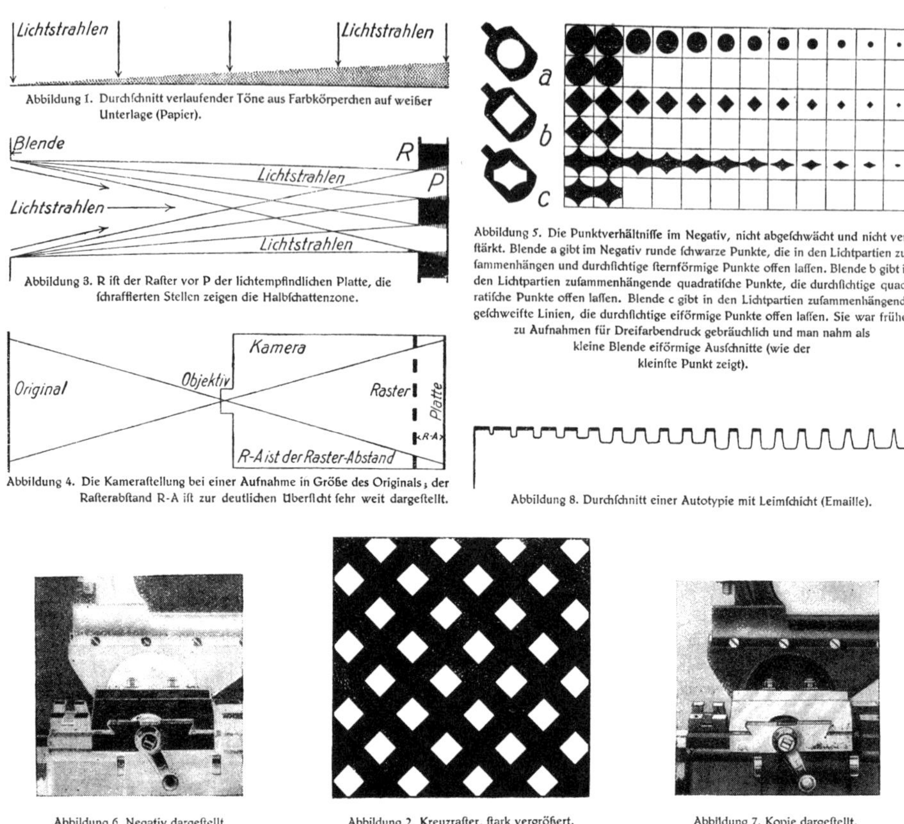

FIGURE 15 Illustration of halftone process, including optical blending of halftone dots, published in Emil Köditz, "Die Photomechanische Reproduktionstechnik," *Typographische Mitteilungen* 21, no. 6 (June 1924), 95. Letterform Archive, San Francisco.

halftone printing, readers had learned to read them as coherent images.[110] Although today it seems "natural," the legibility of halftones depends on the unconscious mental labor of individual perception. In this sense, *Typophoto* is a paradigm for identifying readers not merely as consumers of mass media, but as coproducers of graphic design.

NEW TYPOGRAPHY AND THE ASSIMILATION OF APPLIED PSYCHOLOGY

One of the most important sources for Tschichold's doctrine of New Typography was a 1924 self-published leaflet by fellow German graphic designer Max Burchartz, *Form-Production of Advertising* (*Gestaltung der Reklame*). The work promoted Burchartz's advertising concern in the style of a manifesto, offering

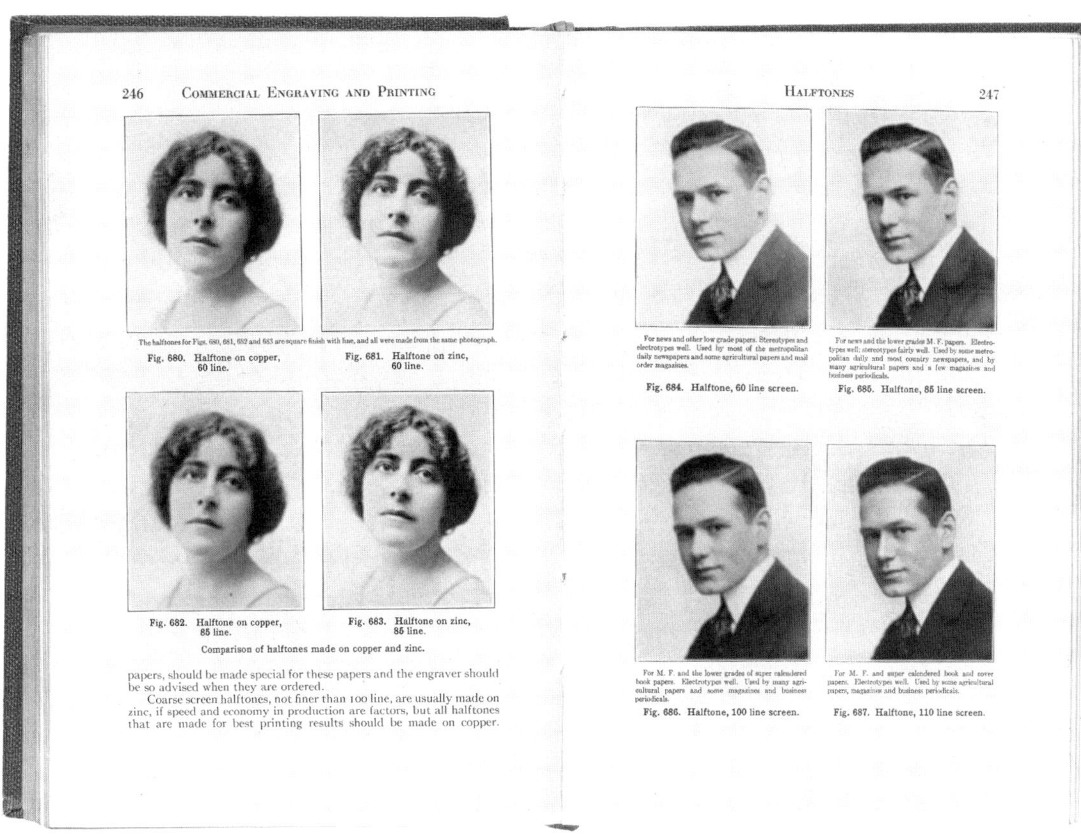
246 COMMERCIAL ENGRAVING AND PRINTING

The halftones for Figs. 680, 681, 682 and 683 are square finish with line, and all were made from the same photograph.

Fig. 680. Halftone on copper, 60 line.

Fig. 681. Halftone on zinc, 60 line.

Fig. 682. Halftone on copper, 85 line.

Fig. 683. Halftone on zinc, 85 line.

Comparison of halftones made on copper and zinc.

papers, should be made special for these papers and the engraver should be so advised when they are ordered.

Coarse screen halftones, not finer than 100 line, are usually made on zinc, if speed and economy in production are factors, but all halftones that are made for best printing results should be made on copper.

HALFTONES 247

For news and other low grade papers. Stereotypes and electrotypes well. Used by most of the metropolitan daily newspapers and some agricultural papers and mail order magazines.

Fig. 684. Halftone, 60 line screen.

For news and the lower grades M. F. papers. Electrotypes well; stereotypes fairly well. Used by some metropolitan daily and most country newspapers, and by many agricultural papers and a few magazines and business periodicals.

Fig. 685. Halftone, 85 line screen.

For M. F. and the lower grades of super calendered book papers. Electrotypes well. Used by many agricultural papers and some magazines and business periodicals.

Fig. 686. Halftone, 100 line screen.

For M. F. and super calendered book and cover papers. Electrotypes well. Used by some agricultural papers, magazines and business periodicals.

Fig. 687. Halftone, 110 line screen.

FIGURE 16 Illustration of effects of printing using screens with different line densities, published in Charles W. Hackleman, *Commercial Engraving and Printing: A Manual of Practical Instruction Covering Commercial Illustrating and Printing by All Processes* (Indianapolis: Commercial Engraving Publishing Company, 1921), 247. Letterform Archive, San Francisco.

sweeping declarations about the nature of commercial design and its impact on society. They were summarized in five pithy maxims: "Good advertising is objective / is clear and concise / uses modern means / has formal punch / [and] is inexpensive."[111] He illustrated each point with an example of his own design work—including the signet for his firm, an advertising poster, and a store window display showcasing his product packaging design. Among the "modern means" named by Burchartz was psychological research: "Good advertising also exploits the results of scientific-psychological research and new perspectives on the development of artistic form-production."[112] Although he did not elaborate on this research directly, his subsequent comments on "formal punch" in advertising illuminate the usefulness of experimental psychology to design, as he understood it.

Burchartz emphasized that advertising design should employ "attention-grabbing form-play" (*Aufmerksamkeit fesselndes Formspiel*) to produce "formal punch" (*Schlagkraft der Form*), drawing a direct link between form on the page and perception. He described the workings of form on the eye and mind of a reader in remarkably physical terms. He argued, rather paradoxically, that the "violent . . . struggle of contrasts" within a design that achieves overall "balance" has a "harmonious . . . effect [on] our senses."[113] Burchartz demonstrated this claim through typographic design: the leaflet incorporates visual contrast between typefaces, type sizes, and the colors red and black. Geometric forms, such as squares and vertical and horizontal rules, lead the eye around the page, and some text is printed sideways, forcing the reader to rotate the leaflet to read it. The legibility of this piece depends on the treatment of typographic elements as perceptual devices, intended to activate the reader both mentally and physically.

Burchartz's treatment of typographic form was predicated on a specific understanding of legibility that was aligned with, if not directly borrowed from, applied psychology. He understood legible graphic form as an immediate, sensory stimulus for memory, recognition, and attention. Yet, he was not unique in describing the perception of printed advertising in physical terms. W. R. Tillerton, for example, claimed that effective advertising must "strike the eye."[114] With the application of "accurate psychology," he continued, "the best advertisement slides into the mind of the consumer without his being well aware of it."[115] This metaphor of the mind as a repository for advertising, where images could stay long after printed matter had been thrown away, was a powerful description of memory-value. The similarity between Tillerton's language and Burchartz's emphasis on "formal punch" shows how applied psychology had become popularized through the shared language of graphic design.

In 1926, German artist and designer Johannes Molzahn published a brochure promoting his own Magdeburg graphic design studio (Figure 17, top).[116] It featured Molzahn's trademark designs, accompanied by an essay claiming that understanding perception was key to effective commercial graphics. He described how form is perceived by the human eye and mind, asserting that a designer's main task is to "determine the graphic representational elements that have the greatest visual impact, and which reflect and preserve the psyche."[117] By insisting that good design begins with understanding vision and cognition, Molzahn centered the psychology of consumption—rather than the designer's intent, the quality of a product, or even the manufacturer—in design praxis.

Like Burchartz, Molzahn regarded psychological science as a crucial tool of advertising design, which also ensured its cost-effectiveness. He described perception as a psychological process akin to photography, by which the eye records images in the mind, as though on the substrate of a photographic negative: "The eye, by virtue of its recording function, is best able to reflect concrete phenomena and to arouse the psyche's deepest and most lasting impressions. Therefore, the mechanism to transform propaganda production must rely primarily on these optical functions."[118] He defined a successful trademark design according to its economic efficiency; like Burchartz, he argued that cheap design was good design. Molzahn drew a direct correlation between monetary economy and "opto-mechanical laws." He made explicit and clear that memory-value, attention-value, suggestion-value were linked to monetary value—something that had been merely implied in the discourse of applied psychology: "The consistent application of a full-fledged, optically and psychically effective brand will save you a high percentage of propaganda costs."[119]

The "economy" of good design, according to Molzahn, should be measured temporally because of the dearth of time, made ever scarcer by the conditions of modern life. The pace of modernity, brought about by new technologies and forms of transportation, "have not only given new form to our thinking, they have also transformed the body and most especially the eye."[120] Molzahn therefore argued that graphics should be designed for a modern viewer who was forced to look at the world with a discriminating glance, which "takes in only a small fraction of myriad optical stimuli."[121] The need for new forms was thus framed not only as good business practice, but also as a necessary response to modernity's effects on human perception.

To emphasize the importance of perception, and his own understanding of graphic form as an object of scientific study, Molzahn compared the consumer's visual apprehension of the trademark to a process of material transfiguration:

> If we take a magnifying glass in hand and position it between the sun and a piece of paper, in such a way that it is in the focus of the lens, it ignites and starts a fire. So we have transformed solar energy into living energy. In this example, we recognized the principle that also builds the symbols of industry and makes them effective. The trademark has the function of the lens; it stands for the lens. At the focal point = concentration point of the industrial symbol, the same transformation process happens: energy production becomes activated in the psyche of the consumer, in approximately the manner shown schematically in Fig. 11.[122]

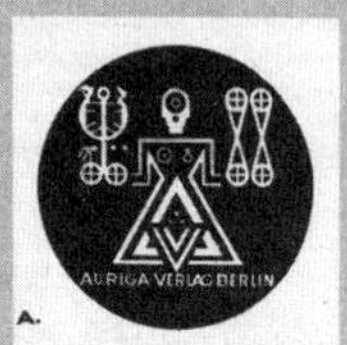

A.

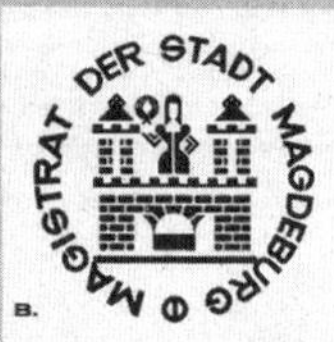

B.

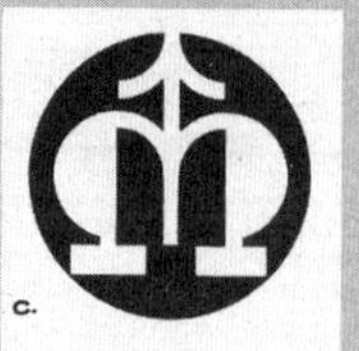

C.

JOHS. MOLZAHN SCHUTZMARKEN

A. AURIGAVERLAG G. M. B. H. BERLIN

B. DIENSTSIEGEL DER STADT MAGDEBURG

C. LUDWIG MOLZAHN WEIMAR

JOHS. MOLZAHN
MAGDEBURG
WERBE-ENTWURF

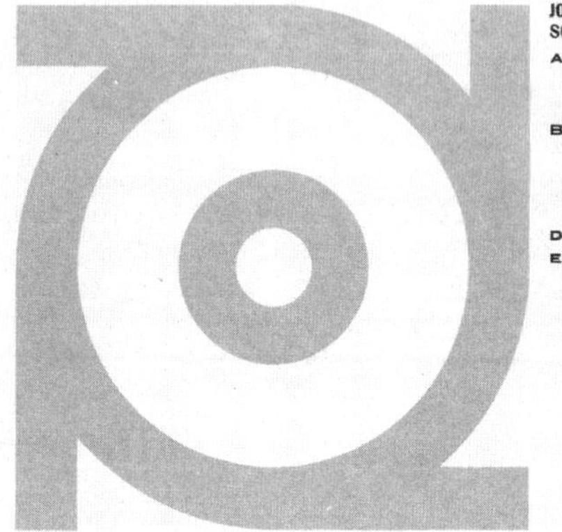

So ist das Warenzeichen immer elementarstes Mittel — Mittler zwischen Produktion und Verbrauch. Keine Organisation kann auf die Dauer existieren und weiterwachsen, wenn sie sich nicht dieses Symbolmittels bedient und als Repräsentationsträger anwendet. Will die Marke diesen Sinn erfüllen, so muß sie auf das weitläufige literarische Wirkungsmittel verzichten und ausschließlich auf optische Funktionsmittel aufbauen, d. h. den Mitteln, die bei kürzestem Zeitmaß das beste und drastischste Merkmalsbild auslösen und der Psyche bewahren. Es ist von der Marke vor allem zu verlangen, daß die Form und Gestaltungselemente einen sehr hohen Grad von optischem Widerstand darstellen, in dessen Brennpunkt sich die Sehstrahlen brechen und konzentrieren; es ist keine Forderung, ihr ein konkretes Motiv, die Darstellung einer Erscheinungsform usw. zugrunde zu legen, so wenig man dieses von irgend einer anderen Mechane verlangt. Der Markensinn ist absolut und die Form wird allein bestimmt von optisch-mechanischen Gesetzen, die die Gestalt nach sich ziehen; hier fordert Funktion eine Form in derselben Weise wie im Maschinenbau. Die Markenfrage ist in Wirklich-

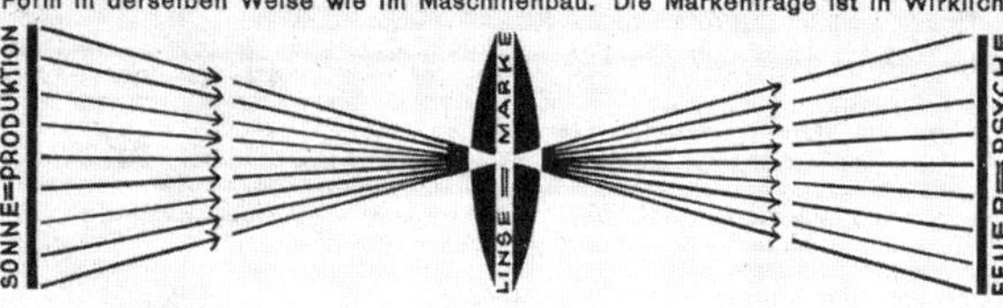

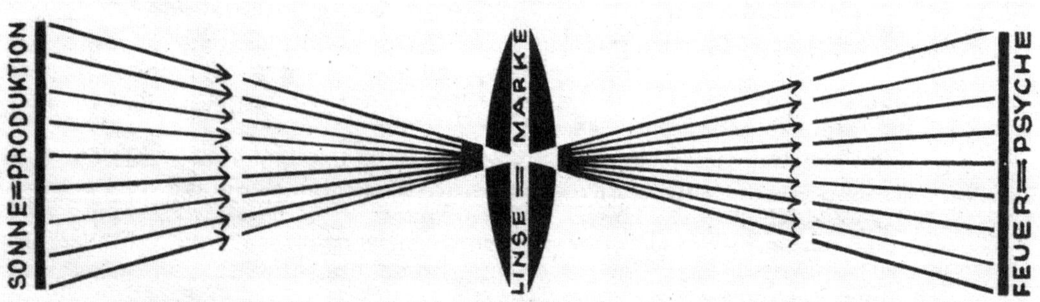

FIGURE 17 Johannes Molzahn, *Ökonomie der Reklame-Mechane*, 1926, interior pages and diagram detail. Typographische Sammlung Jan Tschichold, Bibliothek für Gestaltung Basel. © und Werkdokumentation im Johannes-Molzahn-Centrum ® für Documentation und Publication, Kassel.

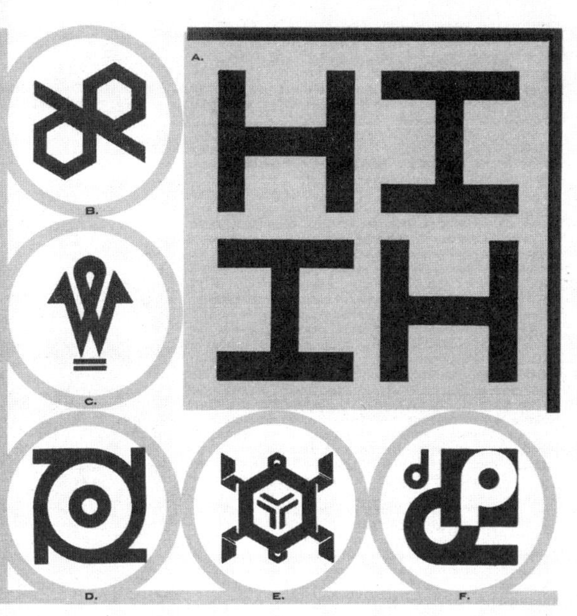

He included a schematic diagram to illustrate the point (Figure 17, bottom). Nothing short of combustible, the trademark's power as a symbolic "concentration point" made it an indispensable mediator between production and consumption. This comparison—and especially the inclusion of a technical diagram—underscored Molzahn's insistence that graphic design was a practice with firm scientific backing. He elaborated by saying that the trademark's "form alone is determined by optical–mechanical laws," deeming trademark design, like the design of a machine, as "not primarily an artistic problem, but rather a technical–scientific and living–psychic one."[123] Molzahn's idea of functional form came straight from perceptual psychology's rhetoric of mechanized vision.

These brochures by Burchartz and Molzahn are just two artifacts of New Typography's assimilation of the rhetoric of applied psychology. Yet, the link between applied psychology and New Typography is far richer than a mere matter of unidirectional influence. New Typography's concept of *Typophoto* also suggests a way of understanding the hybridity of visual culture produced in early experimental psychology. For New Typography, *Typophoto* signaled the shared aspiration of a network of designers to use graphics to control vision by combining type and photographic images. In the context of perceptual psychology, *Typophoto* connotes the mechanization of human perception; the understanding of graphic forms as optical devices; and the production of photographic images in print as scientific data.

American and European graphic designers adopted and parroted the rhetoric of applied psychology to secure the legitimacy of their profession in the 1920s. As a result, the value of graphic design was articulated and understood primarily in terms of efficiency. As is made abundantly clear in Molzahn's trademark brochure (written for an audience of potential corporate clients), appeals to the efficiency of visual communication and reading supported profit-driven capitalism using science as an explicit justification. Molzahn collapsed the speed and profitability of well-designed graphics into the term "economy." Typical of New Typography, both Burchartz and Molzahn offered guidelines not only for successful design, but also for reading their own work as such.

Contemporary graphic design textbooks and professional manuals retain the idea that legibility is determined by efficiency and cost-effectiveness, expressed in somewhat subtler language. For example, one textbook from 2007 offers the following definition: "Legibility is achieved by controlling the qualities and attributes inherent in typography that make type readable. These attributes make it possible for a reader to comprehend typographic forms with the least amount of difficulty."[124] Although this claim may on its surface sound indisputable, it assumes that reading is predicated on speed. We might imagine an alternative definition, suggesting that more effort and time required to decipher a word or image—cast pejoratively above as "difficulty"—could facilitate a reading experience that privileges contemplation over speed. This may well be a definition applicable to New Typography if we resist interpreting modernist designs according to modernist rhetoric. Doing so suggests that New Typography's ethos was motivated by capitalist interest, veiled in scientific terms, which demanded a legibility synonymous with efficiency.

3

TYPOPHOTO AND THE NEW PHOTOMONTAGE, 1928–1933

Photomontage will be the means of expression of the future. It enables a new type of combination of fragments of reality—on all levels of logic, into an illogical bond—as well as a field for the desire for fantasy.

—MAX BURCHARTZ, "HANDSCHRIFT-TYPE, ZEICHNUNG-FOTO" (1926)

It should be pointed out to our comrades that the fetishism of fact is not only not needed, it's also pernicious for photography.

—ALEXANDER RODCHENKO, "A CAUTION" (1928)

In 1927, the Frankfurt-headquartered Bauer Type Foundry commissioned Heinrich Jost to design a prospectus to promote the release of Futura, a sans serif typeface designed by German typographer Paul Renner that quickly became New Typography's signature typeface (Plate 9). Jost's design featured photomontage as Futura's ideal companion. Photography and typography converge in this design as a visual fantasy that celebrates urbanization, industrialization, and mass communication—all harnessed by the creative experimentation of the graphic designer. The prospectus touted photomontage as "a new means of expression that combines the precision of photographic reporting with the optical charm of the free formation of space."[1] This claim was illustrated by Jost's playful arrangement of halftones, the effect of which was to merge the space represented in the photographic fragments with the space of the printed page. On the brochure's cover, the disembodied, scissor-wielding hand of the monteur looms over a skyscraper and Futura letterforms. In the interior spread of the prospectus, a factory rises above a mass of people. The back cover shows that the real work of controlling modern experience—through the manipulation of form, material, and perception—is done at the photomonteur's worktable.

When Jan Tschichold first adopted *Typophoto* as a tenet of New Typography, he championed photographic illustration as precise, efficient, and objective.[2] However, as the Futura prospectus shows, in practice the New Typographers used photography as much more than a tool for objective representation. Indeed, Tschichold's writings from around 1930 suggest the significant refinement of his own thinking about photography and typography—both in terms of the relationship between visual and verbal representation and how that relationship is informed by the graphic design process. In *Die Neue Typographie,* he had distinguished *Typophoto* from photomontage by describing the latter as a process of cutting, arranging, and pasting by hand, but paid no such attention to the material construction of *Typophoto.*[3] By emphasizing photomontage as a process of handwork, he had implied *Typophoto* as a product only of machine work—supporting his claim that photographic illustration fortified type with technological precision, efficiency, and objectivity.

After the publication of his first book, Tschichold came to understand photography as a set of experimental techniques that, when used in design, evoked active construction and affective response in the minds of readers. This shift was encapsulated in a second treatise on New Typography: the book *The Captured Glance* (*Gefesselter Blick*), edited by architects and designers Heinz and Bodo Rasch in 1930. This compendium brought together photography-based art and graphics by a number of designers associated with New Typography, including Willi Baumesier, Max Burchartz, Johannes Canis, Walter Cyliax, Franz Krause, El Lissitzky, and Piet Zwart. Their experimental uses of photography suggested the interdependency of functionalist graphic design and surrealist art, in effect proposing an alternative definition of New Typography to the one Jan Tschichold had proposed in 1928.

This chapter centers the New Typographers' uses of experimental photographic techniques in visual communication to destabilize the relationship between word and image, evoke consumer desire, and implicate readers as coproducers of graphic design. Tschichold's unpublished writings from the late Weimar era suggest that he sustained a major preoccupation with photomontage in graphic design. Around 1930, he planned to author a book on photomontage, which was never realized. This chapter reconstructs the designer's intended argument using his extant, unpublished outline and related notes for the book, *Fotomontage* (ca. 1930–31). It recovers Tschichold's thesis that "the new photomontage" encompassed a capacious set of practices, including experimental photographic techniques and artistic collage, the manipulation of the halftone as *Typophoto,* and the cut-and-paste processes of graphic design. In this book, he intended to identify the techniques and representational strategies of experimental photography as integral to modern visual communication. He had also come to understand *Typophoto* as a medium of composite image-making intimately related to nonphotographic collage and printmaking practices of Dada and surrealism.

Tschichold's thinking about visual communication and photography in this period was deeply influenced by German art historian and critic Franz Roh, who became an important collaborator and interlocutor when Tschichold moved to Munich in 1926. Indeed, an advertisement from 1930 announced Tschichold's *Fotomontage* book as the fourth installment of Roh's Fototek series.[4] Given that Tschichold had originally named photomontage as an artistic technique antithetical to the objectivity of *Typophoto,* it is striking that Roh would charge Tschichold with the task of editing this book and writing its introduction. Yet, the collaborations of Tschichold and Roh were part of a larger shift in New Typography that took place around 1930. Tschichold's plan for *Fotomontage* was one of many publications and exhibitions about graphic design and photomontage in the early 1930s. These contemporaneous projects help unpack the substance of Tschichold's own unrealized book on the subject, framing this project as a handbook for the mass dissemination of Roh's theories of photography and montage.[5]

Photography proved particularly valuable in commercial design precisely because its capacity for mimetic representation could be manipulated through the evocative arrangement of photographic fragments in relation to text. Like the visible halftone, the fragmentation of photomontage signaled to readers that they were consuming the products of sophisticated graphic manipulation. The New Typographers sought to produce word–image combinations imbued with what André Breton—in describing images that connote a utopian future or fantasy apart from any direct referent in the real world—called "the marvelous."[6] Breton was particularly fascinated by what he deemed the "convulsive beauty" of photographic images: by isolating a moment or image of the world, photography could reconfigure nature as a sign, arresting both space and time. Rather than see photography as a seamless representation of reality, the surrealists relished how the medium could violently disrupt a sense of continuity in representations of the world.[7] New Typography similarly sought to destabilize photography as mimetic representation, betraying a strong kinship between surrealist photography and what Moholy-Nagy called "superphotography" in advertising.[8]

Tschichold's unrealized book on photomontage foregrounds an important paradox: New Typography encompassed a dialectic between its own aspirations toward the universal legibility and objectivity of visual communication and the strategies of Dada and surrealism that the New Typographers employed in practice. In order to be "functional," commercial design had to incite desire through combinations of word and image that upended the expectation that text should explain images and, in turn, that images should illustrate text. Attention to the dependency of functionalist graphic design on surrealist strategies illuminates the extent to which the Weimar craze for rationalization and standardization was fueled by utopian fantasy and experiments with the human mind. When we look back on New Typography's legacy, the movement is perhaps best understood as emblematic of Weimar Germany's utopian aspirations, rather than as an example of rationalization that actually took place.

PHOTOMONTAGE, OLD AND NEW

All that remains of Tschichold's book for the Fototek book series is an outline consisting of a four-page typescript and one page of handwritten notes.[9] However, these notes represent nearly a decade spent thinking and writing about photography and graphic design. The outline is rich with ideas that correlate to public discourse in contemporaneous exhibitions and publications. Advertisements for Fototek promised that the book *Fotomontage* would illustrate "significant possibilities that lie in this new manner of form-production" with "excellent examples."[10] An unattributed announcement for Fototek published in December 1930 noted the timely relevance of the book: "Especially Tschichold's book on 'Photomontage' will be awaited with impatience, since this new area—so important to our graphic arts—has not been worked on to this day, although there exists already a wealth of excellent material of great beauty."[11] The contemporary appetite for a monograph on photomontage was whetted not only by the technique's prominence in avant-garde art, but equally, by graphics that circulated en masse through print advertising.

From his outline for *Fotomontage,* it appears that Tschichold had three major goals for this unrealized book. First, he proposed that the technique of photomontage was not a new invention, but rather had a history that had begun in the nineteenth century. “This [book] is a historical survey,” he wrote, “a conscious historical document, showing what is good and bad. Examples and counterexamples.”[12] He intended to situate what he called “the new photomontage” as a reinvention of the technique in early twentieth-century avant-garde art—namely constructivism, futurism, Dada, and surrealism—as well as in modernist graphic design.[13] A key ambition of this publication was to show that contemporary graphic design was inextricably linked to avant-garde art.[14] However, Tschichold resisted rehearsing a narrative about the “invention” of photomontage by modernists. By identifying the origins of the technique in the nineteenth century and by elaborating its applications in design, Tschichold boldly offered a counternarrative to one propagated most forcefully by Raoul Hausmann who, in his talk delivered at the opening of the 1931 Berlin exhibition *Fotomontage,* defended Dadaists as “the first photomonteurs.”[15]

Both Hausmann and Tschichold sought to claim photomontage for different ends. For Hausmann, insisting on the future importance of photomontage ensured the continued relevance of Dada. He defended the “free” use of photomontage as a technique for art-making and dismissed its “practical application” in design.[16] Tschichold, on the other hand, wanted to expand the definition of photomontage by illuminating meaningful connections between many applications of the technique, including advertising. The diverging agendas of Hausmann and Tschichold were brought together by Dutch artist and designer César Domela-Nieuwenhuis, hung side by side somewhat uneasily in his 1931 exhibition, *Fotomontage.*[17] Domela-Nieuwenhuis included examples of various applications of photomontage, including political propaganda and commercial graphics. Although Hausmann agreed to loan his own work to the exhibition, he objected to the inclusion of commercial design by Tschichold, László Moholy-Nagy, Herbert Bayer, and others. In a letter to Hannah Höch written around the time of the opening, Hausmann referred to these designers as “our descendants”—pointed language that emphasized the primacy of Dada. He dismissed their work as “quite weak” and praised Höch’s contributions to the show by comparison.[18]

Tschichold’s unrealized book and Domela-Nieuwenhuis’s exhibition shared both a title and a thesis about photomontage as a paradigm for dissolving the boundaries between art and design, and between historical and modern cultural production. Like Tschichold, Domela-Nieuwenhuis defined photomontage as a capacious category and proposed contemporary experiments with photography as part of a longer tradition, rather than a clean break from it. The exhibition's first gallery displayed nonphotographic works from the eighteenth and nineteenth centuries, referred to in the catalog as "curiosities that can be seen as precursors of photomontage."[19] Some of these works were borrowed from the collection of the Museum für Kunst und Gewerbe Hamburg, directed by German art historian Max Sauerlandt.[20] Domela-Nieuwenhuis's exhibition followed Sauerlandt's radical conviction that modern art belonged in museum collections and exhibitions to enliven the entire history of art for a contemporary audience.[21] Sauerlandt's collecting supported Domela-Nieuwenhuis's attempt to think about modernism historically.

Fotomontage also borrowed from the local collection of German photography historian Erich Stenger, reflecting his interest in the wide-ranging applications of the medium.[22] For example, Domela-Nieuwenhuis showed a late eighteenth-century collage by Christian Gottlob Winterschmidt, *Quodlibet with Perpetual Calendar*, borrowed from Stenger.[23] The collection also included hand-colored photomechanical reproductions of paintings, such as Hermann Wilhelm Vogel's *Three-Color Printing According to the Procedure: Vogel–Ulrich* (*Dreifarbendruck nach Verfahren: Vogel–Ulrich*) of 1892, to which butterfly specimens were pinned. Stenger acquired at least one image of a headless soldier from the late nineteenth century, created as a "template" for a photographic portrait to be added with montage (Plate 10).[24] Stenger historicized photography as a technology that touched every aspect of modern life. In doing so, he implicitly defined the medium somewhat broadly, including techniques of "manipulation" such as photomontage and spirit photography.[25] In his own unpublished notes, Tschichold also cited Stenger's collection as proof that the modern technique of photomontage had noteworthy historical precedents.[26]

In his catalog essay for *Fotomontage*, Domela-Nieuwenhuis firmly dismissed any need to pinpoint photomontage's origins: "Photomontage was not invented, as is frequently claimed, but rather evolved out of a contemporary need for new forms of expression and combinations of materials. For this reason no one can claim to have been the sole creator of the medium."[27] This framing echoed Aloïs Riegl's theory of *Kunstwollen* (will to form) by proposing photomontage as a formal–material tendency that emerged as a response to modernity, rather than as a narrowly defined technique that could be claimed definitively by the avant-garde.[28] By characterizing photomontage as historically rooted in the nineteenth century, Tschichold similarly suggested that the origins of photomontage could not be easily identified—a position that Hausmann regarded as both threatening and false.[29]

Hausmann, Tschichold, and Domela-Nieuwenhuis did concur on one important score: all three vehemently characterized photomontage as thriving and socially relevant around 1930. Sabine Kriebel has framed Domela-Nieuwenhuis's essay as a defense against a cacophony of declarations in the German press—including art and advertising journals—that the medium of photomontage was a waning trend, or already dead.[30] She has similarly read the remarks Hausmann made at the exhibition's opening—and I would add, the very impetus to make them despite his evident misgivings about the show—as a defensive rebuttal to those claims. Yet, Hausmann also called for the "disciplining" of both photomontage and film for future use, condemning their application in commercial design.[31] Though Domela-Nieuwenhuis refused to endorse an origin story of photomontage, he declared that "it would be quite mistaken to think of it as a mere fad," and stressed that "photomontage is by no means passé, as one often hears, but rather in the initial stage of its development."[32]

Both Domela-Nieuwenhuis and Tschichold cited the deeper history of photomontage, and its relevance to contemporary life, as proof of its staying power. This defense also shored up theories of modernism's broader relevance to both history and modernity. In a review of the exhibition, German critic and art historian Adolf Behne at first credited the Dadaists for "inventing montage," thereby making "the rigid photograph mobile and thinking."[33] However, he also mused, somewhat provocatively, "But . . . is the coat of arms of the old knight shields not the real ancestor of this new art form? Of course, there are the formal beginnings of montage, in those heraldic divisions of the surface, in the combination of half eagles, horse-tailed tails, double heads with mythical creatures, with crenellated walls and gates, with stars, suns, and comets."[34] Behne recognized heraldic images as fantastical, composite forms constructed from preexisting image fragments, describing objects from Sauerlandt's collection in Hamburg as "ancestors of photomontage . . . which anticipate the adhesive images of [Pablo] Picasso and [Kurt] Schwitters."[35] He reinforced and extended the exhibition's thesis by suggesting that photomontage—along with cubism and Dada—had a deeper history. He speculated that modernism had emerged from a tradition of "divisions of the surface" in composite image-making, which transcended the boundaries of medium, material, and purpose. To propose a continuity between medieval heraldry and modernist photomontage was a direct challenge to the avant-garde's self-mythologizing of its own originality.

Tschichold's book outline shows that he, too, had clearly intended to weigh in on this debate about the past and future of photomontage, an ambition that likely predated the opening of Domela-Nieuwenhuis's exhibition. At stake, as Behne suggested, was an understanding of how the extended precipitation and current ubiquity of photomontage had fundamentally changed the way people saw images, both past and present. In one of the few fully formed theses for his own project, Tschichold wrote, "My book wants to offer an overview of the possibilities of photomontage, established on the basis of its previous creation, to prove that the talk of the 'survival' of these graphics is empty chatter."[36] His notes confirm that he would certainly have refuted accusations such as Hausmann's that photomontage had been debased by commercial design, instead framing its broader use as a reinvention that ensured future relevance.

Tschichold's second goal was to produce a publication that would serve as both a theoretical text and a practical handbook, offering prescriptions for "good" and "bad" photomontage illustrated by examples and counterexamples. The didacticism of this premise recalls his publications, including *Die Neue Typographie* (1928) and *Eine Stunde Druckgestaltung* (1930). He had made a case for New Typography in a similar manner: He situated the movement historically as a natural progression of typography and printing (understanding history as a teleological development), and he emphasized the diverse applications of New Typography as a universal design program, providing examples and counterexamples of his thinking. Yet, from the outline of *Fotomontage,* it is clear that this book would also have departed somewhat from the format of Tschichold's other publications.

His intent was to blend the format of the design handbook with the theoretical premise and visual argument of *foto-auge: 76 fotos der zeit* (1929), a book he made in collaboration with Roh, published in response to the Deutscher Werkbund exhibition *Film und Foto* (1929–31), which described and illustrated myriad uses of photography from its invention to the present day.[37] The book *foto-auge* was an important prototype for Roh's Fototek series on photography, inaugurated the following year. It consists primarily of a visual essay of photographic and photography-based images, preceded by Roh's introduction, "Mechanism and Expression: The Essence and Value of Photography" (printed in German, French, and English). Textually and visually, the book posited photography as a conduit for new ways of seeing by presenting a range of visual experiences produced through the medium. It included anonymous press and archival photographs; aerial, astronomical, and X-ray photographs; designs for book covers, posters, and advertisements; as well as collage and photomontage by numerous photographers, including some associated with Dada and surrealism. These examples presented photography as inherently heterogeneous, riddled with contradictions, and ultimately undefinable according to any one set of criteria. Their sequencing suggested that photographic images are best read dialectically. Each example might spark the reader's mental associations and connections relative to the previous one, or encourage them to flip forward or backward in the book to reference another image.

In his introduction to *foto-auge,* Roh laid out his theory that photography could extend the capacity of the human eye, or even replace it as a superior optical prosthesis.[38] For Roh, photography included not only the mechanical production of images with a camera, but also myriad manipulations with photographic chemistry and printing. He pointed to experimental photography—including photomontage, combination printing, solarization, and photograms—as evidence that the medium had radically altered human vision. The new ways of seeing engendered by photography, he argued, permeated the boundaries between the "isms" of contemporary art; between machine production and handcraft; and between art, design, technology, and science.

Like Roh, Tschichold intended to offer a theory of photomontage as much more than a technique of the avant-garde. His third goal for the book was to situate "the new photomontage" as a paradigm for making, using, and perceiving images. He intended to show that the myriad applications of photomontage were part of a general, modern impulse toward montage that transcended boundaries between mediums, between fine and applied art, and between techniques of production. The first extant page of the typescript lists a number of different applications as subcategories of photomontage, with shorthanded names of artists and designers under each one, indicating possible examples.[39] We can assume, based on the formats of the two extant Fototek publications, that these names were placeholders for images that together would have constituted a photographic essay—likely consisting of sixty reproductions—preceded by Tschichold's written introduction.[40] It is telling that he included the category of *freie fotomontage* (free, or nonfunctional, photomontage) in the outline, but offered no potential examples, instead enumerating its many uses.

The first applications of photomontage listed in the typescript are *politische fotomontage* (political montage, exemplified by the work of Georg Grosz and John Heartfield) and *fotomontage als witz* (photomontage as joke or satire, exemplified by Hannah Höch and László Moholy-Nagy). As examples, he may have used works incorporating photomontage that had also been reproduced in the book *foto-auge*, such as Grosz's *"The Convict" Monteur John Heartfield after Franz Jung's Attempt to Set Him on His Feet ("Der Sträfling" Monteur John Heartfield nach Franz Jungs Versuch ihn auf die Beine zu stellen)* (1920); Moholy-Nagy's *Leda and the Swan (Leda und der Schwan)* (1925); and Höch's *From Above (Von Oben)* (1927) (Plate 11).[41] These categories named artists who not only were leading figures of Dada, but also worked in advertising or as graphic designers between the Wars.[42]

The typescript pays particular attention to the use of photomontage in various forms of graphic design. These included *fotoplakate* (photographic advertising posters) and photomontage in book design and illustration as applications of the technique by graphic designers.[43] Tschichold may well have used one of his own designs for Phoebus–Palast cinema in Berlin, made in 1926 and 1927, as examples of poster design (Plate 12). These are among the few examples of applied photomontage in his own work. Despite Hausmann's disapproval of the technique's commercial application, Tschichold's poster for the film *Die Frau Ohne Namen* (1927) anticipated what Hausmann would later describe as "photography and printed texts combined and transformed into a kind of static film."[44]

Importantly, the typescript points beyond examples of handheld printed matter to include the design and representation of built space as the purview of both experimental photography and graphic design. Yet another application identified in the outline is *fotomontage in der architektenzeichnung* (photomontage in architectural drawing), naming Swiss architect Le Corbusier and Czech architect Jaromír Krejcar as potential examples. These notes may well have referred to representations of built architecture by Le Corbusier or Krejcar, who both employed photomontage in different forms, or to preparatory architectural drawings that integrated photographic elements. Le Corbusier used extensive airbrushing to isolate the "pure" forms of his Villa Schwob, built in 1916, in photographic reproductions for the journal *L'Esprit nouveau*.[45] He also used photomontage to create what he called a "parallel discourse" with images in *L'Esprit nouveau* as well as in his books *L'Art décoratif d'aujourd'hui* (1925) and *Vers une architecture* (1929) (Figure 18).[46] Krejcar used photomontage to envision his 1923 Olympic department store in Prague, emphasizing its structure as an assembly of pure geometric forms and its exterior planes as ready-made surfaces for advertising (Figure 19).[47] Both architects demonstrated a savvy awareness of the habits of the modern reader, who might only flip through a book or magazine, skimming for visual content.

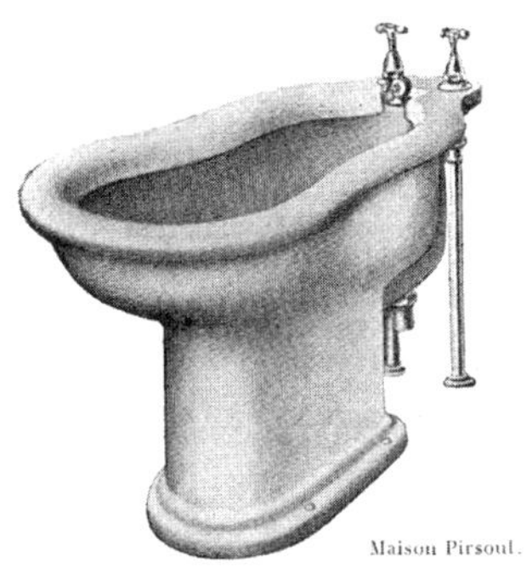

AUTRES ICONES
LES MUSÉES

Il y a les bons musées, puis les mauvais. Puis ceux qui ont pêle-mêle du bon et du mauvais. Mais le musée est une entité consacrée qui circonvient le jugement.

FIGURE 18 Le Corbusier, *L'Art décoratif d'aujourd'hui* (Paris: G. Crès et Cie, 1925), unpaginated. Copyright F.L.C. / ADAGP, Paris / Artists Rights Society (ARS), New York 2024.

In the category of *fotomontage in der ausstellungsarchitektur* (photomontage in exhibition architecture), Tschichold named Moholy-Nagy and German graphic designer Joost Schmidt. Moholy-Nagy and Schmidt had become known for their experiments with photography in the design of exhibitions and advertising signage under the auspices of the Bauhaus sculpture workshop, which Schmidt reestablished in Dessau in 1928.[48] Commercial projects of the Bauhaus sculpture workshop under Schmidt's direction included a display promoting Junkers water heaters at the 1929 *Gas and Water* trade exhibition in Berlin, attributed to Schmidt and fellow Bauhaus instructor Xanti Schawinsky, as well as Schmidt's display for an association of canned fruit and vegetable manufacturers at the 1930 *International Hygiene* exhibition in Dresden. Of Moholy-Nagy's use of photomontage in exhibition design, Tschichold may well have had in mind the first room of *Film und Foto* (1929).[49] Schmidt

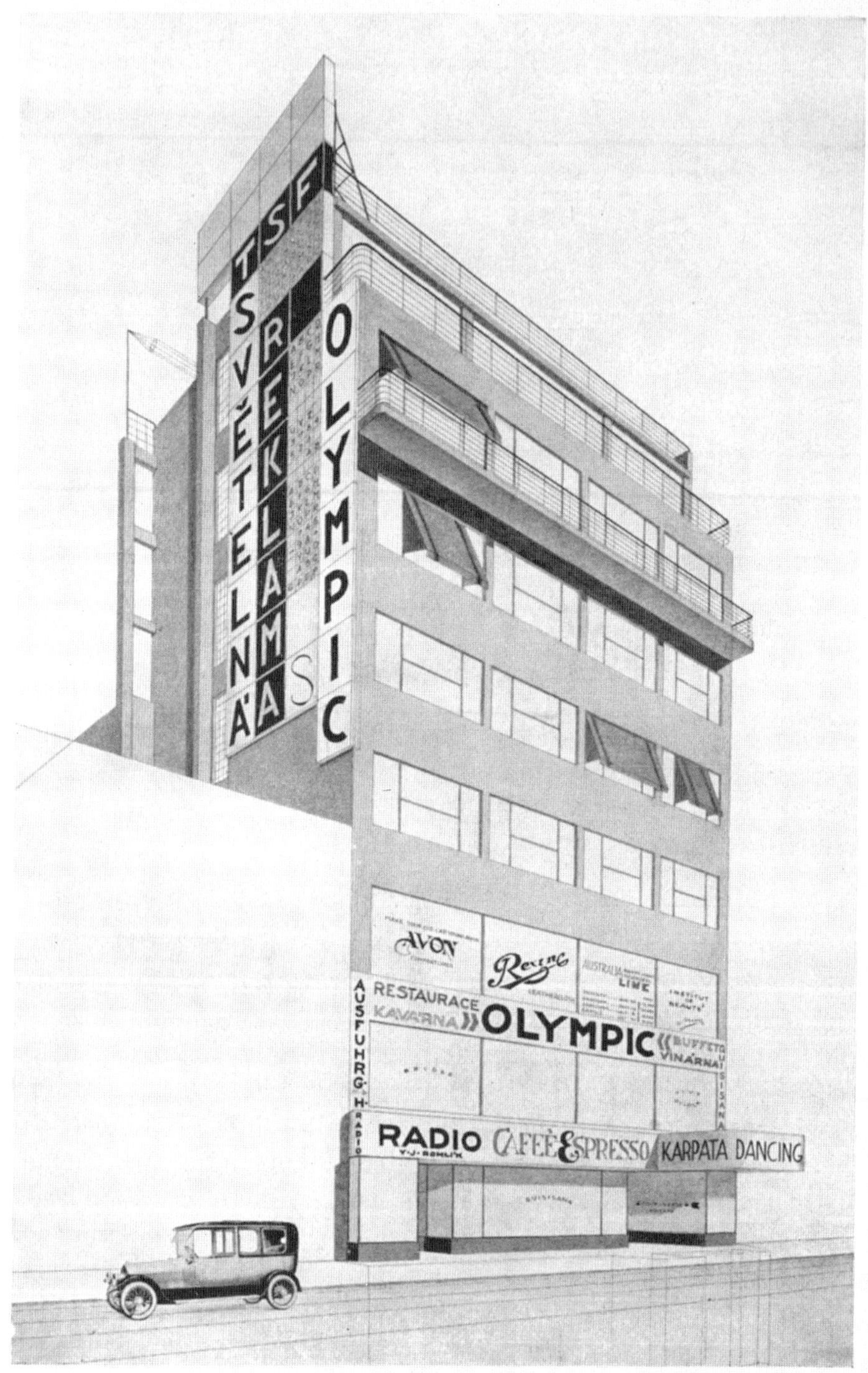

Projekt obchodního a kancelářského domu **„Olympic“** v Praze
Проэкт торгового и канцелярского дома »**Олимпик**« в Праге
Projekt des Büro- und Geschäftshauses **„Olympic“** in Prag

1923

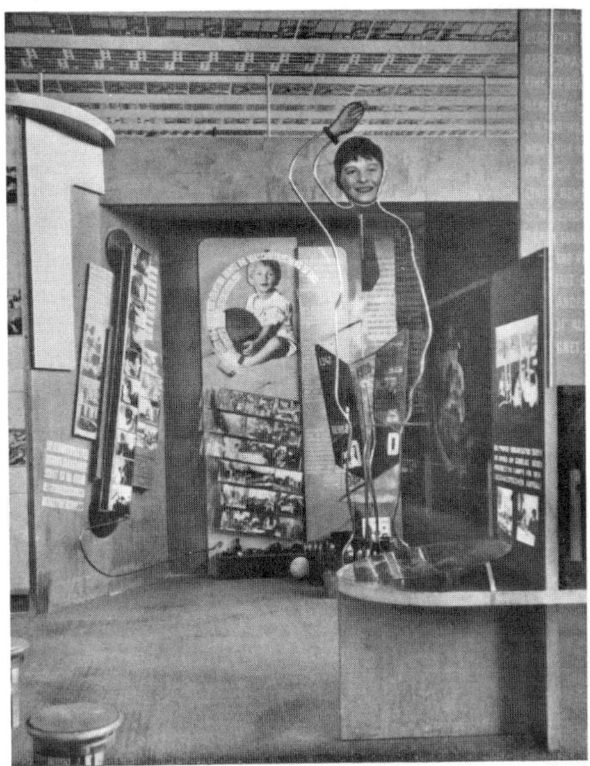

Child Welfare Section in the Soviet Department of the Dresden Hygiene Exhibition. The extremes of naturalism and modern geometry are combined with entire success

FIGURE 20 Documentation of El Lissitzky's design of the Soviet section of the 1930 *International Hygiene* exhibition in Dresden, reproduced in Jan Tschichold, "Display That Has Dynamic Force: Exhibition Rooms Designed by El Lissitzky," *Commercial Art*, January 1931, 24. General Research Division, The New York Public Library. Copyright 2024 Artists Rights Society (ARS), New York.

and Moholy-Nagy presented photography and text as detached surfaces—often suspended on wires or freestanding armature and seemingly exempt from the rules of architectural construction—which suggested the exhibition as an extension of the magazine, allowing visitors the freedom to navigate space and information alike.[50]

Tschichold named El Lissitzky as an exemplar of photomontage in both architectural drawing and exhibition architecture. Long influenced by Lissitzky's typography,[51] Tschichold featured his designs for the Soviet sections of the 1930 International Hygiene Exhibition and the 1928 International Press

FIGURE 19 Drawing with photomontage by Jaromír Krejcar, reproduced in Karel Telge, *Práce Jaromíra Krejcara* (Prague: Nakladatel Václav Petr, 1933), 27. Getty Research Institute, Los Angeles (90-B18208).

Exhibition in Cologne, commonly known as *Pressa,* in an article for *Commercial Art,* "Display That Has Dynamic Force: Exhibition Rooms Designed by El Lissitzky," published in January 1931 (Figure 20).[52] He praised Lissitzky's "visual design of the exhibition space and its contents," which incorporated "glass, mirrors, celluloid, nickel and other materials; by contrasting these new materials with wood, lacquer, textiles and photographs," as well as type in various thicknesses, sizes, colors, and orientations.[53] The result was an exhibition space that Tschichold described as "a sort of stage on which the visitor himself seemed to be one of the players."[54] These examples would have demonstrated photomontage as a means of sensory immersion in exhibition design. As in the window display of a department store, the intermingling of photographic materiality with other surfaces and textures in Lissitzky's exhibitions was intended to subsume the viewing public into these environments and therefore into the ideology they promoted.[55] At the same time, these immersive spaces cultivated visitors as active, embodied participants. In a set of notes that appears to be related to the *Fotomontage* typescript, Tschichold wrote that the "value [of photomontage] consists in the fact that one can use it to form optical associations."[56] Thus, he sought to enumerate its seemingly limitless applications in design as demonstrations of how to see and move through the modern world.

FRANZ ROH AND NEW TYPOGRAPHY: BETWEEN REPORTAGE AND *GESTALTUNG*

Tschichold's capacious concept of "new photomontage" betrayed the strong influence of Franz Roh. During his years living in Munich, Tschichold became personally and professionally acquainted with Roh as a neighbor, friend, and collaborator.[57] After they edited *foto-auge* together in 1929, Roh inaugurated the Fototek series on "new photography" in 1930, in which eight books were planned. They were to include thematic volumes on police photography, kitsch photography, nude photography, and sports photography as well as a monograph on El Lissitzky, including "Fotos und Typofotos."[58] In 1930, the first and only two books in the series were published: monographs on László Moholy-Nagy and German photographer Aenne Biermann, both designed by Tschichold.[59] The uniformity of their covers and layouts suggests that Tschichold's typography would have served to unify the series visually, despite its range of subject matter.

A page of handwritten notes for Tschichold's *Fotomontage* makes explicit reference to Roh's ideas and ongoing discussions with Tschichold in the late

1920s about the nature of photographic representation and the relationship between fine and applied art. In these notes, Tschichold referenced several texts by Moholy-Nagy and Roh to be reprinted or excerpted in his own book. One such note reads:

> Roh on the glued photographic image
> extreme fantasy with extreme sobriety,
> freest composition with realistic imitation
> cubist nesting of pure illustrations
>
> Tsch:
> "constructivist" versus "organized"[60]

Here Tschichold quoted directly from Roh's brief discussion of photomontage in his 1925 book *After Expressionism: Magical Realism, Problems of Recent European Painting* (*Nach-Expressionismus: Magischer Realismus, Probleme der neuesten europäischen Malerei*), which introduced the term "magical realism" to describe contemporary trends in painting (including *Neue Sachlichkeit* and surrealism) and, to a lesser extent, photography.[61] Perhaps Roh's single most enduring idea about photography was that its potency as a tool of communication and means of expression inhered in its contradictions, especially its dual capacity to show objective reality and to visualize the imaginary. This idea was illustrated in Paul Citroen's *Metropolis (City of My Birth)* (*Weltstadt [Meine Geburtsstadt]*), a collage of photographic fragments made in 1923, one of the few photographic images represented in *After Expressionism* (Figure 21). The inclusion of Citroen's photomontage underscored Roh's view that the medium of photography was defined as much by its uses—including the arrangement and pasting together of fragments—as by production with a camera or in a darkroom. This was a position with which Tschichold, as a graphic designer, could easily align himself.

Roh rejected any singular understanding of the photographic medium. He understood photography's social and artistic relevance to reside in its inconsistency. Rather than devise a theory of medium specificity to fit his own beliefs about photographic representation, he raised questions about how a single medium could be used in so many contradictory ways. How could one devise a comprehensive theory of photography that could encompass, rather than deny, such inconsistencies? How could photography be so thoroughly elusive—often seeming to operate according to its own logic and fixing images

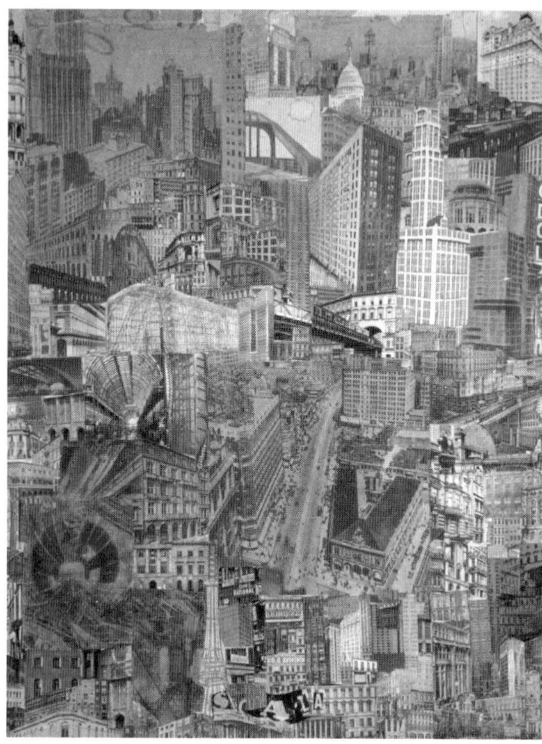

FIGURE 21 Paul Citroen, *Weltstadt (Meine Geburtsstadt) (Metropolis [City of My Birth])*, 1923, photomechanical reproduction of collage. The Museum of Modern Art, New York. Bridgeman-Giraudon / Art Resource, NY. Copyright 2024 Artists Rights Society (ARS), New York / c/o Pictoright Amsterdam.

outside and beyond the scope of human vision—and yet be trusted as an accurate and reliable medium of reportage, a tool of journalism, medicine, and law? Roh recognized photography's artistic value as a direct extension of its contradictions. In Moholy-Nagy's terms, Roh understood photography to be a "reproductive" and a "productive" medium, holding these modes perpetually in tension. This dialectic became embedded in the term *Typophoto* in the late 1920s and early 1930s as a paradigm for verbal–visual communication under the auspices of New Typography.

Roh upheld Moholy-Nagy's photographic work as exemplary of the dialectic inherent in the photographic medium. In his introduction to *60 Fotos: László Moholy-Nagy* (1930), Roh championed him as a figure of art historical importance and as an exemplar of photography's relevance to contemporary art. According to Roh, Moholy-Nagy's turn to working with photography was prompted by dissatisfaction with abstract painting, which failed to capture "the whole range of the human."[62] Unlike abstract painting, he recognized in photography the possibility to satisfy "the craving for expression of what is contained in *external objects*."[63] He praised Moholy-Nagy for harnessing photography's capacity to produce new forms and to capture the essence of objects in the world, reproduced as images.

Roh described photography, especially in Moholy-Nagy's work, as mediating between two poles: the reporting of experience at one end, and pure formal experiment at the other:

> Experience and formation, that often had a troubled mixture yesterday, are separated more emphatically today. They are directed to their specific poles and placed in ingenious opposition to each other. The modern emphasis on problems of form on the one hand (the most liberal and unencumbered possibilities of formation), and on the other hand the keenness with which the concept of "reportage" is emphasized, reportage in all fields, are characteristic.
>
> Photography is above all *reporting*. But between reporting and forming [*Gestaltung*] there is after all only a difference in degree, no absolute distinction.[64]

He identified photography as a means of representing what is extrinsic to the camera (objectifying external objects as images) as well as what is entirely intrinsic to photography (formal experiment made possible by the photographic apparatus and by the properties of photochemistry). In proposing that "there is . . . only a difference in degree" and not an "absolute distinction" between reportage and pure abstraction, he identified poles located at opposite ends of a spectrum of photographic representation. Like Moholy-Nagy, Roh understood photographic "realism" to be predicated on, rather than undermined by, construction—choices made by photographers, including mechanical and chemical manipulations. Photography's capacity for reporting and forming imbued the medium with its unique capacity to create reality, rather than merely re-present it.

Tschichold applied Roh's theory of photography as a more sophisticated framework for defending *Typophoto* in visual communication than he had initially proposed. He came to understand objective visual communication and propaganda as two poles on a spectrum of graphic representation. Although, in *The New Typography,* he emphatically declared the photographic halftone and sans serif type as equivalently "objective," he also acknowledged photography and typography as fundamentally different modes of representation that fused in a dynamic visual contrast.[65] His notes for *Fotomontage* suggest that, in the years immediately following the publication of his first book, he continued to reflect on reading as an active process of optical and cognitive negotiation between photographic and typographic communication. Despite the decisive tone of *The New Typography,* his acknowledgment of the contrast between photography and type alluded to unresolved questions of how images and text work together—or clash—in representing and conveying information. Perhaps most importantly for New Typography, Roh acknowledged that *Neue Sachlichkeit* and surrealism were not opposite approaches to image-making, but rather two sides of the same coin: an idea succinctly captured in the term "magical realism."[66] He believed that surrealist expression was latent in photography's ostensible trustworthiness. Tschichold came to recognize this quality of photography as well, and eventually understood it as key to the medium's efficacy as visual communication.

Tschichold's notes for *Fotomontage* also suggest Roh's influence on his understanding of photomontage as a technique that encompassed a spectrum of processes, involving both manual labor and machine production, which were to be addressed directly in Tschichold's book for Fototek. His notes include the following fragments:

> Glued photographic image
> Glued image out of parts of manual graphics [*Manualgraphik*]
> Mechanical graphics [*Mechanographik*][67]

Here, Tschichold established a dialectical relationship between *Manualgraphik* (graphics made by hand) and *Mechanographik* (graphics produced by machine), especially in the "glued photographic image." Again, Tschichold quoted Roh, who had described photomontage as "bare, glued photographic images" (*bloßen Fotoklebebilder*).[68] In doing so, he called explicit attention to montage as laying bare a way of making and, by extension, a way of reading. The dialectic of manual and machine-made graphics was key to Roh's theory about the interrelation of different kinds of paper-based contemporary art, including experimental photography, printmaking, and collage. Tschichold's reference to the "glued photographic image" in the typescript suggests that his book would address photomontage as both process and product of art and design. He had intended to write about how visual communication, like collage, results from manually cutting, arranging, and recombining fragments to create new wholes—effectively acknowledging graphic design as a form of montage, and thus of constructing meaning, as opposed to the objective communication of information.

STÜCKUNGSGRAPHIK: NEW TYPOGRAPHY'S SURREALIST UNDERBELLY

In 1927, Franz Roh's article "Max Ernst und die Stückungsgraphik" appeared in *Das Kunstblatt*.[69] In this short text, he effectively offered a theory of images that, in the hands of Tschichold, became a way to understand "the new photomontage" as an umbrella term for composite image-making in both art and graphic design. The article reflected Roh's interest in the collages of Max Ernst, which he first became aware of through reproductions in two books, both published in 1922: *Repetitions* (*Répétitions*) and *The Misfortunes of the Immortals* (*Les malheurs des immortels*), both of which featured Ernst's prints made from collages, reproduced with poems by French surrealist Paul Éluard.[70] The article started with a discussion of Ernst's printmaking, including *Histoire naturelle* (1926), a recently published portfolio of collotype prints created from Ernst's self-described "frottage" process.[71] *Histoire naturelle* took its name from more than thirty scientific volumes published between 1749 and 1788 by Georges Louis Leclerc, comte de Buffon, on the propagation of animal and plant species through biological reproduction.[72] These books introduced the modern concept of sexual propagation in biology using the metaphor of graphic reproduction, aptly illustrated with a series of engravings. Roh's discussion of Ernst's printmaking included reproductions of two images from *The Misfortunes of the Immortals*, identified in the captions simply as woodcuts, though Roh was interested in them as images that resulted from multiple processes of reproduction.

What began as Roh's focused account of printmaking by Max Ernst opened onto a much larger theoretical meditation on interrelated practices of contemporary graphic art. Roh used these examples of Ernst's surrealist prints—all of which were mechanical reproductions of works constructed by hand out of layered fragments—to introduce a contemporary phenomenon he called *Stückungsästhetik* (pieced-together aesthetic). This term described the visual quality of images created through any number of layered, hybrid techniques of graphic image-making, mechanical and manual. The term *Stückungsgraphik* (pieced-together graphics) appears only in the article's title, referring to a sphere of graphic practices including (and combining) printmaking, collage, and photomontage. Roh identified *Stückungsgraphik* as a disruption of another false binary: that of *Maschinenarbeit* (machine work) and art.[73] Like the capacious word "photography," *Stückungsgraphik* encompassed both the processes and products of these techniques.

Much of this short article was given over to a discussion of experimental photography, which Roh regarded as definitive proof of the interdependence of art and technology. He effectively argued that surrealism was unbound by medium, defined instead by a collective impulse to recombine image fragments into new wholes. He dispelled the notion that creative photography was merely aberrant to a purely mechanical process, noting—as he had elsewhere—that every photograph is the result of a series of human decisions. "Since a dispute has erupted lately over the function and limit of the mechanical in art," he wrote,[74] "it must be remembered that there is a human spirit behind machine work."[75] As evidence, Roh named cameraless photography, photographs made from multiple exposures, and photomontage, as well as the *Photoklebebild* (glued photographic image). He described the latter as a technique of physical rearrangement that puts photographic representations into dialectical relationships: "The human hand has once more intervened in those black-and-white pages, which we call photomontage, where a completely new structure is created out of speaking segments of reality (glued photographic image)."[76] For Roh, both experimental photography and Ernst's printmaking exemplified the expression of multiple meanings in a single image created through layered mechanical and manual techniques.

Roh's theory of *Stückungsästhetik* folded photomontage into a family of composite, graphic image-making practices encompassing both photography and nonphotography. Under the rubric of "new photomontage," Tschichold included not only hybrid and experimental photography, but also contemporary forms of nonphotographic composite images. The typescript names many subcategories of photomontage: photo-collage, photo-drawing, photo-painting, photo-sculpture, and, of course, *Typophoto*. However, Tschichold also identified a number of nonphotographic hybrid forms under the umbrella of photomontage, including *typomontage* (montaged typography), Roh's *stückungsgraphik, graphikmontage* (pieced-together graphics, graphic montage), and *zeichnungsmontage* (montaged drawing or illustration).[77] This capacious idea of "new photomontage" supposed that contemporary typographic and photographic practices shared an impulse toward creating hybrid images with highly associative meaning—collectively known as montage—using both mechanical and manual means of combining, layering, and stacking fragments.

We cannot know precisely what *typomontage, graphikmontage,* and *zeichnungsmontage* referred to, or how their meanings might have differed. However, they suggest that what Tschichold had called "elemental typography" in his first book, *Die Neue Typographie,* could also be understood as "montage." Consider, for example, the relationship between two abstract letterpress prints by Piet Zwart, both made in 1925, and his designs for a suite of ephemera for the

Fortoliet Concrete Factory from 1926 (Plate 13). In the abstract prints, Zwart used letterpress to layer and combine elements of varying sizes, thicknesses, and qualities, testing how these forms could be oriented and printed to maximize the use of two complementary colors. In the Fortoliet ephemera, heavier blocks of color constitute parts of letterforms and refer to physical blocks of concrete, punctuating both the company's name and its product. The abstract prints demonstrated how the limited tools of the type case and the constraints of two-color printing could be used in unlimited combinations to experiment with new possibilities of form. What began as *graphikmontage* clearly informed Zwart's *typomontage* for Fortoliet, resulting from formal play as much as economic necessity. Zwart also made use of abstract elements to construct a corporate trademark, a potential example of *zeichnungsmontage*—the combination of abstract forms to create a new form imbued with symbolic value. By emphasizing graphic design as a practice of montage, Tschichold implicitly linked the representational strategies of Dada and surrealism to two important aspects of graphic design: semiotic play with word–image combinations, and the physical combination of fragments into new, unified wholes.

The link between graphic design and surrealism was supported by the many examples of surrealist photomontage that Tschichold had in mind for his book. The typescript reads like a dictionary of terms for hybrid photographic practices, some of which were elaborated with schematic definitions. Subcategories of "the new photomontage" included *fotomalerei* (photo painting), naming Max Ernst as an example.[78] He identified the *fotoklebebild* (glued photographic image) and *stückungsgraphik* (pieced-together graphics)—which he attributed to Roh—as closely related. He described the latter, for which he gave the most examples, as "a new, unified image composed of old drawing parts / ernst, capeli, teige, mesens."[79] Here, he referred again to Ernst, as well as British surrealist P. Capeli, Czech constructivist Karel Teige, and Belgian surrealist Edouard Léon Théodore Mesens. Some of these terms also appear in *foto-auge* (1929), which is useful for unpacking their meanings and speculating about which examples Tschichold may have reproduced in his unrealized book.[80] The plates in *foto-auge* included two collages by Max Ernst, each identified as a *fotomalerei*. Plate 33 reproduced *The Massacre of the Innocents* (1920), a hand-colored photograph to which Ernst applied gouache, watercolor, and ink. Plate 43 reproduced *Approaching Puberty* (*The Pleiades*) (1921), painted in oil and gouache on paper with collaged photographic fragments. From these examples, it is clear that *fotomalerei* denoted any combination of paint and photographic image—whether photographic paper acted as the main material substrate, or photographic elements were added to a painted image on a nonphotographic surface. Undergirding the entire, unfinished project of Tschichold's *Fotomontage* book was Roh's theory of *Stückungsästhetik:* a framework for considering the relationship between technique and representation—how the physical layering of image fragments creates dialectical relationships between them.

EXPERIMENTAL PHOTOGRAPHY AS A DESIGN TECHNIQUE

One of the most notable aspects of Tschichold's unpublished book was its intended focus on the omnipresence of experimental photographic techniques in both contemporary art and graphic design. Among the many photography-based techniques named in the outline under the capacious rubric of "new photomontage" were darkroom methods that had, in the 1920s, become emblematic of New Vision: "photo-composition, also known as photo-combination, created using purely photographic means (copying several recordings on a plate: photogram, etc.), instead of scissors and glue, as a meaningful superimposition and penetrating fixing of light."[81] Tschichold referred here to darkroom experiments with printing multiple exposures on the same print, known as combination printing, as well as cameraless photography, a practice of exposing photo-sensitive paper directly to a controlled light source to record the shapes of objects passed between the paper and light source, creating images known as photograms. He noted these techniques as "purely photographic," in contradistinction to the cut-and-paste process of photomontage, yet at the same time identified them as interrelated.

Tschichold's outline for *Fotomontage* points to a broader fascination with photographic materiality in Weimar culture. By referring to the action and "fixing of light" as "purely photographic means" of image-making, Tschichold considered how photography could produce images unique to its own procedures, both technological and chemical. Due to its scientific applications in the late nineteenth century, cameraless photography held particular fascination for artists working in Weimar Germany.[82] Images made from the direct fixing of light on photographic emulsion were imbued with the capacity to make the invisible visible to the human eye using a technique and visual language unique to photography. Artists such as Moholy-Nagy, Lissitzky, Christian Schad, and Man Ray experimented with light as a material that could fix motion, register facture, and generate novel, abstract forms. If the photographic medium in general connoted a modern way of seeing, cameraless photography enabled the beholder to see through opaque surfaces, as though replicating the penetrating action of light itself.

The *Fotomontage* typescript named Moholy-Nagy and Lissitzky as examples in the category of "photo-composition," referring specifically to Lissitzky's "self-portrait," a combination print also known as *The Constructor*, made in 1924, which also graced the cover of *foto-auge*. Next to Moholy-Nagy's name, Tschichold indicated an example with the placeholder *zeissfotogramm*.[83] Though it is unclear precisely what this note means, *zeiss* likely referred to Zeiss AG, a German manufacturer of optical instruments including camera lenses, spectacles, microscopes, and telescopes, founded by Carl Zeiss in 1846 and headquartered in Jena. On a trip to Jena with Walter Gropius and a group of Bauhaus students in 1925, Moholy-Nagy visited the Sternentheater (now known as Zeiss Planetarium), which was then under construction and opened in 1926 as the world's first permanent planetarium.[84] In his 1929 book *Von Material zu Architektur*, Moholy-Nagy included a photograph of the geodesic steel dome of the planetarium in Jena, seen from below with construction workers appearing to float in midair (Figure 22). Not only did Moholy-Nagy's encounter with Zeiss Planetarium clearly affect his thinking about new possibilities of architectural construction, it may also have informed his experiments with the representation of cosmic space in his photograms. Tschichold may have had in mind a celestial photogram reproduced in *60 Fotos: László Moholy-Nagy* (1930) with the caption "Lightning running through astral gleam."[85]

Tschichold's discussion of experimental photography in *Fotomontage* would by no means have been his first. The outline for *Fotomontage* culminated nearly a decade of writing about and collecting examples of art and design that incorporated combination prints, negative prints, and photograms, as well as photomontage. In an article for the British journal *Commercial Art* published in December 1930, likely written around the same time he outlined the book for Fototek, Tschichold defended "composite photography"—which he used as an umbrella term that included photograms, multiple exposures, and photomontage—in commercial graphic design.[86] He described successful uses of composite photography in advertising as a technique not intended to fool the eye of the beholder, but rather as one that "enables us to build up optical associations."[87] Experimental photography held far more value in commercial design as a visual stimulus in the minds of readers than as a mere tool of representation.

Die Neue Typographie included a brief discussion of the photogram, attributing its advent "as an art form" to Man Ray.[88] It also included two examples of photograms in advertising: a 1924 advertisement by Lissitzky for Pelikan ink; and an insert by Piet Zwart for Nederlandsche Kabelfabriek (Netherlands

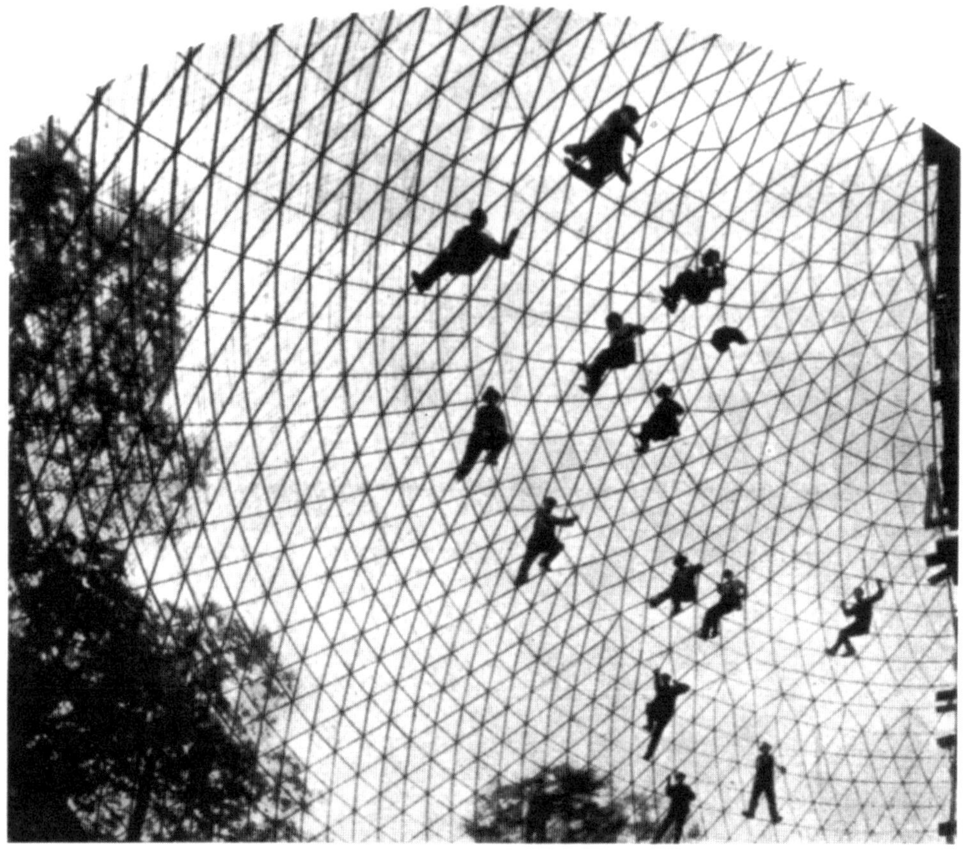

foto: schottwerke / jena

abb. 208 bau des skeletts für ein planetarium der zeisswerke

eine neue fase der besitznahme von raum: eine menschenstaffel in schwebend durchsichtigem netz, wie eine flugzeugstaffel im äter.

FIGURE 22 László Moholy-Nagy, *Von Material zu Architektur* (Munich: Albert Langen Verlag, 1929), 235. Copyright 2024 Estate of László Moholy-Nagy / Artists Rights Society (ARS), New York.

Cable Works), made circa 1925, advertising paper insulation for high-tension cables. These examples represent two important ways that graphic designers employed the photogram in the 1920s: as a technique for using light as typographic material and as a means of illustrating the materiality of a particular product for sale. Lissitzky's Pelikan piece used stencils and an ink pen and bottle—presumably the company's own products—as props to create an advertisement made from the action of light and shadow on sensitized paper (Figure 23).[89] Zwart's advertisement includes a photogram that registers the

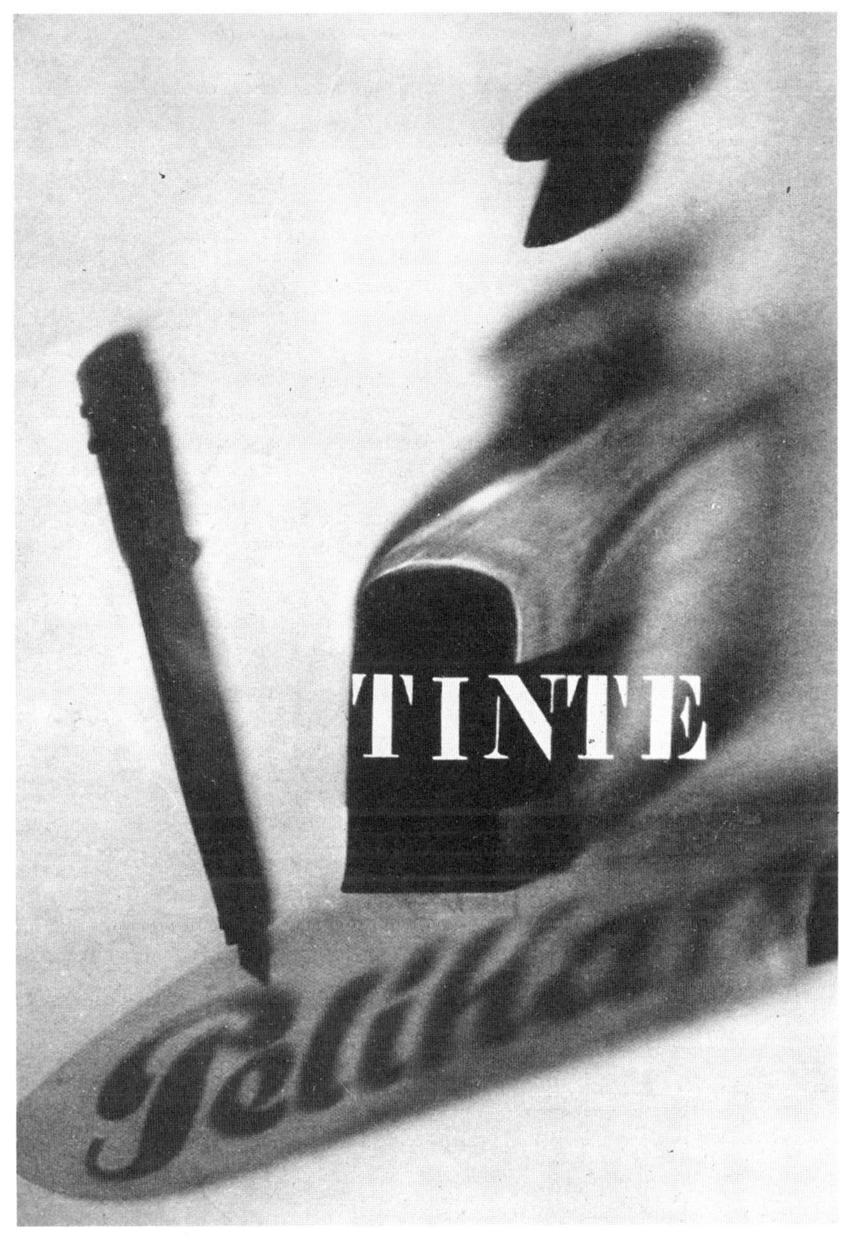

FIGURE 23 El Lissitzky, *Pelikan Tinte*, 1924, gelatin silver print, photogram, 8 5/16 × 5 13/16 in. (21.1 × 14.7 cm), The Museum of Fine Arts, Houston, Museum purchase funded by the Caroline Wiess Law Accessions Endowment Fund, The Manfred Heiting Collection, 2002.1550. Photograph Copyright The Museum of Fine Arts, Houston; Will Michels. Copyright 2024 Artists Rights Society (ARS), New York.

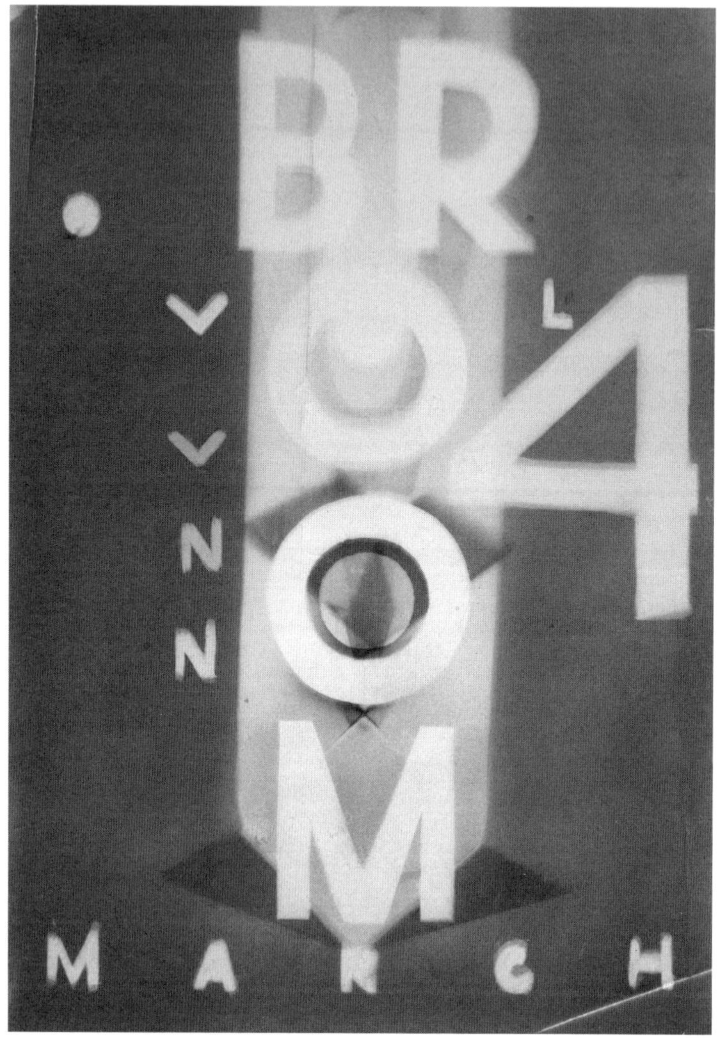

FIGURE 24 László Moholy-Nagy, cover design for *Broom* 4, 1922, contact print. Digital Image Copyright CNAC/MNAM, Dist. RMN-Grand Palais / Art Resource, NY. Copyright 2024 Estate of László Moholy-Nagy / Artists Rights Society (ARS), New York.

FIGURE 25 Mockup for the cover of *Insel-Almanach, 1929*, circa 1929, gelatin silver print (photogram). Nachlass Jan Tschichold, Deutsches Buch- und Schriftmuseum der Deutschen Nationalbibliothek, Leipzig. Courtesy of Creative Common.

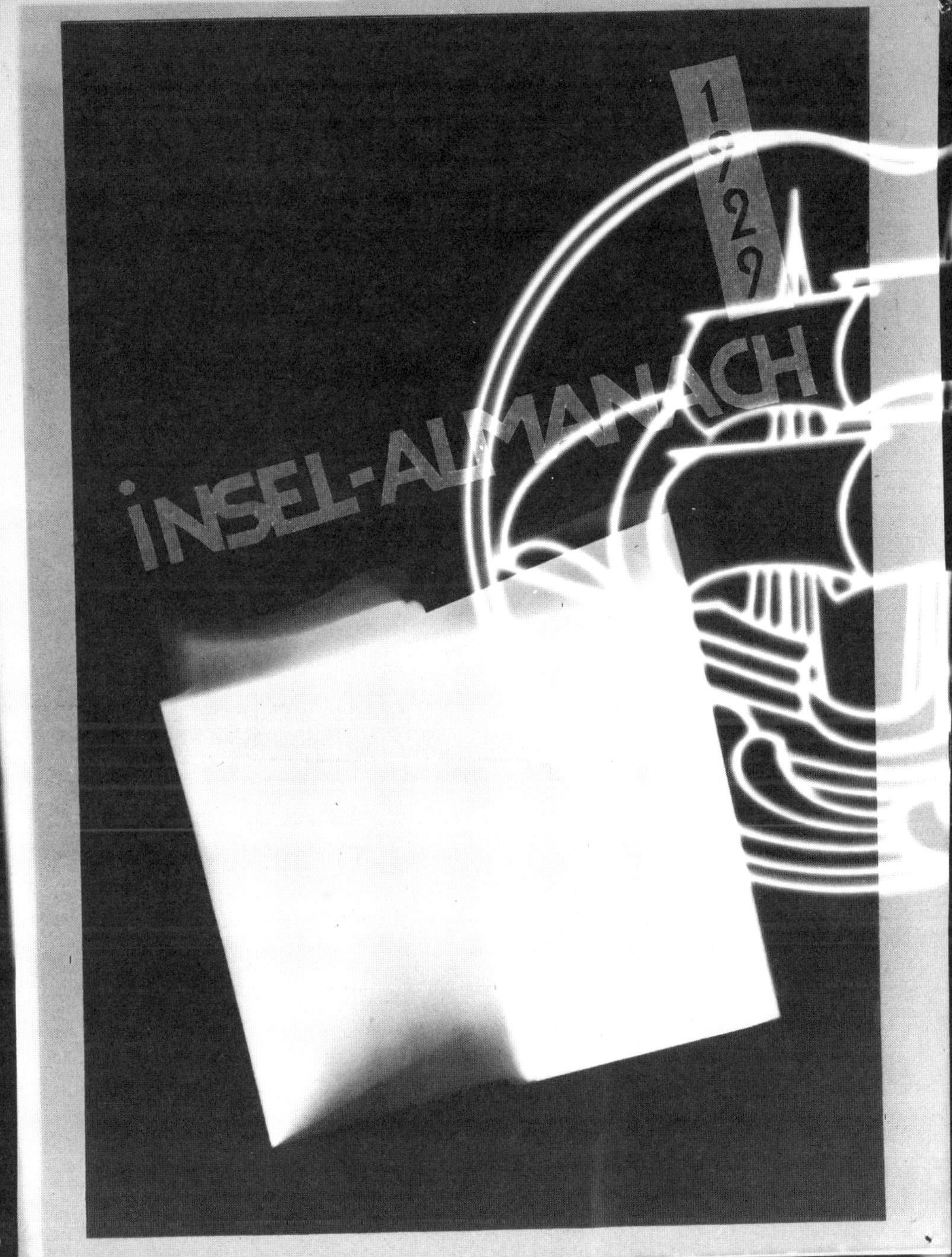
1929
INSEL-ALMANACH

fineness of paper insulation, so thin that it appears nearly translucent, in contrast to the opaque metal cable, which appears solidly bright white. The vertical form of the cable echoes the elongated stems of two *H*'s that appear to cast shadows in the form of horizontal lines of text. Both designs use the photogram as a technique to synthesize word and image, suggesting a kind of reversal of other iterations of *Typophoto:* they show how photographic material could be used to create typographic form, just as typographic material (dot patterns in ink) could be used to create photographic form (the halftone).

In its distillation of photography down to its most fundamental meaning—writing with light—the photogram was a means of demonstrating how photography could not only complement typography, but actually produce it. Moholy-Nagy created a photogram as a cover design proposal for the fourth issue of the American avant-garde journal *Broom* (Figure 24). In 1931, he included a contact print made from one of a series of photograms on the cover of *Foto-Qualität,* a special issue of the German graphic design journal *Qualität* (Plate 14).[90] These examples underscore the positive–negative reversal of photographic chemistry as a corollary to the reversal of letterforms on the bed of a press. They call attention not only to the process of photography as a means of constructing typographic composition, but also to how all typography is physically constructed, whether on a letterpress or light table.

Tschichold himself made a series of photograms for a proposal to Insel Verlag for the cover of the Leipzig publisher's 1929 annual, which was never put into production (Figure 25). He used cameraless photography to create an image of a book as well as the publisher's trademark, name, and date, using stencils. These prints evidence Tschichold's trial-and-error process of using light to record the tactility of the book as an object. These images literalize Tschichold's idea that book design must evolve to include photography by rendering the book itself as photographic material. Evidently, photographic techniques had influenced not only Tschichold's idea of illustration in modern graphic design, but also his recognition of *Typophoto* as a way to understand typography and photography as materially intertwined, and even interchangeable.

TYPOPHOTO IN THREE DIMENSIONS

In *Die Neue Typographie,* Tschichold had discussed color as a key element of New Typography, and in the *Fotomontage* typescript, he explicitly included it as part of the definition of *Typophoto.* The term first appears in a two-part definition of photomontage:

11. photomontage text = typophoto
photomontage and color[91]

Color is an element that would certainly have illuminated the link between Dada and surrealism and New Typography that Tschichold intended to draw in *Fotomontage*. Looking at commercial work by the New Typographers, such a link is easy to imagine, especially in deciphering what work color does in their designs. A 1926 advertising insert by Max Burchartz and Johannes Canis for Orion vacuum cleaners, for example, features two women peering into a schematically rendered room, loosely suggested by a plane of red ink that frames the scene (Plate 15). They appear in the midst of conversation; advertising copy animates their expositional exchange about the health and economic benefits of an electrical vacuum cleaner and where to purchase it. There is a clear distinction between the space of reality—the photographic depiction of the two women, who act as surrogates for potential consumers—and that of fantasy, connoted by the color planes that constitute the vaguely articulated architectural space. The red color blocks highlight each photographic fragment as a different type of illustration: the two women represent reality in the present, while the boisterous crowd represents the excitement and desire we are meant to feel as consumers, and the vacuum represents the object of desire—a future reality. Within a single design, photography's contradictions are laid bare through montage, and color signals the juxtaposition of fantasy and reality.

The supernatural effect that Tschichold ascribed to the combination of photographic with type, abstract elements of color, and the white substrate of the page was especially useful in designs featuring intangible phenomena that resisted illustration. Consider, for example, covers by German designer Walter Cyliax for the journal *Die Elektrizität*, published between 1928 and 1930 (Plate 16). In each of these designs, Cyliax animated the elusive phenomenon of electricity using montage, combining photographic fragments with text and other graphics printed in a single, striking color. Rather than functioning as straightforward illustrations, each cover focuses on a particular use of electricity—such as powering a refrigerator or incubating chicks on a farm—through designs presented to the beholder as visual puzzles. Reading these designs begins as an attempt to decode their meanings. Yet their visual potency lies in their resistance to being easily interpreted. Instead, visual dissonance between the illusionism of photography and the synthetic quality of typography and colorful graphic elements creates a destabilizing effect. These designs might evoke excitement about the many uses of electricity or dread for an increasingly mechanized world. They provide visual and affective stimulus from which the beholder must construct meaning.

Typophoto appears again on the third typed page of the *Fotomontage* typescript, along with references to several examples:

> photomontage (general term)
>
> is the assembled form-production [*gestaltende einbau*] of one or more photographs, or parts of photographs, on a surface regardless [of] whether it is partially or completely covered. the quality of the work depends first and foremost on the power of form-production [*gestaltugskraft*] of the author,[92] secondarily on the quality of the photos used. when typography is added to photomontage, it is called typophoto.
>
> examples: burchartz, bochumer verein
> tschichold, bellisana
> bad typography with bare photos
> good typography with bare photos (bayer)
> calendar for franzsche book publisher (counterexample)[93]

Tschichold indicated that *Typophoto* results "when typography is added to photomontage." His examples of "good" *Typophoto* include a prospectus design by Burchartz and Canis for the Bochumer Verein, a touchstone for New Typography in Tschichold's publications (Plate 17).[94] This montaged prospectus depicts an amalgam of machine parts arranged asymmetrically on the page with the company's trademark printed in black in the upper left corner. It showcases no fewer than seven different products of the Bochumer Verein, overlapping and appearing to float dynamically in undefined space against a gray background. Burchartz and Canis used the disparate scale of the photographic fragments to simulate the regression of deep space—not for the purpose of realistic illusion, but to draw the reader's eye deliberately around the page. The centripetal arrangement of the fragments frames a bolt of red ink at the center, against which the manufacturer's name appears in white. Color creates not only visual contrast between text and image, but also a tension between the three-dimensional space of photography and two-dimensional typographic space.

The emphasis on color and photomontage in Tschichold's revised definition of *Typophoto* was part of an evolving approach to New Typography as not only a set of principles for creating typographic form, but as a corresponding

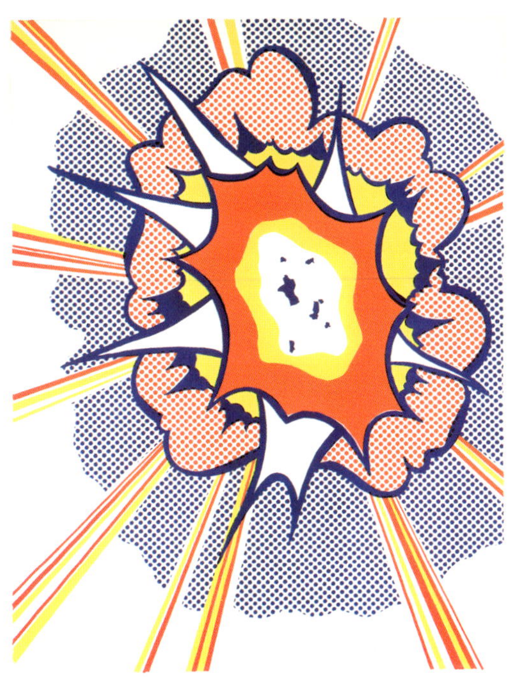

1 Roy Lichtenstein, *Explosion*, 1965–66, lithograph on paper. Tate, presented by the Museum of Modern Art, New York, 1976. Copyright Estate of Roy Lichtenstein. Photograph: Tate.

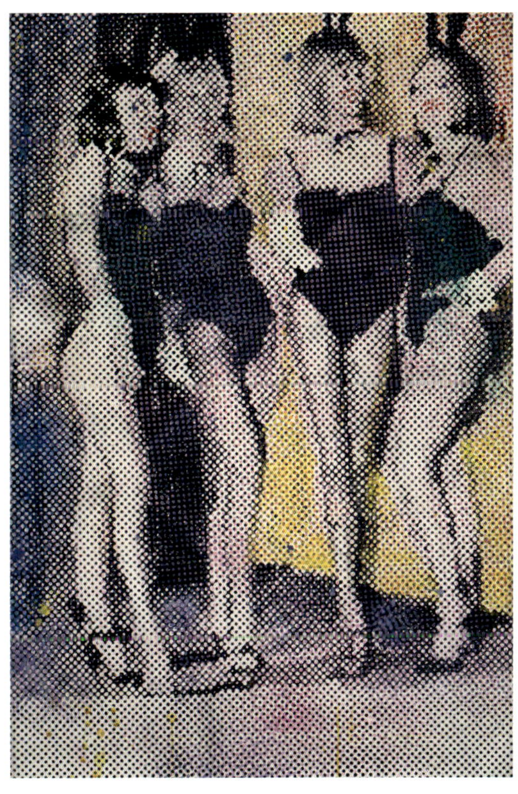

2 Sigmar Polke, *Bunnies*, 1966, synthetic polymer on canvas, 58 3/4 × 39 1/8 in. (149.2 × 99.3 cm), Joseph H. Hirshhorn Bequest and Purchase Funds, 1992. Lee Stalsworth Hirshhorn Museum and Sculpture Garden. Copyright The Estate of Sigmar Polke, Cologne / ARS, New York, 2024.

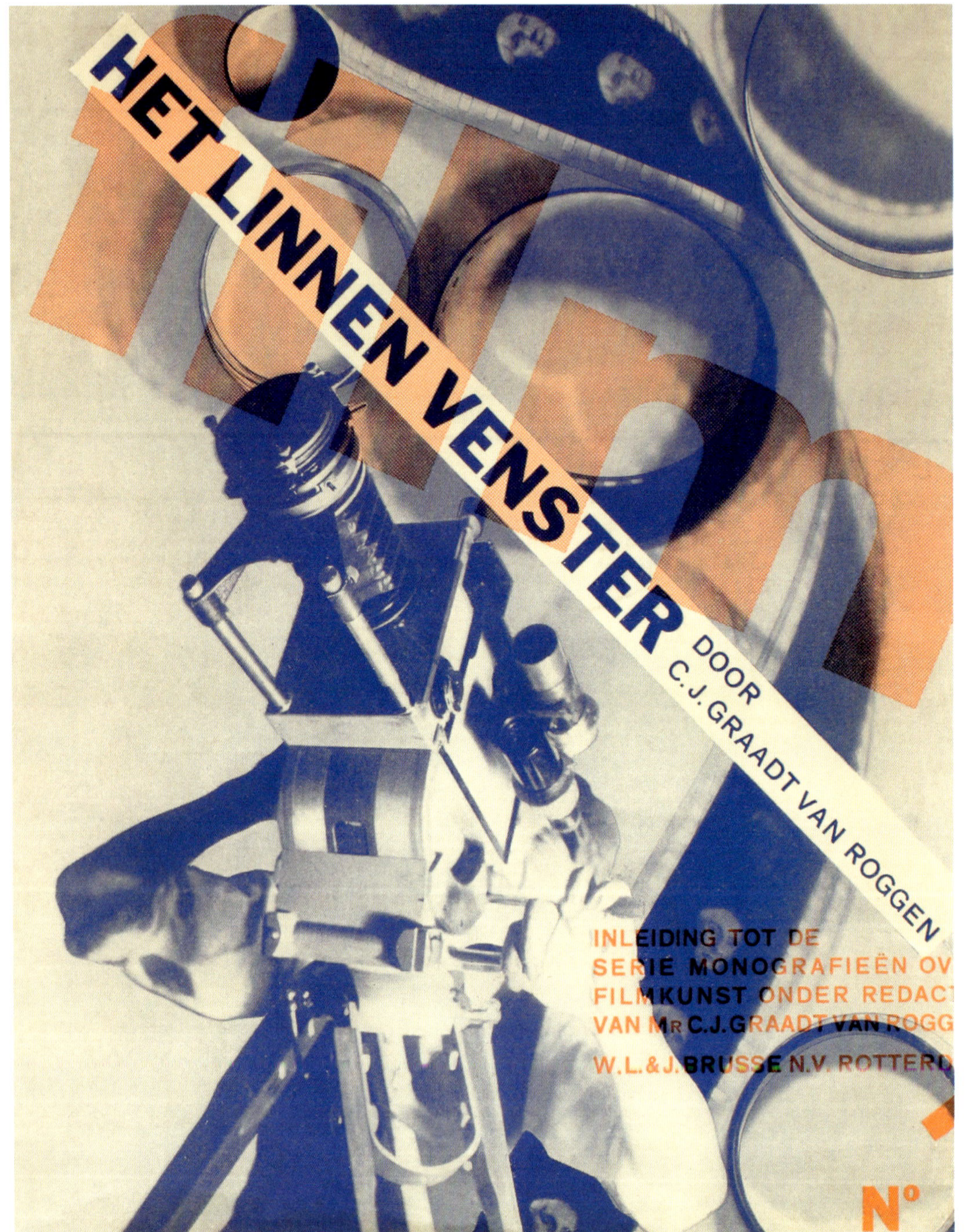
HET LINNEN VENSTER
DOOR
C.J. GRAADT VAN ROGGEN
INLEIDING TOT DE
SERIE MONOGRAFIEËN OV
FILMKUNST ONDER REDACT
VAN Mr C.J. GRAADT VAN ROGG
W.L.&J. BRUSSE N.V. ROTTERD
N°

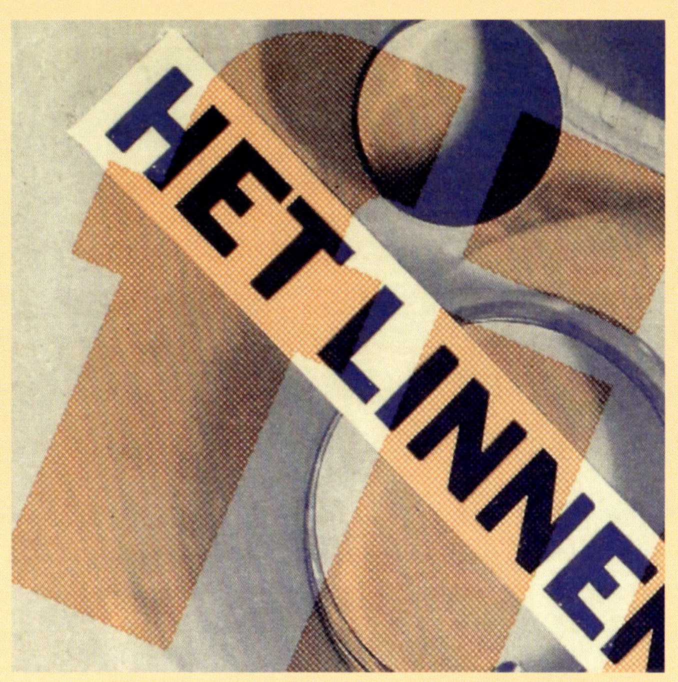

3 Piet Zwart, cover of C. J. Graadt van Roggen, *Het Linnen Venster* (with detail), 1931, offset lithograph. Collection Merrill C. Berman. Copyright 2024 Artists Rights Society (ARS), New York / c/o Pictoright Amsterdam.

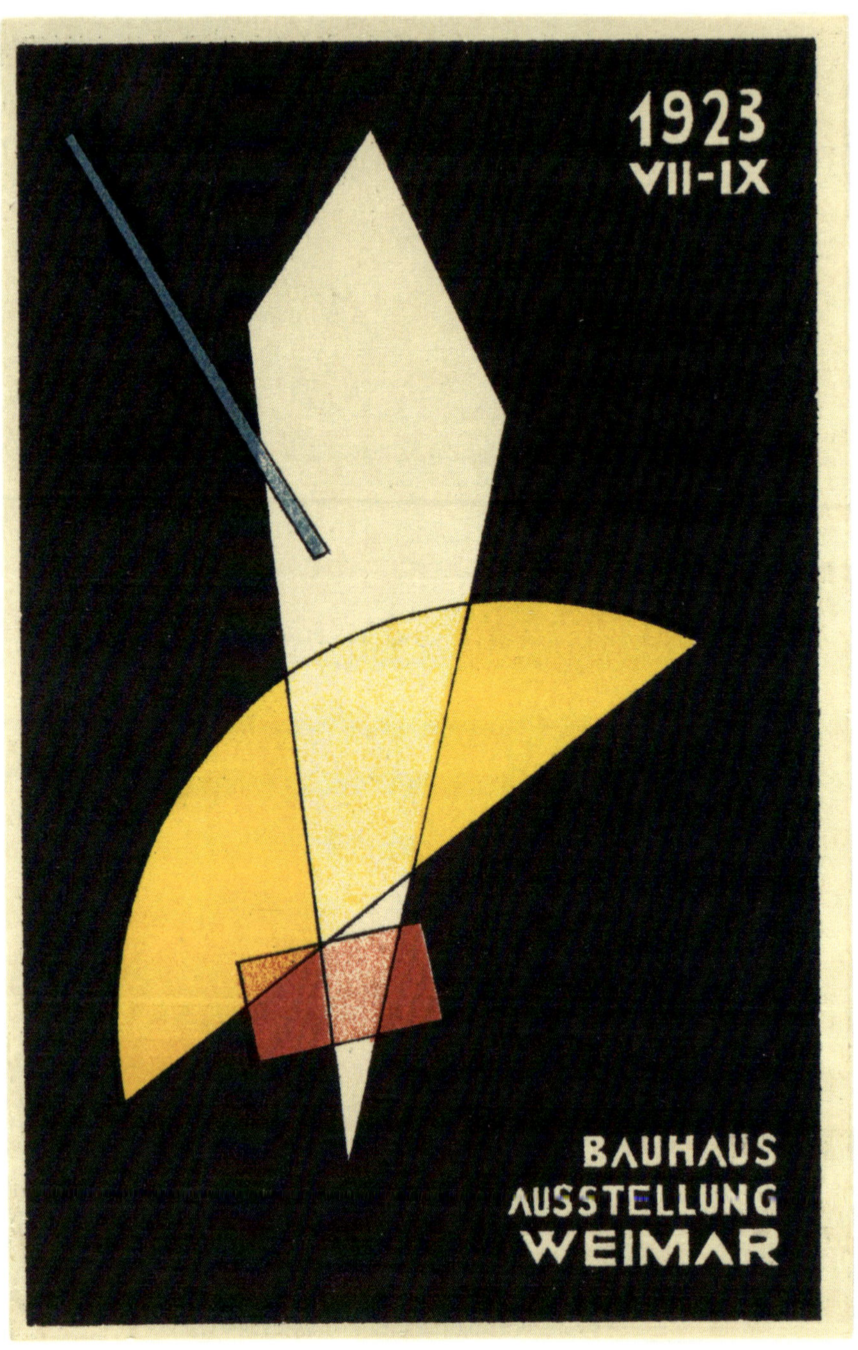

4 László Moholy-Nagy, *Bauhaus Ausstellung Weimar Juli–Sept, 1923, Karte 7*, 1923, lithograph. Digital Image Copyright The Museum of Modern Art / Licensed by SCALA / Art Resource, NY. Copyright 2024 Estate of László Moholy-Nagy / Artists Rights Society (ARS), New York.

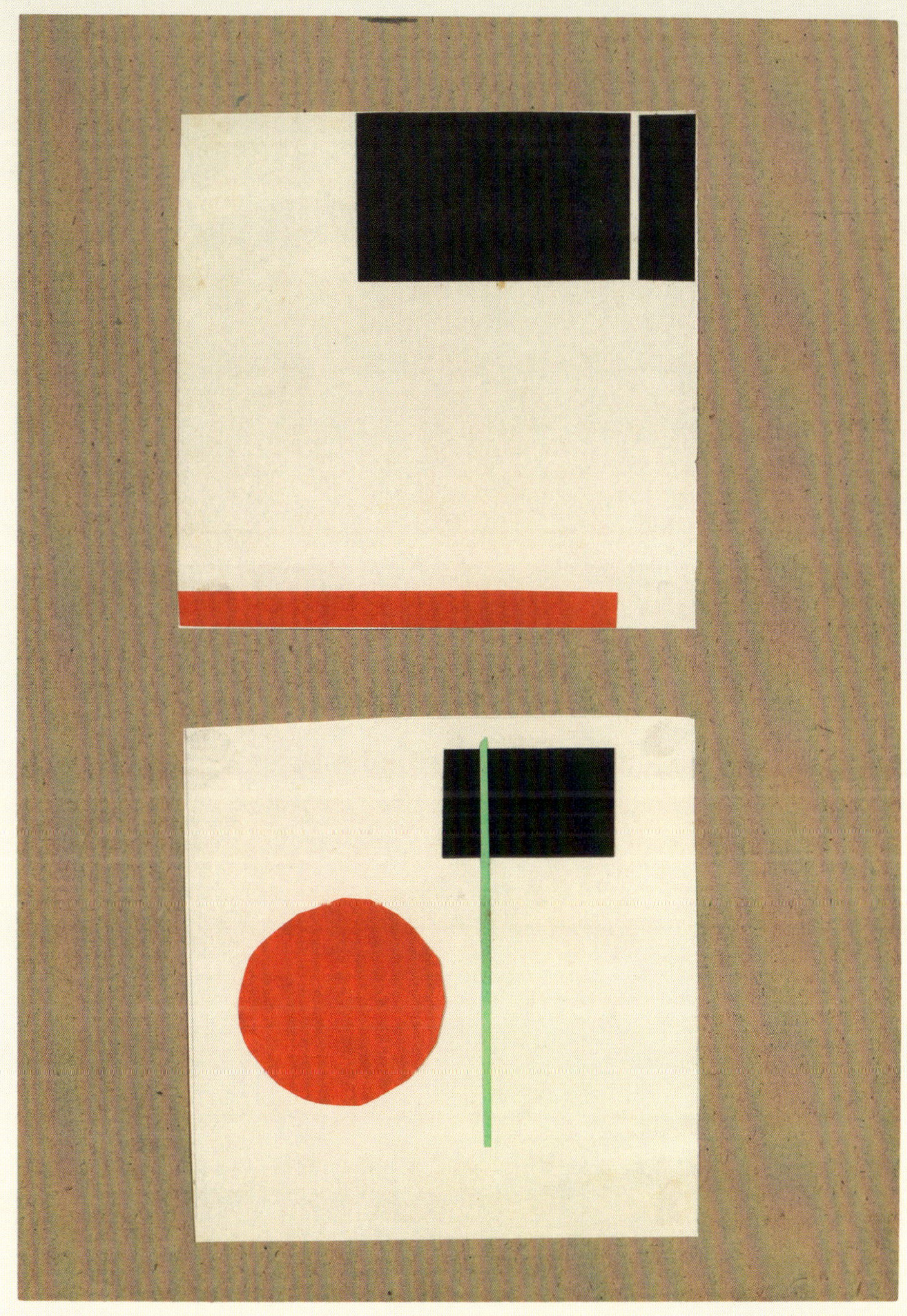

5 Jan Tschichold, untitled collage, date unknown, paper and paste. Box 24, Nachlass Jan Tschichold, Deutsches Buch- und Schriftmuseum der Deutschen Nationalbibliothek, Leipzig. Courtesy of Creative Commons.

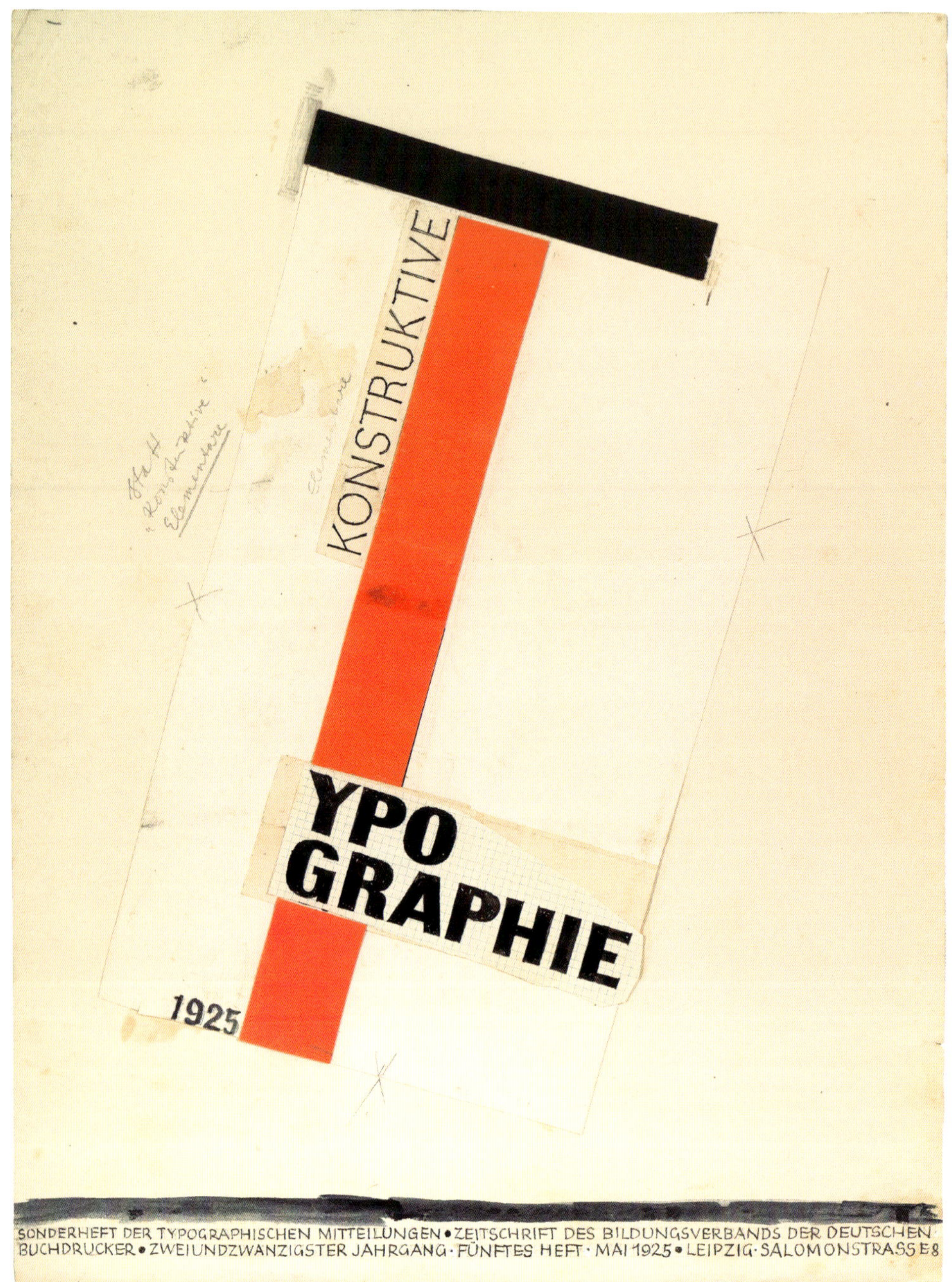

6 Jan Tschichold, mock-up for the cover of *elementare typographie*, circa 1925, ink, gouache, pencil, paper and paste. Box 72, Nachlass Jan Tschichold, Deutsches Buch- und Schriftmuseum der Deutschen Nationalbibliothek, Leipzig. Courtesy of Creative Commons.

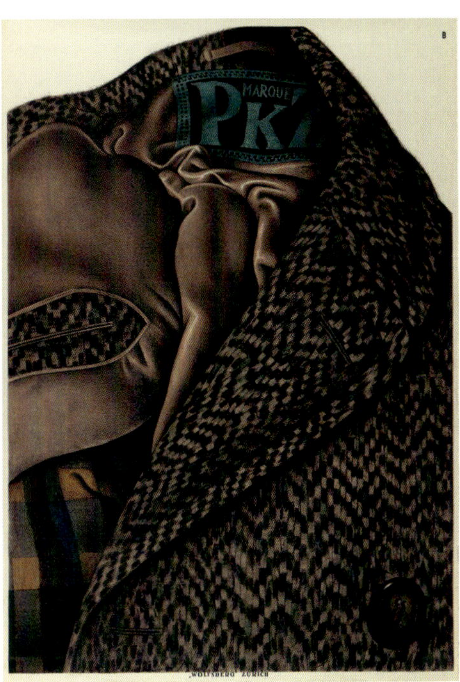

7 Otto Baumberger, advertising poster for PKZ, 1923, offset lithograph. Museum für Gestaltung Zürich. Photograph: Courtesy of the Museum für Gestaltung Zurich, Poster Collection, ZHdK. Copyright 2024 Artists Rights Society (ARS), New York / ProLitteris, Zurich.

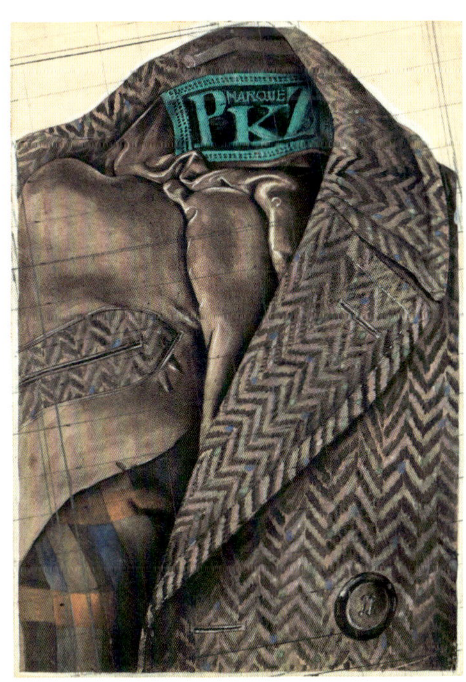

8 Otto Baumberger, sketch for PKZ advertising poster, 1923, pencil, ink, gouache. Museum für Gestaltung Zürich. Photograph: Courtesy of the Museum für Gestaltung Zurich, Poster Collection, ZHdK. Copyright 2024 Artists Rights Society (ARS), New York / ProLitteris, Zurich.

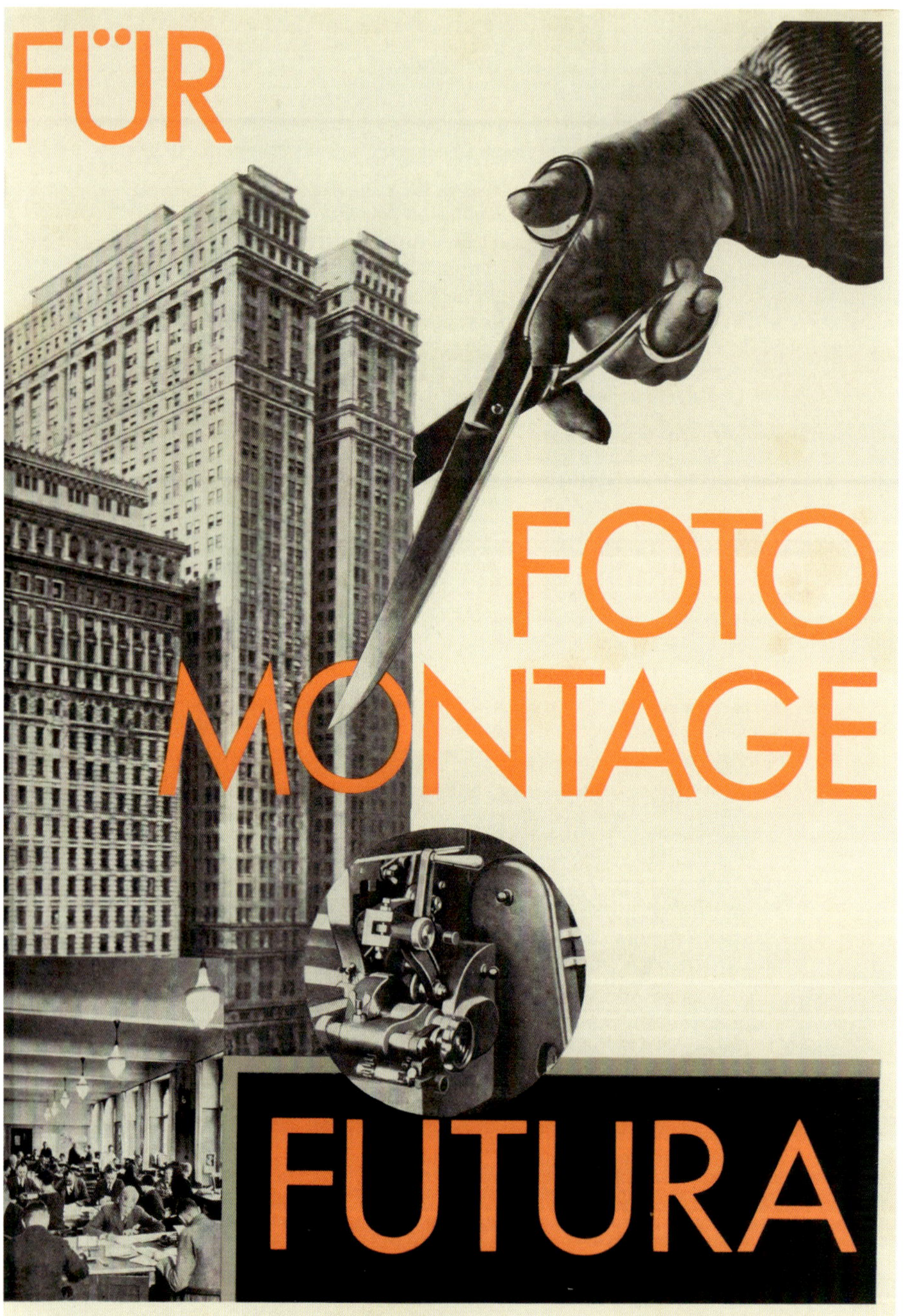
FÜR
FOTO
MONTAGE
FUTURA

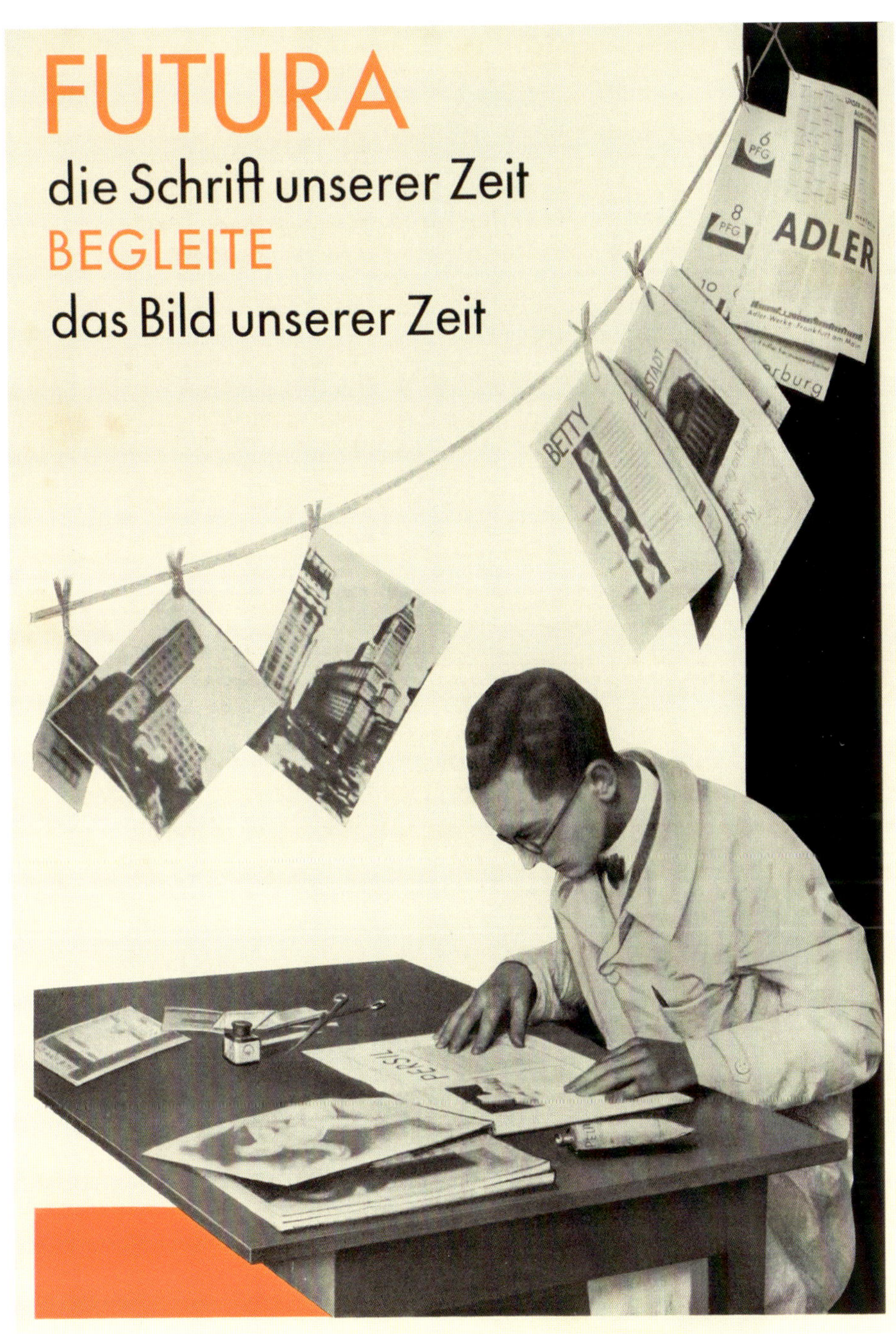

9 Heinrich Jost for Bauer Type Foundry, Futura prospectus (front and back cover), 1927, offset lithography. Letterform Archive, San Francisco.

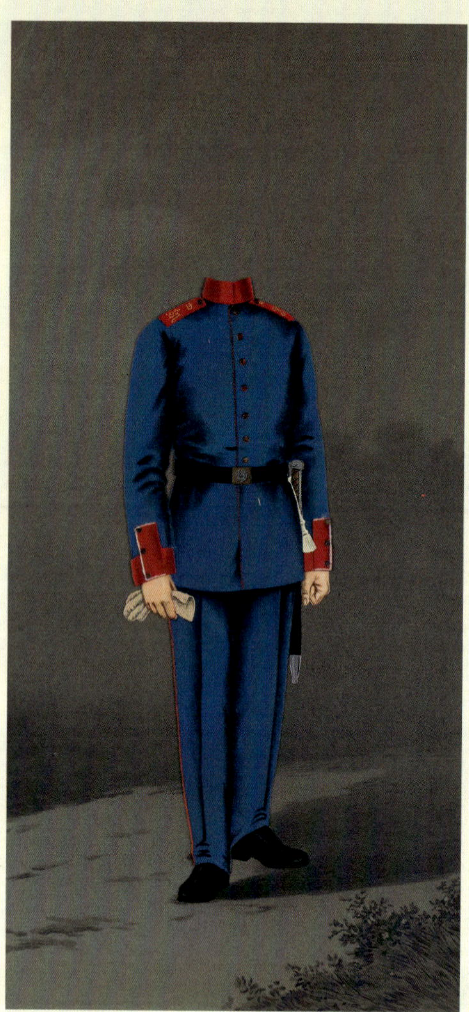

10 Unattributed template for a photomontage (Royal Bavarian Infantry Regiment), medium unknown, second half of the nineteenth century. Rheinisches Bildarchiv Cologne. Copyright Rheinisches Bildarchiv Cologne (rba_d035538).

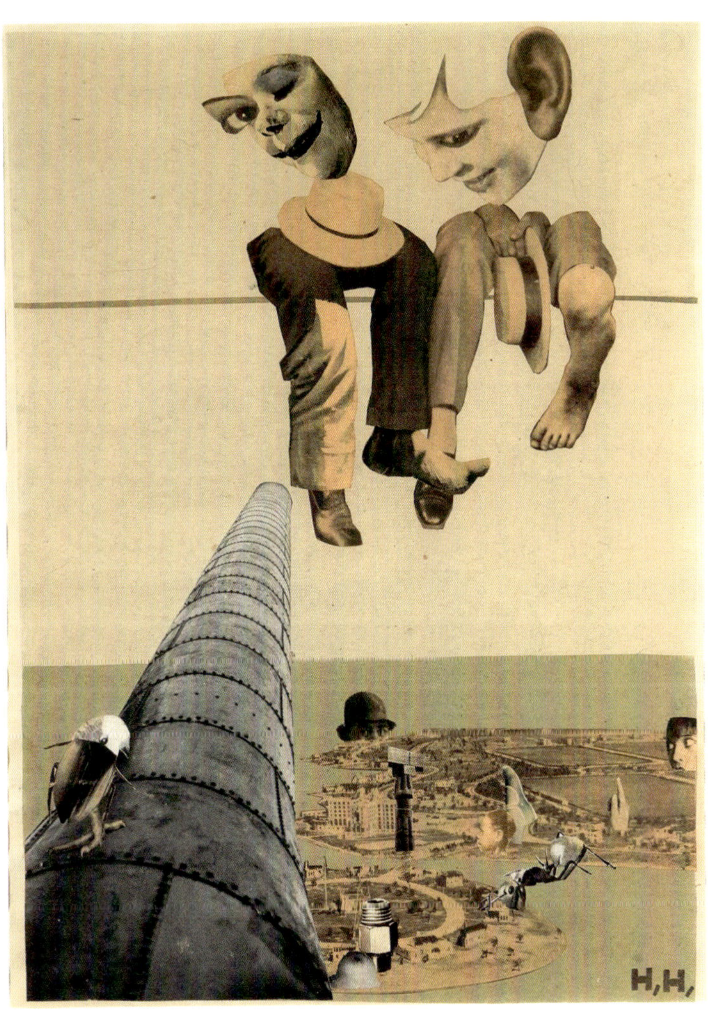

11 Hannah Höch, *Von Oben* (*From Above*), 1926–27, collage and photomontage on paper on cardboard, 12 × 8⅞ in. (30.5 × 22.5 cm), Des Moines Art Center's Louise Noun Collection of Art by Women through Bequest, 2003.323. Photo Credit: Rich Sanders, Des Moines. Copyright 2024 Artists Rights Society (ARS), New York / VG Bild-Kunst, Bonn.

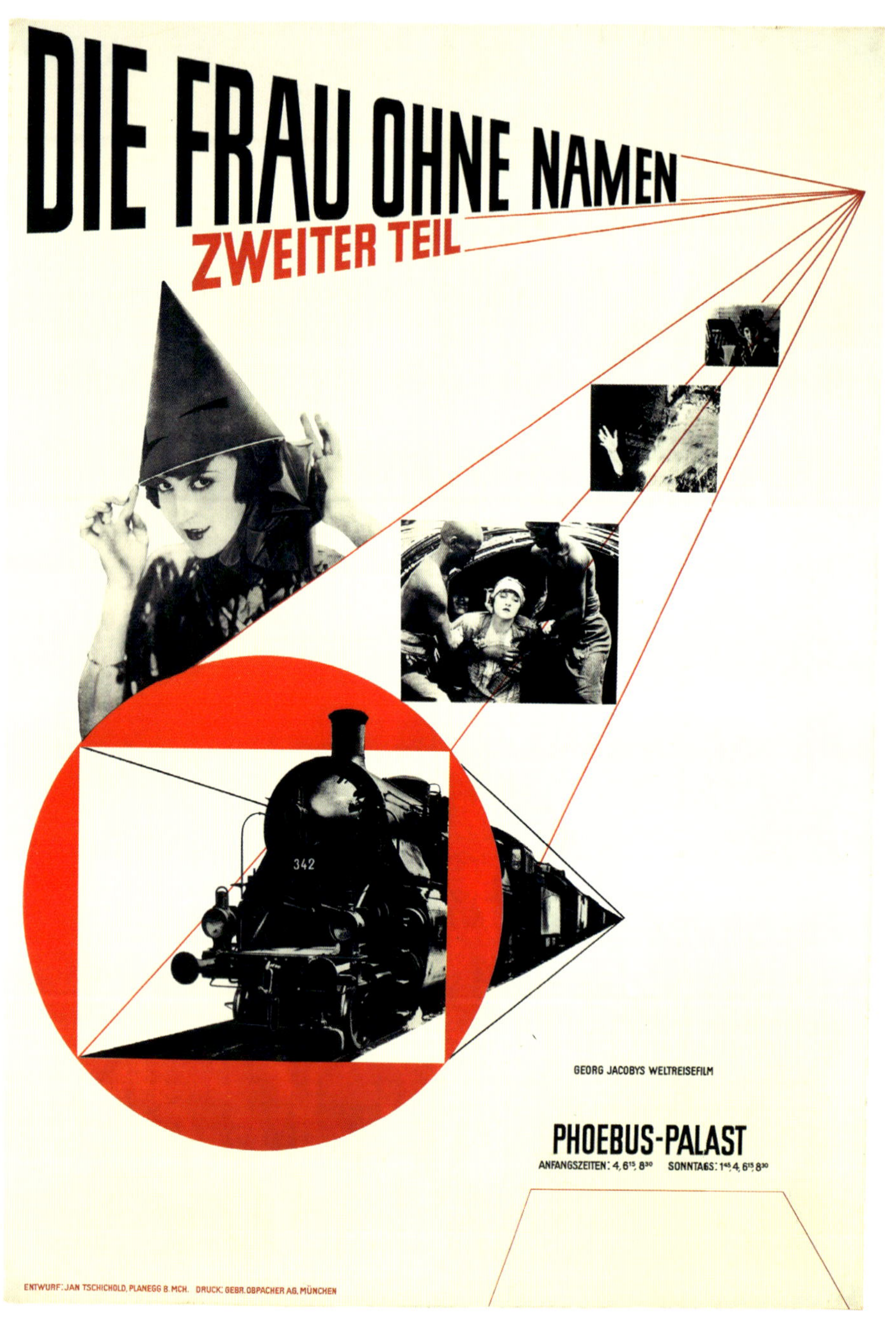

12 Jan Tschichold, *Die Frau Ohne Namen*, 1927, offset lithograph. The Museum of Modern Art / New York, NY / USA. Courtesy of Creative Commons. Digital Image copyright The Museum of Modern Art / Licensed by SCALA / Art Resource, NY.

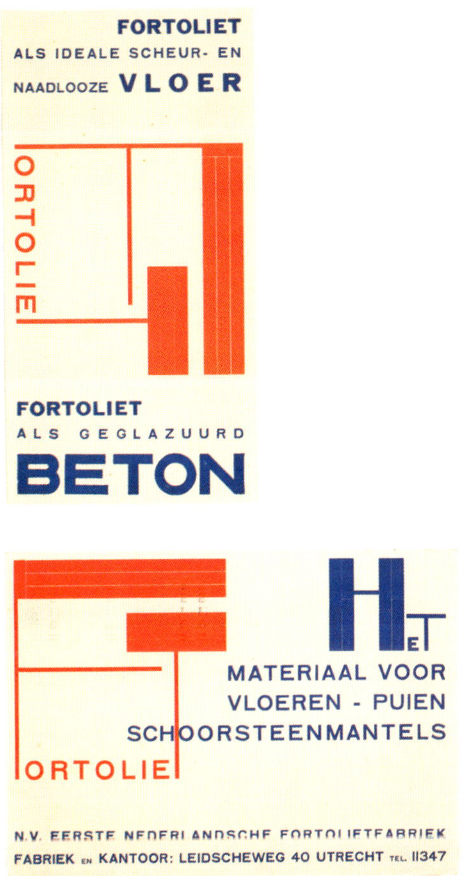

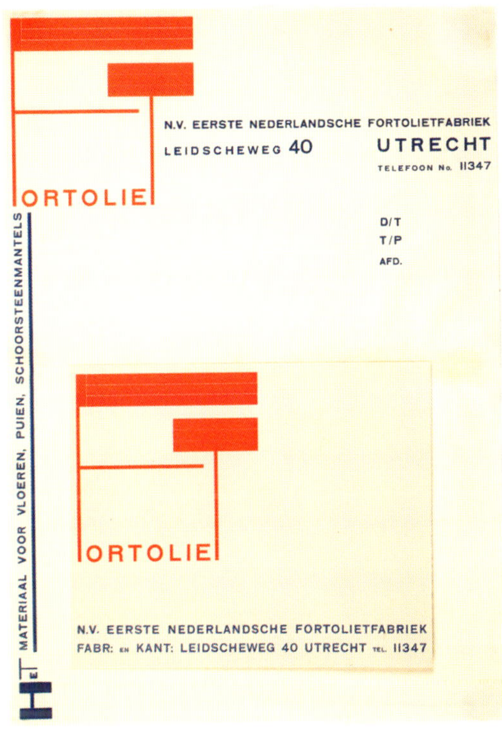

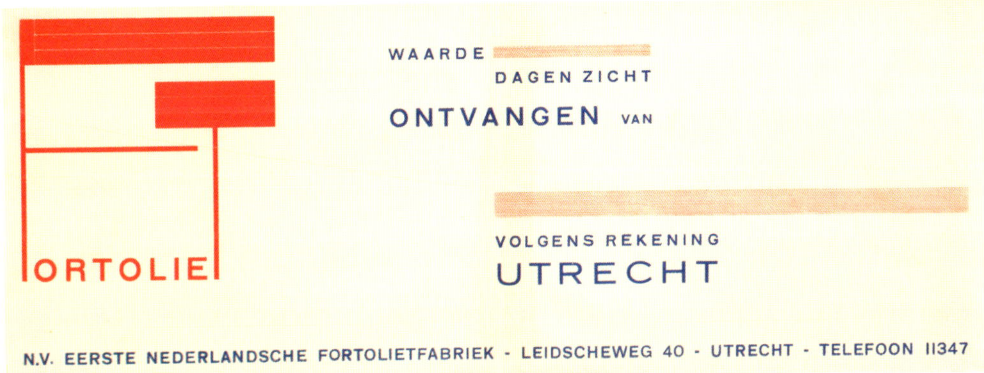

13 Piet Zwart, suite of ephemera for Fortoliet Concrete Factory, 1926, letterpress. Merrill C. Berman Collection / MoMA. Collection Stedelijk Museum, Amsterdam. Copyright 2024 Artists Rights Society (ARS), New York / c/o Pictoright Amsterdam.

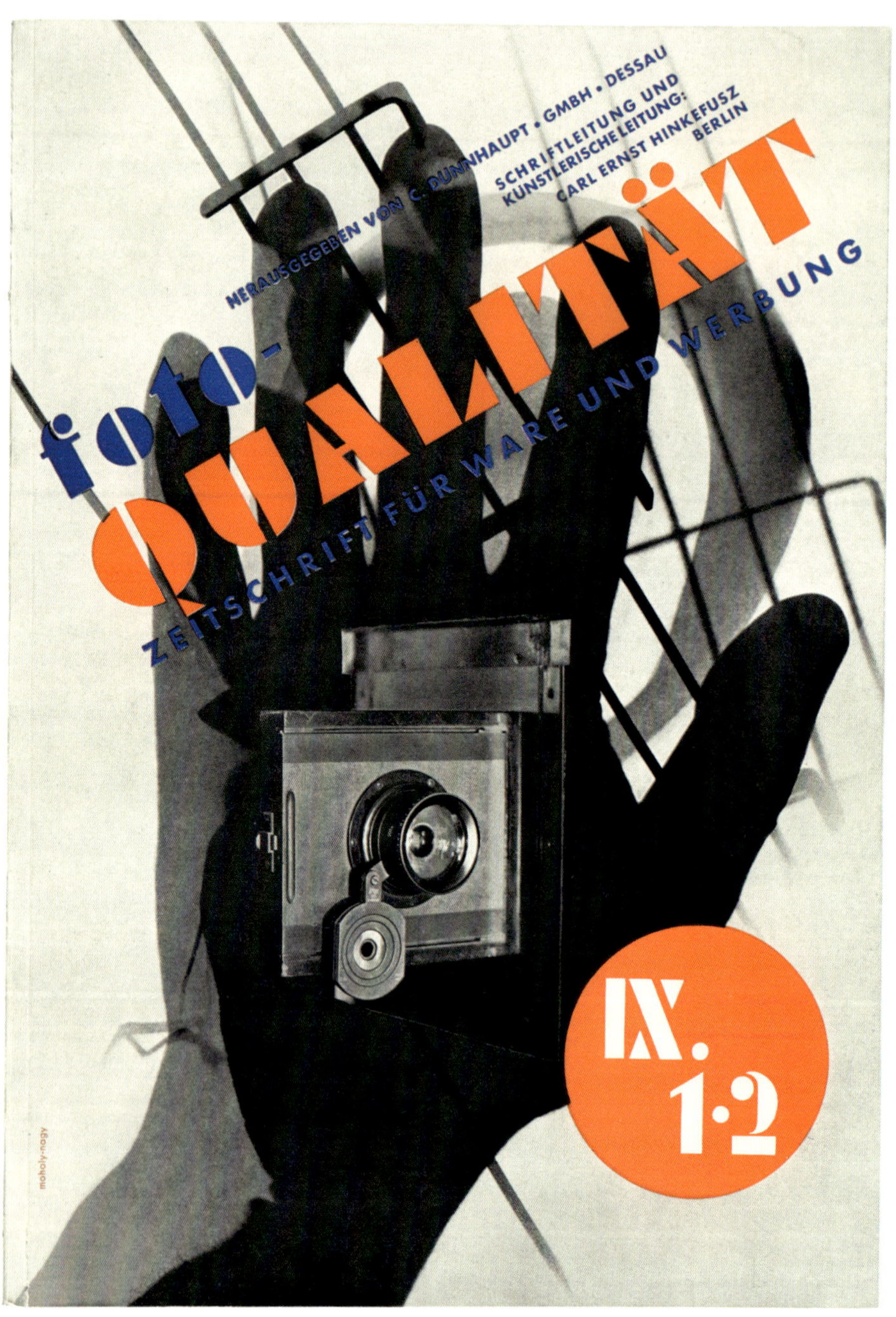

14 László Moholy-Nagy, cover of *Foto-Qualität*, 1931, offset lithography. Getty Research Institute, Los Angeles (930030). Copyright 2024 Estate of László Moholy-Nagy / Artists Rights Society (ARS), New York.

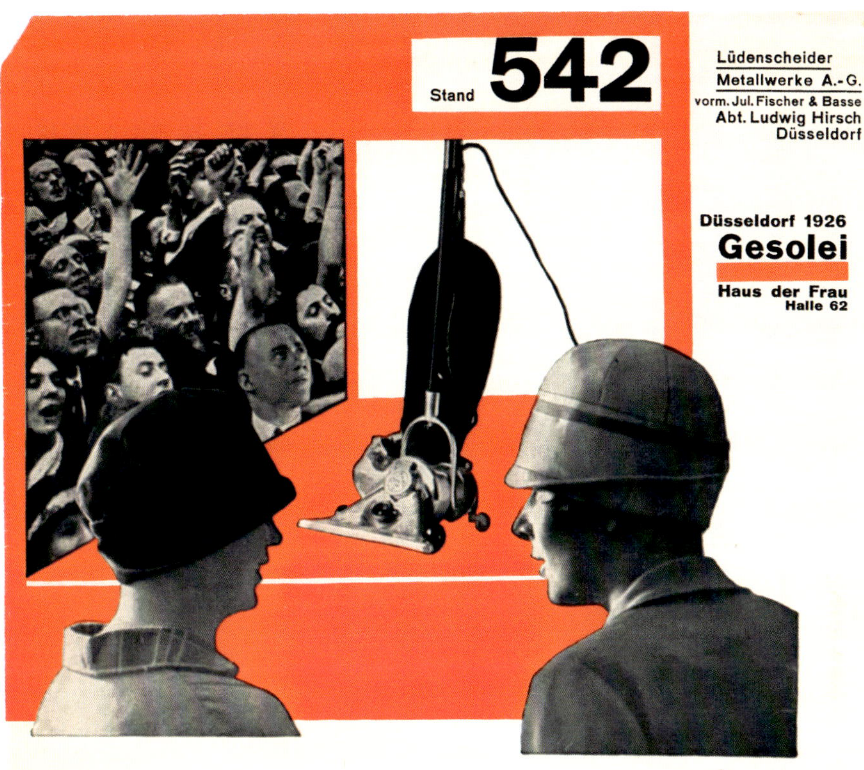

„Du weißt gar nicht, welcher Vorteil Dir entgeht, so lange Du noch keinen elektrischen Hausreiniger hast. Ich kann mir kaum noch vorstellen, wie ich ohne ihn auskam. Sogar von den Büchern und unter den Schränken hole ich den Staub mit dem „Orion“ fort. Ich habe das Gefühl, alles ist sauberer als früher und meine Wohnung ist gesunder. Man braucht nur einmal den Beutel des „Orion“ selber auszuschütten, dann graut einem davor, was an Schmutz in die Zimmer eindringt. Mit Bürste und Klopfer kannst Du diese Berge von Staub und Bazillen nicht fortbekommen. Ich kann Dir nur raten, kauf Dir einen „Orion“.“

„Ich werd mir wohl auch einen kaufen. Nur sag mal, ist der Stromverbrauch nicht teuer?“

„Ach wo, das sind ganz wenige Pfennige für die Stunde. Die sparst Du schnell an Arbeitslohn. Und selbst wenn das nicht wäre, sollte Dir die Gesundheit diese paar Pfennige wert sein. Auch Zeit gewinnst Du, kannst dann spazieren gehen und Dich erholen.“

„Wo kann ich den „Orion“ herbekommen?“

„Durch jedes Haushaltungsgeschäft, auch durch Deinen Installateur. Alles Zubehör — Schlauch, Bürsten, Leitungsschnur usw. — ist stets dabei. Oder schreib an die Fabrik, die Lüdenscheider Metallwerke A.-G., Abtlg. Ludwig Hirsch in Düsseldorf; die schickt Dir Prospekte und gibt Bezugsquellen für den „Orion“ an.“

ORION

15 Max Burchartz and Johannes Canis (werbe-bau), advertising insert for Orion, 1926, letterpress. Digital image copyright the Museum of Modern Art / New York, NY / USA. / Licensed by SCALA / Art Resource, NY. Copyright 2024 Artists Rights Society (ARS), New York / VG Bild-Kunst, Bonn.

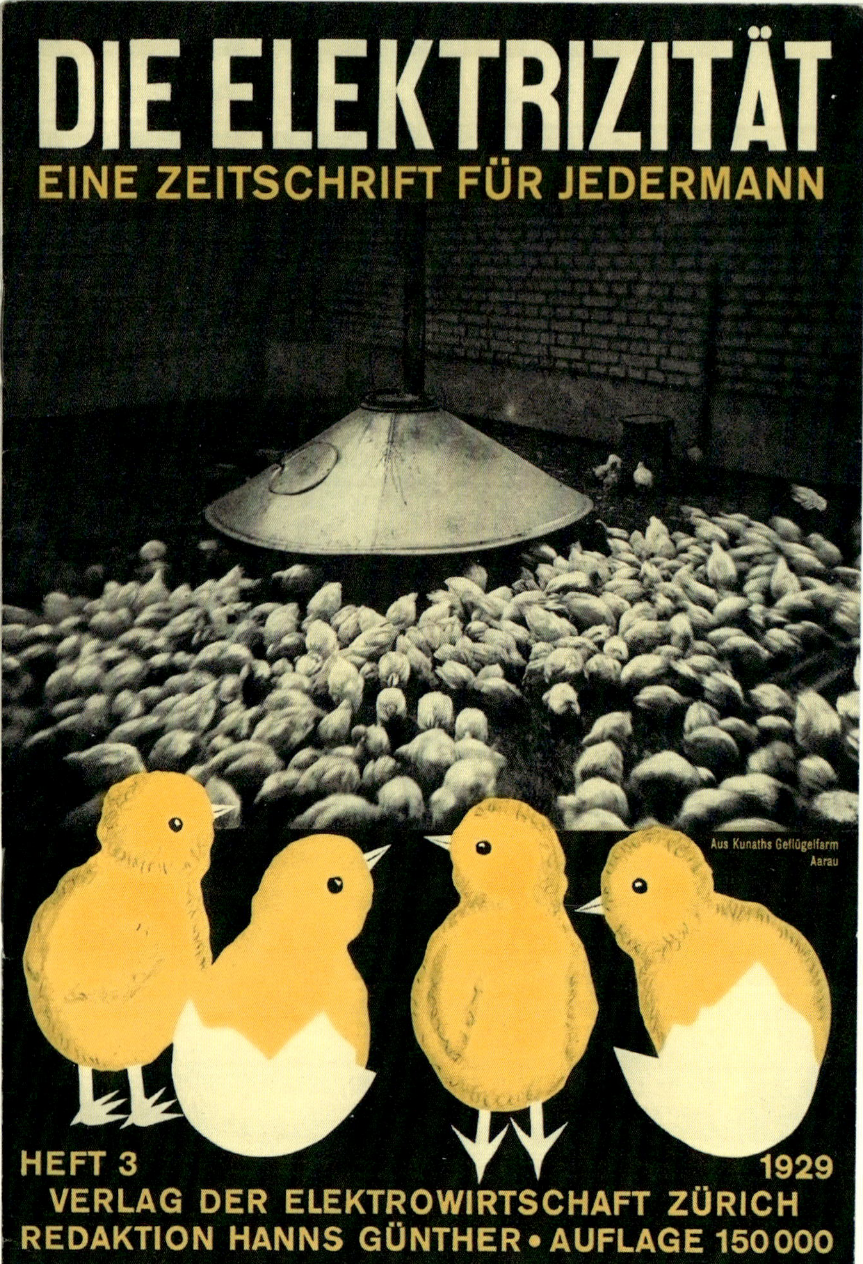
DIE ELEKTRIZITÄT
EINE ZEITSCHRIFT FÜR JEDERMANN
Aus Kunaths Geflügelfarm
Aarau
HEFT 3
1929
VERLAG DER ELEKTROWIRTSCHAFT ZÜRICH
REDAKTION HANNS GÜNTHER • AUFLAGE 150 000

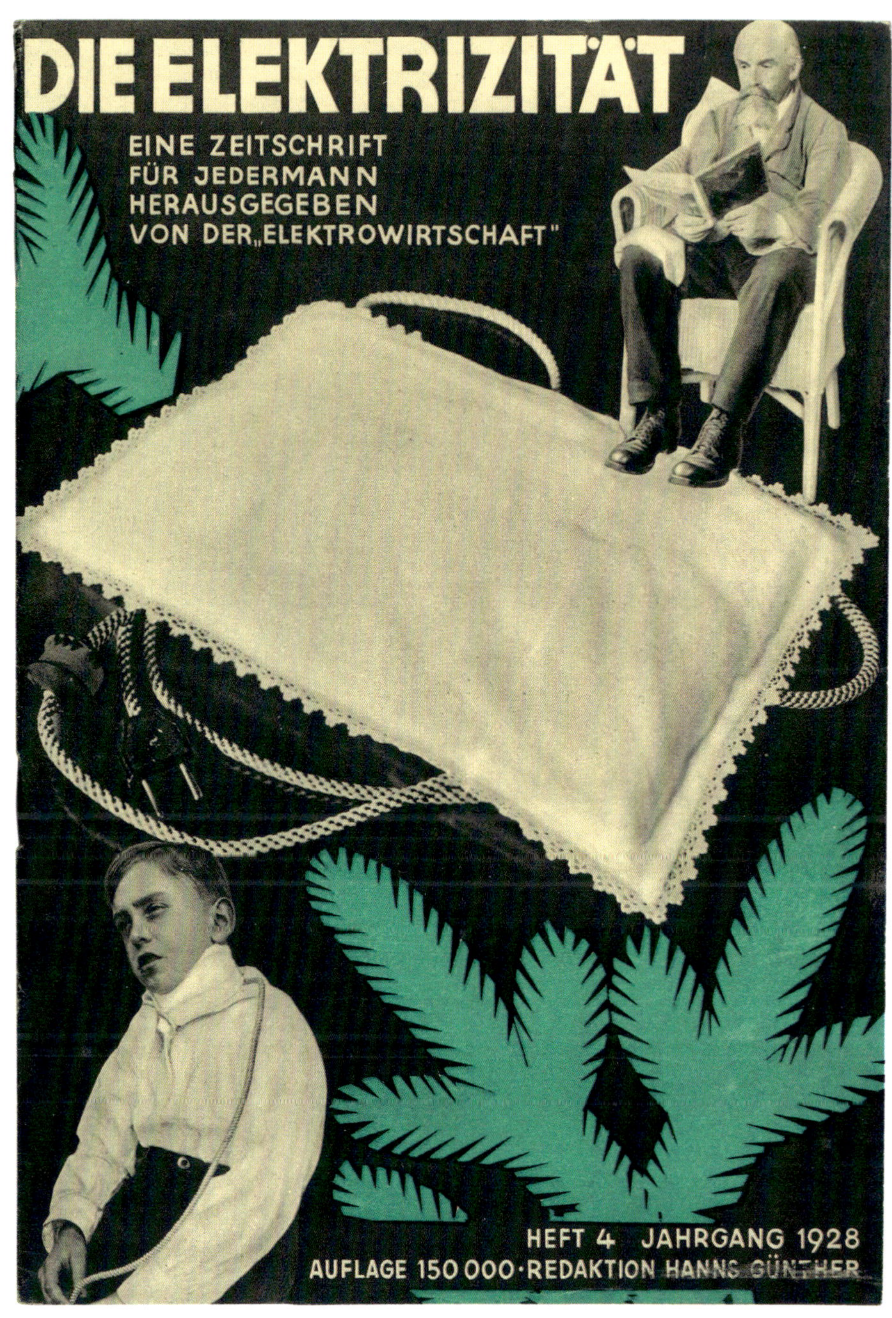

16 Walter Cyliax, cover designs for *Die Elektrizität*, 1928–30, offset lithography. Bibliothek für Gestaltung Basel.

17 ► Max Burchartz and Johannes Canis (werbe-bau), prospectus cover, Bochumer Verein für Bergbau und Gussstahlfabrikation, circa 1928–29, offset lithography. Bibliothek für Gestaltung Basel. Copyright 2024 Artists Rights Society (ARS), New York / VG Bild-Kunst, Bonn.

18 ▼ Max Burchartz and Johannes Canis (werbe-bau), suite of prospectus covers, Bochumer Verein für Bergbau und Gussstahlfabrikation, circa 1928–29, offset lithography. Bibliothek für Gestaltung Basel. Copyright 2024 Artists Rights Society (ARS), New York / VG Bild-Kunst, Bonn.

19 ▼ ► Max Burchartz and Johannes Canis (werbe-bau), suite of prospectus covers, Bochumer Verein für Bergbau und Gussstahlfabrikation, circa 1928–29, offset lithography. Bibliothek für Gestaltung Basel. Copyright 2024 Artists Rights Society (ARS), New York / VG Bild-Kunst, Bonn.

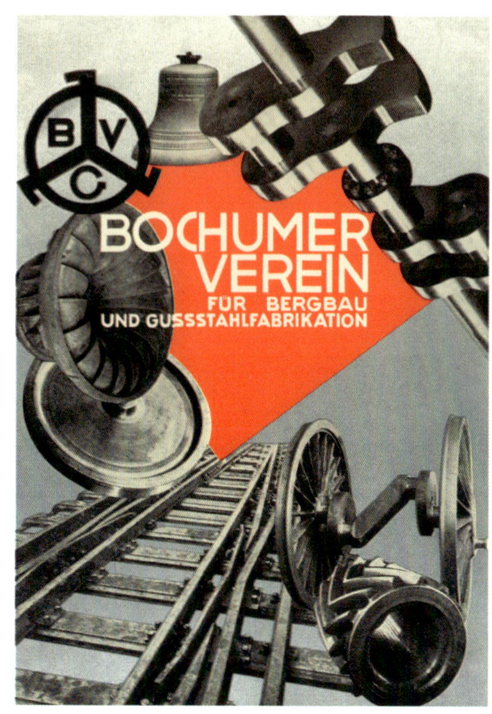

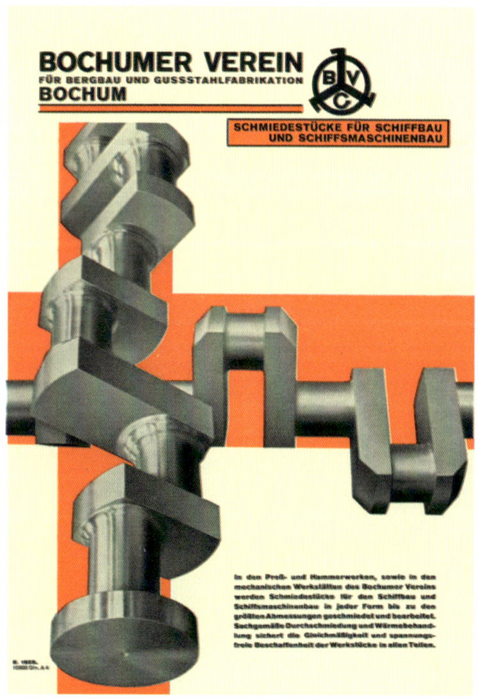

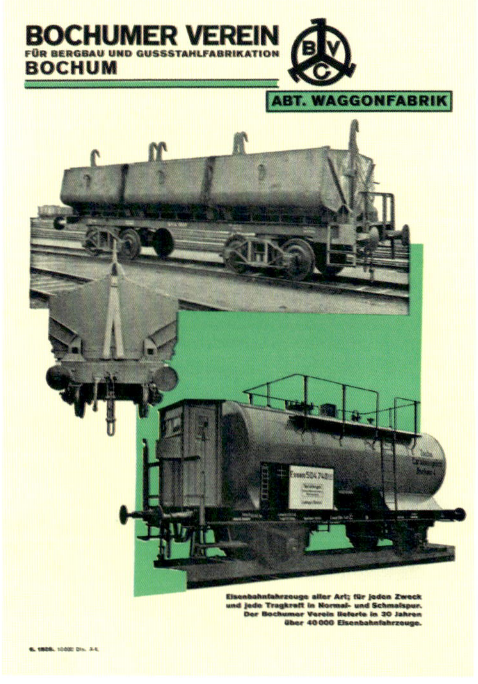

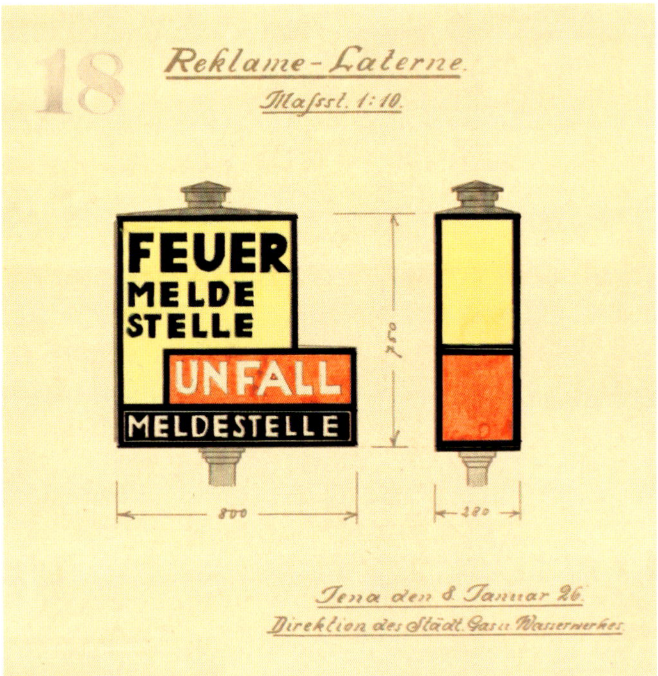

20 ◂ Walter Dexel, *Reklame Laterne*, 1926, ink, graphite, and watercolor on paper. Collection Merrill C. Berman. ▾ Walter Dexel, *farbige Leuchtsäule II*, 1926 (fabricated in 1973), aluminum and plexiglass. Photographs by author.

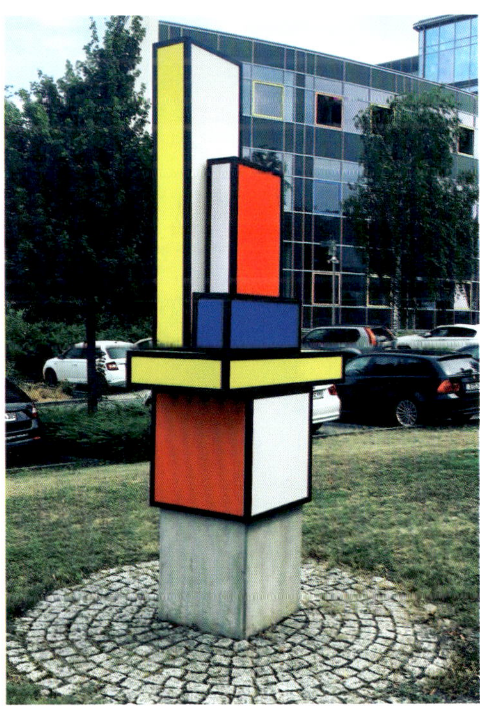

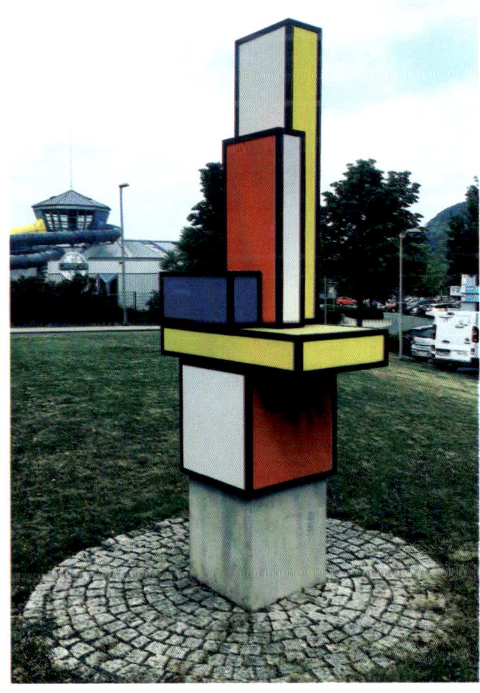

Gefesselter Blick

25 kurze Monografien und Beiträge über neue Werbegestaltung

Otto Baumberger
Willi Baumeister
Bill
Max Burchartz
Johannes Canis
Cyliax
Walter Dexel
Cesar Domela
Hermann Elias
Werner Gräff
John Heartfield
Franz Krause
Geschwister Leistikow
El Lissitzky
Robert Michel
Moholy-Nagy
Brüder Rasch
Hans Richter
Paul Schuitema
Kurt Schwitters
Mart Stam
Karel Teige
G. Trump
Jan Tschichold
Vordemberge-Gildewart
Piet Zwart

Mit Unterstützung des „Ringes der Werbegestalter des Schweizer Werkbundes" u. a.

herausgegeben und mit einer Einleitung versehen von

Heinz und Bodo Rasch

140 Abbildungen

Wissenschaftlicher Verlag Dr. Zaugg & Co., Stuttgart

Gefesselter Blick

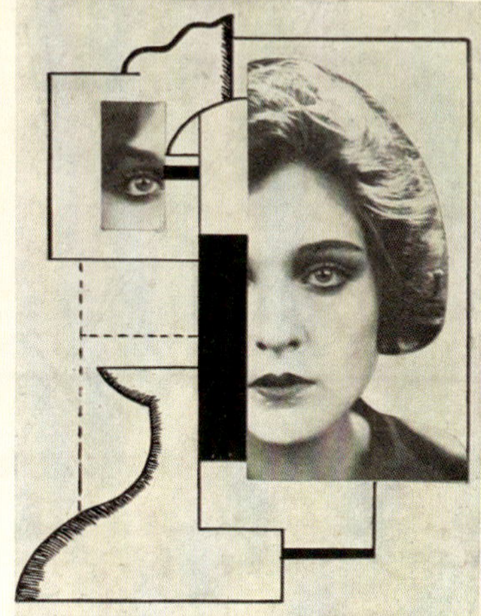

25 kurze Monografien und Beiträge über neue Werbegestaltung

Mit Unterstützung des „Ringes der Werbegestalter des Schweizer Werkbundes" u. a.

herausgegeben und mit einer Einleitung versehen von

Heinz und Bodo Rasch

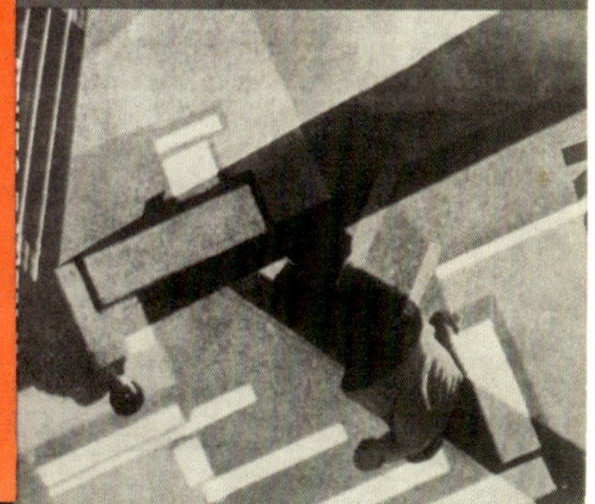

21 Heinz Rasch and Bodo Rasch, eds., *Gefesselter Blick* (Stuttgart: Wissenschaftlicher Verlag Dr. Zaugg and Co., 1930), cover. Letterform Archive, San Francisco. Copyright 2024 Artists Rights Society (ARS), New York / VG Bild-Kunst, Bonn. Copyright 2024 Artists Rights Society (ARS), New York.

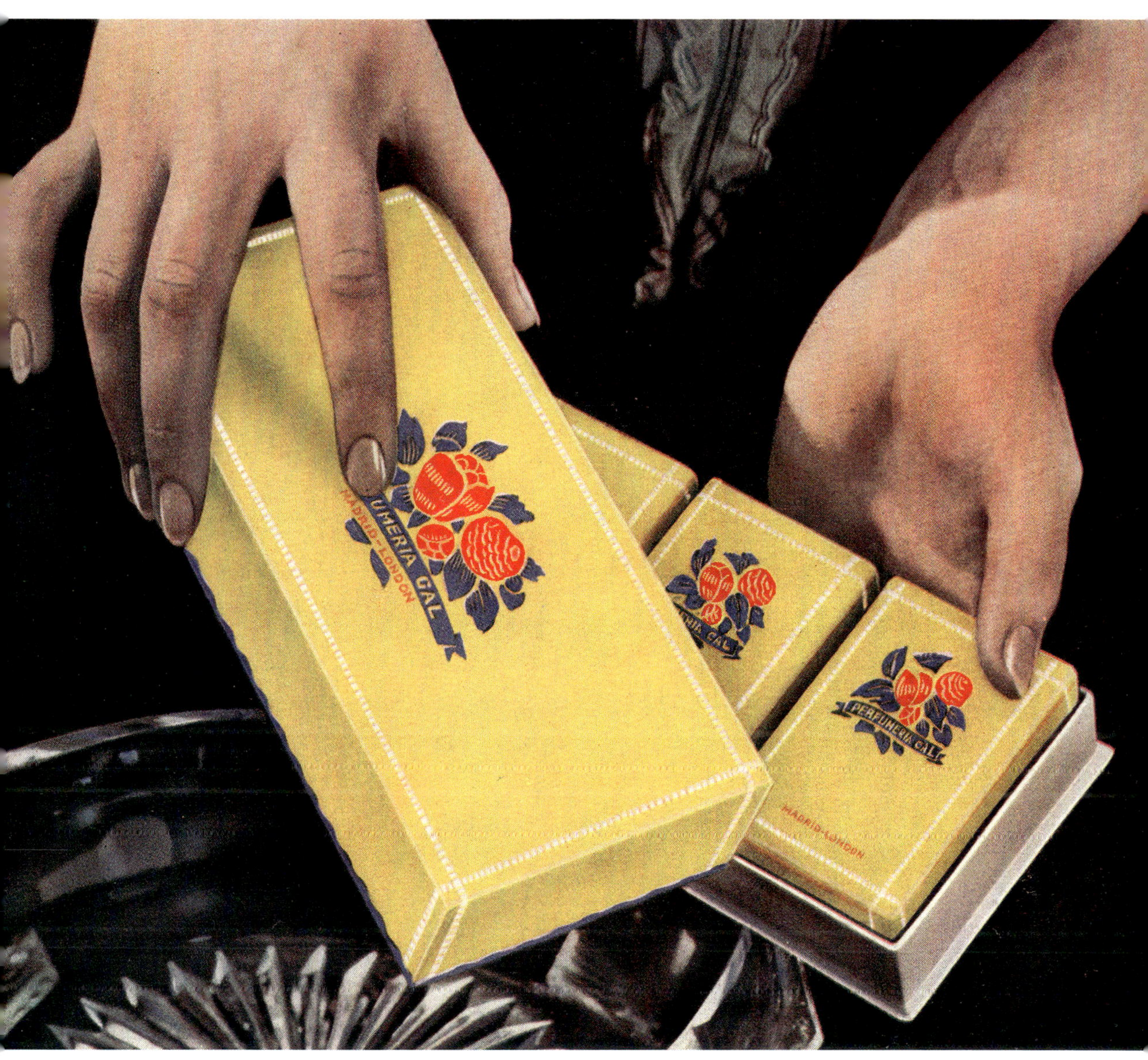

22 Unattributed advertisement for Gal Soap, reproduced in *Commercial Art*, August 1929. General Research Division, The New York Public Library.

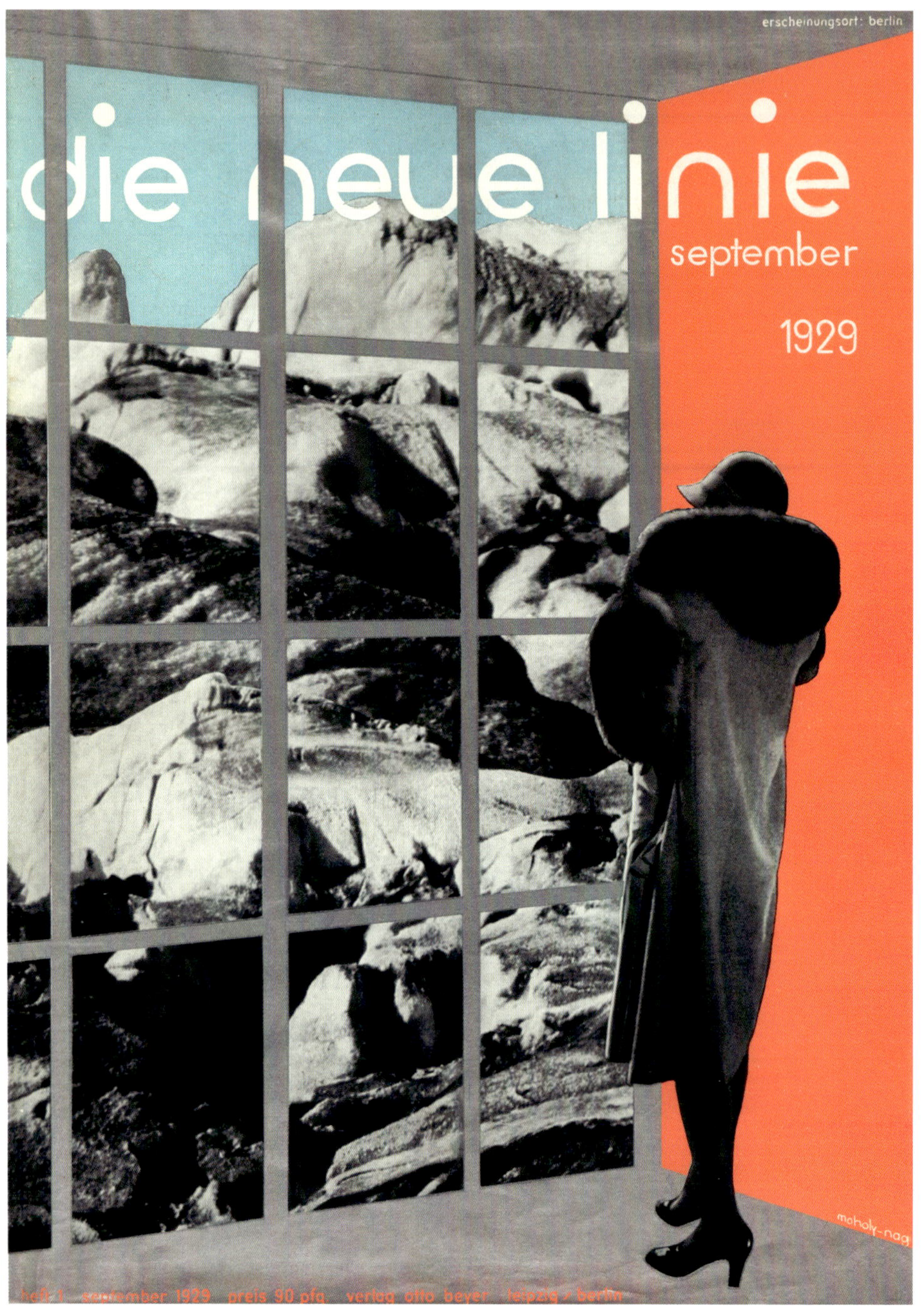

23 László Moholy-Nagy, cover of *die neue linie,* September 1929. Getty Research Institute, Los Angeles (87-S446). Copyright 2024 Estate of László Moholy- Nagy / Artists Rights Society (ARS), New York.

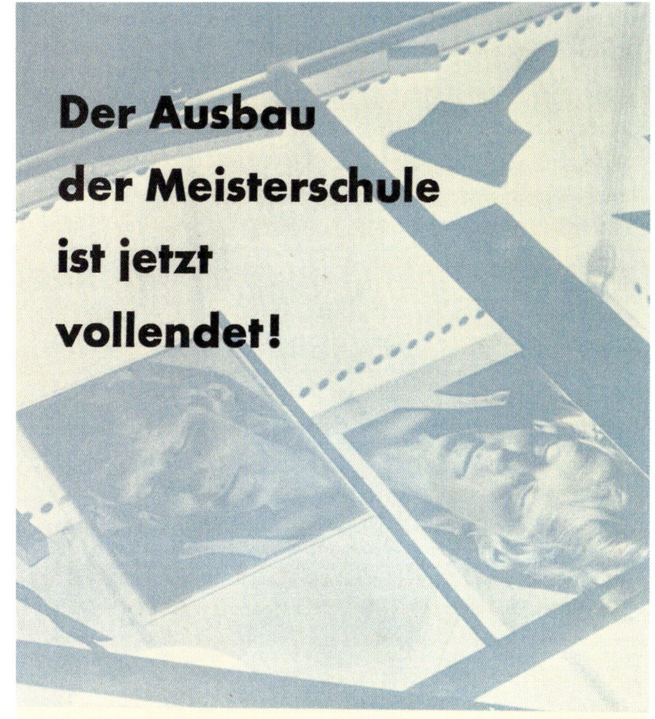

24 Jan Tschichold, pamphlet for the Meisterschule für Deutschlands Buchdrucker, "Der Ausbau der Meisterschule ist jetzt vollendet!," circa 1932, offset lithography, including reproduction of Aenne Biermann photograph. Box 23, Nachlass Jan Tschichold, Deutsches Buch- und Schriftmuseum der Deutschen Nationalbibliothek, Leipzig. Courtesy of Creative Commons.

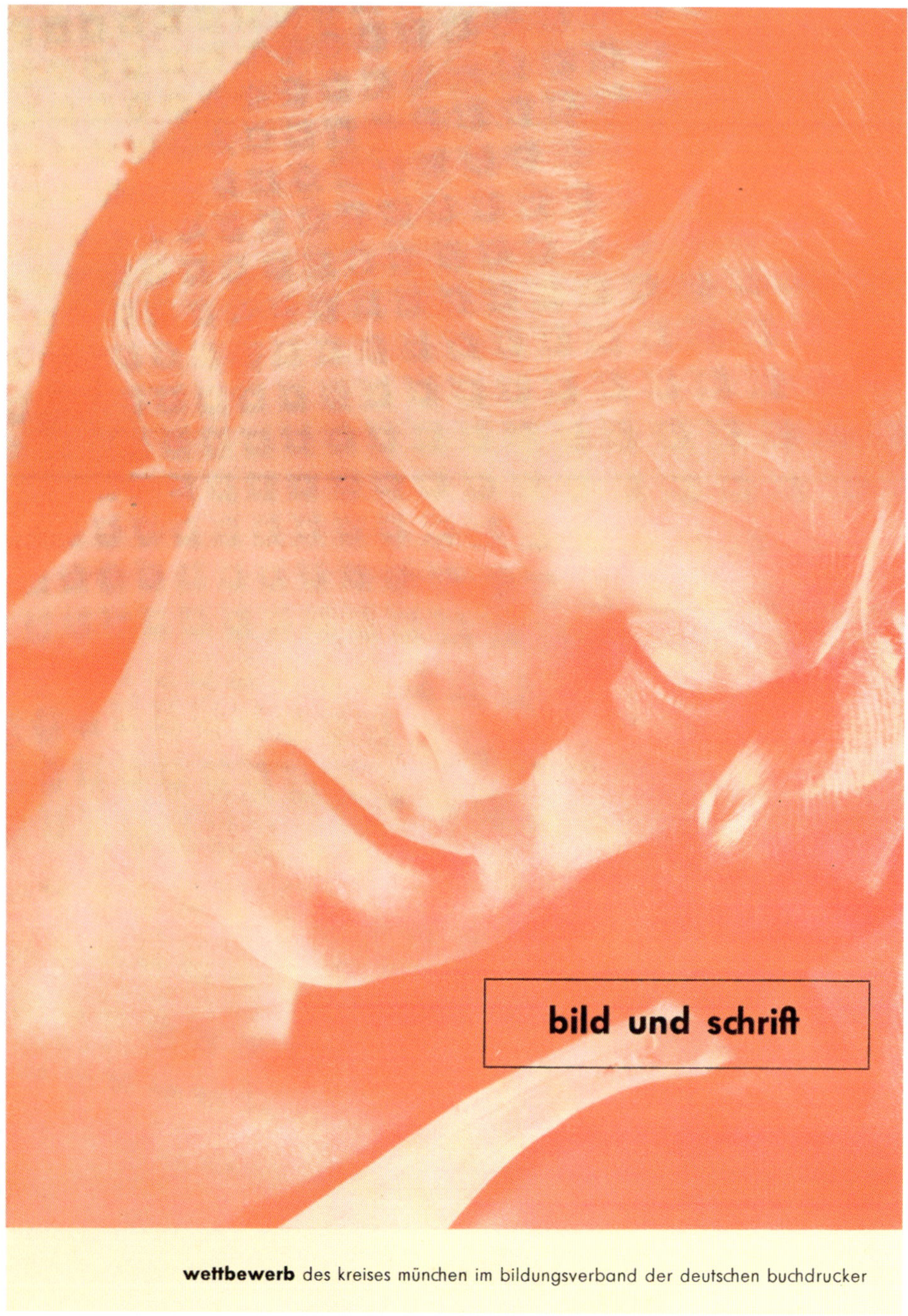

25 Jan Tschichold, *bild und schrift,* circa 1927–31, offset lithograph, including Aenne Biermann photograph. Box 23, Nachlass Jan Tschichold, Deutsches Buch- und Schriftmuseum der Deutschen Nationalbibliothek, Leipzig. Courtesy of Creative Commons.

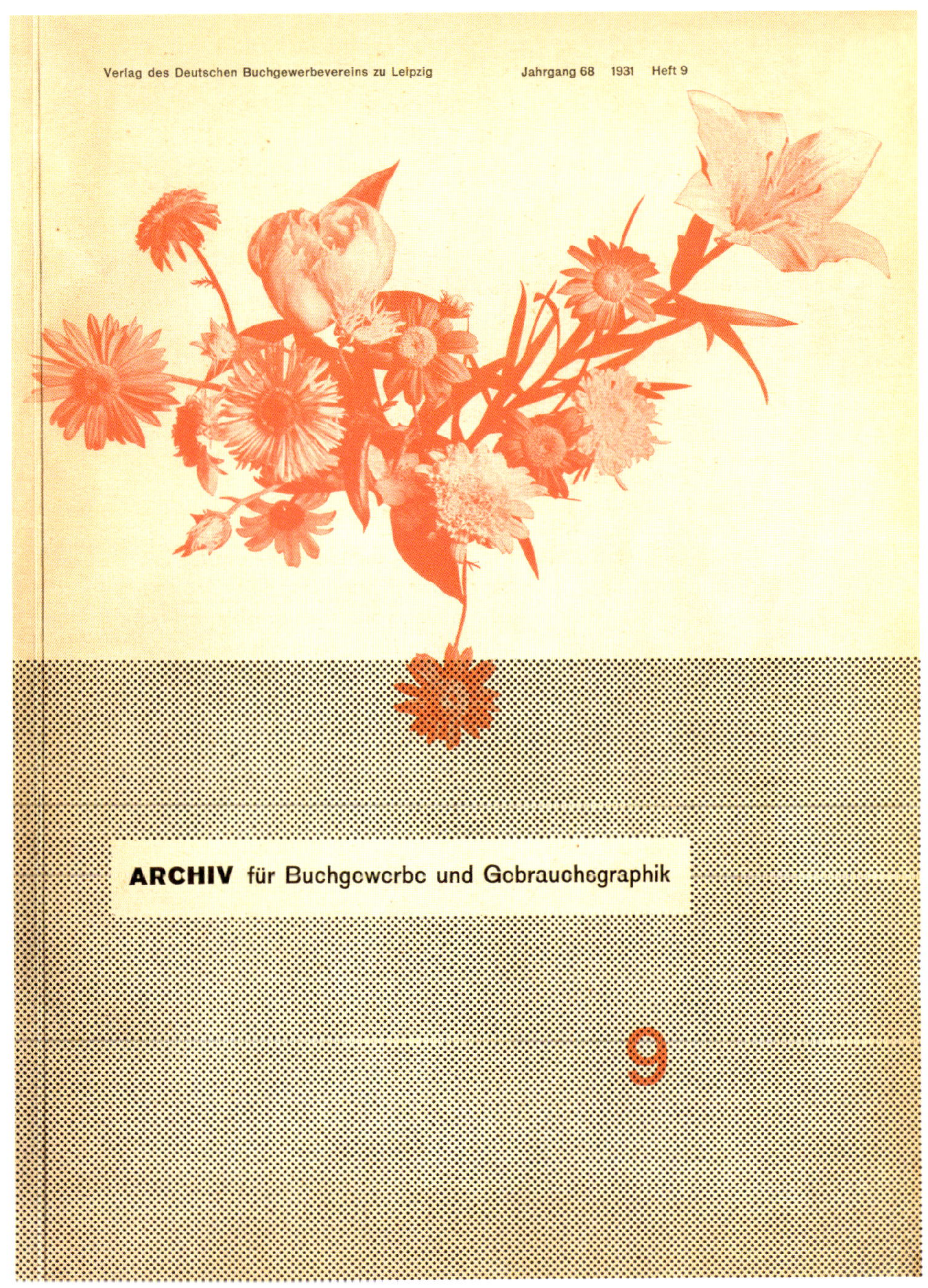

26 Georg Trump, cover of *Archiv für Buchgewerbe und Gebrauchsgraphik* 68, no. 9 (1931). Letterform Archive, San Francisco.

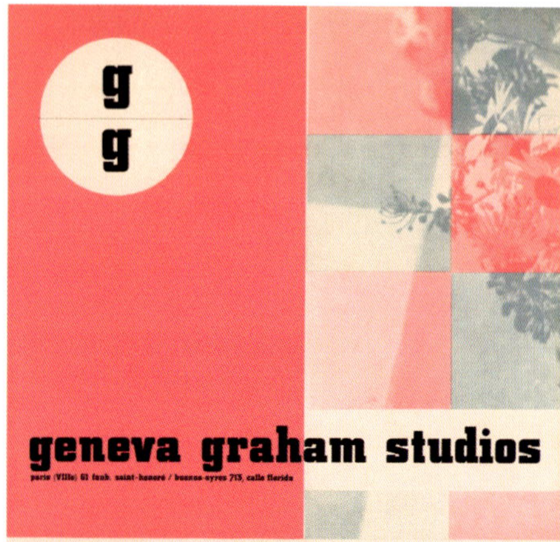

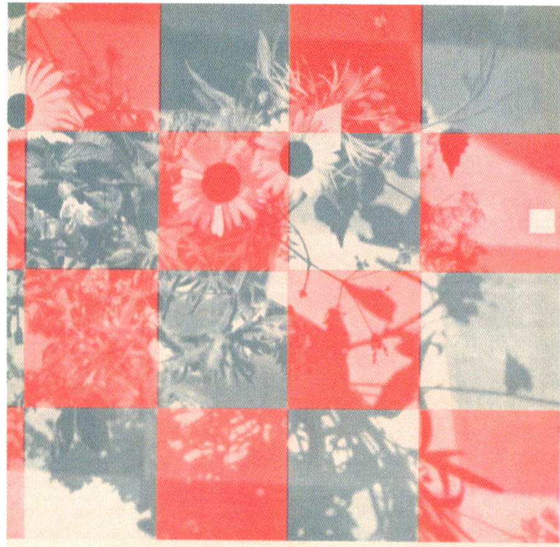

27 Georg Trump, design for Geneva Graham Studios, city prospectus, Berthold AG, circa 1931, offset lithograph. Digital Image copyright The Museum of Modern Art / Licensed by SCALA / Art Resource, NY.

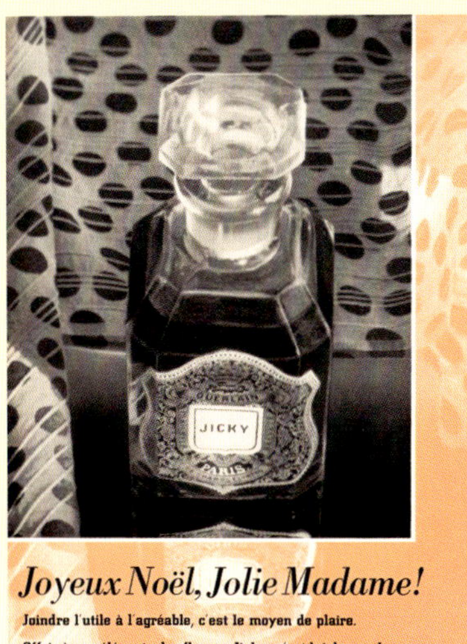

28 Georg Trump, design for Parfumeur Guerlain, circa 1931, offset lithograph. Digital image copyright the Museum of Modern Art / New York, NY / USA. / Licensed by SCALA / Art Resource, NY.

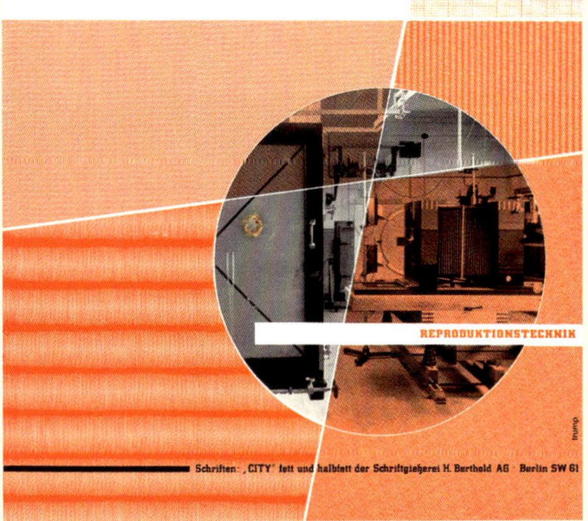

29 Georg Trump, cover, *Deutscher Drucker: Deutscher Buch- und Steindrucker* 27, no. 1 (October 1930). Box 140, Nachlass Jan Tschichold, Deutsches Buch- und Schriftmuseum der Deutschen Nationalbibliothek, Leipzig.

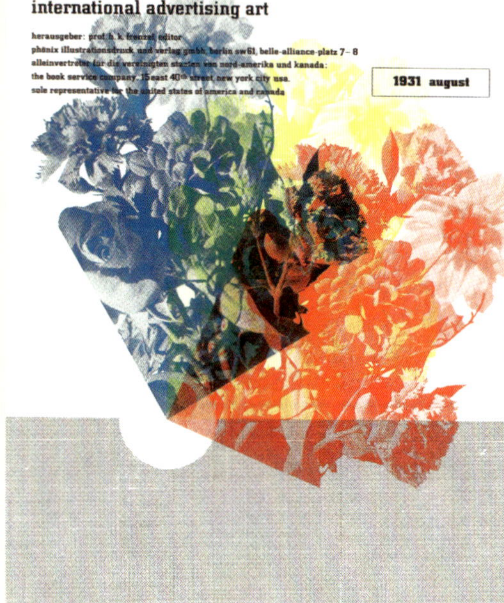

30 ◂ Unknown student designer, unpublished cover design for *Gebrauchsgraphik*, circa 1930–31, offset lithograph. Box 24, Nachlass Jan Tschichold, Deutsches Buch- und Schriftmuseum der Deutschen Nationalbibliothek, Leipzig. ▾ Detail.

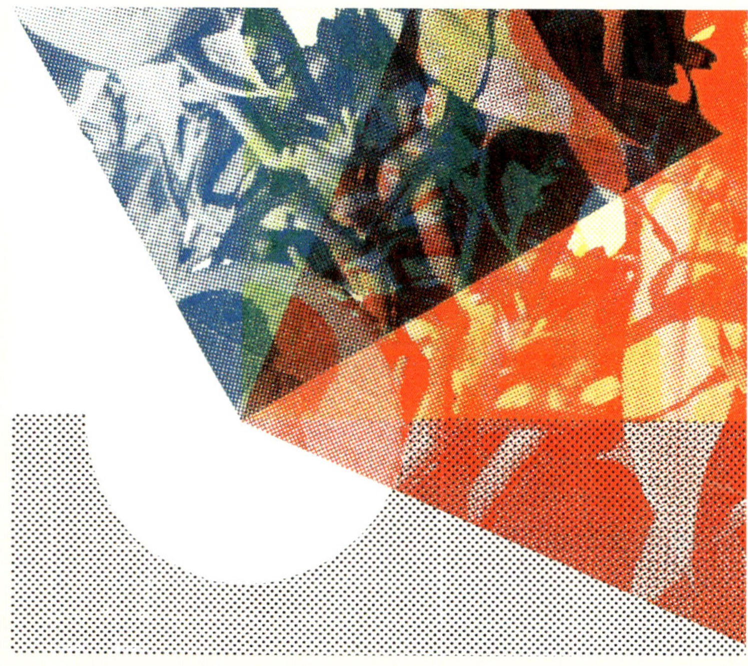

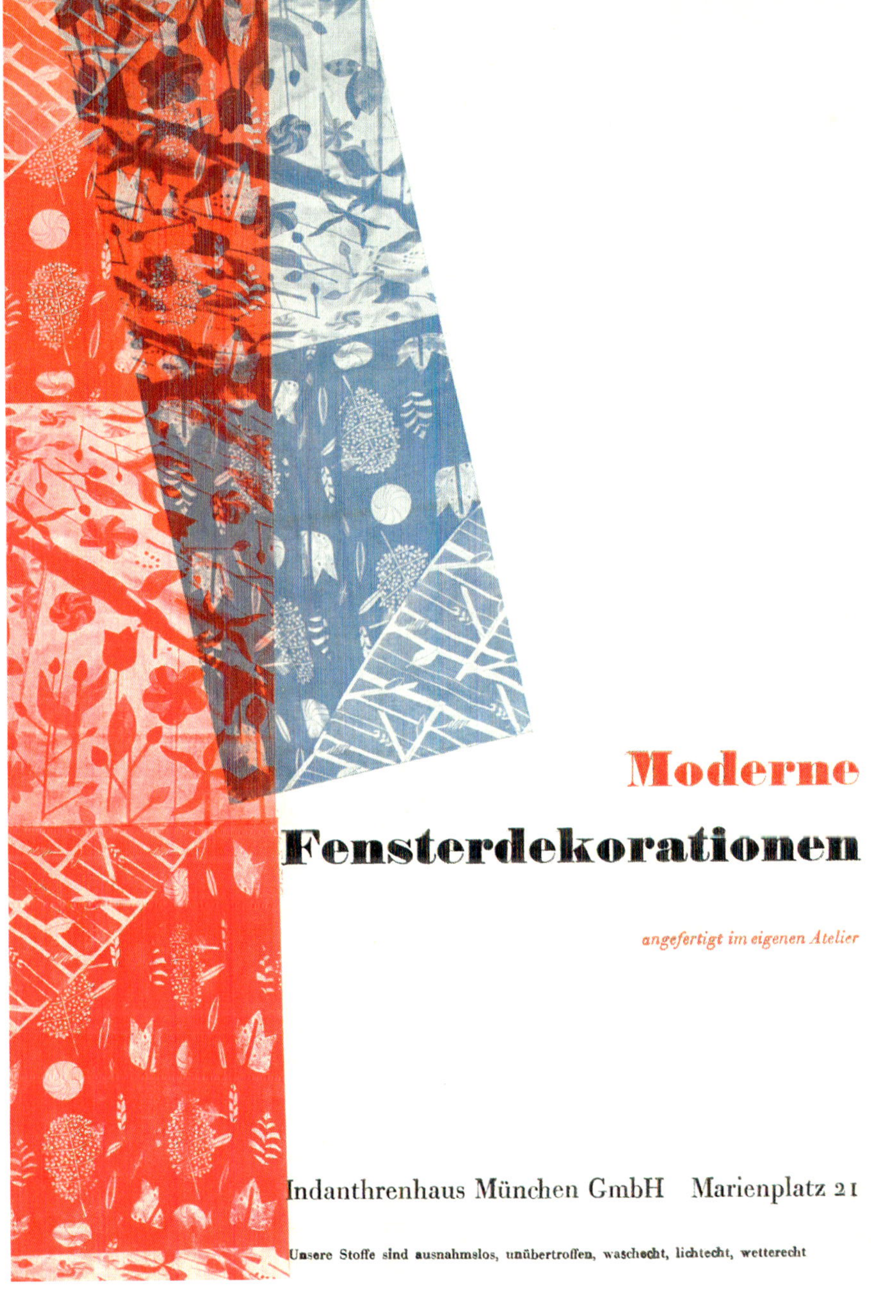

31 Unknown student designer, cover, *Moderne Fensterdekorationen*, brochure for Indanthrenhaus München, circa 1930, offset lithography. Box 23, Nachlass Jan Tschichold, Deutsches Buch- und Schriftmuseum der Deutschen Nationalbibliothek, Leipzig.

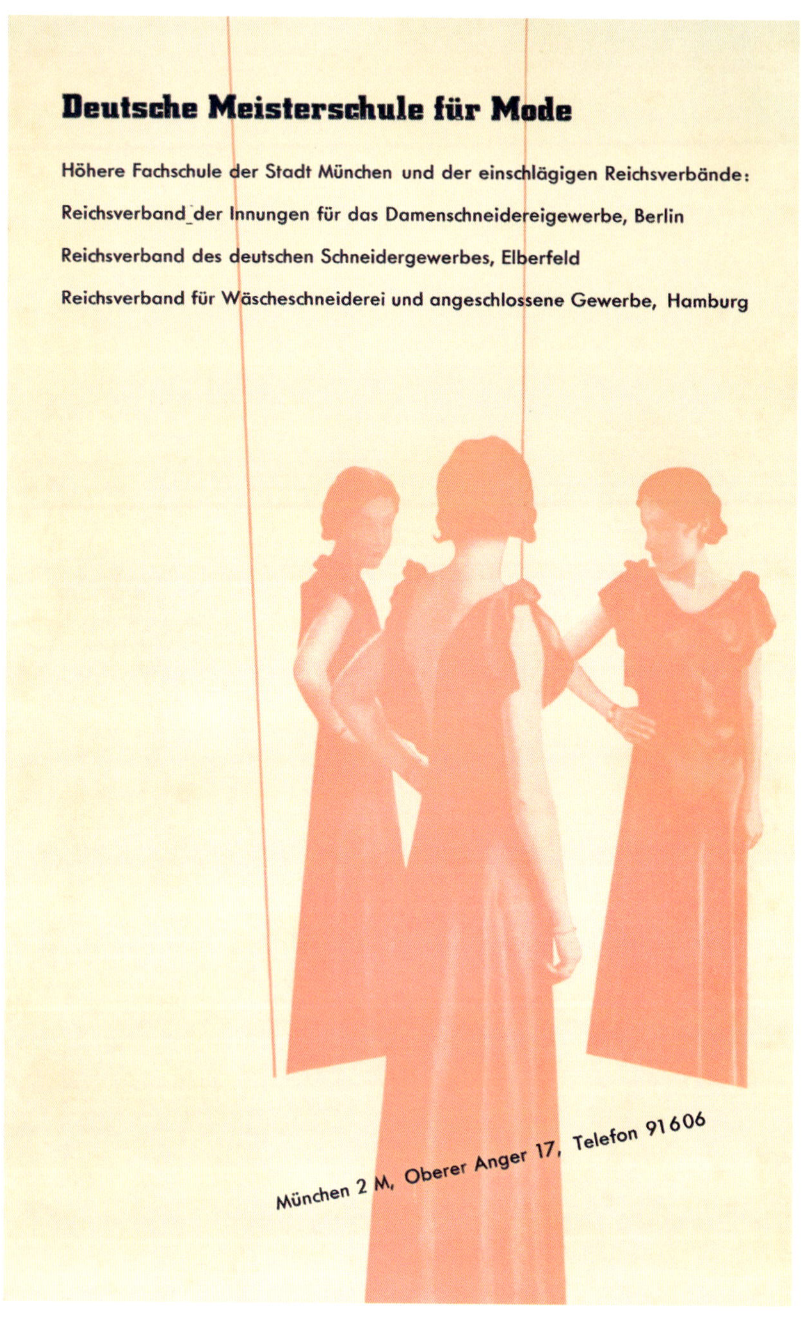

3 2 Unknown student designer, brochure for the Meisterschule für Mode, circa 1930, offset lithography, cover. Box 23, Nachlass Jan Tschichold, Deutsches Buch- und Schriftmuseum der Deutschen Nationalbibliothek, Leipzig.

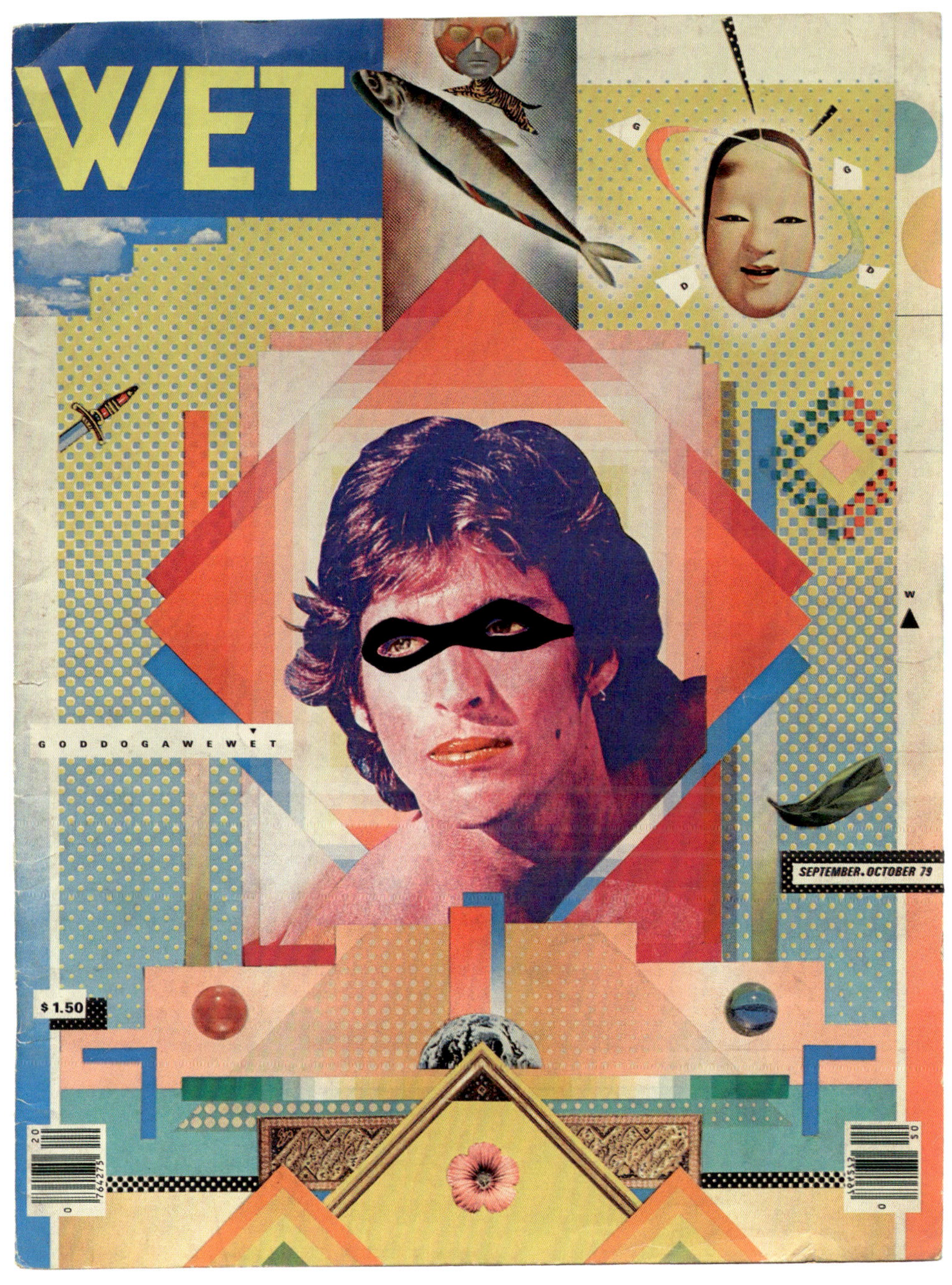

3 3 April Greiman, cover design for *WET*, September/October 1979. Letterform Archive, San Francisco. Copyright April Greiman.

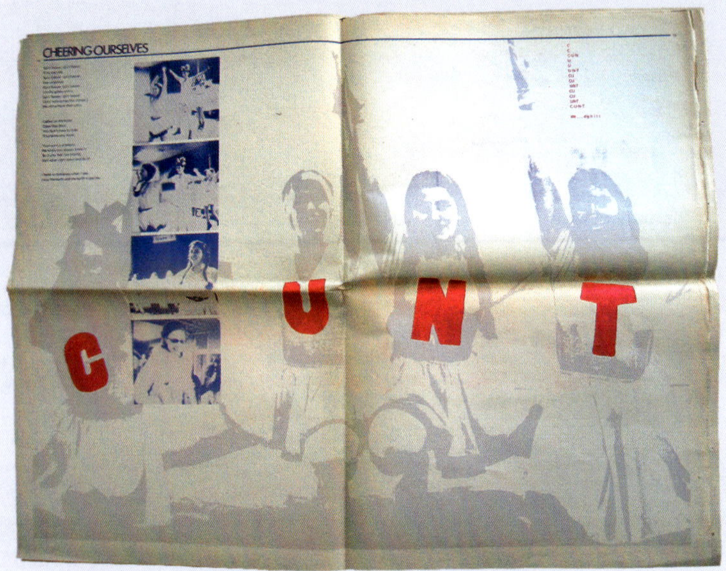

34 Sheila de Bretteville, centerfold of *Everywoman*, 1970. Sheila Levrant de Bretteville. Copyright Sheila Levrant de Bretteville.

framework for their reception. This approach responded to a cacophony of ideas from the fields of graphic design and advertising about the relationship between form and cognition, and how that relationship could be optimized. Many graphic designers came to understand form not solely as the purview of the designer, but as something cocreated by beholders through perception. In 1926, Hermann Frenzel, editor of the prominent German graphic design journal *Gebrauchsgraphik*, remarked on the importance of color to the design of a business prospectus: "The universal joy in color lures the beholder to examine the object more exhaustively."[95] Frenzel set up the primacy of the relationship between beholder and form, insinuating that the graphic designer's primary task was to activate that relationship. He noted that the business prospectus—a type of printed commercial ephemera that was widely recognized by commercial designers as key to the success of heavy industry—had to do the work of advertising while also conveying detailed, technical information to a specialist clientele of factory owners. He remarked that the prospectus must "be full of charm and interesting," while also balancing "the right harmonious accord of art and practical purpose."[96] According to Frenzel, "universal joy," induced in the beholder through color, was as important to the function of the industrial business prospectus as the accurate illustration of machine parts.

Close consideration of color as an abstract, graphic element of New Typography betrays the often-murky distinction between decorative and functional graphic forms. Despite its functionalist rhetoric, New Typography was in practice not a wholesale rejection of typographic ornament. Its practitioners were deeply invested in instilling abstract, decorative elements with optical, cognitive, and affective purpose—an ambition that corresponded to the international maturation of graphic design between the Wars. In 1929, German graphic designer Egon Juda penned an article, "Typography in German Advertising," in the British journal *Commercial Art*. In an unusual move for an adherent of New Typography, Juda pointed out the use of abstract graphic elements as "ornamental" signifiers of "revolutionary tendencies," referring to New Typography's association with international constructivism. He claimed that the use of these elements in New Typography "came originally from an emphasizing of the technical side of typography, of the work itself. Thus we find that what ornamentation there is, is derived from the typographer's matter—from rules, quadrats, points, etc."[97] In other words, the New Typographers used abstract graphic elements, such as vertical rules or abstract halftone patterns, as emblems of the labor involved in typesetting and printing. By illuminating the contradictions of a functionalist design movement that used decoration to express its identity, Juda explicitly described abstract graphic elements used in New Typography as "ornamental" and "decorative": "This manifestation of German typography, realistic as it claims to be, is in the last resort ornamental, and is distinguished from conventional styles only in so far as it derives its decorative forms from the contents of the letter-case and disclaims all other ornament."[98] At the article's conclusion, Juda abandoned the critical tone that had infused his earlier comments; he claimed that "symmetry, balance, and order will frequently have to give way to the principle of 'catching-the-eye,'" and insisted that the diagonal arrangement of type yielded the "highest possible degree of legibility."[99]

Juda's assessment of particular abstract elements can also extend to a number of New Typography's core tropes—including asymmetrical layout, diagonal orientation, use of color, and, not least, photographic illustration—best understood both as "functional" devices intended to catch the beholder's eye and as signifiers of ideological affinity. As Robin Kinross has noted, Tschichold's "arguments may employ the terms of use, need, and function, but they are deeply and explicitly infused with the idea that form must be created and that it must be the form of a new age."[100] More than simply a formula for optimal legibility, the "functionalism" of New Typography—like its architectural counterparts—manifested as a visual idiom, which fetishized technology and industrial production,[101] and combined abstract and representational forms through montage. Moreover, this visual idiom married the tropes of international constructivism with trends in the field of advertising—a fact that provoked the criticism of an anonymous reviewer for the journal *bauhaus*, accusing Tschichold of appropriating constructivism as merely a formalist approach to commercial design.[102]

The suite of werbe-bau prospectus designs for the Bochumer Verein, from which Tschichold sourced this oft-cited example, shows how Burchartz and Canis used color to mediate between the flat plane of the page and the three-dimensional space represented in photographic fragments (Plates 18 and 19). This suite consists of five unbound leaflets, each folded and collated in a cardstock folder. They were printed in two ink colors: black as well as blue, orange, green, yellow, or magenta. The outer folder is coated in shiny silver ink, a dazzling reminder of the gleaming steel of machine parts manufactured by the Bochumer Verein. Blocks of color create a sense of spatial depth, appearing as solid planes suspended behind, and parallel to, the surface of the page. Machine parts appear to levitate above the page, protruding toward the reader from these furthermost color planes.

The visual effects of these graphic experiments were related to another realm of activity that was integral to the aesthetic of New Typography: the design of illuminated advertisements and retail signage for installation on building facades and electrically lit advertising columns known as *Litfaßsäulen.*[103] Designs for illuminated advertisements and storefront signs by German artist and designer Walter Dexel exemplify the translation of New Typographic principles into three dimensions (Plate 20).[104] Dexel saw the careful arrangement of color planes as crucial to commercial design, explaining that "economical" and "correct, well-chosen color" emphasizes information and "really does the job of catching the eye."[105] The thoughtful application of color, he claimed, was necessary to instantly convey information, thereby capturing the attention of typical urbanites who tried to ignore the distraction of advertising as they rushed through the cityscape.

Despite Dexel's rather pragmatic description of the "economical" use of color in his designs, they nevertheless made use of dazzling optical effects. His signage consisted of interlocking color planes that appeared differently from every angle, as evidenced in a sketch from 1926 and an extant replica of one of his designs from the same year installed in the city of Jena. Rather than treat signage as inert structures or surfaces seen properly from a single viewpoint, Dexel created dynamic spatial constructions out of inert color planes that appeared to shift and change with the bodily movement of passersby. The signs consisted of geometric forms built up in the mind, seen from many angles in varying sequences, creating a dynamic interplay of color and form that played like a mental filmstrip. The illumination of these signs heightened this effect, making blocks of color appear to float in space, especially when lit against a night sky.[106] As in the werbe-bau prospectus designs, there was a dynamic tension in Dexel's illuminated signage between two- and three-dimensional forms, which was activated through perception. While Burchartz and Canis achieved this tension by juxtaposing photographic fragments against color planes, Dexel did so by enhancing color with the basic material of photography—controlled light—in his illuminated signage.

In the werbe-bau prospectus designs, color tempers the contrast between the flatness of typography and the dimensionality of photography. However, this mediation between two- and three-dimensional representation is unresolved, its effect ambiguous. It is unclear whether color creates a sense of order and cohesion in these designs, as Tschichold would argue, or whether it in fact has the opposite effect, introducing visual chaos into the designs. Color sometimes appears as a conduit, and sometimes a disruption, between typographic and photographic elements. It holds photographic and typographic elements together visually, but just barely, anchoring photographic fragments that look like they might otherwise fly off the page entirely. Color enhances our sense of beholding a fantasy—as destabilizing as it is intriguing. Despite the rhetoric of *Sachlichkeit* in the promotion of New Typography, its visual tropes tended to produce "effects that touch the imagination and give you a thrill of sheer surprise," as one commentator put it in 1930.[107]

In exchange for realism, such a design elicits sensation, but one person's fantasy of a technologized future might read as another's nightmare. Likewise, one person's favorite color is the next person's least, but the design is predicated on the idea that both readers are likely to pay attention. Rather than guaranteeing exactly what affective response the design might evoke, color facilitates the movement of the eye through the constructed space of the page, underlining and highlighting pieces of text. By maintaining eye movement, it prevents aimless wandering and overfocus on a single photographic detail.[108]

The exuberant colors in each design for the Bochumer Verein visualized the "joy" and "charm" that Frenzel had called for in a business prospectus. Color served to humanize these assemblages of machine parts. This was necessary because the products of industry are represented here through industrial processes, twice over—mediated by the medium of photography and then reproduced as halftones. Photomontage renders the gleaming metallic forms visible from multiple points of view simultaneously. They are magnified, detached, and abstracted—shot through with technology fetishism. Industrial production is glorified in these designs through formal play, overtly presenting industrial manufacture as the product of fantasy and desire, rather than human labor.

The photographs of machines produced at the Bochumer Verein, which Burchartz and Canis used as source material, were made by Ernst Topp.[109] His photographs show turbines, cranks, wheels, and sprockets as inert and impossibly massive on the factory floor, dwarfing workers who stand beside them. Yet, in the werbe-bau designs, machine parts appear to glide weightlessly through undefined space, untethered by the laws of gravity or physics. The arrangement of photographic halftone fragments against irregularly shaped color blocks evokes the kineticism of machine parts and suggests our own dynamic, shifting point of view as a beholder in unfixed space. Like typography and the Bochumer Verein trademark, these machines seem to lack mass or permanent attachment to any fixed plane. Montage's effect is to fully divorce the prospectus from the conditions of production at the Bochumer Verein.

In these designs, technology is presented as dynamic, exhilarating, and even whimsical—floating high above the hazards and filth of the factory floor.

The true subject of these designs is not the manufacture of machine parts by the Bochumer Verein, but rather photomontage itself. Like the abstract elements described by Egon Juda, photomontage symbolized a utopian belief propagated by the New Typographers—and undoubtedly shared by the German steel manufacturer—that technology would help build a prosperous future. The werbe-bau's use of photomontage is emblematic of what American historian Leo Marx later called the "technological sublime," describing the glorification of technology as a visual motif.[110] Color breathes a different kind of life into these graphic constructions, contrasting sharply with the relentlessly mechanical character of the montaged halftones. Despite the antidecorative dogma of New Typography, both color elements and halftone fragments demonstrate an important paradox of this doctrine: to be clear, legible, and memorable—that is, to be functional—a commercial design must combine the "joy" and "charm" of abstract visual elements with image fragments that operate as connotative, rather than denotative, signifiers of unfixed meaning.

GEFESSELTER BLICK AND READING AS OPTICAL CONSTRUCTION

As Tschichold began outlining his book on photomontage in 1930, German architects, industrial designers, and brothers Heinz and Bodo Rasch were at work organizing *The Captured Glance* (*Gefesselter Blick*). Sponsored by the Graphischer Klub Stuttgart, a local association of printers, typographers, and designers, this exhibition was on view at the Gustav-Siegle-Haus for only four days, February 8–11, 1930.[111] The exhibition was apparently a pretext to publish a book under the same title, which has endured as the definitive compendium of work by members of the loose association of Dutch and German graphic designers associated with New Typography known as the ring neuer werbegestalter (ring of new advertising designers).[112] Initiated by German artists and graphic designers Kurt Schwitters and Robert Michel in 1928, the ring communicated with members through a series of circular letters, soliciting samples of their work from one another for promotion through various public exhibitions and also suggested Schwitters's intent to publish a compendium similar to *Gefesselter Blick*.[113]

Heinz and Bodo Rasch's book contains illustrated textual contributions by twenty-six designers and artists, including Tschichold and Moholy-Nagy, as well as Willi Baumeister, Max Burchartz, Johannes Canis, Walter Dexel, and César Domela-Nieuwenhuis.[114] Each contributor received a letter from Heinz

Rasch soliciting his age, education, examples of his work, and a response to a broad query:

> The book is structured such that each artist will be represented with 2–4 pages for his examples and a right-hand title page, including his name, and dates printed smaller underneath, and his answer to the following survey:
>
> Which principles do you follow in the formation of your typography, or do you actually have principles in mind?[115]

General though this brief was, it was intended to focus responses on the subject of graphic design. Arranged in alphabetical order by designers' last names, the entries made up a directory of expertise in the field.

Gefesselter Blick proposed experimental uses of photography as essential to modern design, thereby offering an alternative definition of New Typography to the one offered by Tschichold in his first book, and more in keeping with the thesis of his unfinished book on photomontage. Most of the contributors to *Gefesselter Blick* submitted short responses on general principles of typography, as instructed. However, Rasch's letter also acknowledged "the diversity of the assembled materials" in the book, acknowledging that its contributors were not strictly limited to members of the ring, nor even to practicing designers.[116] While this book is, on the surface, a compendium about modernist graphic design, its deeper import is as a collective theory of modern perception and photography's role in mass media to engender active reading. Photography is reproduced and described throughout as a medium that necessitates new modes of perception in printed matter.

The book's title established the pursuit of visual attention as graphic design's central challenge: The word "captured" connotes not only the idea of catching one's eye or attention, but also holding or arresting—a sustained, more physically aggressive, and even violent action, and a term often associated with photography. "Glance," by contrast, connotes the fugitivity of an inadvertent look, as when one glances at an advertisement in passing. As the Rasch brothers described in their introduction, a glance must be actively arrested to ensure that an advertisement is actually seen. These connotations address the particular difficulty of commercial design, which has to combat the beholder's resistance to even seeing, let alone reading, an advertisement.

The opening sentence of Heinz and Bodo Rasch's introduction to *Gefesselter Blick* succinctly established visual perception as the book's framing concern: "The means of communicating anything through the human visual sensorium is image and text."[117] In unpacking how word and image are perceived and apprehended, they borrowed German Enlightenment philosopher Gotthold Ephraim Lessing's concept of the fundamental difference between the verbal and the visual: whereas words describe "events" or "functions" (which occur in time), images represent static "conditions" or "objects" (which exist in space).[118] Importantly, Heinz and Bodo Rasch subtly converted what had, for Lessing, been an argument about mimesis into one about mass communication. They did so to tease out a central dilemma of commercial design—that is, how different forms of representation could support the interrelation of advertising copy and illustration toward the goal of eliciting consumer desire.

The Rasch brothers framed modern graphic design as a practice that had the potential to resolve the fundamental tension between verbal and visual representation. Advertising, they claimed, surpassed the limitations of both as a superior, hybrid medium of communication. A promotional brochure for *Gefesselter Blick* declared this in tactile terms: "Commercial graphics is a completely exceptional form of communication, namely a fusion [*Verschmelzung*] of image and word."[119] The idea of image and word merging into a new, unified entity was illustrated in the brochure by a sample design by German architect, artist, and designer Franz Krause for Daimona flashlights, also reproduced in *Gefesselter Blick* (Figure 26). The two-color design depicts a drawn illustration of a diminutive Daimona flashlight within a red circle, cut by a beam of light emanating from the small bulb. The light appears to illuminate a patterned repetition of the manufacturer's trademark, framed by the beam's powerful reach. By incorporating text into this illustration—and effectively rendering word as image—Krause demonstrated the fusion that the Rasch brothers described. They termed the resulting synthesis, located specifically in the broken red circle where "text and image touch each other," as an "eye-catcher" (*Blickfang*) charged with purpose.[120]

Catching the reader's eye and attention was merely the initial step in the cognitive operation of commercial design. Whereas the Rasch brothers characterized the act of reading text as a relatively passive experience, they also suggested that the act of beholding could animate an object or image. They described the perception of images—also referred to as "illustrated objects" (*dargestellten Objekten*)—as an active experience generative of cognitive association in which "the function of an object is triggered in the [mind of the] viewer."[121] By contrast to the immediacy of images, they described text as communication that unfolds in sequence; in this sense, they proposed that film was a visual analogue to text. In drawing this comparison, they posited

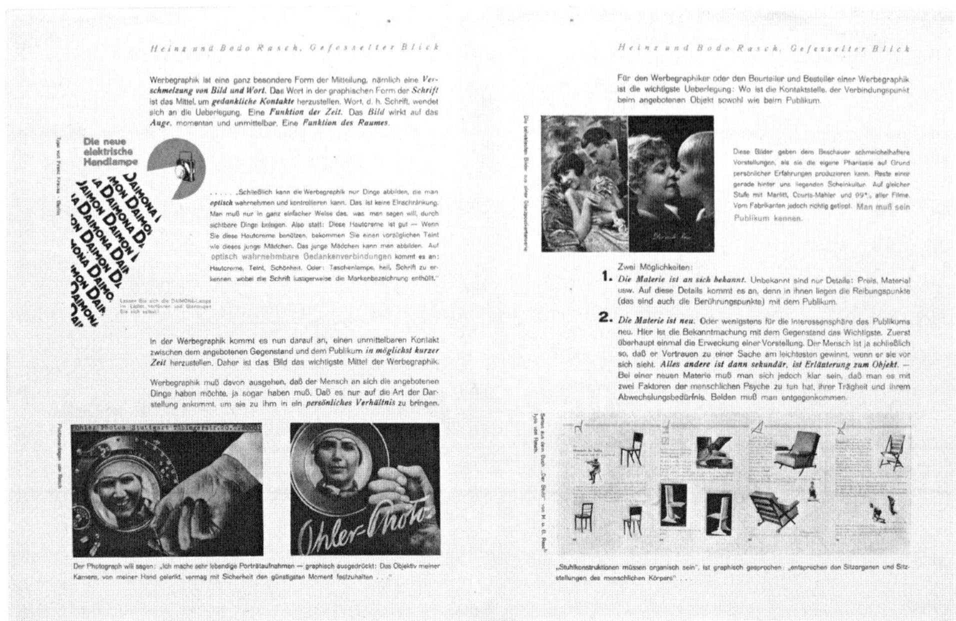

Heinz und Bodo Rasch, Gefesselter Blick

Werbegraphik ist eine ganz besondere Form der Mitteilung, nämlich eine ***Verschmelzung von Bild und Wort.*** Das Wort in der graphischen Form der ***Schrift*** ist das Mittel, um ***gedankliche Kontakte*** herzustellen. Wort, d. h. Schrift, wendet sich an die Ueberlegung. Eine ***Funktion der Zeit.*** Das ***Bild*** wirkt auf das ***Auge***, momentan und unmittelbar. Eine ***Funktion des Raumes.***

Die neue elektrische Handlampe

DAIMON

. . . . . „Schließlich kann die Werbegraphik nur Dinge abbilden, die man ***optisch*** wahrnehmen und kontrollieren kann. Das ist keine Einschränkung. Man muß nur in ganz einfacher Weise das, was man sagen will, durch sichtbare Dinge belegen. Also statt: Diese Hautcreme ist gut — Wenn Sie diese Hautcreme benützen, bekommen Sie einen vorzüglichen Teint wie dieses junge Mädchen. Das junge Mädchen kann man abbilden. Auf optisch wahrnehmbare Gedankenverbindungen kommt es an: Hautcreme, Teint, Schönheit. Oder: Taschenlampe, hell, Schrift zu erkennen, wobei die Schrift lustigerweise die Markenbezeichnung enthüllt."

In der Werbegraphik kommt es nun darauf an, einen unmittelbaren Kontakt zwischen dem angebotenen Gegenstand und dem Publikum ***in möglichst kurzer Zeit*** herzustellen. Daher ist das Bild das wichtigste Mittel der Werbegraphik.

Werbegraphik muß davon ausgehen, daß der Mensch an sich die angebotenen Dinge haben möchte, ja sogar haben muß. Daß es nur auf die Art der Darstellung ankommt, um sie zu ihm in ein ***persönliches Verhältnis*** zu bringen.

Der Photograph will sagen: „Ich mache sehr lebendige Porträtaufnahmen — graphisch ausgedrückt: Das Objektiv meiner Kamera, von meiner Hand gelenkt, vermag mit Sicherheit den günstigsten Moment festzuhalten . . ."

Heinz und Bodo Rasch, Gefesselter Blick

Für den Werbegraphiker oder den Beurteiler und Besteller einer Werbegraphik ist die wichtigste Ueberlegung: Wo ist die Kontaktstelle, der Verbindungspunkt beim angebotenen Objekt sowohl wie beim Publikum.

Diese Bilder geben dem Beschauer schmeichelhaftere Vorstellungen, als sie die eigene Phantasie auf Grund persönlicher Erfahrungen produzieren kann. Reste einer gerade hinter uns liegenden Scheinkultur. Auf gleicher Stufe mit Marlitt, Courts-Mahler und 99 % aller Filme. Vom Fabrikanten jedoch richtig getippt. Man muß sein Publikum kennen.

Zwei Möglichkeiten:

1. ***Die Materie ist an sich bekannt.*** Unbekannt sind nur Details: Preis, Material usw. Auf diese Details kommt es an, denn in ihnen liegen die Reibungspunkte (das sind auch die Berührungspunkte) mit dem Publikum.

2. ***Die Materie ist neu.*** Oder wenigstens für die Interessensphäre des Publikums neu. Hier ist die Bekanntmachung mit dem Gegenstand das Wichtigste. Zuerst überhaupt einmal die Erweckung einer Vorstellung. Der Mensch ist ja schließlich so, daß er Vertrauen zu einer Sache am leichtesten gewinnt, wenn er sie vor sich sieht. ***Alles andere ist dann sekundär, ist Erläuterung zum Objekt.*** — Bei einer neuen Materie muß man sich jedoch klar sein, daß man es mit zwei Faktoren der menschlichen Psyche zu tun hat, ihrer Trägheit und ihrem Abwechslungsbedürfnis. Beiden muß man entgegenkommen.

„Stuhlkonstruktionen müssen organisch sein", ist graphisch gesprochen: „entsprechen den Sitzorganen und Sitzstellungen des menschlichen Körpers" . . .

FIGURE 26 Heinz Rasch and Bodo Rasch, interior page of promotional brochure for *Gefesselter Blick*, circa 1929, unpaginated. The Getty Research Institute, Los Angeles (850513).

the raster as the basic structure of both text and film: "The densest grid, which is the densest resolution of action in an image, is film. Film is function interpreted through images. Text is closely related: text is truly just a film made from symbolic images."[122] They established this structural congruency between text and film to introduce the idea of effective graphic design as a conduit between the human senses. At the center of their description of interrelated media is the raster—a German word that translates to "grid" as well as "halftone"—implicating photography as fundamental to graphic communication. The matrix of the halftone, like the typographic grid, or the grid of a filmstrip or photographic negative, structures the arrangement of words and images on planar surfaces. This visual and spatial arrangement, they argued, evokes the construction of meaning.

They explicitly linked the manipulation of photography in graphic design to the beholder's perception. As a medium apposite to representing static objects and capturing fleeting moments in time, they wrote, photography upended

Lessing's word–image dichotomy. Echoing Moholy-Nagy's idea of modern photographic literacy, the Rasch brothers characterized photography as a hybridized visual language that had superseded verbal communication.[123] Photography was thus well suited to advertising design. Yet, they also noted the photographic tendency to capture "things that do not belong," which might obscure truth by impeding the beholder's "close personal relationship with an object."[124] Photomontage could effectively remove "trivialities" (*Nebensächliche*) so that "realities" (*Eigentlichen*) could be made clearly visible.[125]

Experimental photography, the Rasch brothers speculated, was crucial to drawing the beholder into a printed design. They championed photomontage as a medium that generated meaning and sharpened the interrelation of text and image by causing the beholder's eye to move purposefully across the page. This idea was also expressed by invoking photography as a metaphor for human perception, describing the human eye as a framing device akin to a camera lens that "takes aim" at an object, rendering it an "image fragment" through perception.[126] The Rasch brothers upended the common trope in Weimar writing on photography of the camera as an extension of the photographer's eye, instead describing photomontage as a model for seeing: "The camera must identify itself with the eye of the beholder."[127]

Two images accompany their discussion of photography and perception. In the upper, left-hand corner is a photomontage of a jovial woman's face framed within the lens of a camera.[128] A hand reaches into the space between the lens and the viewer, holding a shutter release and poised to press the button. This disembodied representation of the camera operator, along with the visual suggestion that the lens doubles as a viewfinder, indicates that the image is being visually isolated, framed, and focused by the camera itself—a visualization of the idea that "the camera must identify itself with the eye of the beholder." The lower image is a close-up photograph of a rotary press in the process of printing a newspaper; the lower, gravure cylinder rolls off the upper, impression cylinder to create one of many imprints on a large sheet of paper. This image depicts the high-speed process of rotogravure, a technology that became widely used in the 1920s and revolutionized the quick, cheap reproduction of illustrated periodicals.[129] The pairing of these images suggests the consumption of photographic images in the popular press—facilitated by the savvy arrangement of text and image in layout—as essential to training modern beholders to read visual information.

Photomontage was a compelling metaphor for a new kind of reading, as it suggested that disparate visual elements could be actively constructed into

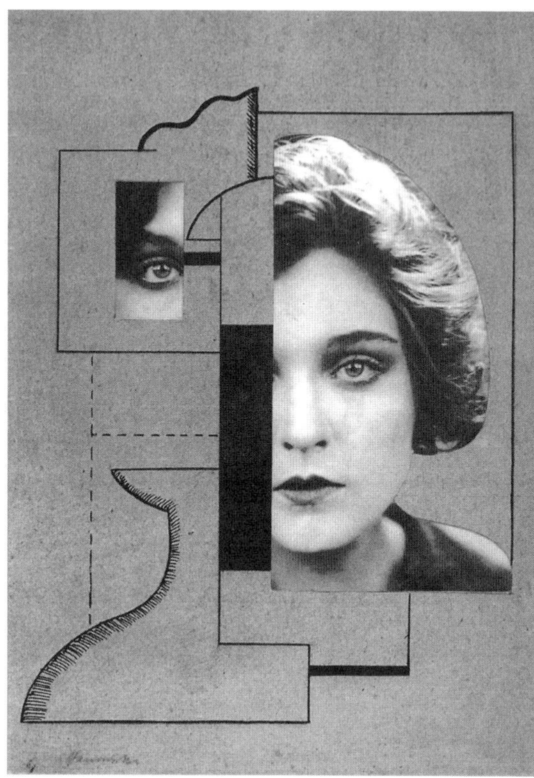

FIGURE 27 Willi Baumeister, *Kopf*, drawing and photo-collage on paper, circa 1923. Archiv Willi Baumeister, Kunstmuseum Stuttgart.

new, meaningful wholes that coalesced in the mind. Like Tschichold's outline for *Fotomontage, Gefesselter Blick* offered examples of optical construction in commercial graphic design as well as a number of other experimental composite images. One such example was identified as a *fotozeichnung* (photo-drawing) by Willi Baumeister, titled *Kopf* (ca. 1923), which embodied the idea of photomontage as a paradigm for modern perception (Figure 27). The term *fotozeichnung* also appears in Tschichold's book outline, citing Baumeister as an example.[130]

Baumeister's contribution to *Gefesselter Blick* was substantial, including five images, three of which were identified by the term *fotozeichnung*. The first appears with the following caption: "lighthearted photo-drawing. summary of existing picture elements. they become irony themselves. the painter works here like the architect, who must search for the conditions (building place, building purpose) of a form."[131] The image comprises three halftone fragments representing a man's head and several extremities, roughly grafted onto a crude, amorphous line drawing that connects the photographic parts into a visually coherent, albeit anatomically impossible, body. The disjuncture between the halftone fragments and the whimsically drawn human figure call attention to the constructedness of the image. The caption—written by Heinz Rasch,[132] himself an architect—likens the practice of montage to that of architecture: both are processes of construction under certain practical constraints. Both the architect and the monteur offer solutions to a given set of problems, ultimately creating forms that engage the beholder's imagination. Above this image, Baumeister concluded his own remarks with the statement "imagination and fantasy are fertile soil for all speculative–artistic creation."[133]

Reading *Gefesselter Blick* as a definitive survey of New Typography, the pages featuring Baumeister are perhaps the most perplexing.[134] Baumeister's idiosyncratic contributions to *Gefesselter Blick* exemplify the idea that photomontage induces active optical construction as a co-creative act. Pages 20 and 21 reproduce three photographic works by Baumeister, none of which was used in his work as a graphic designer, including *Kopf,* which also appears on the book's title page (Plate 21). This image is reproduced within *Gefesselter Blick,* accompanied by the following caption: "photo-drawing. a photograph like many others . . . . . . the constructive structure is so strict that the foreign element [*fremdkörper*] of photography will become completely fused with it. the rhythmic dislocations create continuous movement, which the eye of the beholder must continually follow.—result: kinetic."[135]

The Rasch brothers suggested that this image is constructed through perception, in a kind of feedback loop between the "foreign" photographic fragments and the beholder's eye: as the eye attempts to apprehend the image, the disjointed composition of photographic fragments directs its movement, propelled by the visual rhythm of its "dislocations," until disparate forms "become completely fused" into a single image. This is a quintessential example of a constructed image, in the sense first propagated by the Russian avant-garde; this image is not apprehended as a harmonious composition, but rather as an accumulation of dissonant parts that require assembly by an active beholder.[136] The prominence of this image, repeated on the book's title page, suggests optical construction not only as a cornerstone of modernist graphic design, but as a paradigm of modern communication and perception.

Gefesselter Blick proposed a fully integrated method of reading *Typophoto.* Baumeister's contributions to *Gefesselter Blick* exemplify the book's key contribution: the idea that printed, photographic images combined with graphic marks or text activate the reader's fleeting "glance," which in turn incites the mental construction of form and meaning. In keeping with Tschichold's claim that photomontage enabled readers "to form optical associations,"[137] the Rasch brothers advocated for applied photomontage in graphic design as a stimulus for active perception. Beyond the technique of photomontage, the Rasch brothers also proposed that all photographic images in print have trained us to read graphics in a particular way. Their introduction included an image of the façade of a Schocken department store photographed at an oblique angle, which they included as an "example of the spatial observation of text."[138] They described the process of perceiving this image in terms of spatial navigation: the text is first read backwards, as the eye travels from right to left, taking in the depth of space depicted in the photograph; and then from left to right, moving back across the image to read the word "SCHOCKEN." Read in both directions, the letterforms spanning the store's facade are rendered as text and image through the photographic sign. This example illustrated the idea that *Typophoto* held the possibility of integrating word and image through the act of perception.

Gefesselter Blick is perhaps the closest thing to a manifesto that captures the true heterogeneity of New Typography. Rather than summarize an array of practices according to a rigid set of principles written by a single author, the book offers as many perspectives on modern graphic design as it has contributors. Together, the entries offer diverse, sometimes clashing perspectives. Among the multiplicity of voices is that of Heinz Rasch, whose image captions throughout the book create dialogue with each contributor. *Gefesselter Blick* is perhaps most articulate as a manifesto on experimental photography as a crucial link between functionalist graphic design and Dada and surrealism. Photography's assumed link to the "real," which Tschichold had initially lauded as its objectivity, was in fact what made the medium so "functional" as a tool for animating the fictions of advertising.

The "magical realism" of photography that Roh described is perhaps most apparent in photomontage, broadly defined as it would have been in Tschichold's unrealized book. *Gefesselter Blick* offers an understanding of photomontage as a medium that layers mechanical and manual processes, combining photographic fragments with nonphotographic elements to create productive visual contrast and dialectical meaning—an example of what Roh called *Stückungsästhetik*. In doing so, *Gefesselter Blick* expresses the import of photography to New Typography, thereby retooling the meaning of *Typophoto*. In the pages of *Gefesselter Blick* and as Tschichold recognized by 1930, *Typophoto* engendered perception as a kinetic experience of navigating graphic space.

4

TOO MUCH AND TOO LITTLE

Photographic Halftones, Bare and Retouched

In 1924, a peculiar set of illustrations—an array of machine parts and industrial tableaux—appeared in the pages of *Commercial Art,* referenced as good and bad examples of retouching (Figure 28). Eric Simons, a British advertising consultant and regular contributor to *Commercial Art,* used these examples to offer advice to the journal's international readership of advertising designers on the proper procedures for retouching photographic halftones, especially commercial illustrations for heavy industry. Simons warned against excessive retouching and critiqued one image (his Figure 5) as "obviously over-retouched, full of hard edges," referring to line work and washes that had been added to enhance the definition of a microscope.[1] However, he also dismissed an example of a completely unretouched halftone (his Figure 3) as "lifeless and dull."[2] Simons praised his Figure 7 as an illustration in which retouching had been used judiciously to find a balance "between boredom and interest," yet he provided no further explanation.[3] The illustrations go further than words in clarifying conventions of retouching, yet the reader is still left with only the vaguest sense of their purpose. Despite their arrangement on the page in a grid, these illustrations are numbered nonsensically, an inadvertent echo of Simons's futile attempt to articulate a clear set of rules for retouching in a field still struggling to justify its use.[4]

The commercialization of the halftone process in the 1880s had enabled photographic images and text to be printed from a single plate, effectively combining photography and typography into the medium that László Moholy-Nagy would eventually call *Typophoto*. However, this combination was neither simple nor stable. The material and visual translation of photographs into halftones invited new manipulations of photographic images in print. These manipulations opened onto new understandings of what photography could do—and sparked controversy about its very nature. Photography and visual communication historian Estelle Jussim once proposed that a "medium," in the context of visual communication, can be broken down into two parts: the "channel," or material and physical processes and components, and the "code," what she describes as "the structure imposed upon a message that permits that message to be transmitted"—what William Ivins called "syntax."[5] In Jussim's terms, the halftone process transformed photography through the channel of printmaking and the code of the abstracted halftone grid. Photographic images were then recoded through retouching according to the visual conventions of hand-drawn commercial illustration.

Practices of retouching and surrounding debates reflected a lack of consensus among printers and graphic designers about the communicative and persuasive efficacy of photography. As halftones began to appear in the illustrated press, retouching quickly became commonplace among designers, printers, and advertisers. Yet, the practice was by no means uncontroversial, largely due to the wide range of visual effects produced through the modification of photographs—including negatives, prints, and halftone images—at every stage of production.[6] The unassuming term "retouching" encompassed a wide array of alterations made by hand and aided by machines. Retouching encompassed an array of techniques, employing tools including ink washes, varnishes, acid-based retouching fluids, graphite, watercolors, Conté crayons, pastels, brushes, rulers, T squares, tracing paper, etching knives, and straight razors.[7] The most valuable tool for commercial retouching in the 1920s was the airbrush, a machine used to add pigment to photographic images using highly controlled air compression.[8] These tools were employed to trace, outline, and visually define certain elements of an image while smoothing out or erasing others; they could excise unwanted details and conjure new ones. The resulting images were true hybrids of painting, drawing, printmaking,

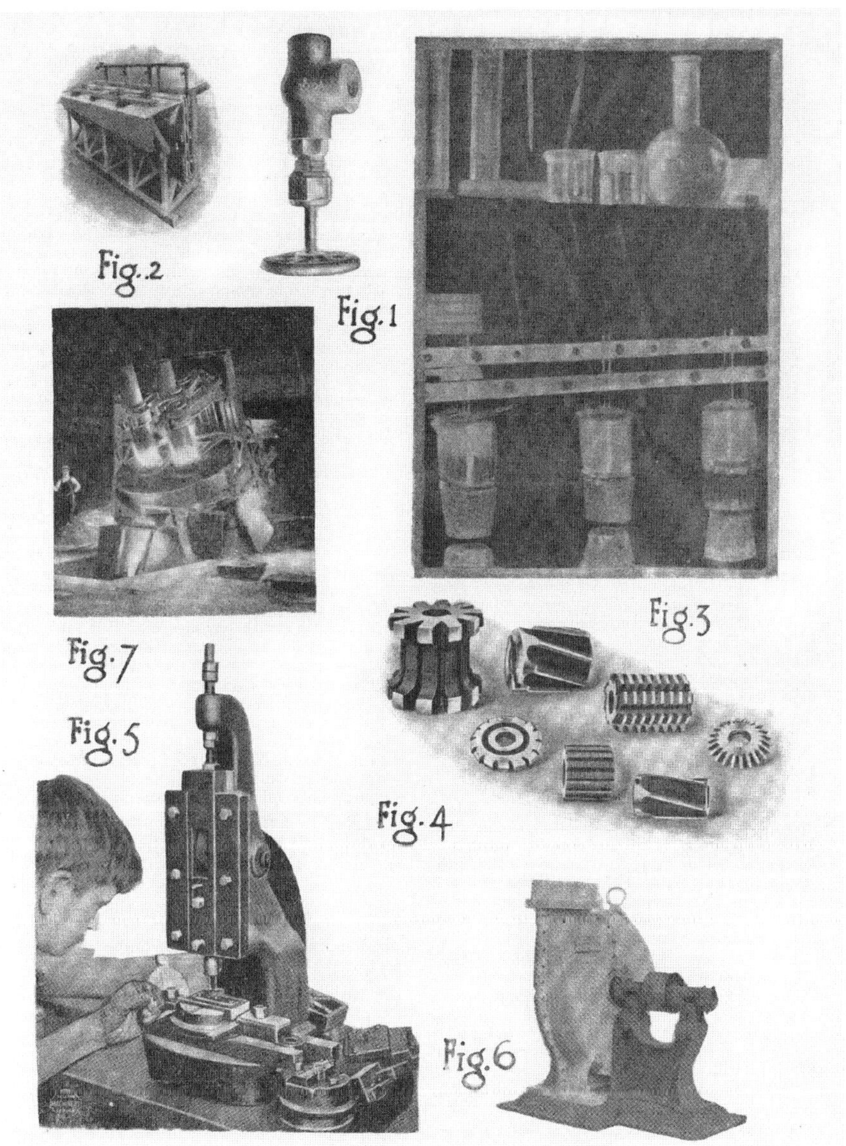

FIGURE 28 Anonymous illustrations reproduced in Eric N. Simons, "The Art of Illustrating Engineering Products," *Commercial Art*, February 1924, 409. General Research Division, The New York Public Library.

and photography. Collapsing these interventions into the term "retouching" obscured the extent to which they fractured, multiplied, and complicated the meaning of a photograph in print.

The conundrum of retouching is key to a broader understanding of how photography was conceptually and materially reinvented in commercial graphic design. When we consider the material hybridity of photographic images in print, it is no wonder that there was so much confusion and disagreement among commercial designers about the true nature of photography and its usefulness to design. The practice of heavily retouching prints, negatives, and halftones was so commonplace in the interwar era that the photographic basis of many halftones is visually undetectable to the contemporary eye. "Photography" could look like almost anything. Yet, conveniently, these uncanny hybrid images exemplified photography for many commercial designers who wanted to manipulate the look and meaning of photographs while capitalizing on their supposed trustworthiness. Embedded in *Typophoto* were practices and discussions of retouching that surrounded and included New Typography. This context was crucial for New Typography's embrace of photomontage, and for a broader understanding of how theories of photography shaped the graphic design profession.

ARTISTIC REALISM: REDEFINING PHOTOGRAPHY IN COMMERCIAL GRAPHICS

Although photographic halftones had circulated in magazines and newspapers since the late nineteenth century, their use remained fraught into the 1930s.[9] Many graphic designers still regarded the integration of photographic halftones into design with ambivalence and skepticism. At issue was whether photography was suited to both the accurate representation of products for sale and the more elusive task of persuasion, which required an understanding of how visual form could act as a cognitive and affective stimulus in the consumer mind.[10] In the words of Walter Raffé, a British graphic artist and author of one of the first published treatises on graphic design,[11] "We must appeal to emotion and desire as well as to vision."[12] He pondered whether the designer should attempt a "detailed realistic representation of the commodity to be advertised; or whether he will avoid this aim, in part or entirely, and will concentrate rather on suggestion of the pleasurable character of the commodity or service in relation to the consumer."[13] German designer Walter F. Schubert similarly pondered whether photography could be both practical and artful. He claimed that "technical photography" was the best medium for depicting machines, but questioned how it could be integrated into "an attractive design."[14]

At stake in this discourse were larger questions about photography's efficacy as a medium of representation, communication, and artistic expression. Practitioners and users of photography debated whether the medium was governed by its own unique set of rules, and therefore suited to certain uses over others. How could photography be a tool of science, law, and industry as well as a medium of artistic expression? Among artists, these questions sparked stylistic debates that were foundational for graphic designers' discussions of photographic illustration. In the late nineteenth and early twentieth centuries, proponents of pictorialist photography used labor-intensive darkroom and printing techniques—including combination printing, carving into negative and print emulsion, and an array of retouching practices—to create unique, handcrafted photographs with subtle tonality. Often drawing on allegorical subject matter, pictorialists emulated painting to secure photography's status as art.[15] In reaction to pictorialism, "straight photography" emerged as a style that explicitly rejected the manipulation of photographic negatives and prints.[16] Champions of straight photography instead favored sharp focus and precise detail, claiming these traits as unique to the medium. With its insistence on photography's medium specificity and suitability for depicting visible "reality," straight photography was a style that came to define realism in photography more broadly.

In Weimar Germany, appeals to photography's medium specificity were expressed through the idea of New Objectivity (*Neue Sachlichkeit*). Albert Renger-Patzsch, Karl Blossfeldt, and August Sander used sharp focus to verify the camera's "objectivity," or capacity to bring forth the true essence of a subject, whether live or inanimate.[17] In 1929, Renger-Patzsch described how photography had effectively replaced painting as a means of representation, insisting that "photography works faster and with greater precision and greater objectivity than the hand of the artist."[18] This ethos had important implications not only for art, but also for product photography, imbuing "photographic" qualities of sharp-focused, black-and-white images with inherent trustworthiness.[19] These associations were crucial for the commercial viability of photographs by Hans Finsler, Aenne Biermann, and Walter Peterhans. Many graphic designers cited photography's detailed precision as proof of its superiority over drawing as an "honest" medium of commercial illustration.[20] Yet, the extensive manipulations that fall under the umbrella of "retouching" were so routine in the translation of photography into print as halftones that graphic designers came to regard them as inherent to the medium.

Paradoxically, to retain the visual characteristics associated with photographic "objectivity," photographic images in print were enhanced through nonphotographic techniques. Consequently, interwar design discourse on "photography" often served to mask the composite nature of *all* photographic images in print. These techniques included the practice known as "vignetting," in which a select part of a photographic image was excised from its frame so that its border appeared soft and faded, used "to avoid hard edges in printing."[21] This technique produced images that appeared to emerge from the substrate of the page (Figure 29). While vignetting tended to soften the sharpness of a photographic image, "outlining" and "re-etching" (or "staging") referred to heightening contrast, either by emphasizing existing lines, or lightening certain parts of an image to create pure white tones.[22] Generally speaking, these techniques were used to either emphasize or deemphasize the visual details of an image, and to alter or erase its background. They were so commonplace that they were usually regarded as entirely necessary to the process of transferring photographic images onto printing plates, and therefore inherent to printed photographic images.[23] As the result of many stages of material manipulation, printed photographic images were also amalgams of subject matter, which combined the image of a photographic referent with elements of fantasy, drawn and etched by hand.

Graphic designers in the 1920s effectively redefined the efficacy of photography for advertising design as what Raffé called "artistic realism." While photography was well suited to capturing the details of a product, it could fall short of the kind of emotional truth that advertising required. "The paradox emerges," he wrote, "that photographic realism . . . is not nearly realistic enough for adequate impression. Only skillful artistic realism will suffice, in the selected realism for facts that are stated simply, direct, unconfused and hence suggestive."[24] Implied in this commentary is that "suggestive" design was also inherently more artistic; a design that became adequately imprinted on the mind of a beholder had the added benefit of conveying the artistic skill of a designer. Schubert argued that even a prospectus for heavy industry "must not dispense with a certain dignity; it must compel the beholder through force and strength of line and color."[25] Proponents of heavy retouching understood the practice not as a rejection of photographic realism, but rather as a necessary revision of the idea. Retouching, like the technique of photomontage, yielded the "selective realism" of illustrations that were both materially linked to, but selectively removed from, the specificity of their contexts. "The object which matters is fully detached from the rest of the machine," another unattributed commentator described, "and yet intimately connected with it."[26]

In the 1920s, retouching mimicked the still-popular style of nonphotographic commercial illustration, and the status of photographic illustrations

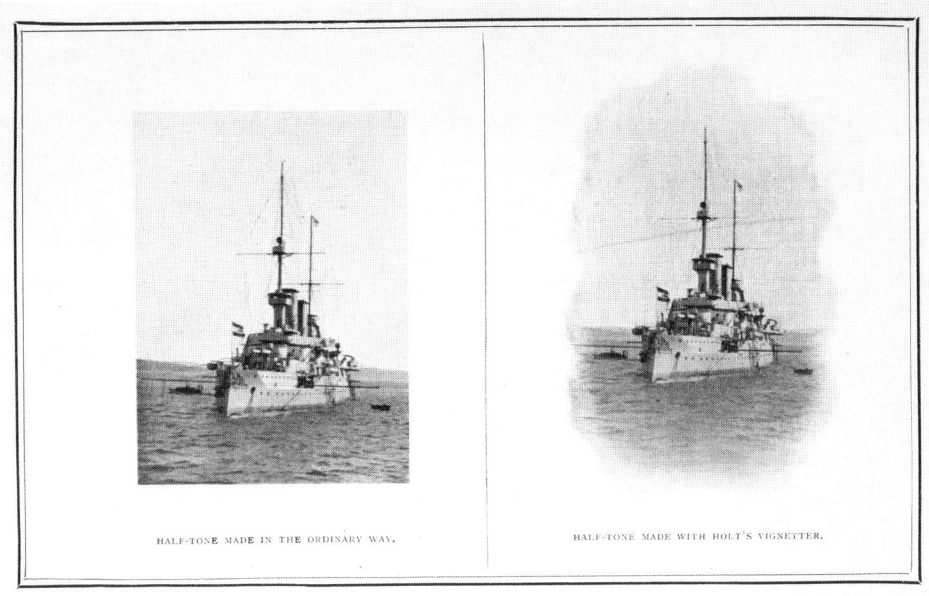

FIGURE 29 Illustrations of the difference between an unvignetted and vignetted halftone, reproduced in Julius Verfasser, *The Half-Tone Process: A Practical Manual of Photo-Engraving in Half-Tone on Zinc, Copper, and Brass* (London: Iliffe and Sons, 1904), 264.

was further complicated by the persistence of hand-drawn illustrations. Modern advertising began in the mid-nineteenth century with the reproduction of drawn illustrations, mostly translated into line engravings and reproduced as lithographic posters.[27] The early advertising poster featured visual interpretations of commodities by artists rather than mimetic representations of them, thereby establishing the visual idiom of drawing as advertising's native tongue. In Germany, the prewar popularity of the *Sachplakat* established the visual codes of drawing as "objective" representation in a commercial context.[28] Commercial artists like Lucian Bernhard depicted commodities schematically, privileging the visual appeal of clean lines and blocks of color, rather than mimetic accuracy or naturalism. The introduction of photographic illustration was regarded by some as a threat to the interpretive license and artistry of advertising, particularly due to photography's capacity to capture the details of an actual object or its surroundings, whether desired or not. The retouched photographic illustration emerged as a middle ground between the harsh truth of photography and the pure aestheticism of the nineteenth-century advertising poster. This hybrid image type allowed for a blending of reality and fantasy—a territory occupied decisively by twentieth-century advertising.

Designers and advertisers who defended photography in commercial illustration contemplated whether what was commonly accepted as the medium's inherent honesty could also be persuasive and emotionally evocative. Heinz Giebelhausen, writing for *Die Reklame*,[29] asserted, "The goal of representing a product as not only true to nature, but also appealing, interesting and promotional, can certainly be achieved by photographic means."[30] Gilbert Russell likewise described photography as a democratic medium capable of "lifelike reproduction" with broad public appeal, and therefore ideal for advertising.[31] He drew a subtle but important distinction between "photographic accuracy" and "realism," advocating for the savvy and selective use of photography to control the effects of light and shadow to create "vivid" and "life-like" illustrations of commodities.[32] Although Russell called the airbrush "an abominable instrument" if overused, retouching was used to temper the harshness of photographic "realism" but retain its "accuracy."[33] The latter has been described by Andrés Mario Zervigón as a "sense of realness" evoked in beholders by photography, especially photomontage.[34] Though photomontage was a technique used by commercial designers since photography's introduction to advertising, the vast majority did not name it as such.

It was precisely the balance between reality and fantasy that could be achieved with photographic illustration that appealed to many designers. French designer R. L. Dupuy, for example, insisted that photography's capacity to be surprising and inventive inhered in its "documentary reproduction of the object or scene that is being represented."[35] The examples accompanying Dupuy's article included commercial photographs by Lucien Lorelle, André Vigneau, and Laure Albin Guillot, who exploited extreme contrasts in black-and-white photography and ghostly effects of light and shadow in surrealist photograms to suggest commodities come to life, as expressions of the uncanny. General trust in photography, according to Dupuy, imbued the medium with the power of suggestion, which psychologists unanimously agreed was advertising's most important quality.[36] German psychoanalyst Edmund Heilpern wrote in *Die Reklame*, "Man constantly produces wishful fantasies that he is never happy without. Recognizing these illusions is the first task of the advertiser. Then he has a thousand connecting points and his task is to link desires and goods together."[37] Advertisers recognized that a single photographic image of a product could operate as evidence and fantasy, simultaneously testifying to the presence of an object and imagining a desired future for its possession and use. Advertising harnessed the temporal slippage in photography to declare that "*this has been* and *this will be*," as Roland Barthes would later write.[38] Designers recognized how photographic images could function like the fetish object, living in the consumer's mind as a latent image of unfulfilled desire, an aspirational surrogate for future satisfaction.

Like Russell, Max Burchartz emphasized the superiority of photography as a direct expression of a person or object. Writing for *Gebrauchsgraphik*, he compared an expressionist drawing by Oskar Kokoschka and an unidentified photograph that had first appeared in the art journal *Der Querschnitt* (Figure 30). The lines of Kokoschka's drawing, Burchartz argued, read as expressions of the artist himself, "but these impressions have nothing or very little to do with the woman who sat in front of the artist as he drew."[39] He touted the photograph, by contrast, as an objective expression of the sitter herself, and thus as a tool for recognition: "the photograph gives us a clear idea of the appearance of the depicted person. we would recognize her when she meets us in the street. the softness of the lighting and the richness of tonal nuances correspond to the impression we have when we see for ourselves the object in reality."[40] Photography was most useful, in Burchartz's estimation, to convey "appearance," or the unmediated visual "impression" of a person or thing, especially through tonal gradations and subtleties of light and shadow. His emphasis on appearance as the expression of a photographic referent, rather than as faithful mimesis, echoes the subtle difference drawn by Gilbert between "photographic accuracy" and "realism." This distinction was critical for the recoding of photography in the context of commercial illustration: the impressionistic "accuracy" of photography had to be decoupled from its association with unforgiving naturalism, imbued instead with suggestive power. This quality of photography was useful in two important ways: it was used to offer vivid impressions of commodities and to implicate the consumer–reader in the space and narrative of an advertisement.

Advertisers repeatedly cited the usefulness of photography for the representation of products for sale. Champions of photographic illustration argued that it could give the impression of physically instantiating a product, rather than merely representing it, thereby compelling the consumer–reader to vividly imagine it in their possession. Marcus Adams, for example, praised photographic illustrations as "exact representatives" of products, anthropomorphized as charismatic surrogates for tangible objects: "In some cases the

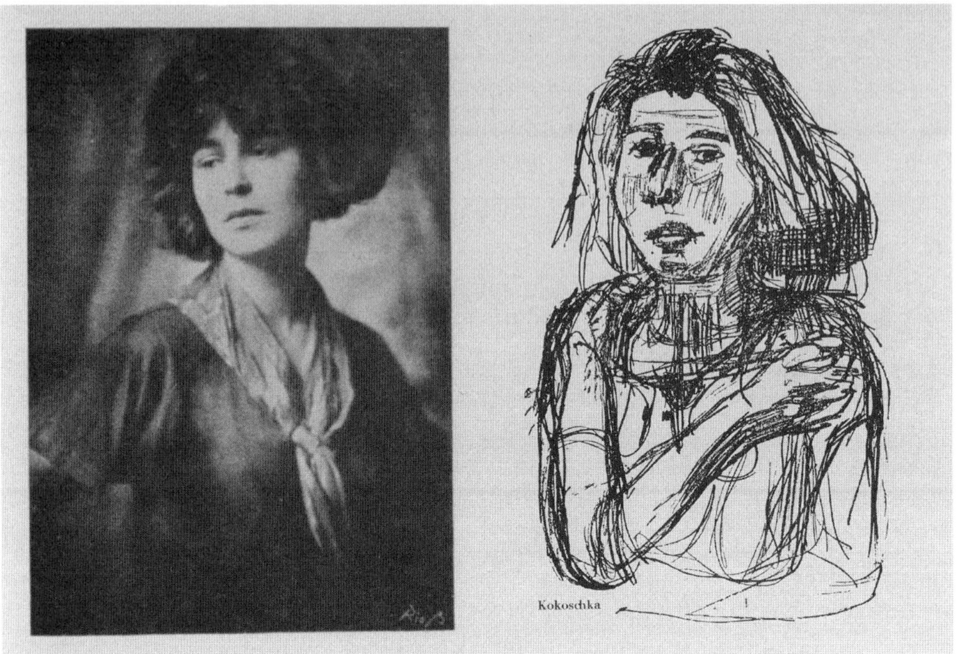

FIGURE 30 Illustrations included in Max Burchartz, "handschrift-type, zeichnung-foto," *Gebrauchsgraphik* 3, no. 8 (August 1926): 41, including reproductions of Frieda Gertrud Riess photograph and Oskar Kokoschka drawing. Letterform Archive, San Francisco. Copyright 2024 Fondation Oskar Kokoschka / Artists Rights Society (ARS), New York / ProLitteris, Zurich.

drawing utterly fails to convey the charm of the goods, whereas a photograph if properly taken has the advantage of making you quite at home with the object and familiar with all the details, thus having the peculiar fascination of making you really feel the goods are in front of you are really yours."[41]

Charles Wormald likewise lauded sophisticated uses of photography in advertising to suggest a narrative, or to evoke affective and extravisual sensations:

> It is one thing to photograph a motorcar or a bottle of perfume, it is quite another to put up a photographic picture of a motor, illustrating the car

> and all the pleasures of ownership, the thrill of speed, the beauty of open spaces, etc., etc., or in the case of a good perfume all the quality and dignity, beauty and fragrance of the perfume, the charm of its bottle and case, and to suggest its desirability to the fair consumer. The successful portrayal of all this on paper is something that cannot be told or even taught, it is psychological, something that can only be "felt," and therein lies the art.[42]

Both Adams and Wormald alluded to photography's indexicality as key for inciting consumer desire. Photographs seemed to evoke and animate the intangible aspects of using and living with commodities, a quality that Wormald recognized as both persuasive and artful.

Such defenses of photography suggested that its persuasive power was not in conflict with, but rather was enhanced by, its truthfulness. These defenses were fortified by a false distinction between photographic and nonphotographic illustration. "Besides," Adams added, "photography has a very good name for telling the truth, whereas a painting or drawing might well be imaginary."[43] Retouching disrupted this distinction: the addition of painted or drawn elements often enabled photographic images to function as evocative representations of desire. Thus, some defenses of photographic illustration masked the importance of retouching by appealing to the purity of the photographic medium. In his own defense of photography as a means of commercial illustration, Giebelhausen contended that, in the hands of the right artists, photography could be as expressive as drawing in depicting commodities. His examples included what he described as "simple" and "naturally lit" product photography for Maggi tea and Neuerburg cigarettes, which showed that certain "possibilities and stimuli" were evidently "slumbering in the photographic plate."[44] This reference to the latent image of the photographic negative underscored the material link between these photographic images and the products they pictured, thereby implicating photography as a direct, unmediated means of bringing forth its referent.

In blending reality and fantasy, photographic illustrations could also implicate readers not only as consumers of an advertisement, but as part of its contents. Designers used photography to picture human figures in variously intimate scenarios, sometimes addressing the reader directly, with the intent of evoking a sense of urgency or even fear about the consequences of not purchasing a product. In one advertisement for Chlorodont toothpaste, for example, a menacing male figure emphasized by an exaggerated shadow occupies the majority of the advertisement's frame. This archetypal dentist points

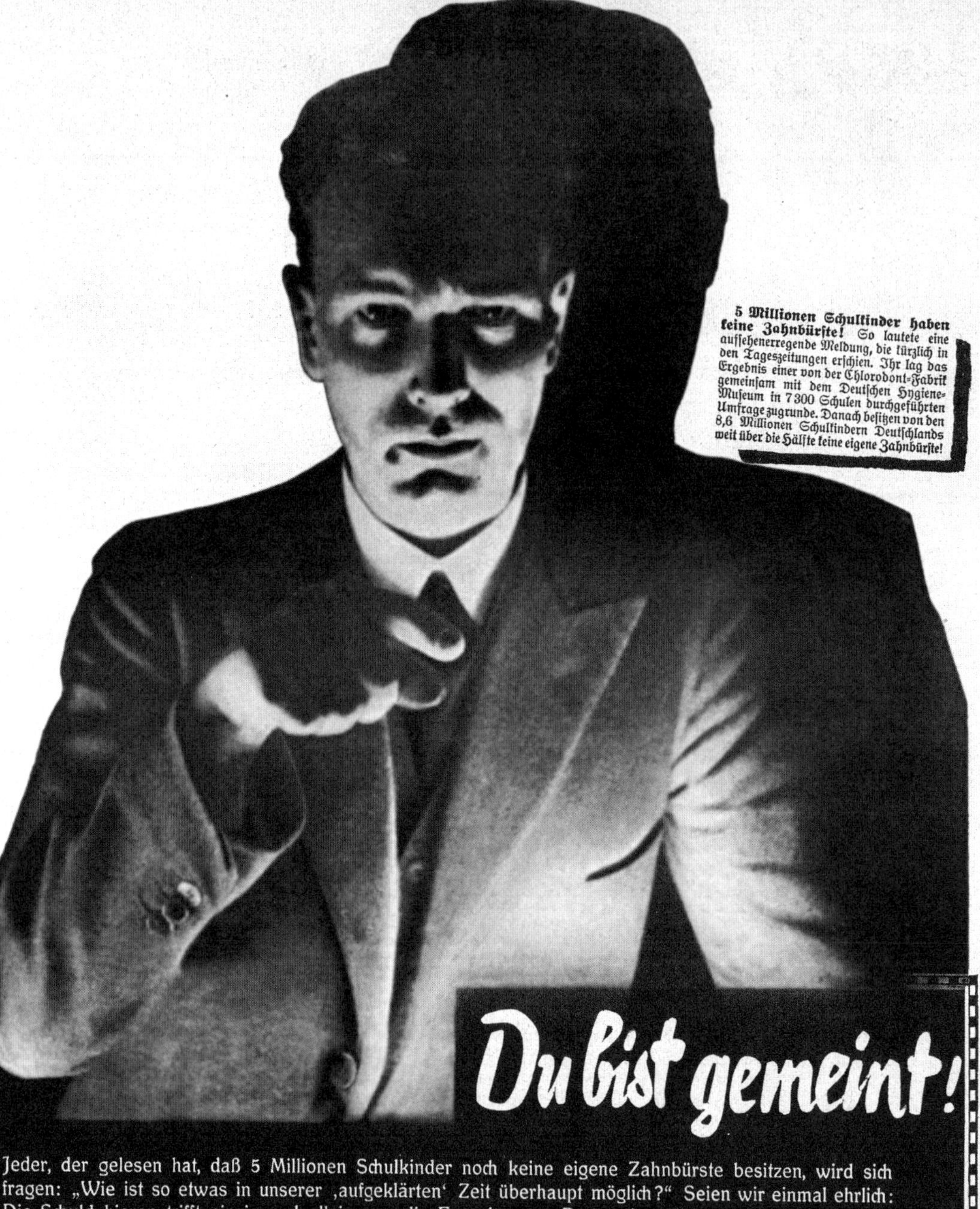
5 Millionen Schulkinder haben keine Zahnbürste! So lautete eine aufsehenerregende Meldung, die kürzlich in den Tageszeitungen erschien. Ihr lag das Ergebnis einer von der Chlorodont-Fabrik gemeinsam mit dem Deutschen Hygiene-Museum in 7300 Schulen durchgeführten Umfrage zugrunde. Danach besitzen von den 8,6 Millionen Schulkindern Deutschlands weit über die Hälfte keine eigene Zahnbürste!
Du bist gemeint!
Jeder, der gelesen hat, daß 5 Millionen Schulkinder noch keine eigene Zahnbürste besitzen, wird sich fragen: „Wie ist so etwas in unserer ‚aufgeklärten' Zeit überhaupt möglich?" Seien wir einmal ehrlich: Die Schuld hieran trifft einzig und allein uns, die Erwachsenen. Denn wie sollen die Kinder zu regelmäßiger Zahnpflege erzogen werden, wenn die Erwachsenen nicht mit gutem Beispiel vorangehen? Aber noch tut die überwiegende Mehrzahl unseres Volkes nichts für die Gesunderhaltung der Zähne! Dabei läßt sich hier doch mit etwas gutem Willen und — Chlorodont so leicht Abhilfe schaffen! Jeden Abend und Morgen Chlorodont — das macht die Zähne blendend weiß und erhält sie bis ins hohe Alter gesund!
Chlorodont

directly at the reader, accompanied by the text, "Du bist gemeint!" (This means you!) (Figure 31). This advertisement targeted parents with small children, warning of the health risks to children who did not routinely brush their teeth with toothpaste.[45] Other advertisements used photographic fragments to evoke a romantic connection between a man and woman, or to suggest the love between a mother and child. A commentator writing in *Die Reklame* praised an advertisement for Vasenol skin cream for featuring a photograph of a smiling baby to elicit a mother's emotional response.[46] Whether meant to induce fear, romantic desire, or maternal affection, the isolation of human figures against a monochrome background, and their seamless integration with type, was intended to dramatize the emotional impact of their interactions with one another or directly with the consumer–reader. This visual isolation was achieved through the techniques of photomontage and retouching.

Direct address implicated the consumer–reader somatically within the world of an advertisement. Sabine Kriebel has described the absorptive quality of photomontaged designs by John Heartfield, especially for political propaganda, which similarly engage the body of the beholder.[47] Though commonly associated with Heartfield as an innovator of photomontage in graphic design, this strategy was arguably pioneered by many anonymous advertising designers working contemporaneously through the combination of photomontage and retouching. One of the most ubiquitous tropes of photography-based advertising was that of the disembodied hand, or pair of hands, usually pictured holding, utilizing, or pointing to a product for sale (Plate 22, Figure 32). Especially in Weimar Germany, where renewed interest in the physiognomy of human hands gained popularity through books and magazines, this trope saturated commercial and political graphics alike (Figure 33).[48] In advertising, photographically illustrated hands typically appeared as surrogates for the hands of the consumer.[49] Their resemblance to the reader's actual hands—in view as they held open and flipped through the pages of a magazine or newspaper—was heightened through photographic representation.[50] Disembodied hands invited the somatic projection of readers into the graphic space of a newspaper or magazine, often pictured cut off at the frame of an advertisement where the page ended and the body of the consumer began.

FIGURE 31 Designer unknown, advertisement for Chlorodont toothpaste, reproduced in *Berliner Illustrierte Zeitung*, 1935. Getty Research Institute, Los Angeles (89-S484).

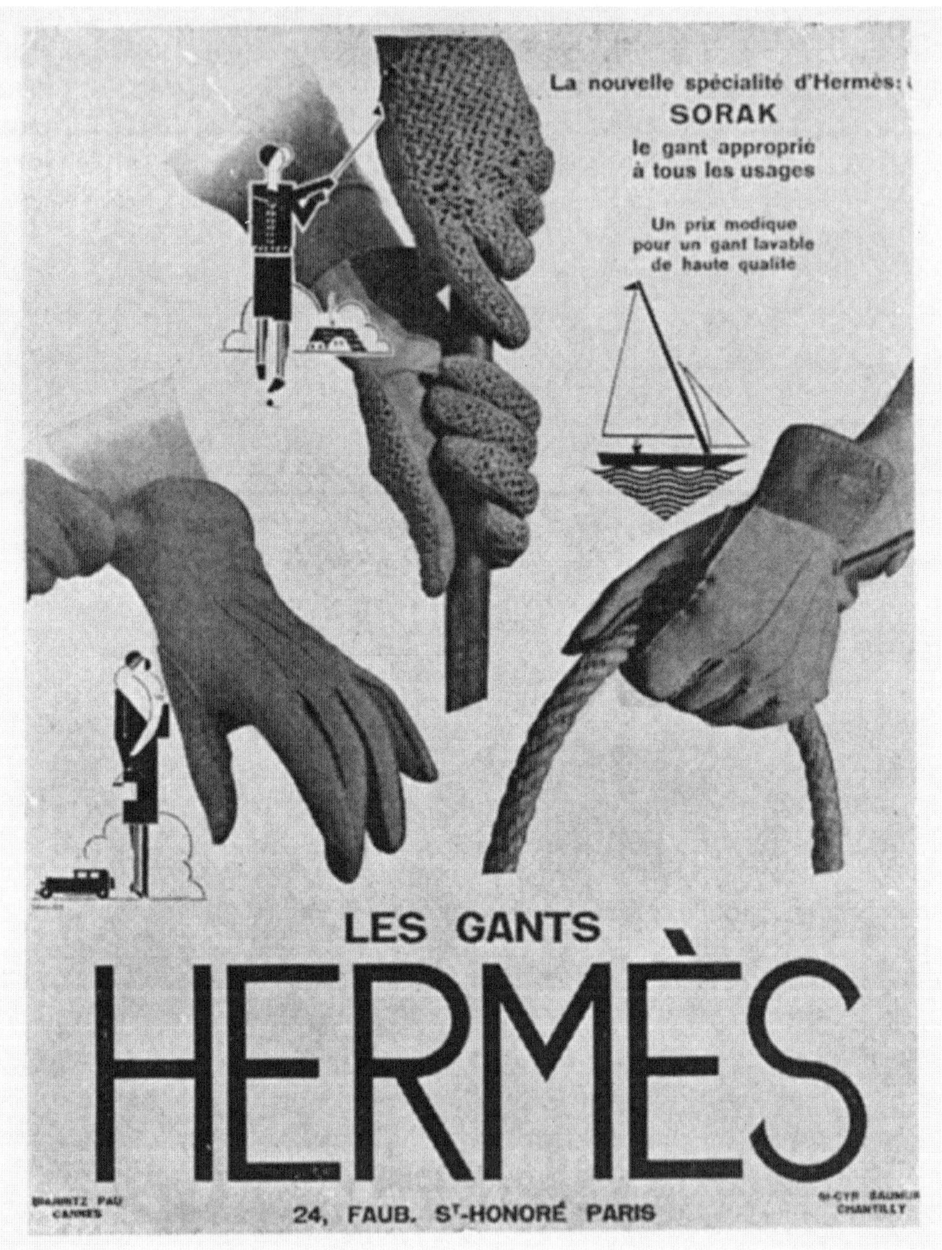

FIGURE 32 Unattributed advertisement for Hermès gloves, reproduced in *Arts et métiers graphiques*, September 1929. Letterform Archive, San Francisco.

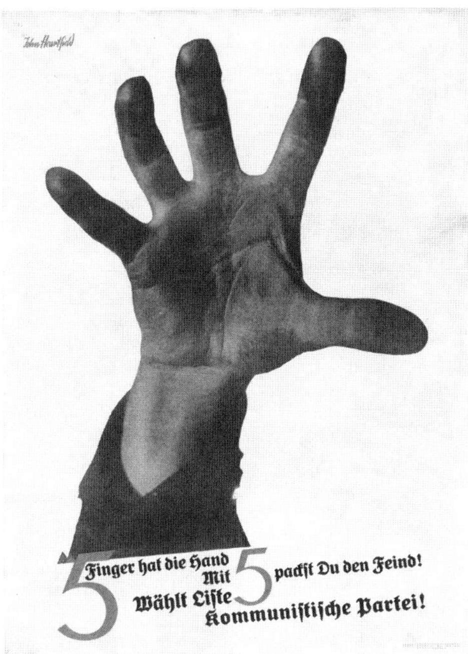

FIGURE 33 John Heartfield, poster design: "5 Finger Hat die Hand" (1928). Digital Image Copyright The Museum of Modern Art / Licensed by SCALA / Art Resource, NY. Copyright The Heartfield Community of Heirs / Artists Rights Society (ARS), New York, 2024.

As Kriebel has argued, this trope evidences awareness on the part of graphic designers that reading and perception were not only visual experiences, but also haptic ones.[51] Moreover, this trope tacitly emphasized advertising as a participatory medium through which meaning is coproduced by designers and readers—implicating consumption itself as an active choice rather than as passive persuasion. This notion, however subtle, was crucial at a moment when advertisers sought to distance capitalist consumerism from the nefarious connotations of political propaganda.

Yet, in some cases the visual effects of retouching leveled the visible differences between machine and human, creating what Terry Smith has described as an uncanny equivalency in advertising "between the tactility of treated machine and the metallic sheen of bright flesh."[52] In an advertisement for Mouson hand lotion printed in the *Berliner Illustrierte Zeitung* in 1935, for example, two hands extend from out of frame into the advertisement, demonstrating the superiority of Mouson's product (Figure 34). The advertisement boasts that Mouson absorbs into the skin, giving the appearance of "smoothness without shine" (*Glätte ohne Glanz*), illustrated by the hand and forearm that reaches diagonally from the top of the advertisement, around which its

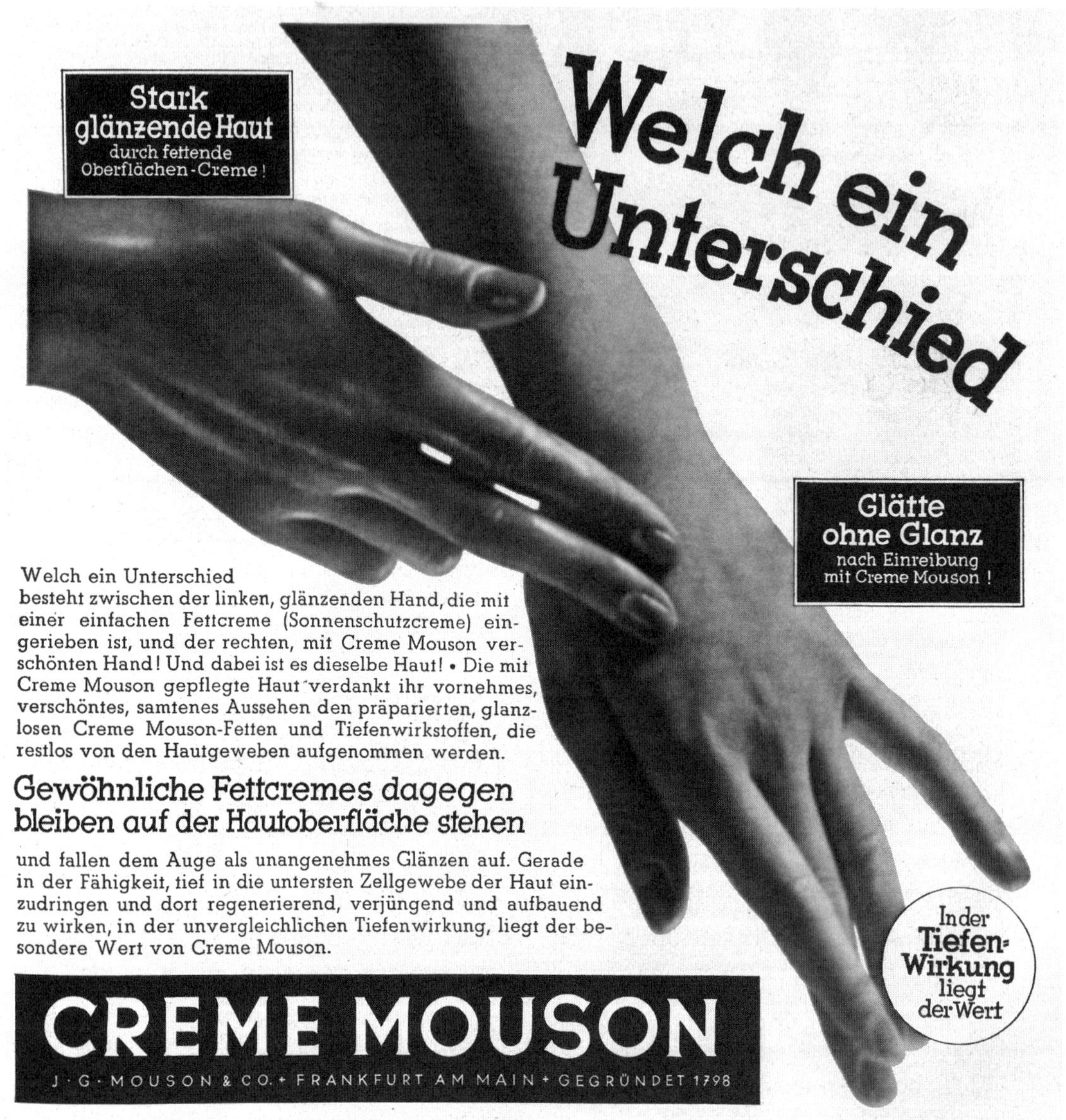

FIGURE 34 Designer unknown, advertisement for Mouson hand lotion, reproduced in *Berliner Illustrierte Zeitung*, 1935. Getty Research Institute, Los Angeles. Getty Research Institute, Los Angeles (89-S484).

layout is arranged. By contrast, another hand reaches into frame from the left, showing "intensely shiny skin" (*Stark glänzende Haut*) coated with a different hand cream. The shinier hand has an altogether inhuman quality, appearing waxy in texture. Both photographic fragments have been retouched to enhance the visual contrast that they are meant to illustrate, making it difficult to discern whether the shiny hand belonged to a human or mannequin. This ambiguity, which Smith called "the homogenization of consumer and product," was exploited in commercial design to reinforce a harmonious vision of both ideal commodities and consumers.[53]

"THE PHOTO WAS NOT ENOUGH": THE LIMITS AND ETHICS OF RETOUCHING

While some designers celebrated the possibilities of photographic illustration, others expressed doubt about how to retain craft in photography-based design and whether the aesthetic of drawn illustration could work in photographic illustration. Some denounced photography's capacity for detail as a threat to both the designer's control over representation and the generalized impression—as opposed to specific description—that advertisers often wished to convey about a given product. In an article printed in *Gebrauchsgraphik* by Traugott Schalcher, "Advertising and Naturalism," the Swiss artist and advertising designer delivered an ambiguous critique of retouching photographic images, a technique he associated with the commercial success of American advertising (and what he deemed the questionable taste evident therein).[54] Schalcher grappled with how to reconcile the "naturalism" of photography with, in his view, the need for archetypal artistic representations of greater truths in commercial design. He concluded that photography was insufficient for such a task.

In scrutinizing the shortfall of naturalistic photography as a means of visual persuasion, Schalcher confronted the medium's capacity for detail as a distinct problem for advertising: "Does the photo suffice to awaken the buyer's wish to possess any goods? One would think so. And yet the photo was not enough. It gave too much and too little."[55] To correct for photography's propensity to magnify "the most trifling fault . . . with exaggerated clarity," he described retouching as "a method of completely repainting the photographic copy with the airbrush," which ultimately rendered "all the variations in tone and color inseparable from every photographic reproduction."[56] He continued, "The concrete picture of the object photographed becomes more abstract through the re-touching process, since it loses the individual characteristics, proper only to itself."[57] Rather than describing the retouched halftone as purely photographic, he celebrated its ability to go beyond photography's medium specificity to bring forth a sense of objecthood through abstraction. His comments echoed those of German luminary Siegfried Kracauer, a contemporary of Schalcher, who famously critiqued photography as a lifeless, diminished representation of its referent, likening it to the "sediment" of memory.[58] Kracauer deemed photographs "too little," to borrow Schalcher's words, and lamented the loss of uniqueness and expressive depth that were equally elusive for designers like Schalcher.

Formal abstraction, Schalcher argued, not only made retouched halftones easier to reproduce, but more importantly, also imbued them with a kind of archetypal truth: "The re-touched picture does not show *a* machine, but *the* machine."[59] Such erasure of specificity was especially useful for commercial illustration, which was meant to be more generally evocative than particularly descriptive. Photography could express much more than it represented. Ultimately, for Schalcher, the virtual obliteration of the photographic image through retouching—and the effectiveness of the resulting hybrid images—suggested that only non-photographic images should be used in advertising. He championed the discursive potential of images that did not purport to photorealism, even suggesting their agency as conduits for an active exchange of ideas between advertisement and consumer: "We wish not only to see, but to converse, to take part in thinking and in creating. The naturalistic picture does not excite the imagination. The resolve to buy, however, is a matter of the power to buy—and of imagination."[60] Whereas photographs foreclosed consumer fantasy, according to Schalcher, nonphotographic illustrations invited and encouraged it.

In addition to the anxieties of many commercial designers about photography's undiscerning ability to capture unwanted details, there were also ethical concerns about both photomontage and retouching. Those who cast doubt on the visual credibility of retouched halftones referred to techniques of manipulation as photographic "stunts," as in a 1931 article by David Charles in *Commercial Art* dedicated to photography.[61] Charles identified different techniques used to punch up specific aspects of photographic images: for example, to create visual contrast and make products stand out against a background; to tell a compelling story (especially through photomontage); or to make an object or scene look dreamlike or nostalgic (through manipulation of camera focus). Like many of his contemporaries, Charles struggled to reconcile the general regard for photography as a "realistic" medium with the manipulations that it seemed to invite. Many designers contemplated how photography could be trustworthy while also aesthetically compelling and persuasive.

Though photographic halftones populated some of the most widely circulated advertisements and commercial graphics before World War I, many were virtually unidentifiable as such. Retouching was commonly used to erase "imperfections" or unwanted details from photographs, to mask the raster pattern imposed by the halftone screen, and to add visual definition that the "bare" halftone lacked. The practice of retouching mimicked the visual language of drawing and painting to mask the mechanical regularity of the dot matrix.[62] Gerry Beegan has therefore noted that "it is more accurate to speak of 'semi-mechanical' rather than mechanical reproduction" of mass-circulated images in the late nineteenth and early twentieth centuries.[63] Early twentieth-century retouching is therefore emblematic of the artificiality of "photography" as a distinct medium, which has never been a stable or static category. Paradoxically, designers often depended on nonphotographic techniques of retouching to achieve precision, mimesis, and exacting detail—considered to be intrinsic qualities of photography. Beegan notes that in some cases, the softening effects of the airbrush intentionally mimicked the artisanal process of hand-drawing.[64]

What is clear from looking at retouched photographic images from the 1920s, and from the discourse surrounding this practice, is that they rendered photography and drawing indistinguishable. Moreover, their hybridity was key to the communicative efficacy of photography as commercial illustration. "Photographic" was less a description of a medium apart from drawing and more a matter of degrees of realism in any given image. Depending on the subject or message of an advertisement, different characteristics of photography or drawing might be more or less desirable.

A 1912 catalog designed by Peter Behrens showcasing a line of teakettles produced by the German electricity company Allgemeine Elektrizitäts-Gesellschaft (AEG), for example, featured photographic halftones of three teakettles retouched to distinguish between different combinations of material and finish (Figure 35).[65] One page features three octagonal teakettles: one made of brass with a smooth, matte finish; another made of copper with a stippled, wrought texture; and a third made of smooth, nickel-plated brass. These textures are exaggerated through retouching, conveying both their relationship as a set and their potential for individual customization. An unattributed article titled "The Art of Retouching the Photograph," printed in the December 1923 issue of *Commercial Art,* was one of

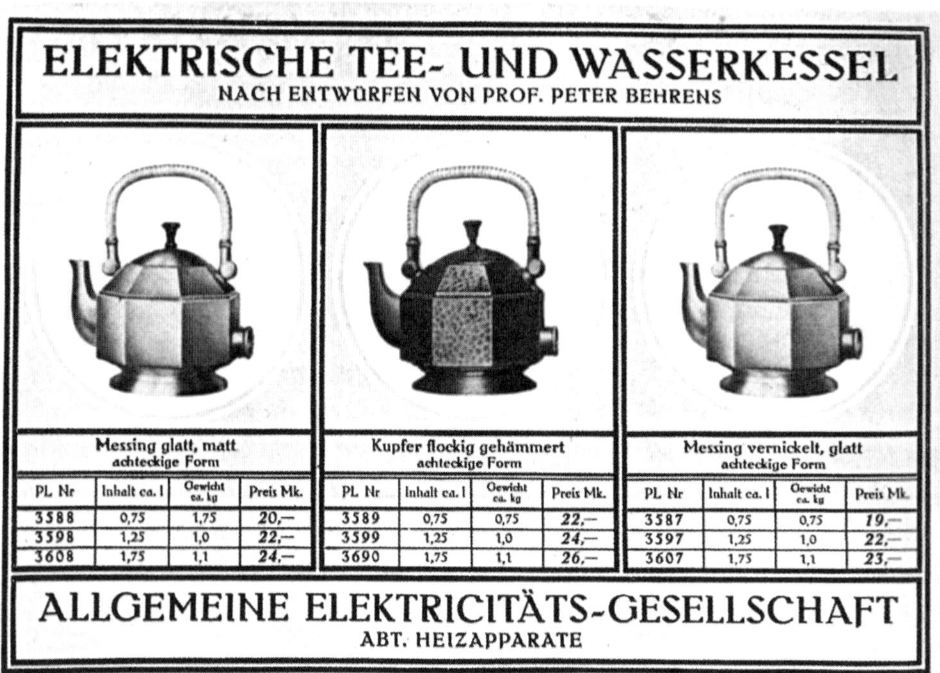

ELEKTRISCHE TEE- UND WASSERKESSEL
NACH ENTWÜRFEN VON PROF. PETER BEHRENS

Messing glatt, matt
achteckige Form

PL. Nr	Inhalt ca. l	Gewicht ca. kg	Preis Mk.
3588	0,75	1,75	20,—
3598	1,25	1,0	22,—
3608	1,75	1,1	24,—

Kupfer flockig gehämmert
achteckige Form

PL. Nr	Inhalt ca. l	Gewicht ca. kg	Preis Mk.
3589	0,75	0,75	22,—
3599	1,25	1,0	24,—
3690	1,75	1,1	26,—

Messing vernickelt, glatt
achteckige Form

PL. Nr	Inhalt ca. l	Gewicht ca. kg	Preis Mk.
3587	0,75	0,75	19,—
3597	1,25	1,0	22,—
3607	1,75	1,1	23,—

ALLGEMEINE ELEKTRICITÄTS-GESELLSCHAFT
ABT. HEIZAPPARATE

FIGURE 35 Peter Behrens, catalog design for Allgemeine Elektrizitäts-Gesellschaft, 1912.

many that described commercial photography as a hybrid medium produced jointly by photographers, retouchers, engravers, designers, typesetters, and printers.[66] The author warned of the difficulty of photographing objects with particularly reflective surfaces, such as metal, which require the careful control of light and shade to avoid glare. Failure to do so was common, especially in the representation of machines and machine parts: "The consequence is that the resulting photograph calls for so much retouching that the final illustration has very little of the photograph left."[67]

The article praised the skillful retoucher's ability to "bring out parts that are essential," a skill cultivated through intimate knowledge of the product depicted.[68] This point was illustrated by a photographic image of an Avery typewriter slashed down the middle with a diagonal line, an illustration that, according to its caption, "contrasts the retouched parts of a typewriter with the fuzziness produced by the camera, and proves the necessity of sharpening

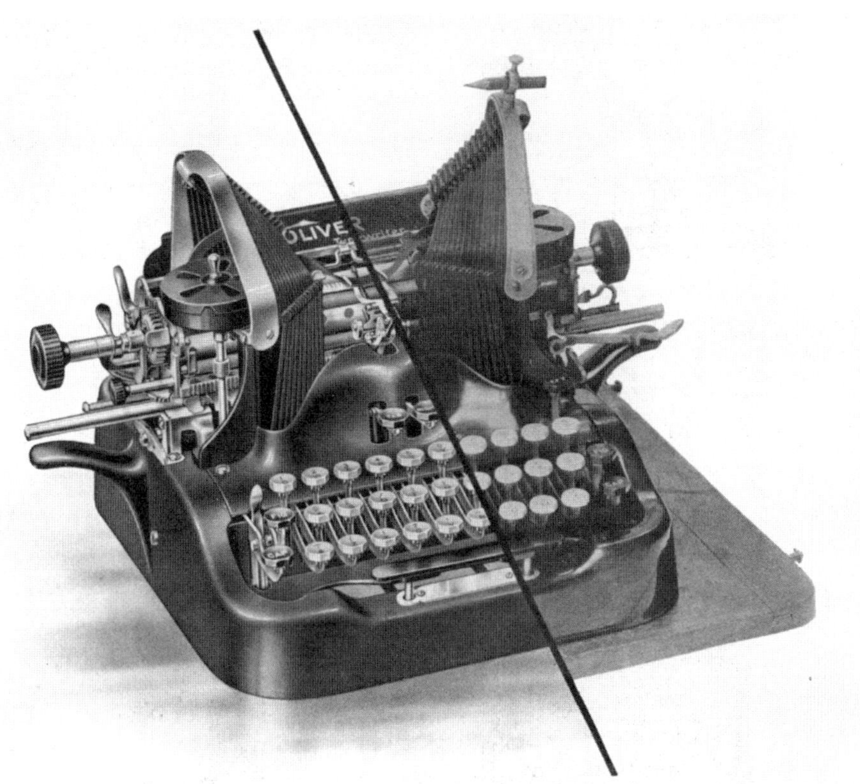

FIGURE 36 Anonymous illustration reproduced in "The Art of Retouching the Photograph," *Commercial Art,* December 1923, 340. General Research Division, The New York Public Library.

up the details" (Figure 36).[69] This bifurcated image, shiny and sharply detailed at left and muddled by gray tones at right, highlights the striking visual dissonance between retouched and unretouched halftones. This image shows how retouchers used their tools to alter composition, sharpen and highlight certain details, and balance light and shade.

On the facing page, an advertisement for Farringdon Studios, a London-based studio that specialized in photographic retouching, features a similar side-by-side comparison of retouched and unretouched versions of an illustration created for an engineering catalog (Figure 37). The article's description of the need for skillful retouching easily describes this advertisement:

> In the plant the object to be photographed is necessarily surrounded by irrelevant details. . . . Such a background is the reverse of helpful. It must be removed before the engraving is made. Ordinarily this is done by the retoucher as he attends to other details. . . . Frequently a photograph is called for that will give prominence to a part or an accessory of a machine, and at the same time show the machine itself, as subdued surroundings. This could be accomplished by the photographer by the manipulation of several photographs, but the retoucher can shine, who can so well differentiate between the tone-values of the machine that he knows exactly which parts to reduce and which to strengthen.[70]

Farringdon Studios "reduced" the grime of the machine and transformed it into a shiny gleam, thereby visually "strengthening" the metallic quality of its surface. The machine had been "detached" from the murky space of the factory in which it was photographed and effectively placed in the undefined but hermetic white space of a showroom—easily simulated by the white space of the magazine page—anchored spatially by the suggestion of a gleaming, checkered floor. The edges of the image are soft, visually fading away, an example of the technique of vignetting. Retouching has also removed the square frame of the photographic image, silhouetting the machine's form and visually isolating particular component parts.

Elsewhere in *Commercial Art,* Eric Simons warned of the potentially dangerous homogenizing effects of retouching:

> You know the sort of thing! A machine stares at you from the page. It looks as though it has been carefully prepared for the South Kensington Museum. . . . Every real and vivid thing has been smoothed and whittled out of it by the dreary hand of the retoucher. It does not move; it is shining and glossy; there is no dirt and grease about it. It is cold and still, resting in a kind of static perfection till the end of all time; an exhibit; a curiosity; perhaps an abortive experiment. But a working machine—Never![71]

Retouching, when done badly, had the potential to drain an image of life and to create a false visual equivalency between objects as dissimilar as teakettles and typewriters. Simons went so far as to suggest that bad retouching could

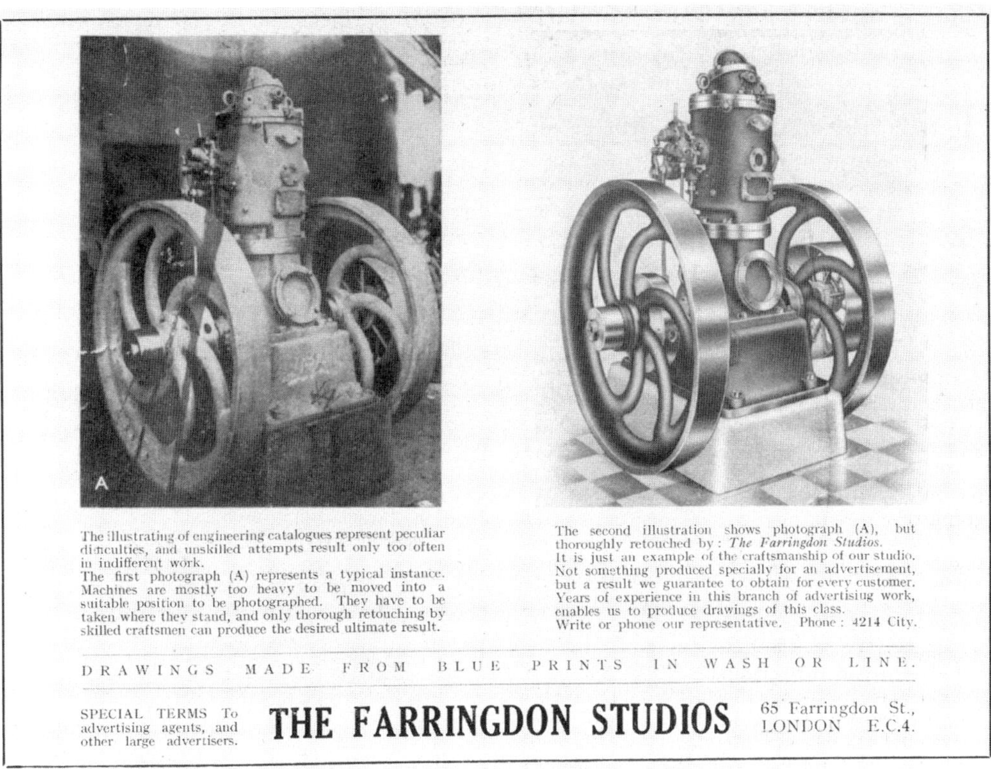

FIGURE 37 Unknown designer, advertisement for Farringdon Studios reproduced in *Commercial Art*, December 1923, 341. General Research Division, The New York Public Library.

condemn both an advertisement and the machine it depicted to impotency. The harsh and potentially alienating realities of glare on a metallic surface or the dirty and dangerous conditions of a factory, which the camera could not help but capture, were removed to create a sense of familiarity and inviting tactility that would charm and entice potential consumers. Despite Simons's protest, visual homogenization in the rendering of different kinds of objects through retouching implies that conveying a feeling of luxury and comfort is more important than providing accurate depictions of products and their uses.

Designers used both photomontage and retouching to emphasize the objecthood of products for sale. By removing photographic fragments from their square or rectangular frames and using retouching to enhance surface texture, they rendered illustrations more like objects in space. Free of the limitations of both photography and drawing, products appeared not as representations in advertising, but as tangible objects. In this sense, the Farringdon Studios advertisement, the bifurcated Avery typewriter illustration, and Behrens's catalog of AEG teakettles are all examples of *Typophoto* in commercial design avant la lettre. These three examples are telling of the agenda that motivated the practice of retouching halftones: they each evoked an idealized version of industrial manufacture as clean and accommodating, producing fantastical commodities that were nevertheless showroom- and storefront-ready. In this composite form of photographic illustration, objects appeared as though brought forth from the planar surface of the printed page.

PURE ILLUSTRATIONS: NEW TYPOGRAPHY REFRAMES RETOUCHING

In 1927, László Moholy-Nagy wrote, "The appeal of what is new and still unused is one of the most effective factors in *advertising*; therefore it is appropriate . . . to include *photography* in advertising."[72] Yet, he also conceded that "photography in advertising is not an alien concept."[73] Photographic images had long been present in commercial illustration, but as we have seen, they were often converted "into the language of painting or drawing," as Moholy-Nagy described it, "never allowing the photographic model to appear as such."[74] He called instead for making photography in print visible as such, thereby implicating the halftone as a pure form of photography that had been hidden and corrupted through excessive retouching. He defended "bare" (or unretouched) halftones on the grounds that photography was an inherently graphic medium—that is, more akin to writing and typography than to painting or drawing. The heightened visibility of photography in advertising would, in his view, secure its status as a productive medium of communication, rather than merely an artistic "model" or a means of reproduction.

Like Moholy-Nagy, Paul Renner also understood the halftone not as a printed translation, but rather as an unmediated form of photography with unique creative potential. In a 1930 article published in the German architecture and design journal *Die Form,* Renner lauded the originality of modernist design born from industrialization: "Today, photography does not want to be anything but itself. . . . A technique can only be intellectually mastered when its inherent laws are acknowledged and understood. . . . The new photography, the new architecture, the new house-hold utensils, and the new typography have gained their specifically modern quality from this kind of imaginative response to the challenge of expressing their inherently mechanical quality."[75] Renner recognized the creative efficacy of both contemporary photography and typography as "inherently mechanical." The same year, his book *Mechanized Graphics* (*Mechanisierte Grafik*) was published, in which he deemed photography a mechanical process akin to printmaking.[76] The clearest expression of photography as a graphic medium was the halftone. Though he did not address retouching explicitly, Renner's appeal to mastering the "inherent laws" of photography implied retouching as a problematic erasure of the halftone's compatibility with type.

Discourse among the New Typographers about the visibility of the halftone did not amount to a wholesale rejection of retouching, but rather a rhetorical reframing of the manipulations of photography necessitated by printing technology. As we have seen, many designers in the 1920s called attention away from retouching as a practice of manipulation by referring to retouched photographic images simply as "photography." In doing so, they denied any meaningful distinction between photographic prints and halftones, let alone between retouched and unretouched halftones. For New Typography, the term "photomontage" stood in for all the processes of construction and manipulation, including retouching, which made *Typophoto* possible. Photomontage was a key term for New Typography because of its association with constructivism and its connotations of making visible, rather than hiding, the labor of graphic design, typesetting, and printing. Ironically, however, the term also collapsed a number of techniques that were necessary to combine photography and type on the printed page—including the many procedures encompassed by the capacious term "retouching."

New Typography borrowed this rhetorical reframing, in part, from discourse on photomontage in the context of art. For example, Franz Roh offered an ambiguous description of Paul Citroen's arrangement of fragments in his 1923 photocollage *Metropolis* (*City of My Birth*) (*Weltstadt* [*Meine Geburtsstadt*]) as a "cubist nesting of pure illustrations."[77] The visual and spatial play explicitly attributed to photomontage was not only the product of cutting photographic fragments, pasting them in new configurations, and rephotographing the resulting compositions. The visual effects of photomontage were also the result of selectively rejecting some conventions of retouching while retaining others. Rather than add background elements that imitated photographic representation, as in the Farringdon Studios advertisement, the New Typographers tended to isolate objects completely, often excising background illustration altogether. Resistance to this convention, as much as

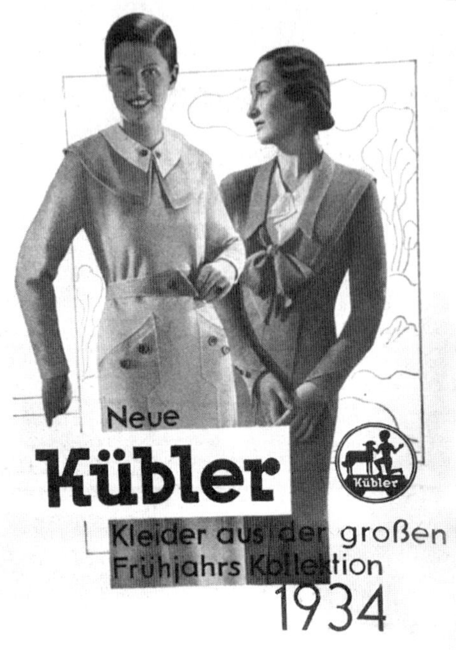

FIGURE 38 Willi Baumeister, advertisement for Paul Kübler and Co. women's wear, reproduced in *Berliner Illustrierte Zeitung*, 1934. Archiv Baumeister, Kunstmuseum Stuttgart. Copyright 2024 Artists Rights Society (ARS), New York / VG Bild-Kunst, Bonn.

photomontage, created in advertising what Roh had described as "cubist nesting" in Citroen's work—the complete evacuation of depth of field in exchange for a depiction of the city as continuous, simultaneous, and relentlessly visible.

In an advertisement for Kübler women's wear printed in the *Berliner Illustrierte Zeitung* by Willi Baumeister, photographic fragments were cleanly cut from their frames (Figure 38). Here, Baumeister used photography as "pure illustration" in the sense that it appears visually distinct from elements drawn by hand, rather than blended together. A schematic line drawing of a bucolic outdoor scene in the background heightens the visual contrast between photography and drawing. The advertisement exploits expectations of photographic realism to visualize fantasy—a paradox that Roh called "magical realism."

New Typography's defenses of photographic halftones as "pure illustrations" in graphic design were predicated on a clear—if completely artificial—distinction between mechanized labor and handcraft in graphic design.[78] This distinction was created through placing rhetorical emphasis of the practice of photomontage, while deemphasizing retouching. While both photomontage and retouching were in fact manual processes, the former carried the connotations of mechanized production, owing to the term's origins in the verb *montieren* (to assemble, to install). However, as Otto Bettmann described in 1931, the visual power of photomontage depended on the material hybridity of the halftone in combination with various retouching techniques. It was through deft and selective retouching, as much as the careful arrangement of photographic fragments, that photomontage could be rendered visually seamless. In an article addressing photomontage both as a conceptual technique and as a set of processes, Bettmann emphasized the "paradoxical blend of realism and fantasy" as a fusion of parts into a new, coherent whole: "The stimuli of a fantasy image are combined with the attraction of representations that carry the accent of truth. Photographic images are believed because they reflect the world as we know it. Montage does not change them in principle, but only fuses them to each other in a new sense, emphasizing the essential."[79]

Much of his discussion of photomontage was dedicated to the balance of color, tonal values, and composition achieved through drawing, underpainting, and airbrushing.[80] Yet, he also warned that "all such processes are pointless if they are not determined and united from the outset by the intention of a clear-cut artistic whole."[81] Among Bettmann's examples of successful photomontage was a poster by Tschichold, in which, according to Bettmann, "image direction and type direction seem balanced. Tonally, the typeface blends in with the black and white of the picture and the background, so that it no longer appears as a foreign body but as a support to the overall structure."[82] In this design, Tschichold used photomontage to bridge typographic and photographic space by making type appear as part of the wall depicted photographically, and in turn by using typographic elements to make the represented architectural space cohere perceptually.

In the context of commercial design, the fusion of photographic and typographic elements into a legible whole was crucial: advertising was intended as an imaginary reality in which consumers could locate themselves physically and emotionally. Although he warned against overretouching, Moholy-Nagy's attitude was certainly more complicated than an outright rejection of the practice. He advocated for the judicious use of retouching in combination with photomontage to create what he called "super-photography," or *Photoplastik* (photo-plasticity):[83]

> Illustrated magazines are trying to produce a realistic representation of "nonsensical" subjects by cleverly retouching parts of the picture or introducing elements that do not belong in it. . . . These photomontages are the precursors to the new and future "photo-sculptures."

> My goal is to produce photo-sculptures which [*sic*]—although composed of many photographs (copied, pasted, retouched)—create the controlled and coherent effect of a single picture equivalent to a photograph. . . . This method allows us to depict a seemingly organic super-reality.[84]

By referring to photomontages that had been rephotographed and retouched as *Photoplastiken,* Moholy-Nagy linked the pliability of photographic material to the representation of a "seemingly organic super-reality." He advocated montage and retouching as techniques intended not to trick the beholder, but to stimulate their awareness of the plasticity and constructedness of graphic design.

The "super-reality" made possible by *Photoplastik* was evident in Moholy-Nagy's own commercial work, especially his first cover of the high-end, luxury women's lifestyle magazine *die neue linie.*[85] Moholy-Nagy designed the cover of the magazine's first issue, which was published in September 1929 (Plate 23). Along with fashion, interior design, travel, and architecture, the magazine showcased some of Germany's most experimental graphic design, featuring a number of cover designs by Moholy-Nagy as well as Herbert Bayer, Otto Arpke, and Georg Teltscher. With a circulation of over forty thousand readers, the magazine was one of the most publicly accessible examples of Moholy-Nagy's graphic design work. He established photomontage as a signature feature of the large-format magazine's bold covers, announcing the relaunched publication as the domain of both modernist graphics and the modern woman.

In this design, Moholy-Nagy constructed a scene in which a woman stands in front of a floor-to-ceiling window. She looks out onto an untamed, rocky landscape and wears an elegant, fur-lined coat, shiny high heels, and a cloche hat. She is turned away almost completely so that no part of her body, not even a sliver of her face, is visually accessible. The coat is a proxy for the woman wearing it. The scene is interrupted by a palpable tension between illusion and material reality. The magazine cover is presented dually as a picture plane, recessing in space, and as the stubbornly flat surface that it is. Halftone fragments read simultaneously as a picture of a woman standing in front of a window and as flat planes arranged against other flat planes. The longer we look, the more the woman appears to float bizarrely in vaguely defined architectural space. Unlike in Tschichold's poster design, the letterforms of the magazine's title float indeterminately, unassimilated into the illusion of the scene. Type is instead a stubborn reminder that the only real surface is the paper on which the design is printed, a fact that Moholy-Nagy did not try to hide. The materiality of the magazine reminds us of the illusion that Moholy-Nagy has deftly constructed: iridescent silver ink pops out in contrast to bright red and blue ink and muted grays of photographic halftones, heightening the sense of realism suspended in a fantasy.

New Typography's reframing of retouching in terms of photomontage invited readers to see photography as graphic material rather than as a model for nonphotographic illustrations. Replacing the term "retouching" with "photomontage" suggested that New Typography had recovered the purity of photographic images, finally unconcealed. Championing the halftone as a symbol of its technology fetishism, New Typography aspired to reinvent photography in advertising, no longer beholden to what they regarded as outmoded conventions of prephotographic illustration. Photomontage also connoted a heightened sophistication among readers, who were assumed to be adept at recognizing the constructedness of modern design. This expectation of the reader underlies Moholy-Nagy's inaugural cover for *die neue linie*, which invited readers to see how photomontage could both create and interrupt narrative and spatial cohesion. Such a design challenged the overly simplistic assumptions about photography's "naturalism" that had dominated graphic design in the profession's earliest decades. Though photomontage had long been used in combination with retouching techniques, New Typography's rhetorical embrace of photomontage perpetuated discourse in the graphic design and printing world about the nature of photography and its persuasive possibilities.

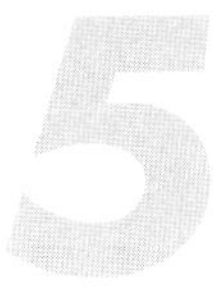

TYPOPHOTO AND THE PROFESSIONALIZATION OF GRAPHIC DESIGN

Munich Meisterschule für Deutschlands Buchdrucker, 1927–1932

There is no doubt that the graphic culture of the future will make a far greater use of photography than today. Photography will be as expressive of our age as the woodcut was of the Middle Ages. For this reason it is absolutely necessary for every graphic professional, even today, to develop creatively all the techniques of photography and reproduction as far as possible and prepare them for the higher demands that will surely be made of them in the near future.

—JAN TSCHICHOLD, *THE NEW TYPOGRAPHY: A HANDBOOK FOR MODERN DESIGNERS* (1928)

The story of New Typography tracks closely with the consolidation of the graphic design profession in Germany, which included graphic arts education reform. Modern printing technologies not only made the production of printed matter easier, faster, and cheaper, but they also facilitated training graphic designers in a wider array of professional skills. Given how formative the founding of professional schools around the turn of the twentieth century was for the nascent graphic design profession in Germany, surprisingly few have been studied.[1] While schools like the Dessau Bauhaus trained freelance designers—a relatively atypical model—far more schools were established in the early twentieth century that offered instruction in many aspects of graphic design, including the histories and traditions of printing, calligraphy, and bookmaking.[2] This chapter examines the founding curriculum and student work of one such school: the Meisterschule für Deutschlands Buchdrucker, located in Munich (referred to hereafter as the Meisterschule).[3] The school exemplified institutions where German graphic design was shaped by pedagogy, and it was a key site for experimentation with *Typophoto* as New Typography was codified.

On February 1, 1927, German typographer Paul Renner opened the Meisterschule with the goal of providing a combination of aesthetic instruction, theoretical grounding, and practical experience for future printing house proprietors.[4] The school was established in partnership with the Union of Munich Printing-House Proprietors (Verein Münchner Buchdruckerei Besitzer) and with funds from the German Printers Association (Deutscher Buchdrucker-Verein), an investment that personally benefited its members.[5] Indeed, a Meisterschule pamphlet printed circa 1932, designed by Jan Tschichold, explicitly specified that the school's main purpose was to train the sons of Deutscher Buchdrucker-Verein members: "The intention of the Deutsche Buchdrucker-Verein at the founding of the school has been achieved: the sons of its members and other ambitious young forces of the German book trade now have the opportunity to prepare **systematically and methodically** for their profession in Munich."[6] The muted, blue halftone illustration in the pamphlet depicts the disembodied process of offset printing, specifically the transfer of a photographic image onto a printing plate. This imagery highlighted the school's adoption of modern printing technology, emphasizing it as key to the "systematic" and "methodical" approach boasted by the pamphlet (Plate 24).[7]

In 1926, Renner had left his post at the Frankfurter Kunstschule, where he taught a preliminary course in typography, to direct the Graphische Berufsschule (Professional School for Graphics) in Munich,[8] which shared a campus with several other state- and city-sponsored trade schools. Renner soon established a new school—the adjoining Meisterschule.[9] Upon returning to Munich, he also began corresponding with Jan Tschichold with the initial intent of recommending that he take Renner's place at the Frankfurter Kunstschule, but ultimately invited Tschichold to join him in Munich. In June 1927, Tschichold began teaching at the Meisterschule, where he taught typography and calligraphy until immigrating with his family to Switzerland in 1933.[10] Renner's decision to hire Tschichold was motivated by an ambition to bring modernist design to the city of Munich, which Renner feared was retrograde in its resistance to innovation relative to Berlin and Frankfurt.[11]

Though not typically associated with interwar modernism, Munich was a key site for the development of New Typography. In the founding curriculum of the Meisterschule, some of New Typography's guiding principles were codified as pedagogical method. Soon after relocating to Munich in 1927, Jan and Edith Tschichold moved into the newly completed Borstei Wohnsiedlung, where their neighbors included Franz Roh and Georg Trump.[12] Designed by Bernhard Borst, the housing development was built between 1924 and in 1929.[13] Borstei's graphic identity—including the logo and lettering of its house numbers and shop signage—was designed by Eduard Ege, who also taught at the Meisterschule from 1927 until 1958.[14] The first five years of the Meisterschule were exceptionally momentous for the development of New Typography as a graphic design doctrine. While living at Borstei and teaching in Munich, Tschichold published his first book, *Die Neue Typographie* (1928). As he prepared it for publication in 1927 and 1928, he also gave a number of public lectures on New Typography in Munich.[15] He subsequently collaborated with Franz Roh on several books: *foto-auge* (1929), *László Moholy-Nagy: 60 Fotos* (1930), and *Aenne Biermann: 60 Fotos* (1930).[16] It was also during this period that he worked on a never-realized book on photomontage, intended as part of Roh's Fototek series on photography.[17]

Beyond Tschichold's connection to the school, study of the Meisterschule offers an expansive understanding New Typography's impact on the modern graphic design profession.[18] When László Moholy-Nagy introduced the idea of *Typophoto* in 1925, he declared, "The printer's work is part of the foundation on which the *new world* will be built."[19] It was fitting, then, that some of the most inventive explorations of *Typophoto* took place at a school founded to train future print masters. Experimental design at the Meisterschule was not confined to hypothetical designs responding to student assignments. Most of the school's official promotional materials—including brochures, prospectuses, and letterhead—were designed and printed by students, often in collaboration with instructors. The school's importance to New Typography was chiefly in explorations of *Typophoto* by students whose identities remain unknown. Their work is emblematic of the modern design school as a place where students receive training in professional best practices to test the boundaries of materials and technology. While manuals warned against printing halftones in light-colored ink to avoid the muddying of contrast and promoted the printer's ability to render halftone dots invisible, students and instructors at the Meisterschule played with color and abstract raster patterns as visible graphic elements.[20] By calling visual attention to the halftone in design, they made visible the labor of printing, thereby demonstrating how the technologies and skills of modern printing not only facilitated the mass dissemination of graphic design, but in fact made innovative design possible.

CRAFT AND TECHNOLOGY IN THE MODERN PRINT SHOP

Founded in 1927, the Meisterschule was located at Pranckhstraße 2 in Munich, the present-day campus of the Berufliches Schulzentrum Alois Senefelder München.[21] Since 1906, it has been a site for vocational training in typesetting, bookbinding, printing, and papermaking.[22] In an article published in 1931, typography instructor Josef Käufer described the mission of the Meisterschule in succinct terms: "to train the student theoretically and practically to become the head of a printing house."[23] The school's less explicit, but no less important, goal was to combine instruction and training in type design, typesetting, and printing by hand, as well as practices of industrial printing without sacrificing the quality of either. Käufer emphasized the need for future print masters to be trained in an array of skills—including the centuries-old practices of letterpress, calligraphy, punch-cutting, and bookbinding as well as business theory, scientific management, and law. The school claimed this combination as unique to its curriculum. Rather than training specialists in one particular trade, such as typography, the Meisterschule offered typographic instruction as part of a holistic understanding of the printing trade, in preparation for managing a printing house, and to "help [the student] understand the spiritual attitude of his business."[24] He described the Meisterschule as a community in which students gained practical skills and a deeper understanding of printing as a trade, motivated not by the forces of industrialization, but rather by the value of printed matter as an expression of culture.

Käufer characterized the school primarily as a workshop, a functioning printing house where students took turns performing each task, including playing the role of manager. According to Käufer, hands-on training served to unite students as a "working community" bound by a shared "work ethos" cultivated through firsthand knowledge of the challenges of leadership and collaborative work.[25] Students of different backgrounds and skillsets gained experience with a variety of machines, tools, and tasks. The gamut of skills needed in a modern printing house—including layout, typesetting, papermaking, bookbinding, platemaking, etching, and printing—were unified by the vision and managerial dexterity of its proprietor, who was expected to have at least a basic knowledge of all aspects of the graphic design and printing to ensure and balance both quality and efficiency. According to Käufer, this training ensured that each student "will inevitably become a useful member of our profession, regardless of where his special qualifications or predetermined path should lead."[26] His description implied the modern workshop as ideal for training not individual designers, but rather specialists of the trade who were well equipped for any task.

The Meisterschule was founded on the *Werkstatt* (workshop) model, a business type that emerged in the 1890s in Germany, operating as a semiautonomous firm that allowed artists control and ownership over the execution of their own designs.[27] In the context of the print shop, the *Werkstatt* model was intended to preserve the craft of printing and bookmaking by resisting the separation of concept and production that was prevalent in industrialized printing. After World War I, Renner and others sought to revitalize the fine book trade that had flourished prewar, seeing the professional trade school as a place where the values of the *Werkstatt* could be revived. The Meisterschule was founded to prepare future printing house proprietors as crafts- and businesspeople, equipped to maintain artistic and legal control and technical command of their future businesses. It operated as a small-scale firm that enabled students to solve modern design problems using both centuries-old techniques and new technologies.

The balance sought at the Meisterschule between teaching printing as a craft and a modern business was embodied by the career trajectory of its founder. Renner studied fine art at the Akademie der Bildenden Künste München and then studied graphics (*Graphik*) for a year at the Debschitz-Schule in Munich in 1906.[28] The Debschitz-Schule was particularly formative for Renner: the school was structured by workshops where students prototyped design for manufacture, and Renner received training in every aspect of book design.[29] If not a direct model for the Meisterschule, the graphics workshop of the Debschitz-Schule provided a template for the school as a small-scale print shop that retained the values of the early modern printing guild. Renner recognized in Tschichold a typographer who was trained in preindustrial techniques of calligraphy, hand-lettering, and punch-cutting, all of which were taught at the Meisterschule. At the same time, as a vocal advocate for New Typography, Tschichold also represented a new way of promoting type design as an expression of the modern Zeitgeist, which Renner saw as an asset to his new school.[30]

Käufer's description of the Meisterschule was published in a special issue of the *Archiv für Buchgewerbe und Gebrauchsgraphik* largely dedicated to the school and its instructors. It included a prospectus that outlined the two-year Meisterschule curriculum. Elaborating on Käufer's remarks, the published prospectus reflected the school's general aim to combine theoretical and practical training, promoting modern printing as both a craft and business requiring artistic skill, technical acumen, and business savvy. This balance was sought through practical experience as well as in the school's historical and theoretical offerings. Emphasis on the histories of calligraphy, bookbinding, and papermaking at the Meisterschule supported the ambition to retain craftsmanship in the modern print shop. At the same time, its facilities included modern technologies like rotary printing presses and Linotype machines.[31] Images published in another promotional prospectus feature students working with the school's up-to-date facilities and machinery (Figure 39).[32] The diverse facilities of the Meisterschule were meant to prepare students for printing not only books, but newspapers, magazines, and advertising as well. While the workshop environment offered students opportunities to sharpen practical skills and apply theories of business management and law, the Meisterschule also offered lectures on the histories of printing technology and the printing trade.

Typography courses at the Meisterschule were instructed—some jointly—by Tschichold, Käufer, Ege, Trump (between 1929 and 1931), and Herbert Post (starting in 1930).[33] They provided hands-on instruction in the traditional practices of calligraphy, drawing letterforms by hand, bookbinding, and manual typesetting, as well as mechanized typesetting and techniques of photomechanical reproduction. Although not primarily a typography school, courses on type composition (*Satz*) and training through formal writing exercises to help students understand letterforms (*Schriftschreiben*) were staples of the first-year program. These were considered outmoded methods of teaching the skills associated with typography at schools like the Bauhaus, where typographic design was taught through the construction of geometric forms.[34] Students at the Meisterschule were not encouraged to work exclusively with sans serif type, but rather challenged to create multiple specimens for a given assignment using several typefaces, including roman and *Fraktur*. This reflected Renner's belief that skilled designers should be well versed in using all available tools (including typeface) and choosing those best suited to the job at hand. Second-year instruction was dedicated to courses on general theories of business and advertising, as well as printing house management in particular, as students continued honing technical skills.[35] Training at the

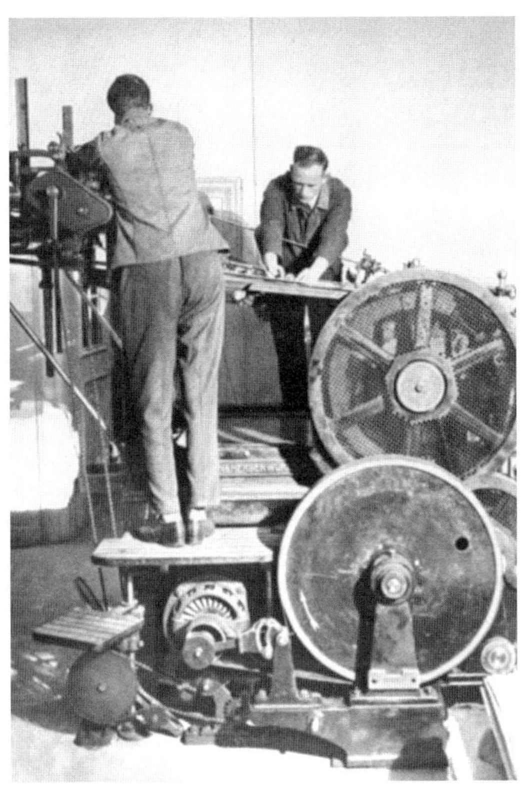

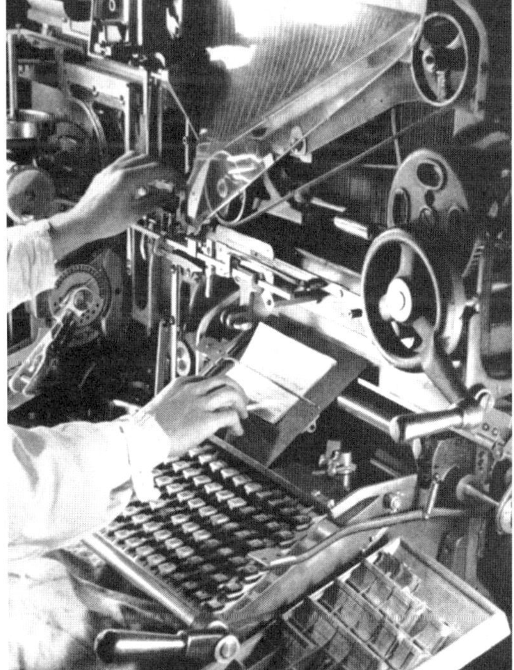

FIGURE 39 Jan Tschichold, prospectus design for the Meisterschule für Deutschlands Buchdrucker, circa 1932, offset lithography, including reproductions of Eduard Wasow photographs. Box 23, Nachlass Jan Tschichold, Deutsches Buch- und Schriftmuseum der Deutschen Nationalbibliothek, Leipzig.

Meisterschule included reprographic techniques such as stereotyping, electrotyping, zincography, etching, lithography, and halftone printing.[36]

The immediate result of this training was the design and production of many printed materials promoting the Meisterschule, as well as those made for neighboring trade schools. Through assignments, students demonstrated that the halftone could be much more than a tool for faithful image reproduction. In their designs, halftones operated as illustrations, optical devices, and compositional elements. Student designers deftly used the halftone as a technology that produced both representational and abstract images, which could be scaled up, printed in a spectrum of colors, and bled off the edges of the page (Plate 25). These designs not only gave the school a unique graphic identity, but also attested to the high quality of its training.

In 1932, the school's prestigious reputation earned its students the opportunity to take a final exam at the Meisterschule in lieu of the official exam traditionally required after a three-year apprenticeship to be certified as a professional printer in Bavaria.[37] By agreeing to this, the Chamber of Craft for Munich and Upper Bavaria (Handwerkskammer für München und Oberbayern) effectively stated that two years of training at the Meisterschule was equivalent to three years of apprenticeship under a master printer. The decision set a precedent for other vocational schools, namely the Meisterschule für das Buchdruckgewerbe Leipzig.[38] Although somewhat controversial, these moves helped solidify the place of modern vocational schools as integral to professional training.[39]

In its holistic operation as a functioning printing house, vocational training at the Meisterschule demonstrated the consolidation of the field of graphic design, represented by the term *Gebrauchsgraphik*. On one level, the school's approach was a practical response to a dilemma that permeated the German printing trade in the early twentieth century and, indeed, German culture more generally: How could established traditions be preserved while keeping pace with innovations in technology and modern business practice? With its roots no shallower than Gutenberg's fifteenth-century printing press, this dilemma was especially urgent for the German printing trade. Yet, the operation of the Meisterschule as both a school and a functioning, modern printing house also made an important statement about graphic design—namely, that the craft and technologies of printing were at the heart of its potential for innovation. Rather than privilege modern design as something that occurs separately from production, the Meisterschule exemplified how skills at every stage of production could drive design innovation. Nowhere was this suggested more forcefully than in the experimental approach to *Typophoto* in student assignments and printed ephemera promoting the Meisterschule.

ANOTHER NEW TYPOGRAPHY: GEORG TRUMP AND THE *BIELEFELDER RICHTUNG*

The instructor who seems to have had the greatest impact on the design aesthetic cultivated at the Meisterschule in its early years was German typographer Georg Trump. Fittingly, the issue of *Archiv für Buchgewerbe und Gebrauchsgraphik* that included Käufer's article on the workshop model of the school also featured a cover design by Trump (Plate 26). Divided in half by a black halftone grid, the design features a play of color and texture between different, layered halftones. One blossom from a spray of flowers, printed in red, spills into the abstract grid, interrupting its uniformity. This floral motif was a signature element in many of his productions. Red ink appears faded where the halftones overlap. This design exemplifies his interest in making visible the materiality of printing—especially individual ink colors and the halftone matrix. Rather than attempt to mimic the tones of a black-and-white photograph by hiding the halftone's raster pattern, the designer exaggerates it, turning the halftone itself into a visual motif. The design achieves a formal elegance, even softness, because of mechanization, not despite it.

Georg Trump's importance to the history of graphic design is primarily as a professor of typography and calligraphy starting in the 1920s, until his retirement from teaching in the early 1950s. From 1926 until 1929, he served as a professor of typography at the Handwerker- und Kunstgewerbeschule in the city of Bielefeld.[40] In 1929, at Renner's invitation, he left Bielefeld to join the faculty of the Meisterschule. Renner had first encountered Trump's work at the International Press Exhibition, commonly known as *Pressa*, held in Cologne in 1928. In 1931, Trump left Munich to direct the Berlin Kunstgewerbe- und Handwerkschule, and returned in 1934 to succeed Renner as director of the Meisterschule for nearly two decades.[41]

In the early 1930s, Georg Trump also established himself as a typeface designer who experimented with the halftone in commercial designs, some published in type specimens (Plates 27 and 28). Many of these designs incorporated color by printing halftones in colors other than black ink, giving photographic images a faded quality, against which text appears to pop. Another hallmark of his distinctive style was the combination of abstract raster patterns in contrast to halftones, which were used for more precise image reproduction. A full-page advertisement for Agfa cameras, for example, is

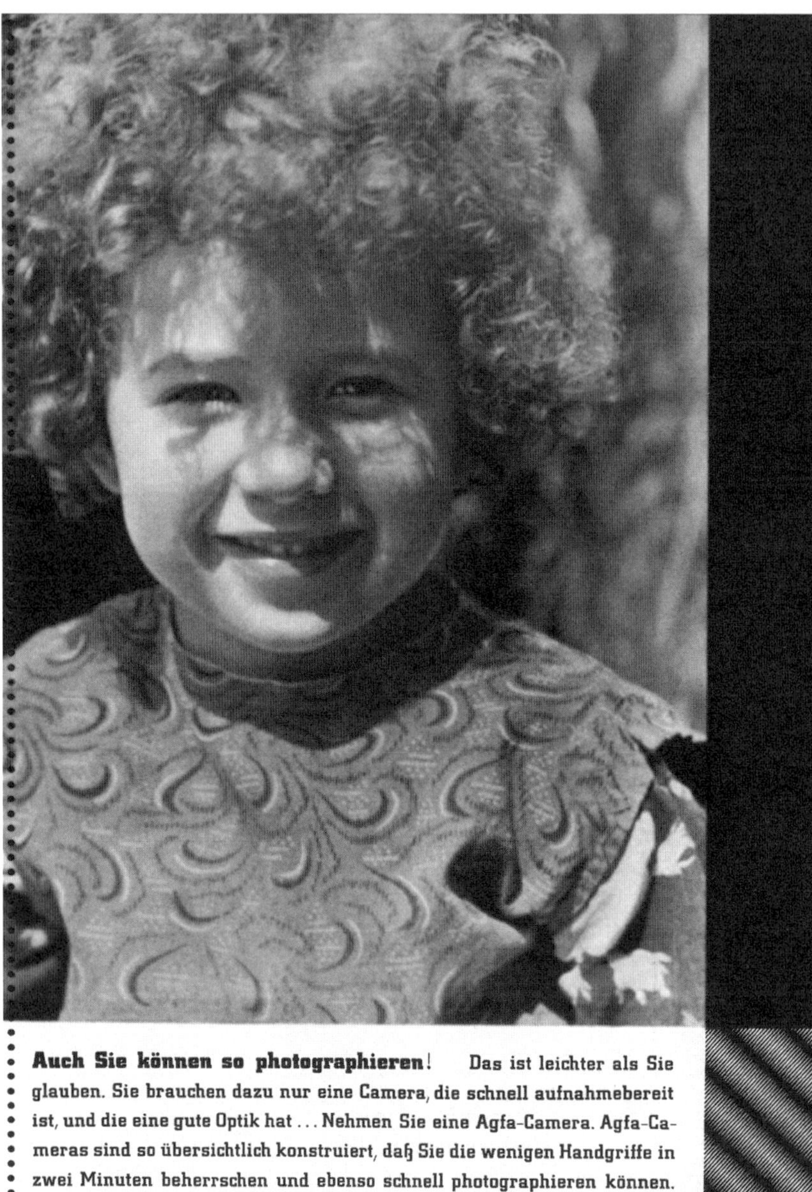

Auch Sie können so photographieren! Das ist leichter als Sie glauben. Sie brauchen dazu nur eine Camera, die schnell aufnahmebereit ist, und die eine gute Optik hat ... Nehmen Sie eine Agfa-Camera. Agfa-Cameras sind so übersichtlich konstruiert, daß Sie die wenigen Handgriffe in zwei Minuten beherrschen und ebenso schnell photographieren können. Die gute Agfa-Optik sorgt für scharfe, sauber durchgezeichnete Bilder. Agfa-Cameras gibt es schon für 36 Mark. Die abgebildete Standard-Rollfilm-Camera Nr. 254 für das Bildformat 6x9 cm mit dem vorzüglichen Agfa-Anastigmaten F:4,5 und dem zuverlässigen Agfa-Automatverschluß kostet 78 Mark.

AGFA-CAMERAS

agfa

divided asymmetrically into quarters (Figure 40). Each of its four panels are occupied by a different kind of graphic material: a crisp halftone reproduction of a photographic portrait of a child; a solid monochrome rectangle of black ink; black text printed on the white background of the page; and the Agfa logo printed against a black-and-white, raster-patterned background.

The prominence of the raster in the Agfa advertisement suggests a relationship between the technical dexterity of manipulating and printing halftones and the quality of the camera that captured the image translated on the page. Trump used the visible halftone pattern to explore photography not as an objective image of the world captured by the camera's lens, but rather as a visible screen through which readers must look to see photographs in print. In his work, the raster is a visual reminder that photography is mediated by the mechanisms of printing. When printed as a halftone, photography is visually restructured according to the logic of the grid; in turn, the grid becomes embedded in the photographic image. Rather than exploit the "halftone's ability to masquerade as a photograph," as Gerry Beegan has described, Trump instead celebrated the graphic nature of the halftone as truly photographic.[42] In his hands, the halftone was a unique image type with its own aesthetic possibilities, not a technique meant to operate invisibly. Trump's designs, and those of his students, invited readers to relish the visual complexity of the halftone, rather than ignore it.

Trump became known in the German printing and graphic design world as the chief exponent of a distinct alternative to Tschichold's New Typography, known as the Bielefeld Direction (*Bielefelder Richtung*). The 1931 issue of *Archiv für Buchgewerbe und Gebrauchsgraphik* featuring the Meisterschule included a profile on Trump by Otto Bettmann, who cited *Pressa* as the event that not only caught Renner's attention, but also brought the designer's work to prominence among a wide circle of German graphic designers.[43] Like many graphic designers of his generation, Trump was trained in typography, but his work was not limited to the graphic arts.[44] Bettmann emphasized the expansiveness of his artistic practice as evidence that craft was at the center of all of his work. According to Bettmann, Trump considered his nontypographic work "his more essential achievements," despite being known primarily as a typographer.[45] Bettmann described the designer's typographic approach as nonformulaic, "artisan-oriented," and consistently responsive to materials.[46]

FIGURE 40 Georg Trump, design for Agfa AG, City prospectus, Berthold AG, circa 1931, offset lithograph. Collection Merrill C. Berman.

These qualities evidently extended to Trump's teaching: "He does not let the students commit themselves to dogmatic forms. He rather forces them to rethink every work from scratch—but it also forces them to remain strictly grounded by technical conditions."[47] Despite his embrace of modern technology and use of ample white space and heavy, geometric typefaces, Trump resisted Tschichold's doctrinaire approach to typography, an attitude that earned him a reputation as an alternative New Typographer.

Yet, this distinction was immaterial to those in the German printing world who regarded any overtly modernist graphic style as a threat to centuries-old tradition, especially as it seemed to infiltrate the way typographers and printers were trained at places like the Meisterschule. Trump's influence on his students in Bielefeld, Munich, and Berlin in the 1920s and 1930s was conspicuous. In January 1932, an editorial was printed in *Typographische Mitteilungen* describing how the designer's departure from Munich to Berlin in 1931 had prompted renewed critique of New Typography (broadly defined) by designers who saw his pedagogical influence as a threat to typographic tradition.[48] The piece referred to a number of letters received by various trade periodicals, including *Offset* and *Deutscher Drucker,* from concerned typographers dismissing and even admonishing outright the work of Trump and the *Bielefelder Richtung.*[49] One such letter accused the New Typographers of being "objectivity fanatics" (*Sachlichkeitsfanatiker*) whose work was devoid of creativity.[50] Defenders of New Typography, such as Bettmann and the editors of *Typographische Mitteilungen,* defended his work against such accusations.

In particular, Bettmann cited Trump's integration of photography into his work as exemplary of thoughtful artistry. He described Trump's designs for André Reuze's 1928 novel about the Tour de France, *Giganten der Landstraße,*[51] as a shining example of Trump's deft handling of photography in graphic design: "Trump boldly approached this task. He gives each picture a special position on the page, a special size, depending on its content and meaning, so that its true unity of type and photo is created."[52] Using photographic halftones as both representational images and as abstract, graphic elements reflected Trump's apparent conviction that artistry and technology were not at odds, but rather should go hand in hand. This was perhaps best expressed in 1930, when he created a cover for *Deutscher Drucker,* one of many German periodicals dedicated to the graphic arts and new printing techniques (Plate 29). The focus of the design is a circular photographic image of reprographic machinery. Its visual continuity is interrupted by vectors that splice the image into asymmetrical segments, filtered with vibrant, orange ink applied in

Winkelhaken aus „Nirosta"? Es bedarf gewiß nur einer Anregung, um eine einschlägige Firma zu veranlassen, für Winkelhaken den Chromstahl, z. B. „Nirosta", zu verwenden. Der Winkelhaken wäre wohl kaum teurer als ein Neusilber„löffel", greift sich aber nicht so leicht ab. Der eiserne Winkelhaken muß von Zeit zu Zeit mit Öl und Bimsstein behandelt werden, was ihm wenig zuträglich ist. Ein Chromstahl-Winkelhaken hätte diese Nachteile aber ganz bestimmt nicht. Heinzel

Die erste deutsche Zeitung. In der Universitätsbibliothek zu Heidelberg befindet sich ein fast vollständig erhaltener Jahrgang einer Zeitung aus dem Jahre 1609. Der Titel lautet wörtlich: „Relation Aller fürnemmen vnd gedenkwürdigen Historien, so sich hin vnnd wider in Hoch vnd Nieder Teutschland, auch in Frankreich, Italien, Schott vnd Engelland, Hisspanien, Hungeren, Polen, Siebenbürgen, Wallachey, Moldaw, Türkey etz. In diesem 1609 Jahre verlauffen vnd zutragen möchten. Alles auf das trewlichst wie ich solche bekommen vnd zu wegen bringen mag, in Truck verfertigen will." Ein Druckort ist nicht angegeben. Der in Schweinsleder gebundene Jahrgang enthält 52 Wochennummern und 115 Quartblätter, jede Nummer durchschnittlich zwei Blätter.

Aus Sowjetrußland wird berichtet, daß die Sowjetregierung eine vollständige Herausgabe der Werke Leo Tolstois veranlaßt habe. Wladimir Tschertkow, Schüler und Freund Tolstois, dem die Gesamtausgabe übertragen worden ist, arbeitet mit einem Ausschuß von Gelehrten und Schriftstellern zusammen. Von den geplanten 90 Bänden liegen 42 im druckreifen Manuskript vor. Die Ausgabe soll nicht nur den Originaltext der Tolstoischen Werke wiedergeben, sondern sie wird auch bisher nicht veröffentlichte Briefe des Dichters, sein Tagebuch und eine Fülle an ihn gerichteter Schreiben aus der ganzen Welt umfassen. In den Archiven der Leningrader öffentlichen Bibliothek wurde, wie die Telegraphenagentur der Sowjetunion meldet, eine Reihe Originalhandschriften Goethes gefunden, einige Gedichte ohne Überschriften im Album des Dichters Schukowskij und nicht veröffentlichte Briefe an Herder.

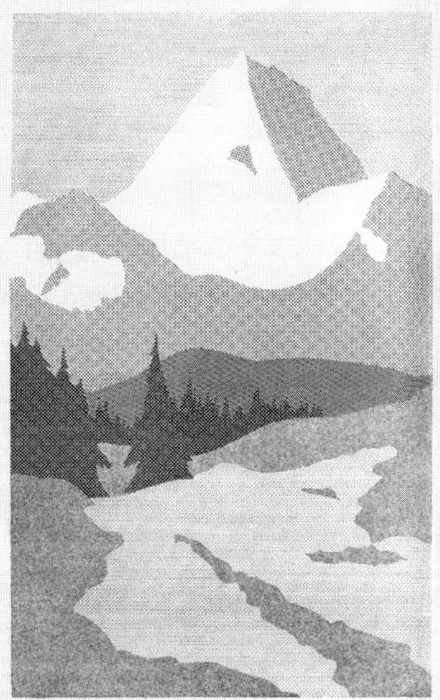

Entwurf von H. Becker

Aus der Verkaufspraxis, September 1931

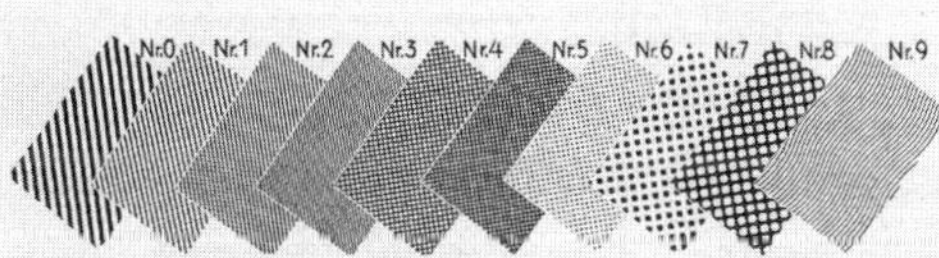

Rasterpapiere für Entwurfsarbeiten in zehn verschiedenen Mustern zeigen uns die Abbildungen auf dieser Seite. Das Anwendungsbeispiel führt die vielseitige Verwendbarkeit derartiger Rasterpapiere für die Entwurfstechnik trefflich vor Augen. Wir haben die besonderen Vorteile auch im Heft 5 hervorgehoben, so daß sich weitere Ausführungen erübrigen. Diese Rasterpapiere, herausgebracht von der Firma Spitta & Leutz, Berlin SW 68, können auch vom Verlag des Bildungsverbandes der Deutschen Buchdrucker bezogen werden

Für den modernen Menschen ist ein Verständnis des großen Geschehens in Natur und Kultur, Politik und Wirtschaft ohne genaue Kenntnis erdkundlichen Verhältnisses undenkbar. Der Augenblick ist daher gegeben, diese Wissenschaft in den Dienst des praktischen Lebens zu stellen und der Zeit zu geben, was sie wünscht und sucht: einen Führer und Berater, der mehr gibt als trockene Schulweisheit. Von diesen Gesichtspunkten ausgehend, darf man das Handbuch der geographischen Wissenschaft, herausgegeben von Prof. Dr. Fritz Klute an der Universität Gießen unter Mitwirkung namhafter Fachgelehrten, als Höchstleistung wissenschaftlicher Arbeit ansehen. Da es unsere Leser interessieren wird, möchten wir nicht verfehlen, an dieser Stelle auf die Anzeige der Firma Artibus et literis, Gesellschaft für Geistes- und Naturwissenschaften m. b. H., Berlin-Nowawes (137) hinzuweisen.

118

FIGURE 41 Advertisement for Spitta and Leutz raster paper (and detail), *Typographische Mitteilungen* 29, no. 5 (May 1932): 118. Letterform Archive, San Francisco.

varying values. The image appears as if through a prism of contiguous, tinted screens or photographic filters. The intended reader—likely a professional printer—is challenged to mentally reconstitute the image, hyperaware of the printing techniques flaunted in this design.

Strikingly, an article in the same issue of *Deutscher Drucker* by Otto Mente discussed the difficulty of reading photographic images through distracting moiré patterns that could result from the halftone process. Mente credited the perfection of offset printing, aided by tilting halftone screens at a forty-five-degree angle, with the prevention of this unwanted visual effect.[53] Yet, Georg Trump's cover design did not simply celebrate the capacity of the offset rotary press to render the halftone matrix invisible; rather, it showed how the grid itself could be useful as an element of visual play with color, texture, and contrast. In his cover design, Trump deftly combined abstract moiré patterns with crisp photographic images reproduced using finer halftone screens. He also experimented with different patterns to facilitate the interplay of line and color, enticing readers to linger over the complexity of the composition before opening the magazine. The cover combined five distinct moiré patterns, each demarcated by an orange panel and thin white border. As in many of Trump's designs, *Typophoto* is presented here as a hybrid medium with endless possibilities for sophisticated visual play with combinations of representational and abstract form.

Trump's cover for *Deutscher Drucker* demonstrated how designers could master the official rules of printing, in part, so they could undermine them. By doing so, he demonstrated technical knowledge and skill, but little deference to professional dogmatism—attitudes he evidently imparted to his students at the Meisterschule. Yet, he was not unique in his use of halftone patterns. An advertisement for raster paper by the firm Spitta and Leutz in *Typographische Mitteilungen* shows that there was a market in the early 1930s for using raster patterns as graphic form (Figure 41). The advertisement includes ten samples of raster-patterned paper, presented like fabric swatches, alongside an illustration of a landscape constructed entirely out of contrasting raster patterns. Experimental uses of the halftone like Georg Trump's suggested a sophisticated understanding of the technologies and materials of modern printing. His approach became a tacit part of Meisterschule pedagogy.

ZUR FARBENLEHRE: COLOR THEORY AND COLOR PRINTING AT THE MEISTERSCHULE

Color theory and color printing were emphasized throughout the Meisterschule curriculum, owing especially to Renner's particular interest in the subject. He authored an undated booklet, *Zur Farbenlehre,* written circa 1930 and printed at the Meisterschule, which outlined his own principles for teaching and applying color theory in design.[54] This text would later become the basis for Renner's 1947 book *Ordnung und Harmonie der Farben. Eine Farbenlehre für Künstler und Handwerker.*[55] One section of Renner's booklet is dedicated to the subject of teaching color theory, which provides a window into instruction at the Meisterschule.[56] In keeping with the school's stated mission to combine theory and practice, he described the application of theoretical principles to hands-on student assignments. He emphasized the importance of teaching students how to see color and recognize color relationships found in nature. He described, for example, assignments in which students were instructed to play with an array of colored paper in different sizes to observe how color relationships appear to change through juxtaposition, and to collect objects in nature for the purpose of similar observation. Given Renner's deep interest in color theory and comments on his pedagogical approach to training designers in the subject, it is not surprising that many extant student assignments from courses at the Meisterschule demonstrate the manipulation of the photographic halftone through color printing.

One such example is an anonymous student design of a speculative cover for the August 1931 issue of *Gebrauchsgraphik,*[57] arguably the most important graphic design journal published in Weimar Germany (Plate 30).[58] Lavishly printed in black, blue, yellow, and red ink, the design epitomizes the manipulation of photography as graphic material by calling particular attention to the malleability of the halftone grid. In this design, the journal's masthead is printed in all-lowercase letters, set in Georg Trump's slab serif typeface City.[59] The black text overlays three triangular photographic images of flowers, which begin in neat wedges at their base and fan out across the page like an abstracted bouquet. The flowers in this design are made from the same printer's stereotype that Georg Trump used in an advertisement for City, which was published by the Berlin type foundry Berthold AG in 1931.[60] Both this specific iconography and the playful approach to color printing and form suggest the strong influence of Trump on his students. Compared to the cover of *Gebrauchsgraphik* that was actually published in August 1931—which reproduced a painting by Munich-based, Polish commercial artist Valentin Zietara in the style of

Sachplakat advertising—this speculative design is unusual in featuring intricate, overprinted halftones, showcasing both an artistic and technical acumen.[61]

Halftones are employed in this design to experiment with asymmetrical composition, primary color relationships, and the optical effects of patterns. The lower quarter of the page is banded with a solid raster pattern printed in black ink, its uniform grid of dots intersected by a half circle and a slice of the red flowers. The photographic print from which these halftones were made was cut such that the wild, unevenly shaped flower heads appear as though they are bursting out of the perfectly geometric right angle that photography has forced them into. The images are confined not only by the photographic frame but by the typographic grid as well. The solid black grid in the lower half of the page echoes the spacing of letters within the regularity of the typographic grid. This part of the design, though purely nonrepresentational, is perhaps the most important: it anchors the colorful, photographic halftones to the band of black text printed at the top of the page. The band of black dots—a pattern that hybridizes text and image—suggests a perceptual mode somewhere between seeing and reading.

The halftone bouquet described above is created through careful arrangement of overlapping fragments, each printed in a different color and rotated clockwise in succession, new colors and patterns created by their overlap. Overprinting of each of the four colors—blue, yellow, red, and black—creates greens, dark blues, pinks, and dark grays. These overlaps make it difficult to discern exactly where each halftone begins and ends, and to see that the floral images printed in blue, yellow, and red ink are in fact identical fragments printed from a single photograph. The reader's eye is compelled to move around the page to solve a visual riddle, dazzled in the process by unexpected juxtapositions of color and form. Abstract forms tangle together like flower stems. The clean corners of each floral halftone meet at the center of the half circle, completed not on the page, but in the mind's eye. Eventually, the underlying structure of the layout becomes clear: the halftones printed in blue, yellow, and red are each right-angled corners, rotated so that they overlap in thirty-degree-angle slivers. Seen this way, the halftones create a partial color wheel, demonstrating the relationships between primary colors. Each halftone is internally structured by the raster grid. Representational, reproductive, and visual possibilities of the photographic medium are harnessed in this design as tools for formal experiment and cognitive stimulation in graphic space.

Beyond the stylistic influence of instructors like Georg Trump, this design demonstrates a sophisticated understanding of color perception among students at the Meisterschule. In Renner's writings and teachings on color theory from the 1930s and 1940s, he sought to balance purely scientific theories of color—based on the empirical measurement of light-producing rays—with a more intuitive and subjective approach to the use of color in art and design. In doing so, he built on the ideas put forward in Johann Wolfgang von Goethe's *Zur Farbenlehre* (1810), a theoretical treatise that sought to distinguish the phenomenon of color perception from visible color. Following Goethe, Renner further bracketed the physical and physiological phenomena of color perception from five basic meanings of "color" as visual or material: as coloring matter (pigment); as an inherent characteristic possessed by an object or image; as an unfixed appearance caused by retinal sensation; as a general family of hues; and as a condition of being "colored," in contradistinction to "colorless."[62] Renner demonstrated a careful understanding of prevailing scientific theories of optics, extending Goethe's position that color is best understood in terms of the "perceived harmonies" created when two or more colors are juxtaposed. Despite all that was known about color through measuring the wavelengths of light rays, he contended this was of little use to artists and designers who sought to create harmonious color combinations in their work.[63]

Much of Renner's 1947 book on color, an expanded version of the Meisterschule booklet, was dedicated to a discussion of how artists and designers should create harmonious juxtapositions of two or more colors in their work. This was based on Goethe's understanding of colors as "dialectical effects," as media theorist Friedrich Kittler put it—that contrasts between colors, and embedded within colors, were integral to understanding them as perceptual phenomena.[64] Goethe had asserted that effective color combinations could create a sense of visual totality.[65] Renner quoted Goethe directly to posit that one must understand the importance of complementary color relationships to create harmonious combinations, thereby satisfying the eye's innate "need for totality."[66] In Renner's words, "[Goethe] believed that the secret of all color harmony could be traced back to the fact that the eye, through looking at any one color, becomes hungry for the complementary color."[67] Understanding the phenomenon of visual perception as stimulus for—and fulfillment of—an innate human desire was crucial for a designer whose goal was to capture the visual attention of a beholder.

Renner advocated for a mix of contrasts—making use of the tension between complementary colors—and harmonies, especially in combining more than two colors. He discussed at length what he called the three "opposition pairs," which he proposed as classifications for any hue: "color direction" (light/dark); "color value" (pure/cloudy); and "color purity" (warm/cold).[68] He insisted that all three aspects of color must be accounted for in evaluating combinations of contrasting and harmonious colors:

> If we want to understand the interchangeable relations between contiguous colors then we must learn to experience each separate color in this threefold contrast in which it is suspended. The cloudier and grayer a color is, the more tension it will have in contrast to all pure and strong colors; the brighter it is, the more tension it will have to all dark colors. And, what a conflagration the contrast of neighboring complementary colors can kindle!
>
> The dialectic relation of contiguous colors gets its tension, its liveliness, through these contrasts of color direction, value, and purity. This dialectic becomes a witty, delightful conversation only if there is in at least one of these three determinants of every hue an agreement or some similarity that joins the colors to one another and creates confidence, without which any harmonious gathering, even of colors, is impossible.[69]

Following Goethe, Renner emphasized the importance of using color relationships to create compositional unity in art or design. Renner's account of the dialectics of color as "a witty, delightful conversation" is telling of what he regarded as the utility of color theory: graphic designers could use the dialectical relationship between colors to create aesthetic discipline in their work, intuited by readers through perception. The "confidence" to which he referred belongs to the reader who, perhaps subconsciously, experiences a sense of harmony in a design. Through the deft handling of color printing and keen understanding of color perception, designers instill their work with a kind of trustworthiness. This is perhaps best demonstrated in the way students played with halftones in their assignments at the Meisterschule, using them as forms embedded with dialectical relationships—between contrasting colors, between abstraction and representation, and between playfulness and control.

Anonymous student designs made at the Meisterschule tested how complementary colors could create compositional unity in design. In doing so, they often demonstrated the complementarity and even interchangeability of photographic images and type as graphic elements. As discussed above in chapter 1 of this book, Tschichold first mobilized the term *Typophoto* to describe how photographic images could operate more like type. Students at the Meisterschule took this a step further by suggesting that type could also mimic certain aspects of photography, bolstering the idea that photographic halftones belonged to the printed page. As graphic material, the halftone could be treated as an element selectively interchangeable with type. Through the manipulation of color and scale, type and halftone could operate together as a complex system of signification masquerading as simple, clean design.

A brochure for bookbinding instruction at the adjoining Graphische Berufsschule, for example, used color halftone printing and sans serif type to convey a tacit message about the value of retaining craftsmanship in bookbinding for the modern printer. The brochure includes halftones printed in blue and red, which appear to recede into the page, while text set in black or a complementary color appears solid and more immediately legible by contrast. The halftones have been transformed into seemingly translucent screens with visible texture and depth using colored ink. The effect is to soften the photographic images, both visually and conceptually. If the halftone, printed in black ink, was meant to instantiate the immediacy of photography in print, the colored halftone had a more ethereal quality, like an image conjured by a dream or memory. The oneiric quality of these images paired with sans serif type evokes a harmonious confrontation between past and present—a nostalgia for the tradition of bookbinding is met with the bold, present-day innovation of modern design.

Color printing and complementary color relationships were also used at the Meisterschule to mimic the chemical aspects of the photographic medium through their translation into graphic elements using the halftone process, thereby suggesting the inherently graphic nature of all photography. For example, the anonymous student design of a brochure titled *Moderne Fensterdekorationen*, produced for the Munich textile manufacturer Indathrenhaus, evoked the positive–negative reversibility of photography just as it overtly aimed to suggest the material luxury of modern drapery (Plate 31). Here, similar photographic fragments are printed in complementary blue and red inks, echoing the reversal between a photographic positive and negative. The halftones also bear evidence of photographic reversal: they alternate panels that appear as positive and negative representations of decorative motifs. They appear to float like filmstrips in a bath of developer, images just beginning to emerge like hazy apparitions from their emulsions. Their translucent quality implies an analogous relationship between the delicacy of photographic materials and fine fabric.

These vegetal forms constituted by light and shadow recall nineteenth-century cameraless photographs, which long predated the avant-garde "photogram," by photographers such as British botanist Anna Atkins.[70] The first volume of her treatise *British Algae: Cyanotype Impressions* (1843) was the first book to include photographic illustrations.[71] Atkins used the cyanotype process to create direct impressions of botanical specimens on chemically treated paper. These two-dimensional images gave a tangible sense of the particular heft, solidity, and translucency of different objects, rendered through the action of light passing through and bouncing off surfaces of varying opacity and transparency. Likewise, the abstracted draperies that grace the Indathrenhaus brochure's cover as halftones appear materially palpable, using the stippled halftone to evoke the translucent surface of a textile penetrated and dappled by light and shadow.

The photographic quality of these halftones is also evoked in their orientation on the page. The halftones are flipped, mimicking how positive and negative images from the same photographic exposure read as mirror images when viewed side by side. The red halftone bleeds off the left-hand side of the page, while the smaller blue halftone—perhaps a direct nod to the cyanotype—bleeds off the top edge of the page, oriented at a slight diagonal so that the halftones intersect. *Moderne* describes not only the dyed textiles made possible by the titan German chemical manufacturer IG Farben, but also the processes of photography, the halftone, and offset printing that have been used to translate chemical dyes into printed form and the translucency of fabric into the language of photography. Like many German commercial designs from the late 1920s that incorporated photographic illustration, the modernity of the product for sale is substantiated by photographic representation, emphasized further by calling attention to the halftone.

Designs such as this one evidence the conscious manipulation of photographic halftones by graphic designers. Savvy design enabled by modern printing technology could approximate the inherent characteristics of photography through purely graphic means. Doing so suggested that the printed page was a natural habitat for the photographic medium. In effect, this use of the halftone implied the merging of two seemingly opposite aspects of photography—what Kaja Silverman has called "liquid intelligence" and "optical intelligence" in reference to photography as a chemical and mechanical process.[72] Students' treatment of the photographic halftone as a graphic element suggested that chemical and industrial forms of photography might be truly complementary, rendered as such through skillful printing.

Design in the early years of the Meisterschule illuminates an important meaning of *Typophoto:* an approach to the printed halftone as a distinct tool of graphic design, definitively native to the printed page, and thus subject to specific criteria for understanding photography in print and what it can do. Whereas Moholy-Nagy and Tschichold, in their discussions of *Typophoto,* emphasized the halftone as a means of translating photography into a graphic medium, students at the Meisterschule took this a step further. Their designs incorporated the halftone as an element always already belonging to the printed page. Rather than trying to emulate photographic prints, they showcased the halftone as a graphic element with which to test the technical limitations of printing. In their hands, halftones were subject to manipulations of scale, color, value, and layout, just like letterforms. Their designs embraced what British philosopher Bertrand Russell in 1923 characterized as the "vagueness" of some photographic images.[73] This concept is key to understanding how designers have consciously used photographic halftones as graphic elements.

Russell attempted to define "vagueness"—in contradistinction to "accuracy" or "precision"—within a larger discussion of representation, both textual and visual, as a central problem of philosophy. He proposed that, whereas representational precision denotes a one-to-one relationship between sign and signified, "a representation is vague when the relation of the representing system to the represented system is not one-one, but one-many."[74] He cited photography as an example of both kinds of relations—in some cases, the medium could emulate the likeness of a particular subject with visual accuracy, producing a specific representation. However, in other instances, photographic images act as more generalized representations. He used the example of a "smudged" photograph depicting a man, which might be used to represent men in general rather than one particular individual. Architect Michelle Chang borrows Russell's term to help explain why "vague" images, namely blurred and pixelated photographic images, are so ubiquitous in twenty-first century architectural rendering.[75]

Both the JPEG and printed halftone are digitized in the sense that they convert the continuous data (or tones) of a photograph into what Lev Manovich has called the "sampled" data of the halftone or pixel grid.[76] Chang's discussion of how twenty-first-century architects make use of blurry or pixelated digital photographs in architectural rendering is valuable in thinking about the efficacy of abstracted or imprecise reproductions of photographs as halftones in graphic design. Chang recognizes that blurred or pixelated photographic images retain the medium's association with accuracy, even while gaining new connotative meaning by virtue of their visual imprecision: "While abstraction can be conceived as a critical methodology for responding to formal intricacy, in raster imagery it is possible to work with both seemingly opposing concepts at once. That is, articulation in the medium can coexist with inarticulation in the content. In raster images, any blurriness makes identifying content difficult, even though the pictorial structure has the capacity to carry millions of discrete bits of information."[77] Chang raises an important paradox of digitized, mass-circulated photographic images: while the halftone or pixel grid is an "articulate"—or data rich—material translation of a single photograph into hundreds or thousands of dots or pixels, it is one that nevertheless disarticulates content. This disarticulation can be useful in transforming the message of an image from too specific to just vague enough. By eroding the visual precision of a photographic image as a sign, it is allowed to signify in far more capacious ways, as Bertrand described.

The disarticulation of photographic images has been useful in graphic design as a means of converting images into a kind of text. In pondering the efficacy of breaking continuous images into quantifiable data, Manovich recognizes digital conversion as more than merely technologically expedient. He writes, "But why, we may ask, are modern media technologies often in part discrete? The key assumption of modern semiotics is that communication requires discrete units. Without discrete units, there is no language."[78] In essence, digitization turns images into elements of communication. Visual information must be broken up into what Manovich calls "discrete units"—whether halftone dots or letterforms—to be read and assigned meaning.[79] He suggests, therefore, that a halftone or JPEG is legible as information in a way that a photograph could never be. Understanding digitization in these terms forces us to understand New Typography's appeal to the "legibility" of halftones in an entirely new way. Tschichold, in *Die Neue Typographie* (1928), made explicit claims to the precision of halftones, and Moholy-Nagy referred to them as "visual facts."[80] In practice, however, halftones were legible as information due to their visual imprecision. At the same time, they were also regarded as faithful translations of actual photographs. The halftone thus accrued status as "information" both by its association with the indexical medium of photography and through its digitization into discrete, legible units.

Students at the Meisterschule flaunted their skills as printers by calling visual attention to the digitization of photographic images in print. In doing so, they also allowed photographs to function flexibly in terms of meaning. When used as illustrations, halftones were sufficiently vague, inviting prospective students to imagine themselves in a classroom or workshop of a vocational school. One such example was a brochure for the neighboring Meisterschule für Mode, designed by students at the Meisterschule,[81] printed in red and black ink, with type set in Georg Trump's City and Paul Renner's Futura.[82] The brochure integrates photography not just as illustration, but also as material that appears as though part of the substrate of the page. In one spread that outlined the departmental structure of the school, for example, it is clear how *Typophoto* could create an organizational logic that eclipsed the typographic grid. Thin, horizontal rules run across the gutter between pages, breaking the grid and unifying the two-page spread into a unified chart of information. The organization of the pages superimposed by the horizontal rules is reinforced by the placement of the photographic image, printed to fit precisely into the upper-left quadrant of the chart.

In an elevated view of an instructor working with two students, the photographic image is printed in a pale red ink, its color muted by the dispersal of ink by the halftone grid, necessarily losing visual information that would normally be legible in a black-and-white photograph. Black rules are printed over the image. The placement of the rules and color of the halftone effectively renders the image a backdrop to the text on the page, rather than an illustration of its contents. This photographic image is representational, yet it functions more like the rules—as an abstract, graphic element that creates spatial logic. The images seem to recede back, their hues and pictorial detail diluted by the pattern of the halftone grid and ink color, given an almost ghostly quality. As such, they suggest the representation of instructor and students as prefigured, rather than captured in the present, by the camera. In this sense, the halftone transforms not only the material of the photographic image, but its temporality as well. Black text, by contrast, appears to pop out from the page toward the reader, insistently present.

On the brochure's cover, black type is again printed over the pale red ink of a halftone fragment, picturing a woman looking at herself in a two-way mirror (Plate 32). Two thin, diagonal rules buttress the thrice-repeated figure of the woman, pictured from three angles, suggesting the mirrored surfaces that we imagine to be part of the photograph from which these fragments were taken. They create a sense of architectural space, even while the text at the top reinforces the flatness of the page. Typographic and photographic elements are brought together subtly by a line of text printed toward the bottom of the page, bearing the school's street address. Printed diagonally, the address follows the bottommost line that cuts off the dress in the woman's reflection. Photographic fragments simultaneously interrupt and rhyme with the arrangement of type on the page.

Throughout this brochure, as in many early Meisterschule designs, photography and type are used as complementary elements—one dark, the other light; one muted, the other saturated—to test the rigidity of the typographic grid and the rules of printing. The resulting designs are characterized by visual complexity using deceptively simple means. However, through the material economy of two-color printing, another kind of complexity is created—on the level of meaning. The ghostly halftones appear like images remembered or imagined, their details lost to both the eye and the mind. They are visually and conceptually vague, more connotative than denotative. As such, they function more like text that requires reader interpretation than as illustration meant to provide a clear and immediate visual account. Just as the materials produced in the early years of the Meisterschule figure the labor of printing into their designs, so do they require the labor of reading. By inviting readers to linger, speculate, or remember, these designs make modern printing itself an object of contemplation, rather than merely an expedient means of delivering information.

EPILOGUE

Halftone Effects

I love all dots. I am married to many of them. I want all dots to be happy. Dots are my brothers. I am a dot myself.

—**SIGMAR POLKE, *POLKE/RICHTER* (1966)**

Images scatter into data, data gather into images.

—**PETER GALISON, "IMAGES SCATTER INTO DATA, DATA GATHER INTO IMAGES" (2002)**

Pixelating or blurring has taken over the role of authenticity. A pixelated picture must surely be authentic if it has unacceptable areas which are concealed. . . . It therefore seems clear that pixels stand for authentification: authentication through authority.

—**THOMAS HIRSHHORN, *PIXEL-COLLAGE* (2016)**

The November 1941 issue of *Gebrauchsgraphik* featured a striking cover design by Wilm Wahl, filled almost entirely by the pattern of a photographic halftone printed in white ink against a black background (Figure 42).[1] Zoomed in so much that the image of a woman's face is almost imperceptible, the design readily exposes the mechanical regularity of the halftone grid. Despite being tilted at a forty-five-degree angle to the page (presumably to avoid moiré effect when printed at intended size), every dot is clearly visible. The logic of the grid overtakes that of the likeness of a human face, the contours of her head and chin lost in an abstract visual field. Wahl's design nodded to the strangeness of an image type that had become entirely commonplace, reminding readers that the halftone was a type of media that they had dutifully learned to ignore through repeated exposure. The blown-up image thwarted the halftone's usual optical trickery, urging readers to consider the imprecision of legibility. Already in the 1940s, the visible halftone pattern read as a vintage throwback to a time when this technology was new.

As in the 1920s, the halftone has continued to bear collective anxieties about how craft in design can coexist with technological change. Starting in the 1970s, as graphic designers began to experiment with digital technologies, the halftone assumed new connotations as a hinge between the profession's predigital era and its transformation by desktop publishing in the late twentieth century. The halftone was a visual artifact of predigital design and, as such, a precursor to the digital pixel grid. April Greiman, a Los Angeles–based graphic designer and former student of Armin Hofmann and Wolfgang Weingart at the Allgemeine Gewerbeschule Basel in the 1970s, was among the first to embrace digital imaging, typography, and layout.[2] Greiman became known in the late 1970s and 1980s for undermining the supremacy of the typographic grid in favor of mining graphic space as a fluid visual terrain between two and three dimensions (Plate 33). Rather than lament the desktop computer as a threat to her profession, Greiman embraced what she called "hybrid imagery," playfully layering and mixing digital and analog techniques, including halftone printing.[3] She used halftones and bright colors as a postmodern motif, creating texture and movement in her designs while resisting the stasis of the page.

The halftone grid has served not only as inspiration for subverting stylistic norms of modern design, but also as a visual means of intervening in sociopolitical discourse. As graphic designer Sheila de Bretteville was in the process of establishing a women's design program at the California Institute of the Arts in 1970, she was commissioned to design a special issue of the feminist newspaper *Everywoman* (Plate 34). Her design was intended to evoke the ethos of women's consciousness-raising, giving equal space to each writer represented therein. Fittingly, her design rejected the typographic grid typical of mainstream newspaper design, employed to denote a hierarchy of information. Instead, she chose to layer large, colorful halftones across full-page spreads. Barbara Kruger, a contemporary of de Bretteville, brought together

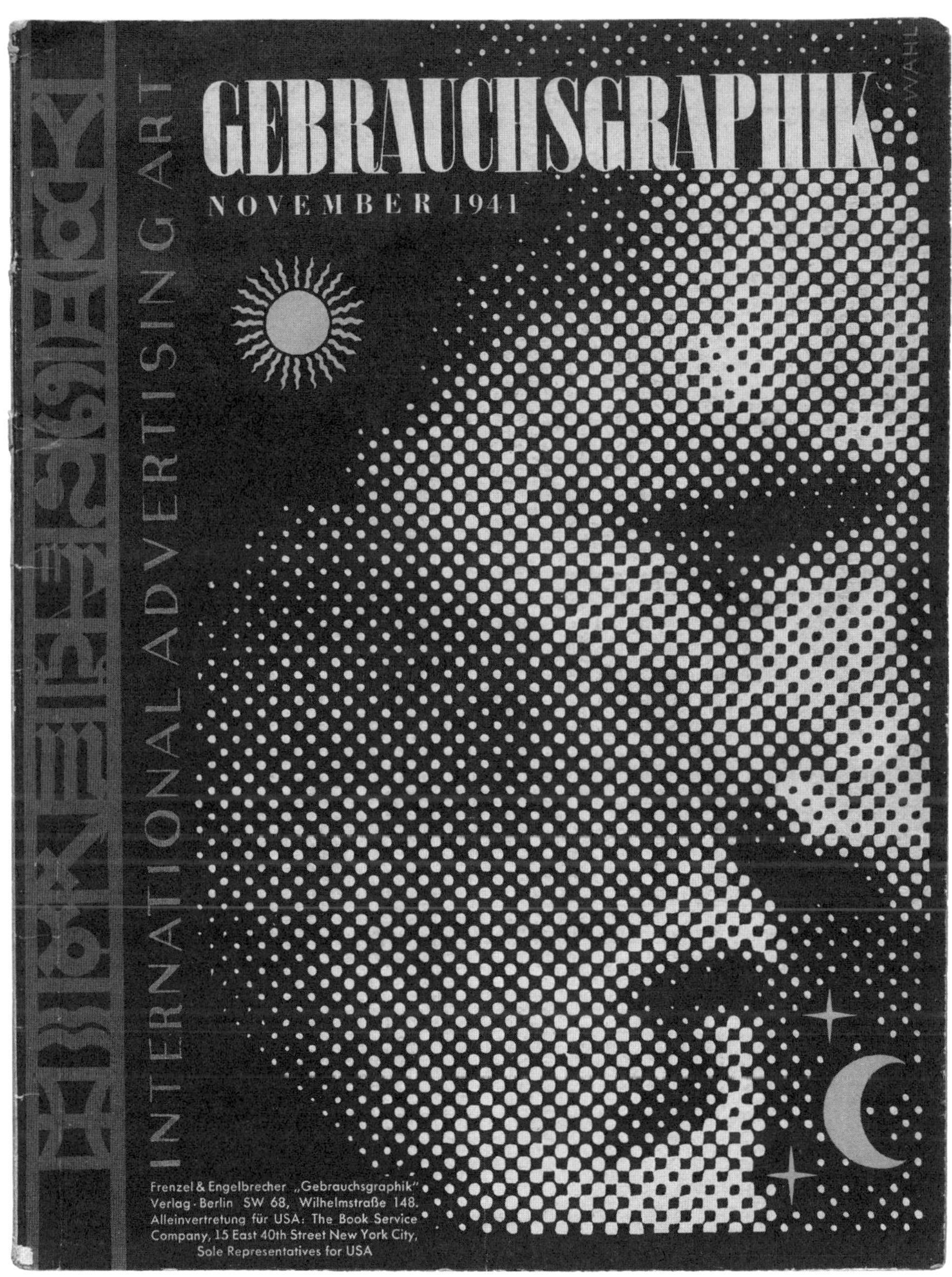

FIGURE 42 Wilm Wahl, cover design for *Gebrauchsgraphik*, November 1941. Letterform Archive, San Francisco.

her training in graphic design with an overtly feminist approach to conceptual art (Figure 43). Since the 1960s, she has used the visual and verbal language of print advertising to exploit elements such as bold sans serif type, direct rhetorical address, and blown-up halftones to subvert the misogynist messages of Western capitalism. Her work calls attention to the black-and-white halftone's alleged neutrality as a vessel of news, evidence, and information. In doing so, she highlights how mechanisms of reproduction—the halftone, the magazine, the newspaper, and photography itself—are used to fortify power structures while allowing them to remain invisible.

In his 1964 book *Understanding Media,* American theorist Marshall McLuhan famously declared that "the medium is the message."[4] He refuted the existence of unmediated content apart from the formal, material, and technological vessels of culture. McLuhan offered "hot" and "cold" to describe different concentrations of information offered by different media. He cited photography as an example of a hot medium, "well filled with data," which requires relatively little effort on the part of a beholder: "A photograph is, visually, 'high definition.'"[5] The "hot" quality of photography, certainly, was recognized by László Moholy-Nagy and Jan Tschichold—which they articulated as legibility, efficiency, and objectivity, which made photographic images well suited to balance the relative coldness of type.

As this study has shown, interwar graphic designers extended the visual possibilities of the photographic halftone far beyond the parameters of *Typophoto* that Moholy-Nagy and Tschichold initially proposed. In practice, the halftone was malleable and ambiguous—a dazzling form tasked with arresting visual attention, which sometimes achieved this goal by slowing down the process of reading rather than by virtue of its efficiency. Halftones commanded attention not necessarily for their clarity and visual succinctness, but because they demanded to be deciphered by readers, occupying a perceptual space between text and image. In McLuhan's terms, the fragmented tonal register of the halftone cools down the "hot" medium of photography. By converting the precision of continuous-tone photography into the vaguely articulated halftone grid, the New Typographers suggested an expanded visual definition of *Typophoto.* They exploited the halftone grid as an optical field that alternately coheres in the mind's eye and remains stubbornly abstract, an almost hypnotic pattern that keeps the eye lingering on the page, struggling—and at times failing delightfully—to make sense of printed form.

The density of visual information that McLuhan described as "hot" is known in today's digital age as high resolution. Film and media scholars Francesco

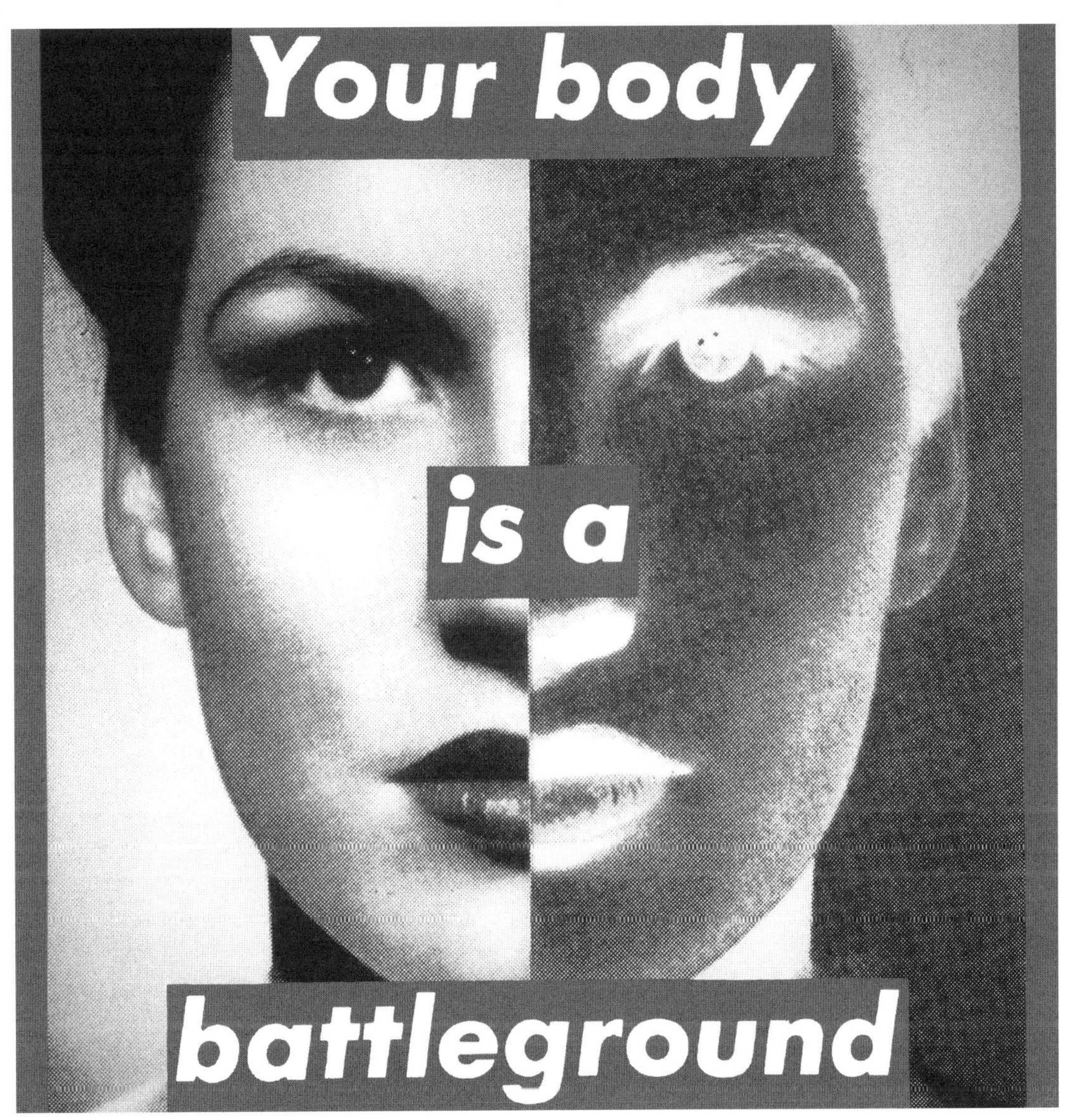

FIGURE 43 Barbara Kruger, *Untitled (Your body is a battleground)*, 1989, photographic silkscreen on vinyl, 284.5 × 284.5 cm | 112 × 112 in., courtesy of the artist, The Broad Art Foundation, and Sprüth Magers.

Casetti and Antonio Somaini have extended McLuhan's theory of "hot" and "cold" media to the materiality of digital images, which they recognize as part of a long history of rasterized images. They explain rasterization in the following way: "To begin with, resolution is a property of images that are *rasterised:* that is, images that are visualised as an orthogonal grid of picture elements or pixels, which represent continuous visual phenomena through a series of distinct, discrete elements. This in itself conditions the *plasticity* of digital images, the transformations they may undergo and the visual artefacts they produce within the rectangular space of a screen, and locates them, from a media-archaeological standpoint, within the *longue durée* of a history of grid-like, point-based images."[6]

Rasterization describes how the form of an image makes visible both the evidence of past material transformation and the potential for further or continuous change. Within the capacious category of "grid-like, point-based images," they include "machine-woven or hand-woven textiles (from Jacquard loom punch cards to *petit point*), pictorial styles such as *pointillisme,* printing techniques such as halftone and Ben-Day dots, all the way up, along a genealogical line leading 'from print to pixels' to the luminous points of cathode ray tube screens and fixed-pixel-array displays (including plasma display panels, liquid crystal displays, light-emitting diode displays, digital light processing projectors)."[7]

This heterogeneous set of images and objects is related not only by the grid structure, but by how they all make plainly visible the in-betweenness of transmediation. A weaving, photographic halftone, and pointillist painting lay bare the record of atomization and reconstitution on their surfaces as formal structure. Each begins with a cohesive image or idea—whether in the mind's eye, sketched on paper, or photochemically printed—which must be fragmented to be put back together.

Since its invention, the halftone has been an object of fascination in art and design. After New Typography emerged nearly a century ago, artists and designers have continued to thematize rasterization, the mechanisms of visual translation, and the distortions of transmediation, printing, and digital projection. The halftone and pixel grid are forms that modern readers have been trained *not* to see. In the hands of artists, halftones and pixel grids are rendered as motifs that remind us as beholders that it is our privilege, and indeed our responsibility, to look closely. As forms that were invented to be ignored, halftone and pixel grids look strange when they are made visible. They become impossible to ignore. Once I began to look for them, I found they are everywhere, hiding in plain sight.

ACKNOWLEDGMENTS

One frozen winter day in February, I hiked a few miles from the small train station in Rye, New York, through sideways-falling snow to an office park where the Merrill C. Berman Collection is housed. As I later pored over a trove of designs, mock-ups, and sketches, I started to understand what this project could become. My memory of that day stands out among hundreds that went into researching and writing this book. From trudging through snow to practicing the art of *Sitzfleisch* for days, weeks, and months on end, this has been one of the most gratifying experiences of my life—especially thanks to the people who lifted me up throughout the process.

Research for this book was generously supported by the American Council on Germany, Central European History Society, Design History Society, and German Historical Institute. At the University of Southern California (USC), where this project began as a doctoral dissertation, research was made possible by the Department of Art History, Visual Studies Research Institute, and USC Graduate School. Its revision, illustrations, and completion were generously supported by the Frances Lehman

Loeb Art Center at Vassar College; I especially want to thank Marianne Begemann, Mary-Kay Lombino, and T. Barton Thurber. I am immensely grateful to everyone at the University of Minnesota Press, including Anne Carter, Shelby Connelly, Euan Lim, Eric Lundgren, Rachel Moeller, Maggie Sattler, and Mike Stoffel, for bringing this book into existence. It is all the better thanks to Nicholas Taylor's expert copyediting, Sandra Friesen's inspired approach to its design, Doug Easton's detailed indexing, and Pieter Martin's thoughtful attention to the project at every stage. I thank two anonymous peer readers for their invaluable feedback.

This project would not be possible without the generosity of many mentors. Megan Luke and Amy Ogata encouraged my intellectual creativity and offered incisive feedback with unrelenting enthusiasm at every stage of this project. Their scholarship as historians of art, design, and visual culture has made an indelible imprint on me and my work. Paul Lerner and Jennifer Greenhill offered indispensable feedback as early readers. Studying with Barbara Heck at Middlebury Language Schools made the depth of my research possible. I remain immeasurably grateful to dear colleagues and mentors, including Gwen Allen, Jennifer Fiore, Corey Keller, Julian Myers-Szupinska, Lucy Oakley, Erin O'Toole, Sandra Phillips, Renny Pritikin, Larry Rinder, George Shulman, and Joree Adilman Weinstein—all of whom have shaped me as a curator and scholar over the years. I first found a love of art history in the high school classroom of Marsha Russell, whose creativity and passion for teaching made me want to be an educator. I will always hold memories of Leigh Markopoulos and Steven Leiber, beloved mentors whose commitments to artists and students continue to inspire so many in their absence. I am exceptionally lucky to have known them both.

Many librarians, archivists, curators, scholars, colleagues, registrars, and collection managers facilitated my research generously. I thank librarians and staff at the Getty Research Institute (GRI), USC Libraries, New York Public Library, Kunstbibliothek der Staatlichen Museen Berlin, and Harvard University Libraries. Thank you to Lydia Smith at Vassar Libraries. Most of this book was written at a reserved desk in a quiet corner of the GRI, an invaluable resource for which I will always be grateful. At the Letterform Archive in San Francisco, Rob Saunders, Kate Long, Elise Carlton, and Stephen Coles welcomed me and offered expertise, and April Harper fielded imaging requests patiently. Gabriele Netsch, Linda Wößner, and Benjamin Sasse facilitated my research in the Nachlass Jan Tschichold at the Deutsches Buch- und Schriftsmuseum in Leipzig, and Stephanie Jacobs offered enthusiasm and encouragement. At the Archiv Baumeister at Kunstmuseum Stuttgart, my sincere thanks are due to Hadwig Goetz and Cristjane Mohringer for their warmth and expertise, to Carla Link-Walesch for assistance with image reproductions, and especially to Felicitas Baumeister for providing thoughtful insights and patiently fielding my granular questions about the work of her late father, Willi Baumeister. I received helpful guidance and advice from Ralf Burmeister at the Berlinische Galerie; Simone Förster, senior curator at the Pinakothek der Moderne in Munich; and Isabel Schulz, director of the Kurt Schwitters Archiv at the Sprengel Museum Hannover. Jolie Simpson and Adrian Sudhalter graciously fielded image requests and facilitated my visit to the Merrill C. Berman Collection. I am especially grateful to Mr. Berman for sharing his superlative collection, and for his interest in my research. Mirjam Brodbeck, director of the Bibliothek für Gestaltung Basel, genially facilitated my visit and fielded image requests. Rolf Kat and Roel Prins made a generous selection of works from the collection available to me at the Stedelijk Museum in Amsterdam.

Colleagues and friends graciously offered ideas and advice: Dan Abbe, Sam Adams, George Baker, Monica Bravo, Sascha Bru, Kathleen James-Chakraborty, Julia Corwin, Virginia Heckert, Karen Huang, James Lee, Ellen Macfarlane, Amanda Maddox, Erin Sullivan Maynes, John Murphy, Nancy Perloff, Emily Pugh, Kristin Romberg, Renee Romero, Jenna Ross, Steffen Siegel, Sally Stein, Paul Stirton, Adrian Sudhalter, Hanna Tulis, Michael Tymkiw, and Andrés Mario Zervigón. An extended community of scholars and friends carried me through the thick of this project; Grace Converse, Dina Murokh, and Robert Gordon Fogelson read chapter drafts tirelessly and provided invaluable insight. I am forever grateful for the love, encouragement, distractions, and uplift offered by dear friends: Jay Alcazar, Sunny Allis, Emily Anderson, Charlie Beckerman, Andrew Bluestone, Nick Branock, Andy Campbell, Lauren Dodds, Courtney Gilette, Jeannie Kenmotsu, Frances Lazare, Natalia Lauricella, Rebecca Pfiffner, Emily Pullen, Emily Purchia, Sophie Joslin-Roher, and Shannon Stagner.

My family has always offered more love and support than I can describe. My parents Betty Littrell and Bennett Brier raised me in a household where books, music, art, and ideas were cherished above all. Their excitement at having an art historian and curator as a daughter is their greatest gift to me. As if that weren't enough, my mother has always been my most enthusiastic reader and was the first editor of these pages. My late grandparents, John Littrell, Rowena

Littrell, and Natalie Brier, helped make my education possible and are with me always. My extended family has cheered me on tirelessly. Ever since I began this project, my wife, Beth Brier, has listened patiently, offered unique insights, and reminded me to be kind to myself—all with empathy and the very best sense of humor. This book will come into the world just a few months after our baby, who is squirming in the womb as I type. I dedicate this book to you, Beth, and to our son Nico.

NOTES

ARCHIVES

Archiv Willi Baumeister, Kunstmuseum Stuttgart
Art Institute of Chicago
Berlinische Galerie
Deutsches Buch- und Schriftmuseum der Deutschen Nationalbibliothek, Leipzig
Getty Research Institute, Los Angeles
Harvard University Libraries, Cambridge, Massachusetts
J. Paul Getty Museum, Los Angeles
Kunstbibliothek der Staatlichen Museen Berlin
Letterform Archive, San Francisco
Merrill C. Berman Collection, New York
Museum für Gestaltung Zürich
The Museum of Modern Art, New York
New York Public Library
Stedelijk Museum, Amsterdam
Typographische Sammlung Jan Tschichold, Bibliothek für Gestaltung Basel

INTRODUCTION

1. *Typographische Mitteilungen* was issued monthly between 1903 and 1933 by the Educational Association of German Printers

(Bildungsverband der Deutschen Buchdrucker), which had over twenty thousand members by 1932. Peter Brooker, Sascha Bru, Andrew Thacker, and Christian Weikop, eds., *The Oxford Critical and Cultural History of Modernist Magazines: Volume III, Europe 1880–1940, Part 1* (Oxford: Oxford University Press, 2013), 972.

2. "Die vorliegende erste Ausgabe der Beilage 'Der Phototypograph' ist entstanden aus der Wunsche der Kollegen, mit der Photogestaltung und der Verwendung der Photographie im modernen Akzidenzsatz näher vertraut zu werden." (This first edition of the supplement "The Phototypographer" arose from the desire of colleagues to become more familiar with photo-design and the use of photography in modern commercial typesetting.) "Was soll und will der 'Phototypograph,'" *Typographische Mitteilungen* 29, no. 1 (January 1932): n.p. All translations in this book are my own, unless otherwise noted.
3. "In immer weiteren Kreisen unserer Kollegen drang die Einsicht durch, dass dies für den gestaltenden Buchdruckergehilfen eine Notwendigkeit ist." (In ever wider circles of our colleagues, the realization that this is a necessity for the creative printer's assistant has prevailed.) *Typographische Mitteilungen* 29, no. 1 (January 1932): n.p.
4. "Die Photogestaltung im typographischen Sinn ist zwar noch Neuland, das erst jetzt beackert werden soll." *Typographische Mitteilungen* 29, no. 1 (January 1932): n.p. I borrow the phrase "conceptual technique" from Craig Buckley, who uses it to describe photomontage as a tool of experimental architecture in the later twentieth century. See Craig Buckley, *Graphic Assembly: Montage, Media, and Experimental Architecture in the 1980s* (Minneapolis: University of Minnesota Press, 2019).
5. The term sometimes appears in scholarship as *Typofoto,* following Moholy-Nagy's original spelling. I have chosen to use the translated version, *Typophoto,* here. One book-length, German-language study of *Typophoto* was published in 1994; Claudia Müller analyzed the term in the context of Moholy-Nagy's *Painting Photography Film* as his ideas related to typography by El Lissitzky, Kurt Schwitters, Guillaume Apollinaire, Stéphane Mallarmé, and at the Bauhaus. Though useful, Müller's is a brief introduction to Moholy-Nagy's ideas and the context of avant-garde typographic experiment between the Wars. See Claudia Müller, *Typofoto: Wege der Typografie zur Foto-Text-Montage bei Laszlo Moholy-Nagy* (Berlin: Gebr. Mann Verlag, 1994). Patrick Rössler has also used the term as a point of departure for analyzing the use of photographic images in Weimar-era book design. See Patrick Rössler, "Neue Typografie, Typofoto und der Buchumschlag zwischen den Kriegen," in *Wissen im Druck: Zur Epistemologie der modernen Buchgestaltung,* ed. Christof Windgätter (Wiesenbaden: Harrassowitz, 2010), 68–99.
6. "sonderheft: elementare typographie," ed. Jan (Iwan) Tschichold, special issue, *Typographische Mitteilungen,* October 1925 (hereafter cited as "sonderheft: elementare typographie").

7. The term “New Typography” also originated in Moholy-Nagy’s writing, appearing in the catalog for the first public Bauhaus exhibition in 1923, in which he also promoted the material, visual, and conceptual hybridity of photography and typography. See László Moholy-Nagy, “Die Neue Typographie,” in *Staatliches Bauhaus, Weimar, 1919–1923* (Weimar: Bauhausverlag, 1923), 141.
8. Jan Tschichold, *Die Neue Typographie: Ein Handbuch für zeitgemäss Schaffende* (1928; repr., Berlin: Brinkmann and Rose, 1987); Jan Tschichold, *The New Typography: A Handbook for Modern Designers,* trans. Ruari McLean (1928; trans., Berkeley: University of California Press, 1995).
9. Tschichold, *New Typography,* 66–67.
10. Previous historical studies of New Typography that resist a face value understanding of functionalism include Maud Lavin, *Clean New World: Cultural Politics and Graphic Design* (Cambridge, Mass.: MIT Press, 2001); and Julia Meer, *Neuer Blick auf die Neue Typographie: Die Rezeption der Avantgarde in der Fachwelt der 1920er Jahre* (Bielefeld: Transcript Verlag, 2015).
11. In keeping with New Typography, the elements of design that optimize the legibility of graphics are still taught today: using the typographic grid, sans serif typefaces, photographic illustrations, lack of typographic ornament, and white space to focus the reader’s eye. See, for example, Rob Carter, Ben Day, and Phillip Meggs, *Typographic Design: Form and Communication,* 4th ed. (Hoboken, N.J.: John Wiley and Sons, 2007).
12. Tschichold, “sonderheft: elementare typographie”; Tschichold, *New Typography,* 87–95. “Halftone” is commonly used to denote both the halftone process and the images it produces. I use the term in both senses throughout.
13. My knowledge of the halftone process as it was practiced between 1923 and 1933 comes from various articles published in trade literature as well as technical manuals, including R. Russ and L. Englich, *Handbuch der Modernen Reproduktionstechnik: Band I, Reproduktionsphotographie und Retusche* (Frankfurt am Main: Verlag von Klimsch and Co., 1927); Charles W. Hackleman, *Commercial Engraving and Printing: A Manual of Practical Instruction Covering Commercial Illustrating and Printing by All Processes* (Indianapolis: Commercial Engraving Publishing Company, 1921); and International Correspondence Schools, *Retouching for Halftones, Part 1* (Scranton, Pa.: International Textbook Company, 1921).
14. William Ivins, *Prints and Visual Communication* (1953; repr., New York: Da Capo Press, 1969), 129, 135.
15. I am indebted to Michael Leja in thinking about the transmediation of photography through the halftone process. See Michael Leja, “Fortified Images for the Masses,” *Art Journal* 70, no. 4 (Winter 2011): 60–83.
16. Lucien Alphonse Legros and John Cameron Grant, *Typographical Printing-Surfaces: The Technology and Mechanism of Their Production* (London: Longmans, Green and

Co., 1916), 487; Dusan C. Stulik and Art Kaplan, *Halftone: The Atlas of Analytical Signatures of Photographic Processes* (Los Angeles: Getty Conservation Institute, 2013), 5; Geoffrey Wakeman, *Victorian Book Illustration: The Technical Revolution* (Newton Abbot: David and Charles, 1973), 138–40; Paul Jobling and David Crowley, *Graphic Design: Reproduction and Representation since 1800* (Manchester: Manchester University Press, 1996), 28. Color halftones were introduced in 1892. See Norma Levarie, *The Art and History of Books* (New York: Da Capo Press, 1968), 279.

17. Siegfried Kracauer, "Photography" (1927), in *The Mass Ornament: Weimar Essays*, trans. Thomas Y. Levin (Cambridge, Mass.: Harvard University Press, 1995), 47.
18. To see photographic halftones as coherent images, an optical illusion allows the human eye to blend the dot matrix. This is described, along with the technical process of halftone production, in manuals such as Hackleman, *Commercial Engraving and Printing;* and Russ and Englich, *Handbuch der Modernen Reproduktionstechnik.*
19. Hito Steyerl, "In Defense of the Poor Image," *e-flux journal*, no. 10 (November 2009): https://www.e-flux.com/journal/10/61362/in-defense-of-the-poor-image.
20. Steyerl.
21. Steyerl.
22. Steffen Siegel, ed., *First Exposures: Writings from the Beginning of Photography* (Los Angeles: J. Paul Getty Museum, 2017), 14.
23. These included Erich Stenger, *Geschichte der Photographie* (Berlin: VDI Verlag, 1929); and Helmuth Bossert and Heinrich Guttmann, *Aus der Frühzeit der Photographie, 1840–70: Ein Bildbuch nach 200 Originalen* (Frankfurt am Main: Societäts-Verlag, 1930).
24. Kenya Hara, *Designing Design*, trans. Maggie Kinsler Hohle and Yukiko Naito (Baden: Lars Müller Publishers, 2007), 19.
25. László Moholy-Nagy is perhaps the most prolific example, leading Matthew Witkovsky to claim boldly Moholy-Nagy's "primary medium" as writing. See Matthew S. Witkovsky, "Elemental Marks," in *Moholy-Nagy: Future Present*, ed. Matthew S. Witkovsky, Carol S. Eliel, and Karole P. B. Vail (Chicago: Art Institute of Chicago, 2016), 21–36.
26. See Sarah Mirseyedi, "Side by Side: The Halftone's Visual Culture of Pragmatism," *History of Photography* 41, no. 3 (2017): 286–310; Gerry Beegan, *The Mass Image: A Social History of Photomechanical Reproduction in Victorian London* (London: Palgrave Macmillan, 2008); Gerry Beegan, "The Studio: Photomechanical Reproduction and the Changing Status of Design," *Design Issues* 23, no. 4 (Autumn 2007): 46–61; Neil Harris, "Iconography and Intellectual History: The Halftone Effect," in *Cultural Excursions: Marketing Appetites and Cultural Tastes in Modern America* (Chicago: University of Chicago Press 1990), 304–17; David Clayton Phillips, "Halftone Technology, Mass Photography, and the Social Transformation of American Print

Culture, 1880–1920" (PhD diss., Yale University, 1996); Robert Taft, "Photography and the Pictorial Press," in *Photography and the American Scene* (New York: Macmillan, 1938), 419–50; Thierry Gervais, ed., *Dispatch: War Photographs in Print, 1854–2008* (Toronto: Ryerson Image Centre, 2014); Thierry Gervais, "Illustrating Sports, or the Invention of the Magazine," in *Getting the Picture: The Visual Culture of the News,* ed. Jason E. Hill and Vanessa R. Schwartz (London: Bloomsbury, 2015), 131–38; Thierry Gervais, "La similigravure," *Nouvelles de l'estampe* 229 (2010): 8–25; Thierry Gervais, *The Making of Visual News: A History of Photography in the Press* (London: Bloomsbury, 2015); and Thierry Gervais, ed., *The "Public" Life of Photographs* (Cambridge, Mass.: MIT Press, 2016).

27. Halftone illustrations became commonplace in some magazines in these decades as well, but the use of halftones for print advertising was unusual until in the 1920s. See Ellen Mazur Thomson, *The Origins of Graphic Design in America: 1870–1920* (New Haven, Conn.: Yale University Press, 1997), 18.
28. Sally Stein, "The Composite Photographic Image and the Composition of Consumer Ideology," *Art Journal* 41, no. 1 (1981): 39–45.
29. This category emerged as the collection and display of photography became more common in North American art museums in the 1970s and 1980s, thereby establishing a system of value for a medium of multiples that could be assimilated by the art market. See Douglas Nickel, "History of Photography: The State of Research," *Art Bulletin* 83, no. 3 (September 2001): 554. I am grateful to curator and art historian Erin O'Toole and photographers Jerry Thompson and John T. Hill for helping me think through this history and invention of these ideas.
30. This history can be traced back to the founding of the Photography Department at the Museum of Modern Art in 1940, following the landmark exhibition in 1937 organized by curator Beaumont Newhall, *Photography, 1839–1937*. This exhibition established a narrative of photography's medium specificity on technical and aesthetic grounds, which continues to dominate the way most museums present and collect photography in the United States. See Beaumont Newhall, *The History of Photography: From 1839 to the Present* (1937; repr., New York: Museum of Modern Art, 1982); and Christopher Phillips, "The Judgment Seat of Photography," in *The Contest of Meaning: Critical Histories of Photography,* ed. Richard Bolton (Cambridge, Mass.: MIT Press, 1992), 15–46.
31. Geoffrey Batchen, "Double Displacement: Photography and Dissemination," in Gervais, *"Public" Life of Photographs,* 39.
32. In his introduction to the English translation of *Die Neue Typographie,* published in 1995, Robin Kinross noted that Tschichold's early announcements of New Typography disrupted "the settled world of the German printing trade" by bringing

international constructivism to an audience of German typographers and printers. See Robin Kinross, "Introduction to the English-Language Edition," in Tschichold, *New Typography,* xvii. Julia Meer has greatly expanded on the context for New Typography by reframing its ideas and practices within the broader context of the emerging profession of graphic design in interwar Germany. See Meer, *Neuer Blick auf die Neue Typographie.*

33. Tschichold also collected materials from the United States and Japan during the interwar era. See Paul Stirton, *Jan Tschichold and the New Typography: Graphic Design between the World Wars* (New York: Bard Graduate Center; New Haven, Conn.: Yale University Press, 2019). An exhibition by the same name was on view at the Bard Graduate Center Gallery in New York, February 14–July 7, 2019.
34. Major repositories of Tschichold's personal papers and collection of graphic design materials from the 1920s and 1930s include the Jan and Edith Tschichold Papers at the Getty Research Institute; the Nachlass Tschichold at the Deutsches Buch- und Schriftmuseum der Deutschen Nationalbibliothek, Leipzig; and at the Bibliothek für Gestaltung, Basel. Additionally, materials are in Zurich, at the Zürcher Hochschule der Künste, the Roche Historical Collection in Basel, and the public library of Saint-Gallen, Switzerland.
35. For thorough discussions of Tschichold's postwar clash with Bill, see Christopher Burke, *Active Literature: Jan Tschichold and New Typography* (London: Hyphen, 2007), 286–99; and Stephen Eskilson, *Graphic Design: A New History* (New Haven, Conn.: Yale University Press, 2007), 288.
36. The principles of Swiss Style graphic design are most concisely aggregated in Armin Hofmann, *Graphic Design Manual: Principles and Practice,* trans. D. Q. Stephenson (New York: Van Nostrand Reinhold, 1965). For an historical overview of Swiss Style design, see Richard Hollis, *Swiss Graphic Design: The Origin and Growth of an International Style, 1920–1965* (New Haven, Conn.: Yale University Press, 2006).
37. Josef Müller-Brockmann, *Grid Systems in Graphic Design,* trans. D. Q. Stephenson (1961; trans., Sulgen: Verlag Niggli, 1996).
38. Müller-Brockmann, 10.
39. Quoted in Burke, *Active Literature,* 293. These statements read as deeply inflected with Tschichold's own guilt as a German in exile, characterizing New Typography as a German phenomenon despite its international network and anti-nationalist ethos.
40. Quoted in Burke, 293.
41. Rosalind Krauss, *The Originality of the Avant-Garde and Other Modernist Myths* (Cambridge, Mass.: MIT Press, 1985), 17.
42. Here I build on work by Patricia Johnston, Elspeth Brown, Robert Sobieszek, and Anne McCauley. See, for example, how Patricia Johnston's monograph on the

advertising work of Edward Steichen engages larger issues of class, gender, and strategies of early American advertising. Patricia Johnston, *Real Fantasies: Edward Steichen's Advertising Photography* (Berkeley: University of California Press, 1997). Elspeth Brown has situated late nineteenth- and early twentieth-century photography within the development of American corporate culture. Elspeth Brown, *The Corporate Eye: Photography and the Rationalization of American Commercial Culture, 1884–1929* (Baltimore: Johns Hopkins University Press, 2005). See also Anne McCauley, *Industrial Madness: Commercial Photography in Paris, 1848–1871* (New Haven, Conn.: Yale University Press, 1994); and Robert Sobieszek, *The Art of Persuasion: A History of Advertising Photography* (New York: Harry N. Abrams, 1988).

43. Studies of New Vision as an avant-garde idea include Christine Kühn, *Neues Sehen in Berlin: Fotografie der Zwanziger Jahre* (Berlin: Staatliche Museen zu Berlin, 2005); and Maria Morris Hambourg, *The New Vision: Photography between the World Wars* (New York: Metropolitan Museum of Art, 1989).

44. I draw on scholarship on the history of advertising including David Ciarlo, *Advertising Empire: Race and Visual Culture in Imperial Germany* (Cambridge, Mass.: Harvard University Press, 2011); Michael Cowan, *Walter Ruttmann and the Cinema of Multiplicity: Avant-Garde–Advertising–Modernity* (Amsterdam: Amsterdam University Press, 2014); Stuart Ewen, *Captains of Consciousness: Advertising and the Social Roots of the Consumer Culture* (New York: McGraw-Hill, 1976); Jackson Lears, *Fables of Abundance: A Cultural History of Advertising* (New York: Basic Books, 1994); Pamela E. Swett, *Selling under the Swastika: Advertising and Commercial Culture in Nazi Germany* (Stanford, Calif.: Stanford University Press, 2014); Pamela E. Swett, S. Jonathan Wiesen, and Jonathan R. Zatlin, eds., *Selling Modernity: Advertising in Twentieth-Century Germany* (Durham, N.C.: Duke University Press, 2007); and Janet Ward, *Weimar Surfaces: Urban Visual Culture in 1920s Germany* (Berkeley: University of California Press, 2001).

45. W. G. Raffé, "The Elements of the Poster: IV Composition: Line and Mass," *Commercial Art*, June 1928, 34.

46. Frederic J. Schwartz, *The Werkbund: Design Theory and Mass Culture before the First World War* (New Haven, Conn.: Yale University Press, 1996), 87.

47. These terms come from Hugo Münsterberg's *Psychology and Industrial Efficiency*, in which the psychologist offered preliminary thoughts on how psychotechnical research and principles could be applied to the quantifiable assessment and improvement of advertising and commercial display methods. See Hugo Münsterberg, *Psychology and Industrial Efficiency* (Boston: Houghton Mifflin, 1913).

48. See Frederic J. Schwartz, *Blind Spots: Critical Theory and the History of Art in Twentieth-Century Germany* (New Haven, Conn.: Yale University Press, 2005); and Schwartz, *Werkbund*.

49. See chapter 1, "Advertising in the Weimar Republic," in Swett, *Selling under the Swastika*, 17–46.
50. The state of the German economy fluctuated wildly after Germany's defeat in World War I and through attempts to stabilize under the Weimar Republic. During a brief period of economic stabilization starting in 1924, catalyzed by American aid mandated by the Dawes Plan, industrial capitalism and consumer culture seemed to promise a way forward, while the German Communist Party gained popularity in the wake of the Russian Revolution. See Detlev Peukert, *The Weimar Republic: The Crisis of Classical Modernity*, trans. Richard Deveson (New York: Hill and Wang, 1992).
51. Kracauer was referring specifically to the cinema as a "cult of distraction," but recognized it as symptomatic of a larger surface culture, especially in advertising films. See Siegfried Kracauer, "Cult of Distraction: On Berlin's Picture Palaces," in *The Mass Ornament: Weimar Essays*, ed. and trans. Thomas Y. Levin (Cambridge, Mass.: Harvard University Press, 1995), 323–29. Originally published as "Kult der Zerstreuung," *Frankfurter Zeitung*, March 4, 1926.
52. Ward, *Weimar Surfaces*, 101.
53. Schwartz, *Blind Spots*.
54. Advertisers frequently wrote about the visual impact of advertisements in physical terms. W. R. Tillertson, for example, claimed that effective advertising must "strike the eye." In combination with the application of "accurate psychology," he continued, "the best advertisement slides into the mind of the consumer without his being well aware of it." See W. R. Tillerton, "Taste as a Commercial Asset," *Commercial Art*, November 1922, 3, 18.
55. In the context of graphic design history, see, for example, Eskilson, *Graphic Design*; Richard Hollis, *Graphic Design: A Concise History* (1994; repr., London: Thames and Hudson, 2001); and Paul Jobling and David Crowley, *Graphic Design: Reproduction and Representation since 1800* (Manchester: Manchester University Press, 1996).
56. See Ellen Mazur Thomson, *The Origins of Graphic Design in America, 1870–1920* (New Haven, Conn.: Yale University Press, 1997), 1–7. Johanna Drucker has similarly described the founding of graphic design as a modern field in terms of its consolidation: "The establishment of professional organizations, publications, and curricula in the early twentieth century consolidated graphic design's distinct identity." See Johanna Drucker, "Philip Meggs and Richard Hollis: Models of Graphic Design History," *Design and Culture* 1, no. 1 (2009): 53.
57. The English-language term "graphic design" was coined in 1922 by the American book and type designer William Addison Dwiggins in his article "A New Kind of Printing Calls for New Design," *Boston Evening Transcript*, August 29, 1922. See Thomson, *Origins of Graphic Design in America*, 7. Though it is difficult to pinpoint

the advent of the term *Gebrauchsgraphik,* several sources suggest that it emerged shortly after World War I. In a 1925 profile on the Bund Deutscher Graphiker for *Commercial Art,* Paul Winkler-Leers wrote, "In Germany as in other countries, the term for commercial art—'Gebrauchs Graphik' (literally 'Applied Graphic Art')—has only recently come into general use. The term 'Gebrauchs Graphik' as opposed to 'Freie Graphik' which means 'Free Graphic Art,' i.e. etching, wood engraving, pen and pencil drawing—embraces all art work, etc., for advertising purposes, and also book decoration, book covers, illustration, fashion drawings and designs, ornamental writing and lettering, ex-libris, etc." See Paul Winkler-Leers, "A Society of Commercial Artists and What It Does," *Commercial Art,* September/October 1925, 204. Jeremy Aynsley has quoted the graphic designer Fritz Ehmcke, writing in 1927 that the term *Gebrauchsgraphik* had not existed fifteen years prior. See Fritz Ehmcke, "Deutsche Gebrauchsgraphik," *Klimschs Jahrbuch,* 1927; and Jeremy Aynsley, *Graphic Design in Germany, 1890–1945* (Berkeley: University of California Press, 2000), 120.

58. For example, the title of an article by Fritz Hellwag, printed in both German and English in *Gebrauchsgraphik* in 1926, was printed as "Die Berliner Gebrauchsgraphik" and "The Commercial Art of Berlin." See Fritz Hellwag, "Die Berliner Gebrauchsgraphik," *Gebrauchsgraphik* 3, no. 5 (May 1926): 3.
59. Aynsley, *Graphic Design in Germany,* 20.
60. The revitalization of German printing was also a motivation of the post–World War I print boom between 1918 and 1924. See Erin Sullivan, "Speculating on Paper: Print Culture and the German Inflation, 1918–1924" (PhD diss., University of Southern California, 2014).
61. Frédéric Barbier, *Gutenberg's Europe: The Book and the Invention of Western Modernity,* trans. Jean Birrell (Cambridge: Polity Press, 2017); Michael Twyman, *Printing, 1770–1970: An Illustrated History of Its Development and Uses in England* (London: British Library; Reading: Reading University Press, 1998), 25–26, 31–35, 51–63.
62. In 1922, this organization was renamed the Verband Deutscher Reklamefachleute (Association of German Advertising Professionals). See Gerard F. Sherayko, "Selling the Modern: The New Consumerism in Weimar Germany" (PhD diss., Indiana University, 1996), 20.
63. The full name of the journal was *Die Reklame: Zeitschrift des Vereins deutsche Reklamefachleute (Advertising: Newspaper for the Association of German Advertising Professionals),* and it was published until 1933. See Sherayko, "Selling the Modern," 19.
64. Ward, *Weimar Surfaces,* 96.
65. This claim was bolstered by the acquisition of advertising posters by museums such as the Museum für Kunst und Gewerbe in Hamburg. See David Ciarlo, *Advertising*

Empire: Race and Visual Culture in Imperial Germany (Cambridge, Mass.: Harvard University Press, 2011), 15.

66. This organization is alternately referred to in historical sources as the Bund Deutscher Graphiker.
67. *Gebrauchsgraphik* was founded by Frenzel in partnership with publisher A. Engelbrecher in Berlin. Frenzel remained editor of *Gebrauchsgraphik* until 1937. See Patrick Rössler, *Eine Zeitschrift als gedrucktes Schaufenster zur Werbewelt: "Gebrauchsgraphik," 1924–1944* (Munich: Stiebner, 2014), 11–15; Aynsley, *Graphic Design in Germany,* 120; Swett, *Selling under the Swastika,* 22.
68. Feature articles in *Gebrauchsgraphik* were printed in both German and English starting in 1927.
69. Teal Triggs, "Graphic Design History: Past, Present and Future," *Design Issues* 27, no. 1 (Winter 2011): 3.
70. See, for example, Philip B. Meggs and Alston W. Purvis, *A History of Graphic Design* (New York: John Wiley and Sons, 2005); Steven Heller and Georgette Balance, eds., *Graphic Design History* (New York: Allworth Press, 2001); Hollis, *Graphic Design*; and Eskilson, *Graphic Design.* In the first major English-language survey of graphic design history, originally published in 1983, Philip Meggs established the narrative of New Typography as the apex of graphic design's natural synthesis of avant-garde sensibility and pure functionalism. See Philip B. Meggs, *A History of Graphic Design* (New York: Van Nostrand Reinhold, 1983). This narrative has been supported by studies of New Typography and Jan Tschichold, such as Cees W. de Jong, ed., *Jan Tschichold: Master Typographer: His Life, Work and Legacy* (London: Thames & Hudson, 2008); Robin Kinross, *Modern Typography: An Essay in Critical History* (London: Hyphen Press, 1992); Martijn F. Le Coultre and Alston W. Purvis, *Jan Tschichold: Posters of the Avantgarde* (Basel: Birkhäuser, 2007); and Ruari McLean, *Jan Tschichold* (Boston: D. R. Godine, 1975).
71. Historical surveys tend to follow the model established by Nikolaus Pevsner in 1936, who championed the emergence of modernism as a teleological progression from nineteenth-century design. The arc of his narrative became a model for writing design history in the twentieth century, and for the positioning of interwar modernism within it as a heroic apex. See Nikolaus Pevsner, *Pioneers of Modern Design: From William Morris to Walter Gropius* (1936; repr., New Haven, Conn.: Yale University Press, 1960). A notable exception, and model for my own study of the historical situatedness of legibility, is Peter Bain and Paul Shaw, eds., *Blackletter: Type and National Identity* (Princeton, N.J.: Princeton Architectural Press, 1998).
72. Meer, *Neuer Blick auf die Neue Typographie.*
73. Levenston proposes integration of the study of written form into linguistics, systematically considering how the visual form of language (including spelling, punctuation,

typography, layout, and translation) affects and creates meaning. In doing so, he proposed to revive the idea of "paragraphemics" (also referred to by Levenston as "graphicology"), coined in 1959 by the linguist Eric Hamp a science for studying typography and layout. See E. A. Levenston, *The Stuff of Literature: Physical Aspects of Texts and Their Relation to Literary Meaning* (Albany: State University of New York, 1992).

74. On this point, I am grateful to Renee Romero for lending her professional expertise as a graphic designer.
75. David Hopkins, *After Modern Art:* 1945–2017 (Oxford: Oxford University Press, 2018), 118.
76. Jennifer L. Roberts argues that the unruliness of the moiré pattern in contemporary art calls for its "study . . . as a 'queering' of print." Jennifer L. Roberts, *Contact: Art and the Pull of the Print* (Princeton, N.J.: Princeton University Press, 2024), 142.
77. See the artist's website, https://www.stephaniesyjuco.com/projects/cargo-cults. Dazzle camouflage is discussed briefly in chapter 2 of this book, in the context of research on perception through the study of optical illusion.

1 PHOTOGRAPHIC LANGUAGE

1. Eugen Gutnoff, "Vergleichende Photobildbetrachtung," *Archiv für Buchgewerbe und Gebrauchsgraphik* 68, no. 3 (1931): 93–99. *Archiv für Buchgewerbe und Gebrauchsgraphik* (*Annal of the Book Trade and Graphic Design*) was published annually by the Verlag des Deutschenbuchgewerbevereins (German Book Trade Association Publisher) in Leipzig.
2. Franz Roh and Jan Tschichold, *foto-auge: 76 fotos der zeit* (Stuttgart: Fritz Wedekind, 1929). The work was published as a compendium to the monumental exhibition *Film und Foto,* organized by the Deutscher Werkbund. Featuring contributions by László Moholy-Nagy, El Lissitzky, Sigfried Giedion, John Heartfield, Hans Hildebrandt, Bernhard Pankok, Jan Tschichold, and Edward Weston, *Film und Foto* opened in August 1929 in Stuttgart and traveled to Zurich, Berlin, Danzig, Vienna, Zagreb, Munich, Tokyo, and Osaka through the summer of 1931. For more on this exhibition, see Ute Eskildsen and Jan-Christopher Horak, eds., *Film und Foto der zwanziger Jahre: eine Betrachtung der Internationalen Werkbundausstellung "Film und Foto," 1929* (Stuttgart: Gerd Hatje, 1979); Olivier Lugon, "Neues Sehen, Neue Geschichte: Laszlo Moholy-Nagy, Sigfried Giedion und die Ausstellung *Film und Foto,*" in *Sigfried Giedion und die Fotografie: Bildinszenierungen der Moderne,* ed. Werner Oechslin and Gregor Harbusch (Zurich: gta Verlag, 2010), 88–105; and Gustaf Stotz, *Internationale Ausstellung des Deutschen Werkbunds Film und Foto* (Stuttgart: Deutscher Werkbund, 1929).
3. These included Erich Stenger's *Geschichte der Photographie* (Berlin: VDI Verlag, 1929) and Helmuth Bossert and Heinrich Guttmann's *Aus der Frühzeit der Photographie,*

1840–70: Ein Bildbuch nach 200 Originalen (Frankfurt am Main: Societäts-Verlag, 1930), as well as Roger Fry's monograph on Julia Margaret Cameron, published in 1926, and Heinrich Schwarz's monograph on David Octavius Hill in 1931. László Moholy-Nagy's *Malerei Photographie Film* (Munich: Albert Langen Verlag, 1925) and Jan Tschichold and Franz Roh's *foto-auge* (1929) explored the dialectical relationship between nineteenth-century and contemporary photography.

4. For in-depth studies of New Vision, see Maria Morris Hambourg and Christopher Phillips, *The New Vision: Photography between the World Wars: Ford Motor Company Collection at the Metropolitan Museum of Art* (New York: Metropolitan Museum of Art, 1989); and Inka Graeve Ingelmann, "Mechanics and Expression: Franz Roh and the New Vision—a Historical Sketch," in *Object:Photo. Modern Photographs: The Thomas Walther Collection, 1909–1949. An Online Project of the Museum of Modern Art,* ed. Mitra Abbaspour, Lee Ann Daffner, and Maria Morris Hambourg (New York: Museum of Modern Art, 2014), https://www.moma.org/interactives/objectphoto/assets/essays/GraeveIngelmann.pdf.
5. The approximate date of Hugo's photograph comes from Bossert and Guttmann, *Aus der Frühzeit der Photographie*. The photograph by Lissitzky is identified as *Untitled (Hand with Compasses)* (1924), in *Situating El Lissitzky,* ed. Nancy Perloff and Brian Reed (Los Angeles: Getty Research Institute, 2003), 131–32.
6. "Hand mit Zirkel eines Architeketen oder Ingenieurs. Komposition von el lissitzky." Gutnoff, "Vergleichende Photobildbetrachtung," 93. Some German quotations from sources referenced here are reproduced entirely in lowercase, as their authors originally wrote them. The penchant for *kleinschreibung* was a signature of New Typography. Designers including Herbert Bayer, Kurt Schwitters, and Jan Tschichold sought to optimize the Latin alphabet as "universally" legible by simplifying letterforms, abolishing letters unique to the German language, and dispensing with the convention of capitalizing German nouns. This practice was strongly advocated by German engineer and theoretician Walter Porstmann in his highly influential book *Sprache und Schrift,* ed. Richard R. Hinz (Berlin: Verlag des Vereins Deutscher Ingenieure, 1920).
7. Gutnoff, "Vergleichende Photobildbetrachtung," 99.
8. Gutnoff, 99.
9. Lissitzky's composite photograph was emblematic of Central European modernism both for its experimentation with the photographic medium and its veneration of the modern engineer.
10. "Heute ist Photographie eine große Sache. Sie hat vom neuen Sehen und neuen Sachlichkeit profitiert. Es genügt ihr schon nicht mehr Bild oder Bildausschnitt zu sein, sie will konstruktieren, läßt sich in Elemente verlegen, die montiert, photomontiert,

werden: Photomontage, Photokombination. Sie drängt weiter und dringt in das typographische Satzbild ein, verdrängt gestaltenden Satz, will mit der Typographie verschmelzen und erscheint als Phototypographie auf dem Plan." Gutnoff, "Vergleichende Photobildbetrachtung," 93.

11. My attention was initially drawn to the repurposing of Lissitzky's *Untitled (Hand with Compasses)* (1924) for Pelikan by John E. Bowlt's discussion of handcraft and machine production in Lissitzky's work. See Bowlt, "Manipulating Metaphors: El Lissitzky and the Crafted Hand," in Perloff and Reed, *Situating El Lissitzky*, 129–52.
12. Moholy-Nagy's experiments with typography can be traced back to a series of paintings and collages made between 1919 and 1921 in which he combined abstracted, industrial forms with letterforms, numerals, and words, as well as abstract lines, using a primary color palette. See Victor Margolin, *The Struggle for Utopia: Rodchenko, Lissitzky, Moholy-Nagy, 1917–1946* (Chicago: University of Chicago Press, 1997), 49–52; and Matthew S. Witkovsky, "Elemental Marks," in *Moholy-Nagy: Future Present*, ed. Matthew S. Witkovsky, Carol S. Eliel, and Karole P. B. Vail (Chicago: Art Institute of Chicago, 2016), 21–36.
13. Moholy-Nagy, *Malerei Photographie Film*. Despite Moholy-Nagy's repeated iteration of this idea, Matthew Witkovsky has proposed that Moholy-Nagy's "primary medium" was, in fact, writing, given that the bulk of his output as an artist, designer, theorist, and pedagogue was in the form of writing. See Witkovsky, "Elemental Marks," 22.
14. Pepper Stetler, *Stop Reading! Look! Modern Vision and the Weimar Photographic Book* (Ann Arbor: University of Michigan Press, 2015), 2.
15. Jan Tschichold, *The New Typography: A Handbook for Modern Designers*, trans. Ruari McLean (1928; trans., Berkeley: University of California Press, 1995), 92.
16. Tschichold, 92.
17. Earlier that year, Moholy-Nagy had joined the faculty of the Weimar Bauhaus as head of the Metal Workshop and director of the Bauhausbücher series. Tschichold traveled to Weimar from his hometown of Leipzig to attend the exhibition. This event was formative for his eventual articulation of a discrete set of principles for graphic design that he believed could embody the spirit of international constructivism. Tschichold's first encounter with the Bauhaus has been repeatedly invoked in religious terms, as his "conversion" to modernism. See, for example, Sebastian Carter, *Twentieth-Century Type Designers* (London: W. W. Norton, 2002), 122; Martijn F. Le Coultre and Alston W. Purvis, *Jan Tschichold: Posters of the Avantgarde* (Basel: Birkhäuser, 2007); and Ruari McLean, *Jan Tschichold* (Boston: D. R. Godine, 1975). For a thorough account of New Typography's relationship to the Bauhaus, see Robin Kinross, "Das Bauhaus im Kontext der Neuen Typographie," in *Das A und O des Bauhauses:*

Bauhauswerbung, Schriftbilder, Drucksachen, Ausstellungsdesign, ed. Ute Brüning and Jeannine Fiedler (Berlin: Bauhaus Archiv; Leipzig: Edition Leipzig, 1995), 9–14.

18. Christopher Burke, *Active Literature: Jan Tschichold and New Typography* (London: Hyphen, 2007), 25, 40.
19. *Staatliches Bauhaus, Weimar, 1919–1923* (Weimar: Bauhausverlag, 1923).
20. László Moholy-Nagy, "Photography in Advertising," in *Photography in the Modern Era: European Documents and Critical Writings, 1913–40*, ed. and trans. Christopher Phillips (New York: Metropolitan Museum of Art, 1989), 88. Originally published as "Die Photographie in Der Reklame," *Photographische Korrespondenz*, no. 9 (September 1927): 257–60.
21. Bauhaus pedagogy, which was developed especially by Wassily Kandinsky, Paul Klee, Johannes Itten, Joseph Albers, and László Moholy-Nagy, was founded on the basic principle that all design and art should begin with abstract form. It drew alternately from theosophy, metaphysics, and psychological science. See Barry Bergdoll and Leah Dickerman, eds., *Bauhaus, 1919–1933: Workshops for Modernity* (New York: Museum of Modern Art, 2009); and Rainer K. Wick, *Teaching at the Bauhaus* (Stuttgart: Hatje Cantz Publishers, 2000).
22. These buzzwords in the fledgling profession of graphic design resonated with trends toward rationalization in Weimar-era design and industrial production, reflected in Jan Tschichold's emphasis on standardization (particularly the adoption of printing and paper standards codified by the Deutsche Industrie-Normen) throughout *Die Neue Typographie: Ein Handbuch für zeitgemäss Schaffende* (1928; repr., Berlin: Brinkmann and Rose, 1987). For more on rationalization and design in Weimar Germany, see Andreas Killen, "Weimar Psychotechnics between Americanism and Fascism," in "The Self as Project: Politics and the Human Sciences," ed. Greg Eghigian, Andreas Killen, and Christine Leuenberger, special issue, *Osiris* 22, no. 1, (2007): 48–71; David Meskill, *Optimizing the German Workforce: Labor Administration from Bismarck to the Economic Miracle* (New York: Berghahn Books, 2010); and Frederic J. Schwartz, *The Werkbund: Design Theory and Mass Culture before the First World War* (New Haven, Conn.: Yale University Press, 1996).
23. Moholy-Nagy, "Die Neue Typographie," in *Staatliches Bauhaus, Weimar, 1919–1923* (Weimar: Bauhausverlag, 1923), 141.
24. "Die Typographie ist ein Instrument der Mitteilung." Moholy-Nagy, 141.
25. "Der Druck korrespondiere mit dem Inhalt durch seine den optischen und physischen Gesetzen untergeordnete Gestaltung. Wesen und Zweck eines Druckes bestimmen den hemmungslosen Gebrauch aller Zeilenrichtungen (also nicht nur horizontale Gliederung), aller Typen, Schriftgrade, geometrischen Formen, Farben, usw." (The print corresponds to content through optical and physical laws, to which

design is subordinate. The nature and purpose of a print determine the unrestrained use of all line directions [not only horizontal arrangement], all types, font sizes, geometric shapes, colors, et cetera.) Moholy-Nagy, "Die Neue Typographie," 141. Here, Moholy-Nagy makes vague reference to principles of experimental psychology. Their influence on graphic design in the 1920s is discussed in depth in the following chapter.

26. "Mit der Elastizität, Variabilität und Frische des Satzmaterials soll eine neue typographische Sprache geschaffen werden, deren Inanspruchnahme nur der Gesetzmäßigkeit des Ausdrucks und seiner Wirkung unterliegt." Moholy-Nagy, 141.
27. Moholy-Nagy was responsible for the catalog's interior, and Herbert Bayer designed its cover.
28. I use the term "construction" here to describe what graphic designers today typically refer to as the "composition" of layout on a page. My use of "construction" follows New Typography's self-identification with international constructivism.
29. The book's square format signaled that industrially printed books could retain an artisanal quality, embodying the Bauhaus ambition to harmonize aestheticism and industrial production. The Dutch design journal *Wendingen*, founded in 1918 by the architect Hendrik Wijdeveld, had likewise adopted a square format. See Martijn F. Le Coultre, *Wendingen: A Journal for the Arts, 1918–1932* (Princeton, N.J.: Princeton Architectural Press, 2001).
30. I am grateful to Robert Gordon-Fogelson for helping me to articulate this design as an example of how the raster pattern of the photographic halftone informed this typographic treatment.
31. Moholy-Nagy also described this phenomenon in the context of cinema, which he regarded as a more advanced use of the action of light and shadow to create form, evolved out of cameraless photography. See Moholy-Nagy, *Malerei Photographie Film*, 39–41.
32. This was a central principle of New Typography as Tschichold articulated it (e.g., *New Typography*, 66–68).
33. See my introduction for a brief explanation of my use of the phrase "abstract graphic elements" to describe nonrepresentational forms in graphic design.
34. Overline, sometimes also referred to as an overbar or overscore, connotes a horizontal rule printed immediately above a line of text, word, or letterform, used (like an underline) for emphasis. See Rob Carter, Ben Day, and Phillip Meggs, *Typographic Design: Form and Communication*, 4th ed. (Hoboken, N.J.: John Wiley and Sons, 2007).
35. The son of a sign painter, Tschichold began his formal training in 1919 at the Königliche Akademie für graphische Künste und Buchgewerbe in Leipzig, where he studied calligraphy with Hermann Delitsch. Under Delitsch, he was trained in the arts and crafts tradition, which promoted the revival of historical scripts and calligraphy

as a mode of personal expression and as a marker of national identity. In 1920, he transferred to the Akademie für Kunstgewerbe in Dresden to work with Heinrich Wieynck. See Burke, *Active Literature,* 17–19. For a more thorough account of Tschichold's formal training and early career as a typography instructor, see Linda Wößner, "Tschichold als Lehrer: Das Fundament," in *Jan Tschichold: Ein Jahrhunderttypograf? Blicke in den Nachlass,* ed. Stephanie Jacobs and Patrick Rössler (Göttingen: Wallstein, 2019), 374–79.

36. Translated in Devon Fore, *Realism after Modernism: The Rehumanization of Art and Literature* (Cambridge, Mass.: MIT Press, 2012), 39.
37. Jan Tschichold, "New Life in Print," *Commercial Art,* July 1930, 7.
38. The trade journal *Typographische Mitteilungen: Zeitschrift des Bildungsverbandes der Deutschen Buchdrucker* (*Typographic News: Journal of the Education Association of German Printers*) was founded in Leipzig in 1903 and circulated among professional typographers and printers in Germany. A comprehensive collection of *Typographische Mitteilungen* from the 1920s and 1930s is included in the Letterform Archive, San Francisco.
39. I use the terms "stem" and "bar" in reference to typographic anatomy according to common usage among graphic designers today. For a full glossary of typographic anatomy, see Carter, Day, and Meggs, *Typographic Design,* 29–46.
40. My observations of the iterative process by which Tschichold created this design were facilitated by access to the largest repository of his own work, to my knowledge, in the Nachlass Jan Tschichold, Deutsches Buch- und Schriftmuseum der Deutschen Nationalbibliothek, Leipzig.
41. Tschichold used "construction" interchangeably with "design" throughout *Die Neue Typographie.*
42. "sonderheft: elementare typographie," ed. Jan (Iwan) Tschichold, special issue, *Typographische Mitteilungen,* October 1925 (hereafter cited as "sonderheft: elementare typographie"). The phrase *elementare typographie* can be translated to mean "elemental typography," referring to the use of basic formal and material elements of typography—including color, line, scale, basic abstract shapes, as well as photographic illustrations—to optimize the legibility and efficiency of a design, rather than using ornamental typography. The word *elementare* also translates as "elementary" or "basic." Tschichold often used *elementare* and *konstruktivist* interchangeably, thereby explicitly referring to New Typography as constructivist graphic design.
43. Jan Tschichold, "Die Neue Typographie," *Kulturschau,* no. 4 (Spring 1925): 9–11. See also Christopher Burke's brief commentary on this manifesto in *Active Literature,* 28–30.
44. Tschichold, "Die Neue Typographie," in Burke, *Active Literature,* 29.

45. Jan (Iwan) Tschichold, "elementare typographie," in Tschichold, "sonderheft: elementare typographie," 192–214.
46. Contributions came from Nathan Altman and El Lissitzky of Russia; Otto Baumberger of Switzerland; Herbert Bayer of Austria; Max Burchartz, Johannes Molzahn, and Kurt Schwitters of Germany; Molnár Farkas and Moholy-Nagy of Hungary; and Mart Stam of the Netherlands.
47. László Moholy-Nagy, "Typographie-Photographie / TYPO-PHOTO," in Tschichold, "sonderheft: elementare typographie," 202–4. This essay is a variant of the short section, "Typophoto," which appeared in *Malerei Photographie Film,* his first Bauhaus book published the same year. The essay in Moholy-Nagy's book is a slightly longer version of what appeared in "sonderheft: elementare typographie." They also differ in that the version in "sonderheft: elementare typographie" is set in a single typeface. See Moholy-Nagy, *Malerei Photographie Film.*
48. Though Tschichold was not outspokenly political and had no known ties to the Communist Party, he borrowed the language of political revolution to promote the formal and technological transformation of typography, bookmaking, and printing. He signaled his association with international constructivism (especially as a follower and friend of Lissitzky) especially through his choice to go by the first name "Iwan" (from his given name, Johannes). Friedrich Friedl has dated this change to circa 1923–24. His name appears as "Iwan Tschichold" in "sonderheft: elementare typographie." See Friedl, "Lernen von Jan Tschichold," facsimile of *sonderheft: elementare typographie,* ed. Jan (Iwan) Tschichold (Mainz: H. Schmidt, 1986), 3. In 1926, upon relocating to Munich as the spread of Nazi ideology in Bavaria made the city increasingly conservative in the late 1920s, Tschichold began going by "Jan" at Paul Renner's request. See Burke, *Active Literature,* 54–56.
49. This was arguably a more urgent question for Tschichold than other designers associated with New Typography, given that he was the one designer among them who was trained as a calligrapher, and thus was more fully immersed in the traditions of lettering than those who had studied fine art or architecture. Carter, *Twentieth-Century Type Designers,* 121.
50. "1. Die neue Typographie ist zweckbetont." Tschichold, "Elementare Typographie," 198.
51. "2. Zweck jeder Typographie ist Mitteilung (deren Mittel sie darstellt). Die Mitteilung muss in kürzester, einfachster, eindringlichster Form erscheinen." Tschichold, 198.
52. "*Innere Organisation* ist Beschränkung auf die elementaren Mittel der Typographie: Schrift, Zahlen, Zeichen, Linien des Setzkastens und Setzmaschine. Zu den elementaren Mitteln neuer Typographie gehört in der heutigen, auf Optik eingestellten Welt auch das exakte Bild: die Photographie. Elementare Schriftform ist die

Groteskschrift aller Variationen: mager—halbfett—**fett**—schmal bis breit." Tschichold, 198; italics and bold are original to Tschichold's text.

53. Tschichold, *New Typography,* 92.

54. *Fraktur* was commissioned by Emperor Maximilian I in 1513 and became the most commonly used form of black letter (or Gothic script) soon after its invention, so much so that it eventually became synonymous with black letter. *Fraktur* appeared alongside roman type through the nineteenth century, but was used to spread and strengthen nationalist sentiment, especially in wartime, in the nineteenth and early twentieth centuries. See Hans Peter Willberg, "Fraktur and Nationalism," in *Blackletter: Type and National Identity,* ed. Peter Bain and Paul Shaw (Princeton, N.J.: Princeton Architectural Press, 1998), 40–49.

55. Debates over the legibility of *Fraktur*—frequently compared to *Antiqua* (or roman type)—began in the nineteenth century and continued into the twentieth, prompting the publication of such books as August Kirschmann's *Antiqua oder Fraktur? (Lateinische oder deutsche Schrift),* vol. 1 (Leipzig: Verlag des Deutschen Buchgewerbevereins, 1907). Proponents of *Fraktur* long advocated for its dominance because of the almost exclusive use of *Fraktur* in Germany, while most other European countries had favored *Antiqua* since the seventeenth century. Others advocated for *Antiqua* as a more international typeface that would help align Germany with the rest of Europe. *Antiqua* had become more popular in Germany during the Weimar era, but *Fraktur* was still frequently used. For more on this debate, see Christopher Burke, "German Hybrid Typefaces, 1900–1914," in Bain and Shaw, *Blackletter,* 38–39; and Hannah J. McMurray, "Winning New Freedom: Intersections of Text and Image in the Art of Kurt Schwitters" (PhD diss., University of Michigan, 2017), 112–17. According to Dutch researcher Gerrit Willem Ovink, who studied typographic legibility in the 1920s and 1930s, the ubiquity of *Fraktur* in Germany made it more legible to Germans, but he also argued that *Antiqua* capital letterforms were more individually legible than individual *Fraktur* letterforms. See *Legibility, Atmosphere-Value and Forms of Printing Types* (Leiden: A. W. Sijthoff, 1938), 115. A discussion of Ovink's work is included in the following chapter.

56. The nationalist and ethnic connotations of *Fraktur* were later weaponized by the Nazi Party to malign avant-garde art and design as "degenerate" and non-German, promoting Aryan racial "purity" in efforts to justify hypernationalism and isolationism. See Burke, "German Hybrid Typefaces."

57. See especially Benjamin Buchloh's discussion of the constructivist notion of "faktura" giving way to "factography" in 1924, in "Faktura to Factography," *October,* no. 30 (Autumn 1984): 82–119. See also Leah Dickerman, "The Fact and the Photograph," in "Soviet Factography," ed. Devin Fore, special issue, *October,* no. 118 (Fall 2006): 132–52.

58. Moholy-Nagy, *Malerei Photographie Film,* 38–40. The book's title was changed from *Malerei Photographie Film* to *Malerei Fotografie Film* in its first reprinting in 1927, adopting a spelling of "Fotografie" in accordance with changes to German orthography (*Rechtschreibung*) promoted as more efficient by the Deutscher Normenausschuss as well as Walter Porstmann in *Sprache und Schrift,* ed. Richard R. Hinz (Berlin: Verlag des Vereins Deutscher Ingenieure, 1920). See Kinross, "Introduction to the English-Language Edition," in Tschichold, *New Typography,* xxxi; and Margolin, *Struggle for Utopia,* 142n41. Though this was the first volume of the Bauhausbücher written by Moholy-Nagy, his mark is visible throughout as designer. For a study of Moholy-Nagy as a book designer for the Dessau Bauhaus, see Alain Findeli, "Laszlo Moholy-Nagy und das Projekt der Bauhausbücher," in Brüning and Fiedler, *Das A und O des Bauhauses,* 22–26.
59. Speculations about the future, and urgent appeals to build a "new world," were common among cultural commentators in Germany during the Weimar era, reflecting a shared sense of urgency around the need to rebuild society in the wake of the physical, psychological, and economic devastation of World War I. For more on these tropes of political and cultural rhetoric in Weimar Germany, see Jeffrey Herf, *Reactionary Modernism: Technology, Culture, and Politics in Weimar and the Third Reich* (Cambridge: Cambridge University Press, 1984); Detlev Peukert, *The Weimar Republic: The Crisis of Classical Modernity,* trans. Richard Deveson (New York: Hill and Wang, 1992); and Eric D. Weitz, *Weimar Germany: Promise and Tragedy* (Princeton, N.J.: Princeton University Press, 2007).
60. Moholy-Nagy, *Malerei Photographie Film,* 39.
61. Tschichold, *New Typography,* 157–58.
62. Paul Jobling and David Crowley have traced the first appearances of photographic halftones in the *New York Daily Graphic,* in 1880, and in the *Illustrated London News,* in 1881, but they have noted that wood engraving continued to be a dominant reproductive technique, used until at least 1900; see *Graphic Design: Reproduction and Representation since 1800* (Manchester: Manchester University Press, 1996). See also Thierry Gervais, "La similigravure: Le récit d'une invention (1878–1893)," *Nouvelles de l'estampe,* no. 229 (March 2010): 8–25.
63. For studies on the relationship between photography, engraving, and printing around the turn of the twentieth century, see Gerry Beegan, *The Mass Image: A Social History of Photomechanical Reproduction in Victorian London* (London: Palgrave Macmillan, 2008); Richard Benson, *The Printed Picture* (New York: Museum of Modern Art, 2008); and Jobling and Crowley, *Graphic Design.*
64. Except for books featuring the work of contemporary photographers, it was still relatively rare to use photographic illustrations, especially for "fine" book printing in

the 1920s. See Kinross, "Introduction to the English-Language Edition," xxxii. Sigfrid Steinberg has noted that there was still a strong tradition of bookmaking in private presses in the 1920s, which tended to strongly favor wood- and linoleum-cut illustrations over photographic ones; see *Five Hundred Years of Printing,* new ed. (London: British Library; New Castle, Del.: Oak Knoll Press, 2001), 186.

65. Tschichold, *New Typography,* 87–95.
66. This concept was introduced in László Moholy-Nagy's article "Produktion-Reproducktion" in *De Stijl* 5, no. 7 (July 1922): 97–101.
67. "Das Wichtigste für die heutige Typographie ist der Verwendung der zinkographischen Techniken, die mechanische Herstellung von photographischen Reproduktionen in allen Formaten." Moholy-Nagy, "Die Neue Typographie," 141. Zincography, to which Moholy-Nagy referred here, was a planometric printing process that used sensitized zinc plates to create larger-scale and more cost-effective reproductions than the use of a lithographic stone. Photogravure was a variant of the zincographic process; as early as 1850, zinc plates were used to transfer photographic images to the printed page. For more on this history, see Lucien Alphonse Legros and John Cameron Grant, *Typographical Printing-Surfaces: The Technology and Mechanism of Their Production* (London: Longmans, Green, 1916), 489; Benson, *Printed Picture,* 222–27; and Dusan C. Stulik and Art Kaplan, *Halftone: The Atlas of Analytical Signatures of Photographic Processes* (Los Angeles: Getty Conservation Institute, 2013), 5. Halftone images produced using zinc or copper plates were also known as "phototones" in the 1920s. See Charles W. Hackleman, *Commercial Engraving and Printing: A Manual of Practical Instruction Covering Commercial Illustrating and Printing by All Processes* (Indianapolis: Commercial Engraving Publishing, 1921), 265. This process was key for the translation of halftones onto printing plates. See John Harthan, *The History of the Illustrated Book: The Western Tradition* (London: Thames and Hudson, 1981), 282.
68. Kinross, "Introduction to thc English-Language Edition," xxxii.
69. Moholy-Nagy, *Malerei Photographie Film,* 38. Emphasis in bold is original to Moholy-Nagy's text.
70. Moholy-Nagy, 38.
71. This is evident from the illustrations reproduced in *Die Neue Typographie,* which represent only a fraction of the designer's vast collection of materials by other designers, amassed in the 1920s and 1930s. These materials are currently divided between Tschichold's estate housed by the Deutsches Buch und Schriftsmuseum, Nationalbibliothek, Leipzig; the Jan and Edith Tschichold papers at the Getty Research Institute in Los Angeles; and the Typographische Sammlung Jan Tschichold, Bibliothek für Gestaltung Basel.

72. These included books, advertisements, posters, letterhead, business cards, book plates, periodicals, and envelopes. The book is filled with prescriptions of "good" and "bad" graphic design, according to the doctrine of New Typography, many of which would have been familiar to anyone who had read "elementare typographie."

73. "Die leitende Idee dieser neuen Typographie, Ausdruck des Zeitgeistes der Gegenwart zu sein, ist richtig, und sieht man von den vielen allerdings wohl auch nicht zu umgehenden Fehlgriffen ab, so finden sich doch auch zahlreiche wertvolle Leistungen, die eine Bereicherung typographischen Gestaltens bedeuten." Rudolf Engel-Hardt, "Neujahrsgedanken zur Typographie," *Klimschs Druckerei-Anzeiger* 57, no. 2 (January 7, 1930): 31. Engel-Hardt's remarks are included in a collection of short statements by German printers and typographers on the state of their field, marking the beginning of the new year. Although these reflections were published five years after the release of "elementare typographie" and two years after *Die Neue Typographie* was published, many discuss Tschichold's formula with urgency, evidence of how deeply felt New Typography's announcements were in the German printing world.

74. "Höchstes Ziel des Buchdruckers muß sein, unter Bejahung des neuen Gestaltungswillens typographische Form und Inhalt aufeinander abzustimmen, d.h. eine Satzweise zu finden, die dem Charakter der Drucksache jeweils entspricht." Engel-Hardt, 31. Though often translated simply as "design," my translation of *Gestaltung* is informed by Detlef Mertins and Michael Jennings's discussion of the complex meanings encoded in this word, in the introduction to their edited volume on the international journal founded and promoted by Hans Richter, Theo van Doesburg, El Lissitzky, Raoul Hausmann, Ludwig Mies van der Rohe, and Werner Graeff. Mertins and Jennings note the intentional slippage in uses of *Gestaltung* by the Central European avant garde between parts of speech, using the term to "refer to form as well as to the process of formation or form-creation or form-giving or even production." Noting the term's connotation of both biological formation and technological production, they translate *Gestaltung* principally as "form-creation," or, when used in the context of constructivism, as "form-production." I use the latter translation throughout to invoke the constructivist connotation of "montage," referring to photomontage as both a product and process of technological assembly. See Detlef Mertins and Michael W. Jennings, "Introduction: The G-Group and the European Avant-Garde," in *G: An Avant-Garde Journal of Art, Architecture, Design, and Film, 1923–1926*, ed. Mertins and Jennings (Los Angeles: Getty Publications, 2010), 5.

75. "Jede Verallgemeinerung oder Überbetonung ist verfehlt, falsch ist auch 'Neue Sachlichkeit' um jeden Preis." Engel-Hardt, "Neujahrsgedanken zur Typographie," 31.

76. He contrasted the *Stahlzeit* to the *Holzzeit* (age of wood) of the Middle Ages. Walter Porstmann, *Sprache und Schrift*, ed. Richard R. Hinz (Berlin: Verlag des Vereins

Deutscher Ingenieure, 1920). Steel was a popular motif in interwar German culture, used especially to evoke experiences of soldiers during World War I. Most famously, Ernst Jünger included it in the title of his memoir, *In Stahlgewittern: Aus dem Tagebuch eines Stoßtruppführers* [*In Storms of Steel: From the Diary of a Shock Troop Commander*] (Berlin: Verlag von E. S. Mittler and Sohn, 1922).

77. Founded in 1917 as the Normenausschuß der deutschen Industrie, the state-run Deutsche Institut für Normung (DIN) establishes and maintains standards for manufacturing, trade, and science. See "DIN—kurz erklärt," Deutsche Institut für Normung, accessed July 31, 2019, https://www.din.de/de/ueber-normen-und-standards/basiswissen. The influence of Porstmann and the DIN on Tschichold is evident in the overarching argument of *Die Neue Typographie,* which closely follows that of Porstmann's *Sprache und Schrift,* as well as in the reproduction of a number of DIN documents for the standardization of paper size and various references to Porstmann in the book. Tschichold was a voracious collector of DIN materials, many of which are included in the Nachlass Jan Tschichold, Deutsches Buch- und Schriftmuseum der Deutschen Nationalbibliothek, Leipzig. DIN standards were a popular subject of debate among printers and typographers in Weimar Germany. See, for example, Robert Eduard Kukowka, "Der Einfluss des DIN-Formates auf die Satztechnik," *Klimschs Druckerei-Anzeiger* 54, no. 14 (1927): 275–77. For studies on Porstmann's influence on New Typography, see Kinross, "Das Bauhaus im Kontext der Neuen Typographie," 10; and McMurray, "Winning New Freedom," 126–31.
78. Tschichold, *New Typography,* 95.
79. Porstmann, *Sprache und Schrift,* 58. Among Portsmann's recommendations for modern script was *kleinschreibung,* the abolition of all capitalization in written language on the basis of efficiency and economy, which Tschichold also advocated in *Die Neue Typographie.* In addition to photography, he also discussed film as a "visual language" of the nineteenth and twentieth centuries.
80. Tschichold, *New Typography,* 87.
81. This was an idea partly borrowed from the Russian avant-garde, namely the Russian futurist literary movement, which sought to level the hierarchy between fine book printing and ephemeral printed matter. Writers such as Vladimir Mayakovsky, Osip Brik, and Viktor Shklovski—in collaboration with visual artists and designers, including Lissitzky and Rodchenko—published and distributed their work through printed journals, such as *Left* and *New Left,* as well as pamphlets and books printed on inexpensive paper. See Evgeny Dobrenko, *Aesthetics of Alienation: Reassessment of Early Soviet Cultural Theories,* trans. Jesse M. Savage (Evanston, Ill.: Northwestern University Press, 2005); Maria Gough, "Faktura: The Making of the Russian Avant-Garde," in "Faktura," ed. Joseph Leo Koerner, special issue, RES: *Anthropology and*

Aesthetics, no. 36 (Autumn 1999): 32–59; Nina Gurianova, *The Aesthetics of Anarchy: Art and Ideology in the Early Russian Avant-Garde* (Berkeley: University of California Press, 2012); and Marjorie Perloff, *The Futurist Moment: Avant-Garde, Avant Guerre, and the Language of Rupture* (Chicago: University of Chicago Press, 1986).

82. Edlef Köppen, "The Magazine as a Sign of the Times," in *The Weimar Republic Sourcebook,* ed. Anton Kaes, Martin Jay, and Edward Dimendberg (Berkeley: University of California Press, 1994), 645. Originally published as "Das Magazin als Zeichen der Zeit," *Der Hellweg* 5, no. 24 (June 17, 1925): 457.
83. Köppen, "Magazine as a Sign of the Times," 644.
84. Siegfried Kracauer, "Photography" (1927), in *The Mass Ornament: Weimar Essays,* trans. Thomas Y. Levin (Cambridge, Mass.: Harvard University Press, 1995), 59.
85. "Die bildliche Darstellung, das Typophoto in Verbindung mit dem Industriesymbol wird die Zukunft der Reklame und die Straße regieren, ebenso wie die Büros und die Stätten der Wirtschaft. Den der phantastische Energieverschleiß unserer Zeit wird die höchste Ökonomie der Organisations- und Verkehrsmittel erzwingen." Johannes Molzahn, *Ökonomie der Reklame-Mechane,* 1926, n.p. A copy of this pamphlet is located in the Typographische Sammlung Jan Tschichold, Bibliothek für Gestaltung Basel.
86. Johannes Molzahn, "Stop Reading! Look!," in Kaes, Jay, and Dimendberg, *Weimar Republic Sourcebook,* 648. Originally published as "Nicht mehr lessen! Sehen!," *Das Kunstblatt* 12, no. 3 (March 1928): 78–82.
87. Molzahn, "Stop Reading! Look!," 648.
88. Molzahn established his studio in Magdeburg in 1923, and Burchartz founded his solo design studio in Bochum early in 1924, partnering with Johannes Canis later that year to establish the firm known as werbe-bau. See Gerda Breuer, "Vom Mahler zum Werbefachmann: Max Burchartz und die Typographie seiner Zeit," in *Max Burchartz, 1887–1961: Künstler, Typograf, Pädagoge,* ed. Gerda Breuer and Julia Meer (Berlin: Jovis, 2010), 84–99; and Annemarie Jaeggi, *Fagus: Industriekultur zwischen Werkbund und Bauhaus* (Berlin: Bauhaus-Archiv/Museum für Gestaltung, 1998), 95–98.
89. This leaflet series was retitled and continued as *werbe-beratung,* produced by the firm werbe-bau. Both leaflets are included in the Typographische Sammlung Jan Tschichold, Bibliothek für Gestaltung Basel. For a comprehensive study of Max Burchartz's work as an artist and designer, see Breuer and Meer, *Max Burchartz.*
90. "Der moderne Mensch geizt mit der Zeit. Wer liest langen Text bei Hunderten von Anzeigen und Plakaten, wer hört auf lange Reden?" (The modern person is stingy with time. Who reads long text on hundreds of advertisements and posters, who listens to long speeches?) Burchartz, *Gestaltung der Reklame,* June 1924, n.p.
91. "Gute Reklame bedient sich neuester zeitgemäßer Erfindungen als neuer Werkzeuge der Mitteilung. Projektion und Film, Grammophon und Radio-Telegraphie bringen

neue Möglichkeiten neben dem Mittel der Typographie." (Good advertising uses the latest contemporary inventions as new tools of communication. Projection and film, gramophone and radiotelegraphy bring new possibilities alongside the medium of typography.) Burchartz, n.p.

92. "Innerhalb der Typoegraphie ergeben sich neue Möglichkeiten auch durch Verwendungphotographischer Verfahren auf neuartige Weise, z.B. durch Retouchen, Eigenart der Aufnahmen und Zussamenstellung verschiedener Aufnahmen bei unterschiedlichen Größe- und Perspektive-Verhältnissen. In der Darstellung ist die Photographie der veralteten Handzeichnung überlegen, sie ist sachlicher, ökonomischer. Schnell herstellbar vermeidet sie die Überbetonung individueller Handschrift, ohne den Ausdruck von Eigenart auszuschießen, dem in der Anordnung noch genügend weiter Spielraum bleibt." Burchartz, n.p.
93. Molzahn, "Stop Reading! Look!," 648.
94. See, for example, Jan Tschichold, "Gute und schlechte Reklametypographie," *Württembergische Industrie* 10, no. 16 (April 20, 1929): 213–16. The same text was republished in 1930 in an unknown publication, as evidenced by a clipping included in the Nachlass Jan Tschichold, Deutsches Buch- und Schriftmuseum der Deutschen Nationalbibliothek, Leipzig (publication unknown, labeled "Wien 1930" in Tschichold's hand).
95. "Fotografie nicht nur als Nebenher, sondern als sprechendes Bild / als Bildtype." This note appears on the back of an envelope scrap, written in pencil. Jan Tschichold, undated handwritten note, Box 74, Nachlass Jan Tschichold, Deutsches Buch- und Schriftmuseum der Deutschen Nationalbibliothek, Leipzig. Underlining is original to Tschichold's text.
96. Moholy-Nagy, *Malerei Photographie Film,* 38–39.
97. Moholy-Nagy, 38.
98. Moholy-Nagy's original line reads, "Typographie ist in Druck gestaltete Mitteilung." See *Malerei Photographie Film,* 37. My translation of this line differs from Janet Seligman's published translation in *Painting Photography Film,* which reads, "Typography is communication composed in type." I have translated *gestaltete* as "formed" and *Druck* as "print," in keeping with Moholy-Nagy's emphasis on the process of printing as the foundation of modern communication.
99. Emphasis in bold is original to Moholy-Nagy's text. Moholy-Nagy, *Malerei Photographie Film,* 39.
100. In her analysis of *Malerei Photographie Film,* Pepper Stetler has sought to privilege Moholy-Nagy's book as a visual and material object that was intended as a manual for the collective training of new vision. While her analysis includes the visual argument of the book's photographic essay, her efforts to decipher this level of meaning ultimately maintain the assumption that the verbal and visual aspects of the book

operate autonomously, just as a purely textual analysis would suggest. See Stetler, *Stop Reading! Look!*

101. This typeface is likely in the Venus–Grotesk family, first released in 1907 by Bauer Type Foundry. See Bauerschen Giesserei, *Hauptprobe in gedrängter Form der Bauerschen Giesserei* (Frankfurt am Main: Bauerschen Giesserei; Barcelona, Madrid: Filialen; Leipzig: Numrich and Co., 1915). It is used throughout to add emphasis to specific lines of text, including Moholy-Nagy's appeal to "the hygiene of the visual." Moholy-Nagy, *Malerei Photographie Film,* 38.
102. Tschichold, *New Typography,* 70.
103. Moholy-Nagy, *Painting Photography Film,* 38–39.
104. Moholy-Nagy noted that this storyboard was originally sketched out between 1921 and 1922, and that he had intended to realize the film in collaboration with Carl Koch. Moholy-Nagy, *Painting Photography Film,* 122.
105. Moholy-Nagy, 122.
106. Emphasis in bold is part of Moholy-Nagy's original text. Moholy-Nagy, 122.
107. Moholy-Nagy, 122.
108. Stetler, *Stop Reading! Look!*, 7.
109. Frederic J. Schwartz, *Blind Spots: Critical Theory and the History of Art in Twentieth-Century Germany* (New Haven, Conn.: Yale University Press, 2005), 47.
110. Schwartz, 47–48.
111. "Die Reklame ist in der heutigen Gemeinschaftsordnung eine Notwendigkeit geworden, eine Folge des Konkurrenztriebes." Mart Stam and El Lissitzky, "Die Reklame," in Tschichold, "sonderheft: elementare typographie," 206.
112. "Die Ware wird genannt"; "Die Ware wird gezeigt." Stam and Lissitzky, 206.
113. "Die photographische Darstellung des reklamierenden Gegenstandes selbst, oder seiner Wirkung, oder beides zusammen, füllen allein die ganze Plakatfläche aus." Stam and Lissitzky, 207.
114. "Für diesen Zweck ist eine photomechanische Reproduktion, mit einem markanten Signet versehen, jeder mehr oder weniger geschickt gezeichneten oder gemalten Abbildung vorzuziehen." Stam and Lissitzky, 207.
115. This image is also reproduced in Heinz Rasch and Bodo Rasch, eds., *Gefesselter Blick* (Stuttgart: Wissenschaftlicher Verlag Dr. Zaugg and Co., 1930), 18.
116. This is according to Bettina Richter, curator of the Plakatsammlung, Museum für Gestaltung Zürich. See Richter, "Otto Baumberger. Poster, Marque PKZ, 1923," Museum für Gestaltung Zürich eGuide, accessed July 2, 2019, https://www.eguide.ch/en/objekt/marque-pkz.
117. Tschichold wrote, "It is surprising how well a small part of a single photograph can sometimes work as a poster, as in the PKZ poster by Baumberger. It is a pillar-poster made from a colour photograph." Tschichold, *New Typography,* 182.

118. For studies of the *Sachplakat* in the context of pre–World War I German poster and advertising design, see Jeremy Aynsley, *Graphic Design in Germany, 1890–1945* (Berkeley: University of California Press, 2000); Susanne Bäumler, *Die Kunst zu Werben: Das Jahrhundert der Reklame* (Munich: Münchner Stadtmuseum, 1996); David Ciarlo, *Advertising Empire: Race and Visual Culture in Imperial Germany* (Cambridge, Mass.: Harvard University Press, 2011); Elizabeth Guffey, *Posters: A Global History* (London: Reaktion Books, 2015); and Schwartz, *Werkbund*, 136–39.

119. *Sachlichkeit* had originally been a key term used and debated by the Deutscher Werkbund, a state-sponsored association of economists, designers, and industrialists who sought to reconcile aesthetic value in design with the mass production of commodities in a newly industrialized economy. The term *Neue Sachlichkeit* was coined by Gustav Friedrich Hartlaub and popularized by his exhibition *Die Neue Sachlichkeit: Deutsche Malerei seit dem Expressionismus*, which opened in 1925 at the Kunsthalle Mannheim, where he served as director. Hartlaub identified *Neue Sachlichkeit* as an anti-expressionist tendency toward realism in German painting after World War I, encompassing both verist and classicist modes of representation. The term became ubiquitous to describe a collective desire for a postwar return to order, which manifested in various aspects of Weimar German culture, including photography, architecture, and design. See Stephanie Barron and Sabine Eckmann, eds., *New Objectivity: Modern German Art in the Weimar Republic, 1919–1933* (London: Prestel, 2015); Herbert Molderings, "The Modernist Cause: New Vision and New Objectivity, 1919–1945," in *Collection Photographs: A History of Photography through the Collections of the Centre Pompidou, Musée National d'Art Moderne*, ed. Quentin Bajac and Clément Chéroux (Paris: Centre Pompidou, 2007): 97–114; and Schwartz, *Werkbund*.

120. For studies on Renger-Patzsch's work for Fagus-Werk, see Annemarie Jaeggi, *Die Moderne im Blick: Albert Renger-Patzsch fotografiert das Fagus Werk* (Berlin: Bauhaus-Archiv / Museum für Gestaltung, 2011); and Jaeggi, *Fagus*. For a study on Finsler's work for Osram, see Klaus E. Göltz, Theo Immisch, Peter Romanus, and Axel Wendelberger, eds., *Hans Finsler, neue Wege der Photographie* (Leipzig: Edition Leipzig, 1991). For further discussion of the still life photography of Renger-Patzsch and Finsler in the context of both *Neue Sachlichkeit* and its utility in advertising, see Megan R. Luke, "Still Lifes and Commodities," in Barron and Eckmann, *New Objectivity*, 229–57.

2 THE MOTIVATION OF FORM

1. László Moholy-Nagy, "Photography in Advertising," in *Photography in the Modern Era: European Documents and Critical Writings, 1913–40*, ed. and trans. Christopher Phillips (New York: Metropolitan Museum of Art, 1989), 87. Originally published as

"Die Photographie in Der Reklame," *Photographische Korrespondenz*, no. 9 (September 1927): 257–60.

2. Moholy-Nagy also noted that psychological science was "still far behind the times, compared to the study of physical laws." Moholy-Nagy, "Photography in Advertising," 87.
3. I am grateful to Grace Converse for her invaluable feedback on an earlier draft of this chapter.
4. Kurt Danziger, *Constructing the Subject: Historical Origins of Psychological Research* (Cambridge: Cambridge University Press, 1990), 28; Ludy T. Benjamin Jr., *A Brief History of Modern Psychology* (Malden, Mass.: Blackwell, 2007), 37.
5. As an amalgam of physiology and philosophy, the discipline of psychology followed an epistemological model that Zeynep Çelik Alexander has called "kinaesthetic knowing," mediation between intellectual contemplation and immediate experience, which she argues was foundational for modernist design, particularly in Germany. Alexander's study is therefore a key text for thinking about the importance of early psychological methods and rhetoric to avant-garde design. See *Kinaesthetic Knowing: Aesthetics, Epistemology, Modern Design* (Chicago: University of Chicago Press, 2017).
6. Among them were G. Stanley Hall, who established the first experimental psychology laboratory in the United States at Johns Hopkins University in 1883; James McKeen Cattell, who in 1889 became the first professor of psychology in the United States at the University of Pennsylvania; and Walter Dill Scott and Hugo Münsterberg, who further developed applied psychology as an academic discipline around the turn of the century at Northwestern University and Harvard University, respectively. Wundt also worked with Oswald Külpe and Karl Marbe, who together founded the Institut für Psychologie at the Universität Würzburg in 1896, another important center for early psychological research in Germany. On the early history of experimental psychology, see Benjamin, *Brief History of Modern Psychology*, 74–92; and Danziger, *Constructing the Subject.*
7. See, for example, Eric N. Simons, "White Space and the Reader's Eye," *Commercial Art*, January 1923, 78.
8. Raymond, "Aspects of the Selling Art, VIII: Continuity of Interest," *Commercial Art*, February 1927, 69.
9. Frank H. Young, "Modern Layouts Must Sell Rather Than Startle," *Advertising Arts*, January 1930, 43.
10. "Die Reklame ist somit nichts anderes als *schriftliche Beratung*, ferner ein Anknüpfen an schon mehr oder minder vorhandene Neigungen, Wünsche, Absichten." Paul Wallfisch-Roulin, "Was ist Suggestion in der Reklame?," *Gebrauchsgraphik*, 3, no. 6 (June 1926): 27.

11. "In diesem Sinne will die suggestive Reklame durch das Mittel der Gedankenassoziation zu einem Starkwerden der oft nur keimartig vorhandenen Neigungen, Wünsche, Absichten führen, das heißt letzten Ende zu einem *Kaufentschluß*." Wallfisch-Roulin, 27.
12. Eric Warne, "Making the Artist Get Your Idea," *Commercial Art*, November 1922, 5.
13. "Photographs That Give Atmosphere," *Commercial Art*, December 1922, 55, 60.
14. Viktor Mataja, *Die Reklame* (Leipzig: Duncker and Humblot, 1910); Hugo Münsterberg, *Psychology and Industrial Efficiency* (New York: Houghton Mifflin, 1913); Christoph von Hartungen, *Reklame Psychologie* (Stuttgart: C. E. Poeschel Verlag, 1921); Theodor König, *Reklame-Psychologie: Ihr gegenwärtiger Stand, ihre praktische Bedeutung* (Munich: Verlag R. Oldenbourg, 1924); Hanns Kropff, *Psychologie in der Reklame als Hilfe zur Bestgestaltung des Entwurfs* (Stuttgart: C. E. Poeschel Verlag, 1934).
15. Among the schools to add *Werbewissenschaft* (advertising science) to their curriculum were the University of Cologne and the Handelshochschulen in Berlin, Mannheim, and Leipzig. See Corey Ross, *Media and the Making of Modern Germany: Mass Communications, Society, and Politics from the Empire to the Third Reich* (Oxford: Oxford University Press, 2010), 215.
16. The portable Leica camera became commercially available in 1925, and rotogravure printing became commonplace in the 1920s for the inexpensive, mass production of newspapers and magazines. See Michel Frizot, ed., *A New History of Photography* (Cologne: Könneman Verlagsgesellschaft mbH, 1998); and Michel Frizot and Cédric de Veigy, *"VU": The Story of a Magazine* (London: Thames and Hudson, 2009).
17. Hermann Frenzel, "Der Prospekt," *Gebrauchsgraphik* 3, no. 6 (June 1926): 4.
18. Frederic Schwartz has shown the interests of New Typography in theories and experiments developed in the German subfield of psychology known as psychotechnics. Julia Meer has also identified the rhetoric of applied psychology among New Typography's influences. See Frederic J. Schwartz, *Blind Spots: Critical Theory and the History of Art in Twentieth-Century Germany* (New Haven, Conn.: Yale University Press, 2005), 66–86; Julia Meer, *Neuer Blick auf die Neue Typographie: Die Rezeption der Avantgarde in der Fachwelt der 1920er Jahre* (Bielefeld: transcript Verlag, 2015), 27–45.
19. "We have a number of careful experimental investigations referring to the memory-value, the attention-value, and the suggestion-value, and other mental effects of the printed business advertisements." Münsterberg, *Psychology and Industrial Efficiency*, 257–58. Münsterberg was among the first to study human will and the visual perception of space as subjects of psychological inquiry. See Matthew Hale Jr., *Human Science and Social Order: Hugo Münsterberg and the Origins of Applied Psychology* (Philadelphia: Temple University Press, 1980), 22.

20. W. Buchanan-Taylor, "Reklame: Wissenschaft Oder Kunst?," *Gebrauchsgraphik* 5, no. 8 (August 1928): 57–58.
21. Psychotechnics was developed by psychologists including Münsterberg, Fritz Giese, Walter Moede, and Emil Kraepelin around the turn of the twentieth century as a German response to Taylorism, indicative of *Amerikanismus* as both an influence and threat to Germany's newly industrialized culture. See Fritz Giese, *Psychotechnik und Taylorsystem* (Langensalza: Wendt und Klauwell, 1920); and Hugo Münsterberg, *Grundzüge der Psychotechnik* (Leipzig: Barth, 1914).
22. For more on this context, see Joan Campbell, *Joy in Work, German Work: The National Debate, 1800–1945* (Princeton, N.J.: Princeton University Press, 1989). For more on Taylorism's influence on industrial design in America, see Terry Smith, *Making the Modern: Industry, Art, and Design in America* (Chicago: University of Chicago Press, 1993). Psychotechnics reemerged in the aftermath of World War I as a strategy for rebuilding the German economy. For more on the popularity of psychotechnics in the Weimar era, see Andreas Killen, "Weimar Psychotechnics between Americanism and Fascism," in "The Self as Project: Politics and the Human Sciences," ed. Greg Eghigian, Andreas Killen, and Christine Leuenberger, special issue, *Osiris* 22, no. 1 (2007): 48–71; and Charles S. Maier, "Between Taylorism and Technocracy: European Ideologies and the Vision of Industrial Productivity in the 1920s," *Journal of Contemporary History* 5, no. 2 (1970): 27–61.
23. Münsterberg, *Psychology and Industrial Efficiency*, 256.
24. Münsterberg, 262–63.
25. Hugo Münsterberg, *Psychology, General and Applied* (New York: D. Appleton and Company, 1914), 430–31. He also cited similar studies on legibility published by American psychologists Walter Dill Scott and Daniel Starch, as well as others he had personally conducted and supervised at the Harvard Psychological Laboratory. These studies tested the legibility of advertisements printed at different sizes and positioned variably on a page, as well as the effects of color and composition on the speed and accuracy with which subjects could recall them.
26. Other variants of these experiments showed that advertisements printed on the right side or upper quarter of the page were more memorable, thereby doubling the "mental value" of the right-hand upper quarter of a page. Münsterberg, 430.
27. Jan Tschichold, "Die Neue Typographie," in *Active Literature: Jan Tschichold and New Typography*, by Christopher Burke (London: Hyphen, 2007), 29–30. Burke notes that Tschichold's emphasis on the importance of economy and brevity is reflective of the context of economic scarcity and recovery in Germany during the Weimar Republic.
28. Tschichold, 29.

29. Gerrit Willem Ovink, *Legibility, Atmosphere-Value and Forms of Printing Types* (Leiden: A. W. Sijthoff, 1938).
30. Ovink, 38–71. Display typefaces were considered most appropriate for headings, titles, and very short lines of text—rather than for larger blocks or longer lines of text—and were often used for signage and poster design.
31. Ovink, 38.
32. Ovink also noted that serifs could impede legibility in cases where one letterform might easily be confused for another, but in other cases, they did not affect legibility. Ovink, 44–71.
33. Gale was one of the many American psychologists trained by Wilhelm Wundt in Leipzig. After returning to the United States in 1895, Gale headed the University of Minnesota's experimental psychology laboratory, where he established a program to study advertising psychology through the development of laboratory experiments and distribution of consumer surveys. For more on Gale's legacy and work, see John Eighmey and Sela Sar, "Harlow Gale and the Origins of Psychology in Advertising," *Journal of Advertising* 36, no. 4 (Winter 2007): 147–58.
34. Eighmey and Sar, 153–54.
35. These results were summarized in Walter Dill Scott, *The Theory and Practice of Advertising: A Simple Exposition of the Principles of Psychology in Their Relation to Successful Advertising* (Boston: Small, Maynard and Company, 1913), 12.
36. Eighmey and Sar, "Harlow Gale and the Origins of Psychology in Advertising," 153–54.
37. E. H. M. Georgeson, "Blue the Favourite Colour: A Practical Test," *Commercial Art*, November 1923, 317.
38. Albert T. Poffenberger, *Psychology in Advertising* (New York: McGraw Hill, 1925).
39. Half of these combinations were painted in pairs of "saturated colors," and the other half were painted in "weak" hues of the same colors. Each group consisted of the following pairs: red–yellow, red–green, red–blue, blue–orange, blue–yellow, blue–green, yellow–green, yellow–purple, yellow–orange, red–orange, and red–purple. Poffenberger, 453.
40. Poffenberger, 455.
41. Subjects were permitted to use the same image as many times as they chose. Poffenberger, 455.
42. This conclusion was especially exemplified by the color yellow. While most subjects reported disliking yellow, it was the color that appeared the most in the pairs chosen as matches with the terms given. Poffenberger, 463.
43. Poffenberger, 462–63.

44. This study was conducted at the Columbia Psychological Laboratory under the supervision of Poffenberger and B. E. Barrows and was first published in the *Journal of Applied Psychology* 8 (1924): 187.
45. The study of perception was a branch of experimental psychology pioneered especially by Münsterberg at the University of Freiburg, where he was appointed from 1887 until 1892. He promoted the basic tenet of applied psychology, arguing that psychological stimulus is directly connected to physiological action, which was sharply criticized by Wundt and G. E. Müller, but praised by American psychologist William James, who invited Münsterberg to teach at Harvard University in 1892. Hale, *Human Science and Social Order,* 22–25. See also Danziger, *Constructing the Subject,* 17–33.
46. Kropff worked as a consultant to department store proprietor Leonard Tietz before taking a position teaching commercial advertising at Vienna University of Economics and Business in 1936. See Meer, *Neuer Blick auf die Neue Typographie,* 325.
47. "Was aufmerksam betrachtet wird, ist klarer." (What is considered attentively is clearer.) Kropff, *Psychologie in der Reklame als Hilfe zur Bestgestaltung des Entwurfs,* 111–12.
48. "Blickt man auf ein Inserat, so sieht man nichts, wenn die Augen über das Ganze schweifen, sondern man erkennt nur die einzelnen Teile, auf denen das Augen ruhen bleibt." Kropff, 111.
49. Kropff, 129–30.
50. American psychologist Walter Dill Scott similarly offered rules for graphic design through critique of sample advertising. See *Theory and Practice of Advertising.*
51. Scott, 164.
52. Scott, 164.
53. "Kombination von Rechtecken und konzentrischen Kreisen. Die Rechtecke sind entweder mathematische Quadrate, doppelte Quadrate oder nähern sich sehr stark dem goldenen Schnitt. Starke Isolierung durch schwarze Flächen." Kropff, *Psychologie in der Reklame als Hilfe zur Bestgestaltung des Entwurfs,* 98.
54. Kropff's writing was almost certainly known to most German graphic designers in the 1920s and 1930s. See, for example, an outline of a course offered in the summer of 1926 by the Schutzverband der Reklametreibenden Österreichs (Austrian Association of Advertising Protection) by Hanns Kropff and Bruno W. Randolph, published in *Gebrauchsgraphik:* "Psychologie in der Reklame: Reklame-Psychologie in Theorie und Praxis," *Gebrauchsgraphik* 3, no. 6 (June 1926): 48–53. The article indicates that at that time, Kropff taught at the Handelshochschule Köln and Randolph was appointed at Columbia University.

55. For a thorough study of abstract form as a tool of contemporaneous psychological experiments in film, see Michael Cowan, *Walter Ruttmann and the Cinema of Multiplicity: Avant-Garde–Advertising–Modernity* (Amsterdam: Amsterdam University Press, 2014).
56. "Die Augen des Menchen haben die Tendenz, nicht auf einen Punkt fixiert zu bleiben, sondern herumzuschweifen. Jedes Herumschweifen des Auges bedeutet aber eine Wanderung der Aufmerksamkeit nach einem anderen Punkt. Dieses Herumschweifen, Abgleiten oder Wandern des Auges ist ein Zeichen für das Fluktuieren der Aufmerksamkeit. Wenn das Auge in Bewegung ist, sieht es nichts, nur in Ruh erblickt das menschliche Auge etwas bestimmtes und der übrige Mechanismus des Körpers verarbeitet es." Kropff, *Psychologie in der Reklame als Hilfe zur Bestgestaltung des Entwurfs*, 110.
57. "So fällt der Blick des Menschen zuerst auf die Mitte der Seite, das heißt auf das optische Zentrum." (One's glance first falls on the center of the page, that is, on the optical center.) Kropff, 119.
58. "Man hat die Augen von Personen photographiert und so festgestellt, wie sie beim Lesen und beim Betrachten von Bildern wandern. Man hat so einwandfrei festgestellt, wie sie sich bewegen, beziehungsweise wann sie ruhen und wann die Aufmerksamkeit wirken kann." Kropff, 119.
59. Louis Émile Javal, "Essai sur la physiologie de la lecture," *Annales d'oculistique*, no. 79 (1878): 97–117, 240–74.
60. The tachistoscope is a mechanical device that displays an image for a specific amount of time. First developed in the 1850s and used by scientists such as Hermann von Helmholtz to study human perception, tachistoscopy served as a tool of experimental psychological study as soon as the field emerged. American psychologist James McKeen Cattell apprenticed with Wundt at the Institut für Experimentelle Psychologie at the Universität Leipzig in the 1880s and designed his own tachistoscope to measure image perception more precisely. Walter Dearborn furthered this work, under the mentorship of Cattell at Columbia University, and published a set of photographic images made with a tachistoscope in 1906. See Ruth Benschop, "What Is a Tachistoscope? Historical Explorations of an Instrument," *Science in Context* 11 (1998): 23–50; and David Sweeney Coombs, "An Untrained Eye: The Tachistoscope and Photographic Vision in Early Experimental Psychology," *History and Technology* 28, no. 1 (2012): 107–17; and Danziger, *Constructing the Subject*, 28.
61. This finding was published in Erdmann and Dodge's coauthored book *Psychologische Untersuchungen über das Lesen auf Experimenteller Grundlager* (Halle: Max Niemeyer, 1898). Gerrit Ovink cited Erdmann and Dodge's findings in Ovink, *Legibility, Atmosphere-Value and Forms of Printing Types*, 71. An earlier version of this theory

was posited in James McKeen Cattell, "The Time It Takes to See and Name Objects" *Mind* 11 (January 1886): 63–65.

62. Miles A. Tinker, "Eye Movements in Reading," *Journal of Educational Research* 30, no. 4 (December 1936): 242.
63. Edmund Burke Huey, *The Psychology and Pedagogy of Reading: With a Review of the History of Reading and Writing and of Methods, Texts, and Hygiene in Reading* (Cambridge, Mass.: MIT Press, 1908).
64. Huey, 24–31.
65. For a thorough discussion of terminology in eye tracking, see Jukka Hyönä, Ralph Radach, and Heiner Deubel, eds., *The Mind's Eye: Cognitive and Applied Aspects of Eye Movement Research* (Amsterdam: North-Holland, 2003).
66. Lisa Cartwright, *Screening the Body: Tracing Medicine's Visual Culture* (Minneapolis: University of Minnesota, 1995), 29.
67. Cartwright, 29.
68. Infographics became conventions of graphic design especially through the development of the Vienna Method of pictorial statistics, a systematic approach to the visual representation of information innovated between 1926 and 1933 at the Gesellschafts- und Wirtschaftsmuseum in Vienna, under the direction of Otto Neurath, by Gerd Arntz, Marie Neurath, and Peter Alma. An in-depth discussion of the Vienna Method is included in chapter 5, below. See also Christopher Burke, Eric Kindel, and Sue Walker, eds., *Isotype: Design and Contexts, 1925–1971* (London: Hyphen Press, 2013); and Frank Hartmann and Erwin K. Bauer, *Bildersprache: Otto Neurath; Visualisierung* (Vienna: Wiener Universitätsverlag, 2002).
69. Raymond Dodge and Thomas Cline, "The Angle Velocity of Eye Movements," *Psychological Review* 8 (1901): 145–57.
70. The device also included a swinging pendulum in the plate holder of the camera, which darkened the edge of the photographic plate at regular intervals, serving as a marker of time in the results recorded on the plate. Dodge and Cline, 145–57.
71. Walter Dearborn, *The Psychology of Reading: An Experimental Study of the Reading Pauses and Movements of the Eye* (New York: Science Press, 1906), 54–55.
72. Tinker, "Eye Movements in Reading," 245. Their experiments were conducted in the 1920s. Miles Tinker noted that these measurements recorded the vertical movement of one eye and the horizontal movement of the other simultaneously. Consequently, the photographs were composite images that amalgamated the independent movement of each of a subject's eye.
73. Guy Thomas Buswell, *How People Look at Pictures; A Study of the Psychology of Perception in Art* (Chicago: University of Chicago Press, 1935), 17.
74. Buswell, 143.

75. Buswell, 143.
76. Buswell, 18.
77. Scott, *Theory and Practice of Advertising,* 14. These "heavy" typefaces are commonly known as display typefaces.
78. Scott, 24.
79. Moholy-Nagy, "Photography in Advertising," 88.
80. I use the term "indexical signs" in reference to the semiotic theory of Charles Sanders Peirce, who categorized a sign that bears a causal relationship to its referent as an "index." See "What Is a Sign?" (1894), in *The Essential Peirce: Selected Philosophical Writings,* vol. 2, ed. Nathan Houser and Christian J. W. Kloesel (Bloomington: Indiana University Press, 1992), 4–10.
81. David Coombs has noted that "tachistoscopy shared with photography a rhetoric of 'exposure times' that makes plain an underlying analogy: what the photographic plate is to photography, the retina and brain are to tachistoscopy. Put another way, tachistoscopic experiments sought to measure a photographic eye." See "Untrained Eye," 108.
82. This played out especially in psychologists' reliance on questionnaires to study the effects of advertising on the behaviors, habits, and beliefs of consumers. Unpublished notes and findings from a number of American studies conducted in the 1920s and 1930s at Harvard University are located at Harvard Business School's Baker Library.
83. Scott, *Theory and Practice of Advertising,* 7.
84. Scott, 14–15.
85. The use of photographic metaphors in early twentieth-century psychology adds to a plethora of technology-related metaphors used by psychologists to understand and describe the workings of the mind. David Leary has argued that "the pervasiveness of twentieth-century psychology . . . is clearly related to its choice of metaphors. By drawing on culturally salient and popular metaphors, psychologists have created a salient and popular discipline." See "Psyche's Muse: The Role of Metaphor in the History of Psychology," in *Metaphors in the History of Psychology,* ed. William R. Woodward and Mitchell G. Ash (Cambridge: Cambridge University Press, 1990), 52.
86. "Der Einfluss der Form des Objektes," in König, *Reklame-Psychologie.* This book was based on König's dissertation, completed at the Universität Würzburg.
87. "In der Reklame wird der Helligkeitskontrast sowohl als Simultankonstrast wie als Sukzessivkontrast wirkungssteigend verwendet." (In advertising, brightness contrast is used both as simultaneous contrast and as successive contrast with increasing effect.) König, 40. Similar concepts were cited by Josef Albers in *Interaction*

of Color (1963; repr., New Haven, Conn.: Yale University Press, 2013), summarizing his theories of color relationships and color perception as he taught them at the Bauhaus and Black Mountain College.

88. König cited studies on color such as Gale's, but synthesized their results in terms of optical-cognitive perception. He also referenced the work of German economist and advertising expert Rudolf Seyffert, who conducted statistical analysis of poster designs and the corresponding profits of the companies who used them to advertise their products. His findings were published in "Die Statistik des Plakates" (*Zeitschrift für Handelswissenschaft und. Handelspraxis* 12 [1919/20]: 228–35), which analyzed the effectiveness of poster design. König, *Reklame-Psychologie,* 40.
89. Scott, *Theory and Practice of Advertising,* 17.
90. I use the term "visual illusions," rather than the more common "optical illusions," to flag the perception of images as an optical-psychic process that entails forming mental images in response to optical perception.
91. In addition to *Visual Illusions,* Luckiesh's books included *The Language of Color* (New York: Dodd, Mead and Company, 1918) and *Light and Color in Advertising and Merchandising* (New York: D. Van Nostrand Company, 1923).
92. Matthew Luckiesh, *Visual Illusions: Their Causes, Characteristics and Applications* (1922; repr., New York: Dover Publications, 1965), 1.
93. Luckiesh, 29.
94. "Optical Illusion in Relation to Poster Art," *Commercial Art,* August 1925, 194.
95. Luckiesh, *Visual Illusions,* 225–32. This type of camouflage was introduced by British marine Norman Wilkinson during World War I. Dazzle patterns—usually comprising stripes painted in contrasting colors—were used during the First World War as devices of visual disorientation that made it difficult to determine the distance, direction, or speed of an enemy vessel. The initial development of the technique in 1917 in Liverpool was overseen by Edward Wadsworth, who was associated with vorticism, along with Lawrence Campbell Taylor. See Jonathan Black, "'A Few Broad Stripes:' Perception, Deception, and the 'Dazzle Ship' Phenomenon of the First World War," in *Contested Objects: Material Memories of the Great War,* ed. Nicholas J. Saunders and Paul Cornish (London: Routledge, 2014), 190–202.
96. Max Wertheimer, "Untersuchungen zur Lehre von der Gestalt, II," *Psychologische Forschung* 4 (1923): 301–50.
97. Edited by Kurt Koffka, Wolfgang Köhler, Max Wertheimer, Kurt Goldstein, and Hans Gruhle, each representing its practice in different cities throughout Germany, the journal's full title was *Psychologische Forschung: Zeitschrift für Psychologie und ihre Grenzwissenschaften.*

98. For a history of Gestalt psychology, see Mitchell G. Ash, *Gestalt Psychology in German Culture, 1890–1967: Holism and the Quest for Objectivity* (Cambridge: Cambridge University Press, 1995).

99. Anne Harrington, *Reenchanted Science: Holism in German Culture from Wilhelm II to Hitler* (Princeton, N.J.: Princeton University Press, 1996), 103–4.

100. Kurt Koffka, *Principles of Gestalt Psychology* (New York: Harcourt, Brace and Company, 1935), 142.

101. Ernst Lau, "Versuche über das stereoskopische Sehen," *Psychologische Forschung* 2 (1922): 1–4. Another version of this image is reproduced in Luckiesh, *Visual Illusions*, 77.

102. Max Wertheimer, "Untersuchungen zur Lehre von der Gestalt, II," *Psychologische Forschung* 4 (1923): 301–50.

103. Though the direct influence of Gestalt psychology on interwar graphic design remains contested among scholars, it is clear that its basic principles of perception were assimilated into postwar American and European design theory, in combination with basic tenets of New Typography. See, for example, Rudolf Arnheim, *Art and Visual Perception* (Berkeley: University of California Press, 1954); and Gyorgy Kepec, *Language of Vision: Painting, Photography, Advertising Design* (Chicago: Theobald and Co., 1944). The influence of Gestaltists on design theory at the Bauhaus was first suggested by Hans Wingler, who noted that a series of lectures on Gestalt psychology were given in 1928 at the Dessau Bauhaus. See Hans M. Wingler, *Bauhaus: Weimar, Dessau, Berlin, Chicago* (Cambridge, Mass.: MIT Press, 1978), 159–60. Evidence of this line of influence on Bauhaus pedagogy may include Josef Albers, "werklicher formunterricht," *bauhaus*, no. 2/3 (1928): n.p. See also Ellen Lupton and J. Abbott Miller, eds., *The ABCs of Triangle, Square, Circle: The Bauhaus and Design Theory* (1993; repr., New York: Princeton Architectural Press 2019), n.p.; and Julia Moszkowicz, "Gestalt and Graphic Design: An Exploration of the Humanistic and Therapeutic Effects of Visual Organization," *Design Issues* 27, no. 4 (Autumn 2011): 56–67.

104. See, for example, the chapter on "Legibility" in Rob Carter, Ben Day, and Phillip Meggs, *Typographic Design: Form and Communication*, 4th ed. (Hoboken, N.J.: John Wiley and Sons, 2007), 73–90.

105. Raymond, "Aspects of the Selling Art, IX: Optical Gearshifting," *Commercial Art*, February 1927, 157.

106. Raymond, 158.

107. Emil Köditz, "Die Photomechanische Reproduktionstechnik," *Typographische Mitteilungen* 21, no. 6 (June 1924): 93–96.

108. See, for example, Charles W. Hackleman, *Commercial Engraving and Printing: A Manual of Practical Instruction Covering Commercial Illustrating and Printing by All Processes* (Indianapolis: Commercial Engraving Publishing Company, 1921); Lucien Alphonse

Legros and John Cameron Grant, *Typographical Printing-Surfaces: The Technology and Mechanism of Their Production* (London: Longmans, Green, and Co., 1916); and R. Russ and L. Englich, *Handbuch der Modernen Reproduktionstechnik: Band I, Reproduktionsphotographie und Retusche* (Frankfurt am Main: Verlag von Klimsch and Co., 1927).

109. Printers also experimented with printing halftones on different kinds of paper, testing their effects on the visibility and precision of images.

110. Here I am indebted to Gerry Beegan's work on the halftone's early integration into the Victorian press in the late nineteenth century. See *The Mass Image: A Social History of Photomechanical Reproduction in Victorian London* (London: Palgrave Macmillan, 2008).

111. "Die gute Reklame ist sachlich / ist klar und knapp / sie verwendet moderne Mittel / hat Schlagkraft der Form / ist billig." Max Burchartz, *Gestaltung der Reklame,* June 1924, n.p.

112. "Als moderne Mittel verwertet gute Reklame auch Ergebnisse wissenschaftlich-psychologischer Forschung und neue Gesichtspunkte der Entwickelung künstlerischer Gestaltung." Burchartz, n.p.

113. "Je heftiger sich der Kampf von Kontrasten äußert und je mehr zugleich eine Ausgeglichenheit im ganzen erreicht ist, um so eindringlicher, erregender und um so harmonischer zugleich wirken Gegenstände auf unsere Sinne." (The more violent the struggle of contrasts, the more balance is achieved overall, and the more urgently, excitingly, and harmoniously objects operate all at once on our senses.) Burchartz, n.p.

114. W. R. Tillerton, "Taste as a Commercial Asset," *Commercial Art,* November 1922, 3, 18.

115. Tillerton, 3.

116. Johannes Molzahn, *Ökonomie der Reklame-Mechane,* 1926, n.p. A portion of this text was reprinted in the April 1926 issue of the Deutscher Werkbund journal *Die Form:* "Ökonomie der Reklame-Mechane," *Die Form* 1, no. 7 (April 1926): 141–45.

117. "Propaganda ist aber ihrem Wesen nach Mitteilung in grafischer Darstellung; es wird nun die Frage sein, die grafischen Darstellungselemente zu ermitteln, die größte optische Wirksamkeit haben, sich der Psyche spiegeln und bewahren." (But propaganda is essentially communication in graphic form; Now the question will be to determine the graphic representational elements that have the greatest visual impact, and which reflect and preserve the psyche.) Molzahn, *Ökonomie der Reklame-Mechane,* n.p. The term "propaganda" was generally used interchangeably with "advertising" by designers and advertisers in the 1920s, before it had become associated with fascism. For a thorough discussion of the term "propaganda" and its many uses and connotations, see Jacques Ellul, *Propaganda: The Formation of Men's Attitudes,* trans. Konrad Kellen and Jean Lerner (New York: Alfred A. Knopf, 1972).

118. "Es bedarf wohl keines Beweises, daß das Auge, infolge seiner optischen Aufnahmefunktion, am besten konkrete Erscheinungen zu spiegeln und der Psyche die tiefsten und nachhaltigsten Eindrücke zu mitteln vermag. Darum wird sich auch der Umformungsmechanismus der Produktionspropaganda in erster Linie auf diese optischen Funktionen stützen müssen." Molzahn, n.p. The phrase *optischen Aufnahmefunktion* implies that the eye functions like a camera, creating a "recording" or "shot" of what it sees that lingers as a latent image in the beholder's mind.
119. "Eine vollwertige, nach optisch-psychischen Wirkungsgesetzen gestaltete Marke in konsequenter Anwendung spart Ihnen einen hohen Prozentsatz der Propagandakosten." Molzahn, n.p.
120. "Haben nicht nur unserem Denken neue Formen gegeben, sie haben auch die Physis und ganz besonders das Auge." Molzahn, n.p.
121. "Das Auge übernimmt aus der Unzahl der optischen Reize nur einen geringen Bruchteil." Molzahn, n.p.
122. "Nehmen wir ein Vergrößerungsglas zur Hand und schalten wir dieses zwischen Sonne und ein Stück Papier in der Weise, daß sich dieses in Brennpunkt der Linse befindet, so entzündet sich dasselbe, es entsteht Feuer. Wir haben also die Sonnenenergie in lebendige Energie umgeformt. Wir haben an diesem Beispiel das Prinzip erkannt, das auch die Symbole der Industrie aufbauen muß, ihnen Wirkung zu verschaffen. Die Marke hat die Funktion der Linse, sie steht für die Linse. Im Brennpunkt = Konzentrationspunkt des Industriesymbols wiederholt sich der gleiche Umformungsprozeß: die Produktionsenergie wird wirksam in der Psyche des Verbrauchers, etwa in der Weise, wie es in der Fig. 11 schematisch dargestellt ist." Molzahn, n.p.
123. "Die Form wird allein bestimmt von optisch-mechanischen Gesetzen. . . . Die Markenfrage ist in Wirklichkeit kein künstlerisches Problem zuerst, vielmehr ein technisch-wissenschaftliches und lebendig-psychisches." Molzahn, n.p.
124. Carter, Day, and Meggs, *Typographic Design,* 73.

3 *TYPOPHOTO* AND THE NEW PHOTOMONTAGE, 1928–1933

1. "Fotomontage ist ein neues Ausdrucksmittel, das die Präzision der fotografischen Aufnahme mit den optischen Reizen freier Raumgestaltung vereinigt." Paul Renner, Futura prospectus, Bauer Type Foundry, n.d. Available at Letterform Archive, San Francisco, in the pages of a March 1929 issue of *Gebrauchsgraphik.*
2. See the section titled "Photographie und Typographie" in Jan Tschichold, *Die Neue Typographie: Ein Handbuch für zeitgemäss Schaffende* (1928; repr., Berlin: Brinkmann and Rose, 1987), 89–98.
3. Jan Tschichold, *The New Typography: A Handbook for Modern Designers,* trans. Ruari McLean (1928; trans., Berkeley: University of California Press, 1995), 87–95.

4. Only the first two books in the Fototek series were published: László Moholy-Nagy, *László Moholy-Nagy: 60 Fotos* (Berlin: Klinkhardt and Biermann, 1930); and Aenne Biermann, *Aenne Biermann: 60 Fotos* (Berlin: Klinkhardt and Biermann, 1930). This advertisement for Fototek was designed by students at the Meisterschule für Deutschlands Buchdrucker, where Tschichold taught from 1927 to 1933, and which is the subject of chapter 5.
5. I am grateful to Adrian Sudhalter for helping me to articulate this important point and for her generosity in helping me think about the longer legacy of Jan Tschichold's unpublished book *Fotomontage,* especially as it relates to her own research on Margaret Miller.
6. Hal Foster, *Compulsive Beauty* (Cambridge, Mass.: MIT Press, 1995).
7. Foster. See also Rosalind Krauss, "The Photographic Conditions of Surrealism," *October* 19 (Winter 1981): 3–34.
8. László Moholy-Nagy, "Photography in Advertising," in *Photography in the Modern Era: European Documents and Critical Writings, 1913–40,* ed. and trans. Christopher Phillips (New York: Metropolitan Museum of Art, 1989), 92. Originally published as "Die Photographie in Der Reklame," *Photographische Korrespondenz,* no. 9 (September 1927): 257–60.
9. These materials are located in box 5, folder 6, Jan and Edith Tschichold Papers, 1899–1979, Getty Research Institute, Los Angeles. Additionally, a typed set of notes that appears related to both *Fotomontage* and *Die Neue Typographie* is included in box 74, Nachlass Jan Tschichold, Deutsches Buch- und Schriftmuseum der Deutschen Nationalbibliothek, Leipzig.
10. "An Hand hervorragender Beispiele wird aufgezeigt, welche bedeutsamen Möglichkeiten in dieser neuen Gestaltungsweise liegen." Fototek advertisement, printed as back matter in Biermann, *Aenne Biermann,* n.p.
11. "Gerade das Buch von Tschichold über 'Fotomontage' wird man mit Ungeduld erwarten, da dieses für unser grafisches Gewerbe so wichtig und neues Gebiet bis heute noch nirgends bearbeitet wurde, obwohl schon eine Fülle hervorragenden Materials von großer Schönheit vorliegt." *Werkbund Gedanken für Volksbildung, Kunsthandwerk und Industrie,* no. 12 (December 16, 1930): n.p.
12. "es gibt einen geschichtlichen querschnitt, will also bewusst historisches document sein, und zeigt auf, was gut und schlecht ist. beispiele und gegenbeispiele." Jan Tschichold, *Fotomontage* outline, 4.
13. The typescript includes a note about "constructivist" design and names futurist painting as an "influence" on contemporary photomontage. He did not explicitly discuss Dada or surrealism, but many of the artists he names as potential examples of different kinds of photomontage were associated with these movements. He

distinguished between historical precedents and current uses of photomontage, naming precursors from the nineteenth century "als urheber der neuen fotomontage" (originators of the new photomontage). Tschichold, *Fotomontage* outline.

14. This was clearly also true of *The New Typography,* which included a section called "The New Art," contextualizing New Typography in part as an extension of modernist tendencies in art that had begun with Impressionist painting. See Tschichold, *New Typography,* 30–51.
15. Hausmann made this statement in a speech delivered at the opening of the 1931 exhibition *Fotomontage* in Berlin, which was also printed in the journal *a bis z.* See Phillips, *Photography in the Modern Era,* 178. Originally published as Raoul Hausmann, "Fotomontage," *a bis z,* May 1931.
16. In his foreword to the exhibition catalog for César Domela- Nieuwenhuis's 1931 *Fotomontage* exhibition, art historian and critic Curt Glaser distinguished between "free" and "applied" photomontage. Hausmann latched onto this distinction to champion the former and dismiss the latter as illegitimate, thereby distancing art (namely Dada) from design. See Adrian Sudhalter and Deborah L. Roldán, eds., *Photomontage between the Wars (1918–1939)* (Madrid: Fundación Juan March, 2012), 17.
17. *Fotomontage* was organized by César Domela-Nieuwenhuis at the Kunstgewerbemuseum, Berlin (today the Martin-Gropius-Bau), on view from April 25 to May 31, 1931, in the museum's atrium. The exhibition also showcased works by graphic designers including Johannes Canis, Georg Trump, John Heartfield, Paul Schuitema, Karel Teige, Friedrich Vordemberge-Gildewart, Kurt Schwitters, and Piet Zwart. See *Fotomontage: Ausstellung im Lichthof des ehemaligen Kunstgewerbemuseums* (Berlin: Staatliche Museen, Staatliche Kunstbibliothek, 1931).
18. "Unsere Nachfahren, Tschichold, Bayer, Errell, auch Moholy-Nagy und Nerlinger sind recht schwächlich, leider." Hausmann, letter to Hannah Höch, April 1931, Berlinische Galerie, BG-HHC K 695/79.
19. "herr prof. stenger ließ uns aus seiner wertvollen fotografiensammlung kuriositäten auswählen, die als vorläufer der fotomontage angesehen werden können." (Mister Professor Stenger allowed us to select curiosities from his valuable photography collection that can be seen as precursors of photomontage.) *Fotomontage* catalog, n.p.
20. In the exhibition catalog for *Fotomontage,* Max Sauerlandt was acknowledged for lending works from the collection of the Museum für Kunst und Gewerbe Hamburg. *Fotomontage* catalog, n.p.
21. Sauerlandt championed German expressionism and was one of the few museum directors to acquire works by members of Die Brücke in the early twentieth century, most of which were confiscated by Nazi authorities in 1937 and remain lost. "History," Museum für Kunst und Gewerbe Hamburg, accessed August 9, 2024, https://

www.mkg-hamburg.de/en/about-us/the-mkg. As one remembrance of Sauerlandt after his death in 1934 stated, his dedication to acquiring modern art "cost him his post" as director of the Museum für Kunst und Gewerbe Hamburg in 1933. See Bernard Rackham, "The Late Max Sauerlandt," *Burlington Magazine for Connoisseurs* 64, no. 371 (February 1934): 95. Sauerlandt's approach to the history and institutional collecting of art is demonstrated in his book *Die Kunst der letzten 30 Jahre* (Berlin: Rembrandt Verlag, 1935).

22. Erich Stenger authored one of several prominent surveys of the medium's early history. His approach to collecting photography and writing its history are evident in his *Geschichte der Photographie* (Berlin: VDI Verlag, 1929), and in his transcribed remembrances, published in Miriam Halwani, ed., *Photographien führen wir nicht . . . : Erinnerungen des Sammlers Erich Stenger (1878–1957)* (Heidelberg: Kehrer; Cologne: Museum Ludwig, 2014).
23. Sudhalter and Roldán, *Photomontage between the Wars*, 17.
24. As Brigid Doherty has shown, Hannah Höch recalled seeing similar mementos of fallen soldiers, which she described as commonplace in domestic spaces before World War I, and identified these objects as seminal for her own experiments with photomontage. See Doherty, "Berlin," in *Dada: Zurich, Berlin, Hannover, Cologne, New York, Paris,* ed. Leah Dickerman (Washington, D.C.: National Gallery of Art; New York: Distributed Art Publishers, 2005), 90–92.
25. Erich Stenger, *The History of Photography: Its Relation to Civilization and Practice,* trans. Edward Epstean (Easton, Pa.: Mack Printing Co., 1939), viii.
26. Jan Tschichold, unpublished notes, page 67, box 74, Nachlass Jan Tschichold, Deutsches Buch- und Schriftmuseum der Deutschen Nationalbibliothek, Leipzig.
27. César Domela-Nieuwenhuis, "fotomontage," in Sudhalter and Roldán, *Photomontage between the Wars,* 129. Originally published as "fotomontage," in *Fotomontage* catalog, n.p.
28. Riegl proposed that a collective will to form developed within a given historical and cultural context, implicating artistic style as a visual manifestation of the unique, shared values of an historical epoch. Riegl developed the concept of *Kunstwollen* primarily in two books: *Stilfragen: Grundlegungen zu einer Geschichte der Ornamentik* (1893) and *Spätrömische Kunstindustrie* (1901). See Henri Zerner, "Aloïs Riegl: Art, Value, and Historicism," in "In Praise of Books," ed. Shirley Robin Letwin, special issue, *Daedalus* 105, no. 1 (Winter 1976): 177–88.
29. Hausmann's objection to the application of photomontage in graphic design was at least partly due to personal animus toward Tschichold. In April 1930, Tschichold received a letter from Hausmann admonishing him for excluding Hausmann from his 1928 treatise on New Typography, specifically in the narrative of modern art

presented in the section "The New Art." See Christopher Burke, *Active Literature: Jan Tschichold and the New Typography* (London: Hyphen Press, 2007), 115. In a letter to Hausmann dated April 3, 1930, Tschichold replied, "ich möchte ihnen in voller ehrlichkeit versichern, dass ich ihren namen nicht absichtlich an den stellen die sie zitieren, weggelassen habe, ich bin mit kurt schwitters wie sie befreundet, und vielleicht nehmen sie veranlassung ihn zu fragen, welche erfahrungen er mit mir gemacht hat." (I would like to assure you, in all honesty, that I have not purposely omitted your name from the passages that you are quoting. Like you, I am a friend of Kurt Schwitters, and perhaps you will have an opportunity to ask him what experience he has had with me.) In the same letter, he also suggested that it was futile to pinpoint photomontage's "reinvention": "ich glaube, dass es zu endlosen und unnützen streitigkeiten führt, wenn man sich ernsthaft darüber unterhalten will, wer die fotomontage neu erfand." (I believe that it leads to endless and useless disputes to seriously discuss who reinvented photomontage.) Jan Tschichold, letter to Hausmann, April 3, 1930, Nachlass Raoul Hausmann, Berlinische Galerie, BG-RHA 1029.

30. Sabine T. Kriebel, *Revolutionary Beauty: The Radical Photomontages of John Heartfield* (Berkeley: University of California Press, 2014), 101.
31. Hausmann, "Photomontage," in Phillips, *Photography in the Modern Era*, 179.
32. Domela-Nieuwenhuis, "fotomontage," in Sudhalter and Roldán, *Photomontage between the Wars*, 130.
33. "Die Dadaisten durch Erfindung der Montage das starre Lichtbild beweglich und denkend machten." (The Dadaists made the rigid photograph mobile and thinking by inventing montage.) Adolf Behne, "Kunst in Berlin: Fotomontage und Große Berliner," *Die Welt im Abend*, May 18, 1931, n.p.
34. "Aber . . . ist nicht das Wappen der alten Ritterschilde der eigentliche Urahn dieser neuen Kunstform? Natürlich, dort liegen die formalen Anfänge der Montage, in jenen heraldischen Aufteilungen der Fläche, in der Kombination von halben Adlern, von Roßschweifen, doppelten Köpfen mit Fabelwesen, mit Mauerzinnen und Toren, mit Sternen, Sonnen und Kometen." Behne, n.p.
35. "Sauerlandt-Hamburg hat vor kurzem die Ahnen der Fotomontage in seinem Museum zusammengestellt, und Domela-Nieuwenhuis hat einen Teil dieses Materials in seine ausgezeichnete Fotomontagen-Ausstellung (Prinz-Albrecht-Str. 7) übernommen, darunter amüsante und köstliche Stücke des 18. Jahrhunderts, die die Klebebilder eines Picasso und Schwitters vorwegnehmen." Behne, n.p.
36. "mein buch will an hand des bisher geschaffenen einen überblick über die möglichkeiten der fotomontage geben und nachweisen, dass die rede von der 'überlebtheit' dieser grafik leeres geschwätz ist." Tschichold, *Fotomontage* outline, 4.

37. Franz Roh and Jan Tschichold, *foto-auge: 76 fotos der zeit* (Stuttgart: Fritz Wedekind, 1929). For studies of *Film und Foto,* see Ute Eskildsen und Jan-Christopher Horak, eds., *Film und Foto der zwanziger Jahre: Eine Betrachtung der Internationalen Werkbundausstellung "Film und Foto" 1929* (Stuttgart: Gerd Hatje, 1979); Olivier Lugon, "Neues Sehen, Neue Geschichte: Laszlo Moholy-Nagy, Sigfried Giedion und die Ausstellung *Film und Foto,*" in *Sigfried Giedion und die Fotografie: Bildinszenierungen der Moderne,* ed. Werner Oechslin and Gregor Harbusch (Zurich: gta Verlag, 2010), 88–105; Gustaf Stotz, *Internationale Ausstellung des Deutschen Werkbunds Film und Foto* (Stuttgart: Deutscher Werkbund, 1929); and Andrés Mario Zervigón, "The Peripatetic Viewer at Heartfield's *Film und Foto* Exhibition Room," *October,* no. 150 (Fall 2014): 27–48.
38. Roh drew heavily from the distinction made by László Moholy-Nagy between photography as a "reproductive" medium that produced mimetic images of the world and as a "productive" medium that could extend the capacity of the human eye and inculcate *neues Sehen* (new vision), a way of seeing commensurate with the technological revolution born of modernity. See especially László Moholy-Nagy, "Production-Reproduction" (1922), in Phillips, *Photography in the Modern Era,* 79–82; and László Moholy-Nagy, *Malerei Photographie Film* (Munich: Albert Langen Verlag, 1925). See also Pepper Stetler, "Franz Roh and the Art History of Photography," in *Object:Photo. Modern Photographs: The Thomas Walther Collection, 1909–1949. An Online Project of the Museum of Modern Art,* ed. Mitra Abbaspour, Lee Ann Daffner, and Maria Morris Hambourg (New York: Museum of Modern Art, 2014), http://www.moma.org/interactives/objectphoto/assets/essays/Stetler.pdf.
39. The outline includes only last names of artists and designers and, in just a few cases, minimal notes indicating specific examples, but for the most part, specific works that Tschichold would have reproduced in his book are unknown.
40. Advertisements for the Fototek series specified that each volume was to include sixty large image reproductions, as in the published volumes on László Moholy-Nagy and Aenne Biermann.
41. Reproductions of these works appear as Plates 49, 55, and 60 in *foto-auge*. The latter also appears in Moholy-Nagy, *László Moholy-Nagy,* as Plate 3.
42. Notably, Tschichold's outline excluded Hausmann. However, in a separate typed set of notes that are likely related to the outline for *Fotomontage,* Tschichold acknowledged Hausmann as an innovator of photomontage in Dada. Tschichold, unpublished notes, page 67, box 74, Nachlass Jan Tschichold, Deutsches Buch- und Schriftmuseum der Deutschen Nationalbibliothek, Leipzig.
43. Tschichold, *Fotomontage* outline, 2–3.
44. Hausmann, "Photomontage," in Phillips, *Photography in the Modern Era,* 178–79.

45. *L'Esprit nouveau* was a journal published from 1920 to 1925 in Paris, primarily concerned with contemporary architecture and design and dedicated to the promotion of the "purist" design movement, led by Amédée Ozenfant and Le Corbusier. The journal was produced under the direction of Paul Dermée and edited, typeset, and printed by Maurice Daratière. For more on purism and *L'Esprit nouveau,* see Carol S. Eliel, ed., *L'Esprit nouveau: Purism in Paris, 1918–1925* (Los Angeles: Los Angeles County Museum of Art and Harry N. Abrams, 2001); and Stanislaus von Moos, ed., *L'Esprit nouveau, Le Corbusier und die Industrie, 1920–1925* (Berlin: Ernst and Sohn, 1987).
46. Cited in Beatriz Colomina, "Le Corbusier and Photography," *Assemblage,* no. 4 (October 1987): 15. Colomina has noted that Le Corbusier used images to "construct the text," rather than to illustrate it. She argues that through his role soliciting advertising for *L'Esprit nouveau,* the architect began appropriating found commercial photography in his own writing and assimilating strategies of combining text and image from advertising.
47. This image was reproduced in Karel Teige's *Práce Jaromíra Krejcara* (Prague: Nakladatel Václav Petr, 1933), but likely circulated in the 1920s as well. Krejcar's use of photomontage was also well known to Tschichold from the cover design for the second issue of the Czech journal *Život,* published in 1922. This design was reproduced as Plate 19 in *foto-auge.*
48. Barry Bergdoll and Leah Dickerman, eds., *Bauhaus, 1919–1933: Workshops for Modernity* (New York: Museum of Modern Art, 2009); Paul Paret, *Experimental Photography from the Bauhaus Sculpture Workshop* (Leeds: Henry Moore Institute, 2007).
49. For more on Moholy-Nagy's exhibition designs, see Jennifer King, "Back to the Present: Moholy-Nagy's Exhibition Designs," in *Moholy-Nagy: Future Present,* ed. Matthew S. Witkovsky, Carol S. Eliel, and Karole P. B. Vail (Chicago: Art Institute of Chicago, 2016), 139–50.
50. Weimar-era exhibitions designed as spatial analogues to flipping through an illustrated magazine are part of a longer history of photography exhibitions, such as Edward Steichen's *The Family of Man* at the Museum of Modern Art, New York, in 1955. See Thierry Gervais, ed., *The "Public" Life of Photographs* (Cambridge, Mass.: MIT Press, 2016); and Fred Turner, *The Democratic Surround: Multimedia and American Liberalism from World War II to the Psychedelic Sixties* (Chicago: University of Chicago Press, 2013).
51. Lissitzky's typographic work was featured heavily in Tschichold's earliest publications on New Typography. See "sonderheft: elementare typographie," ed. Jan (Iwan) Tschichold, special issue, *Typographische Mitteilungen,* October 1925; and Tschichold, *Die Neue Typographie.*

52. Jan Tschichold, “Display That Has Dynamic Force: Exhibition Rooms Designed by El Lissitzky,” *Commercial Art*, January 1931, 22–26.
53. Tschichold, 22.
54. Tschichold, 22.
55. Though these examples of Lissitzky’s exhibition designs were mounted as political propaganda on behalf of Soviet Russia, Tshcichold’s discussion of them (especially in the context of an article for *Commercial Art*) tacitly recognized the strategies of communist propaganda and commercial design as closely related, but not entirely analogous.
56. Tschichold, unpublished notes, page 67, box 74, Nachlass Jan Tschichold, Deutsches Buch- und Schriftmuseum der Deutschen Nationalbibliothek, Leipzig. This phrase is repeated, almost verbatim, in Tschichold’s published article “The Composite Photograph and Its Place in Advertising,” *Commercial Art*, December 1930, 237–49.
57. In 1926, Paul Renner invited Tschichold to teach at the newly founded Meisterschule für Deutschlands Buchdrucker in Munich. According to Ruari McLean and Christopher Burke, Renner originally invited Tschichold to take the position Renner had previously held at the Frankfurt Kunstschule, but then followed up with the invitation to teach in Munich. See Ruari McLean, *Jan Tschichold: A Life in Typography* (London: Lund Humphries Publishers, 1997), 32; Burke, *Active Literature*, 53. When Tschichold moved to Munich in 1926, he and his wife, Edith, became neighbors with Roh while living in Munich’s Borstei housing project. Correspondence in the Jan and Edith Tschichold Papers at the Getty Research Institute indicates that the Tschichold and Roh families sustained a friendship long after the Tschicholds emigrated from Germany in 1933. See also Burke, 105; Inka Graeve Ingelmann, “Mechanics and Expression: Franz Roh and the New Vision—a Historical Sketch,” in Abbaspour, Daffner, and Hambourg, *Object:Photo*, https://www.moma.org/interactives/objectphoto/assets/essays/GraeveIngelmann.pdf.
58. Fototek advertisement. The book on kitsch photography, referred to in advertisements for Fototek as “The Monstrous” (“Das Monströse”), was to draw from the collection of Austrian journalist and collector Raoul Korty. See Ingelmann, “Mechanics and Expression.”
59. Moholy-Nagy, *László Moholy-Nagy;* Biermann, *Aenne Biermann.*
60. “Roh über das Fotoklebebild / äußerste Phantastik bei äußerste Nüchternheit, / freiestes Komponieren bei Wirklichkeitsabklatsch / kubistische Schachtelung bei barem Abbild / Tsch: / ‘Konstruktivistische’ Gestaltung gegenüber ‘organizistischer’” Tschichold, *Fotomontage* notes, n.p.
61. Franz Roh, *Nach-Expressionismus: Magischer Realismus, Probleme der neuesten europäischen Malerei* (Leipzig: Klinkhardt and Biermann, 1925), 46. For an account of

the interactions between Roh and Gustav Hartlaub, who coined *Neue Sachlichkeit,* and their conceptual overlap, see Christian Fuhrmeister, "Hartlaub and Roh: Cooperation and Competition in Popularizing New Objectivity," in *New Objectivity: Modern German Art in the Weimar Republic, 1919–1933,* ed. Stephanie Barron and Sabine Eckmann (London: Prestel, 2015), 41–49.

62. Roh cited Moholy-Nagy's role as a leading figure of the Bauhaus and classified him, first and foremost, as a constructivist. See Moholy-Nagy, *László Moholy-Nagy,* 6.
63. Roh, 6. Just prior to this, Roh wrote, "Moholy's versatility in constructive interests shows that the purism of abstract painting, frequently met with in this modern type of man, does not signify purism in the *totality of life:* the whole range of the human is to be preserved, yet the primary wants of existence are shunted to other districts. Thus, the craving for expression of what is contained in *external objects* remains, but has left painting and the graphic art for the sphere of photography. Moholy considers the camera the most suitable instrument (and manually unsurpassed) to satisfy this craving for the object."
64. Roh, 6.
65. Tschichold, *New Typography,* 96.
66. Roh, *Nach-Expressionismus.*
67. "Fotoklebebild / Klebebild aus Teilen von Manualgraphik / Mechanographik" Tschichold, *Fotomontage* notes, n.p. Underlining is original to Tschichold's text.
68. Roh, *Nach-Expressionismus,* 45.
69. Franz Roh, "Max Ernst und die Stückungsgraphik," *Das Kunstblatt* 11 (1927): 397–400.
70. Virginia Heckert has noted that it was through these publications that Roh first discovered Ernst's work with collage. See *Franz Roh: Photography and Collage from the 1930s* (New York: Ubu Gallery, 2006).
71. Roh, "Max Ernst und die Stückungsgraphik," 400. The portfolio *Histoire naturelle* was published in 1926 by the Parisian Galerie Jeanne Bucher. Ernst's frottage, invented in 1925, involved creating rubbings on paper with crayon or pencil of various found objects or textured surfaces. Ernst would add to the rubbings to create new forms, and the resulting drawings were reproduced using the collotype process, a photomechanical technique known for reproducing fine detail. See Julia Drost and Werner Spies, eds., *Beyond Painting: Max Ernst in the Würth Collection* (Málaga: Museo Picasso Málaga, 2008).
72. Joel Snyder, "Making Photographs Public," in *The "Public" Life of Photographs,* ed. Thierry Gervais (Cambridge, Mass.: MIT Press, 2016), 17–37.
73. Roh, "Max Ernst und die Stückungsgraphik," 399.
74. The "dispute" that Roh referred to here was likely the one catalyzed by a contentious article, "Malerei und Fotografie," by Hungarian art critic Ernst (Ernö) Kallai, which was published in 1927 in the Dutch avant-garde journal *i10.* Kallai, an outspoken

communist who would later become editor of the *bauhaus* journal, argued forcefully against the combination of mechanical techniques and art, particularly on the grounds that photography—unlike painting—lacked facture. This prompted rebuttals by Willi Baumeister, Adolf Behne, and László Moholy-Nagy. See Phillips, *Photography in the Modern Era,* 94–103.

75. "Da heute Streit um eine Funktion und Grenze des Maschinellen in der Kunst entbrannte, muß erinnert werden, daß auch hinter Maschinenarbeit menschlicher Geist steht." Roh, "Max Ernst und die Stückungsgraphik," 399.
76. "Noch einmal starker hat Menschenhand in diejenigen Schwarzweißblätter eingegriffen, die wir Photomontage nennen, wo aus sprechenden Teilstücken der Wirklichkeit ein völlig neues Gebilde getürmt wird (Photoklebebild)." Roh, 399.
77. Tschichold, *Fotomontage* outline, 2–5.
78. Tschichold, 4.
79. "stückungsgrafik (wort von franz roh) dem fotoklebebilde verwandt (klebebild aus manualgrafik) ist eine aus alten zeichnungsteilen zusammengesetzte neue einheit." Tschichold, 4.
80. Most plates bear captions that include the maker's name or image source, along with a short description of the process by which each image was made, in all three languages, with little other information such as titles or dates. These descriptions were most likely written by Roh, given that he authored the book's introductory essay.
81. "fotokomposition auch fotokombination genannt, schafft statt mit schere und klebestoff mit rein fotografischen mitteln (übereinanderkopieren mehrerer aufnahmen auf einer platte, fotogramm usw.) ein als gestaltung sinnvolles über- und nebeneinander verschiedener lichtfixierungen, durchdringungen." Tschichold, *Fotomontage* outline, 4.
82. Most notably, the advent of radiography in 1895 by Wilhelm Röntgen established the X-ray photograph as a tool of medical science. Lisa Cartwright, *Screening the Body: Tracing Medicine's Visual Culture* (Minneapolis: University of Minnesota, 1995), 107–42. For more on Moholy-Nagy's interest in cameraless photography, see Herbert Molderings, "Light Years of a Life: The Photogram in the Aesthetic of Lázsló Moholy-Nagy," in *Moholy-Nagy: The Photograms,* ed. Renate Heyne and Hattula Moholy-Nagy (Stuttgart: Hatje Cantz, 2009), 15–25.
83. Tschichold, *Fotomontage* outline, 4.
84. William Firebrace, *Star Theatre: The Story of the Planetarium* (London: Reaktion, 2017), 79–81.
85. Moholy-Nagy. *László Moholy-Nagy,* Plate 7.
86. Jan Tschichold, "The Composite Photograph and Its Place in Advertising," *Commercial Art,* December 1930, 237–49.
87. Tschichold, 248.

88. However, he also noted that the "simple technique is not new: photograms of flowers, for example, made by simply laying the object on photographic paper, have been known for a long time." Tschichold, *New Typography*, 91.
89. Due to its light background, the final advertisement for Pelikan appears to be a contact print made from the original photogram.
90. *Qualität* was founded and art directed by German graphic designer Carl Ernst Hinkefuss.
91. "II. fotomontage schrift = typofoto / fotomontage und farbe." Tschichold, *Fotomontage* outline, 2. Underlining is original to Tschichold's text.
92. My translations of *gestaltende einbau* and *gestaltungskraft* are again informed by Detlef Mertins and Michael W. Jennings's translation of *Gestaltung* as "form-production." See Detlef Mertins and Michael W. Jennings, "Introduction: The G-Group and the European Avant-Garde," in *G: An Avant-Garde Journal of Art, Architecture, Design, and Film, 1923–1926*, ed. Mertins and Jennings (Los Angeles: Getty Publications, 2010), 5.
93. "fotomontage (oberbegriff) / ist der gestaltende einbau eines oder mehrer fotos oder fototeile in eine fläche, gleichviel, ob diese davon nur teilweise oder ganz bedeck wird. die qualität der arbeit hängt in erster linie von der gestaltungskraft des urhebers ab, erst in zweiter linie von der qualität der verwendeten fotos. kommt zur photomontage typographie, so spricht man von typophoto. / beispiele: / burchartz, bochumer verein / tschichold, bellisana / schlechte typographie mit blossen fotos / gute typographie mit blossen fotos (bayer) / kalender franzsche buchdruckerei (gegenbeispiel)." Tschichold, *Fotomontage* outline, 4. Underlining is original to Tschichold's text.
94. Burchartz and Canis founded the Bochum-based commercial concern, known as werbe-bau, in 1925. The Bochumer Verein für Bergbau und Gussstahlfabrikation quickly became one of the werbe-bau's most important clients. This image was reproduced in Tschichold, *Die Neue Typographie;* and Jan Tschichold, *Eine Stunde Druckgestaltung* (Stuttgart: Dr. Fritz Wedekind and Co., 1930).
95. Hermann Frenzel, "Der Prospekt," *Gebrauchsgraphik* 3, no. 6 (June 1926): 4.
96. Frenzel, 8.
97. Egon Juda, "Typography in German Advertising," *Commercial Art*, December 1929, 258.
98. Juda, 260.
99. Juda, 262.
100. Robin Kinross, "Introduction to the English-Language Edition," in Tschichold, *New Typography*, xxii.
101. For a thorough discussion of the fetishization of technology in design associated with New Typography, see Maud Lavin, *Clean New World: Cultural Politics and Graphic Design* (Cambridge, Mass.: MIT Press, 2001).
102. "jan tschichold: die neue typographie," *bauhaus* 3, no. 2 (1929): 28.

103. These were sometimes also referred to in German as *Lichtsäulen*. The term *Litfaßsäulen* came from Ernst Litfaß, who invented the first freestanding columns for advertising posters in Berlin in 1855. See Sandra Uhrig, "Werbund im Stadtbild," in *Die Kunst zu werben: Das Jahrhundert der Reklame*, ed. Susanne Bäumler (Munich: Münchner Stadtmuseum / Dumont, 1996), 52–56. See also Janet Ward, *Weimar Surfaces: Urban Visual Culture in 1920s Germany* (Berkeley: University of California Press, 2001), 92–95.
104. *Das Neue Frankfurt* was an important platform for the *ring neue werbegestalter* (ring of new advertising designers), and other adherents to New Typography, including Willi Baumeister, Max Burchartz, Walter Dexel, Hans Leistikow, Grete Leistikow, and Paul Renner. The journal showcased their work both in the design of the publication itself and as the subject of articles on exhibition design and advertising.
105. "Sparsam verwendete Farbe hebt die Hauptpunkte der Mitteilung hervor, aber nur die jeweils gut und richtig gewählte Farbe erfüllt ihren Zweck und übernimmt wirklich die Aufgabe des Blickfanges." (Color used economically highlights the main points of the message, but only the correct, well-chosen color fulfills its purpose and really does the job of catching the eye.) Walter Dexel, "Reklame im Stadtbilde," *Das Neue Frankfurt* 1, no. 3 (1926–27): 46. His reference to "correctly chosen color" betrays the influence of De Stijl architecture, especially the designs of Dutch architect J. J. P. Oud, which Dexel cited in the same article. According to De Stijl principles, modern expression in art and design should employ pure abstraction, namely straight lines, square and rectangular forms, and primary colors. See Michael White, *De Stijl and Dutch Modernism* (Manchester: Manchester University Press, 2003).
106. Moholy-Nagy observed this visual effect in painting: "Experiments with painting on highly polished black panels . . . produce strange optical effects: it looks as though the colour were **floating** almost without material effect in a space in front of the plane to which it is in fact applied." László Moholy-Nagy, *Painting Photography Film*, trans. Janet Seligman (1925; trans., London: Lund Humphries, 1969), 25. Emphasis in bold is original to Nagy's text.
107. John Harrison, "What the Camera Can Do for You: The New Photography Enters the Field," *Commercial Art*, June 1930, 257.
108. As discussed in chapter 2, the strategic use of color in graphic design to control eye movement and arrest the reader's attention was a dominant subject of applied psychology in the 1920s and 1930s.
109. Ernst Topp worked as the primary in-house photographer of the Bochumer Verein from 1922 until his death in 1932. See Ralf Stremmel, *Industrie und Fotografie: Der Bochumer Verein für Bergbau und Gussstahlfabrikation. 1854–1926* (Münster: Aschendorff Verlag, 2017).
110. Leo Marx, *The Machine in the Garden: Technology and the Pastoral Ideal in America* (New York: Oxford University Press, 1964). See also Jeffrey L. Meikle, "Ghosts in

the Machine: Why It's Hard to Write about Design," *Technology and Culture* 46, no. 2 (April 2005): 385–92. I am grateful to Amy Ogata for helping me think through the pertinence of Leo Marx's idea of the "technological sublime" to Weimar-era "functionalist" design.

111. According to the recollection of Heinz Rasch in 1989, Willi Baumeister had originally been charged with designing the book, but he had recently accepted a professorship at the Frankfurter Kunstgewerbeschule and declined. Roland Nachtigäller notes that it was likely through Baumeister's close friendship with the Rasch brothers that they came to edit and design the publication. Contributions for the book were solicited at least as early as September 1929. See "Mit Scharfem Auge zum Gefesselter Blick: Die Bruder Rasch und die konstruktivistische Typographie der 1920er-Jahre," in *Der entfesselte Blick: Die Brüder Rasch und ihre Impulse für die moderne Architektur*, ed. Marta Herford (Tübingen: Wasmuth, 2014), 93–94.

112. The ring's membership also included Willi Baumeister, Walter Dexel, Hans Leistikow, Robert Michel, Paul Schuitema, Georg Trump, Friedrich Vordemberge-Gildewart, and Piet Zwart. A slate of exhibitions in Germany and the Netherlands showcased their work between the ring's founding in 1928 and dissolution by 1932. Getty Research Institute, Piet Zwart letters received, 1928–46. Roland Nachtigäller has noted that Schwitters also invited Theo van Doesburg, who declined to join the ring, as well as to Werner Graeff, John Heartfield, Johannes Molzahn, and Hans Richter, none of whom responded to the invitation. Nachtigäller, "Mit Scharfem Auge zum Gefesselter Blick," 93.

113. Letters circulated to members of the ring neue werbegestalter are located in various collections at the Getty Research Institute, Los Angeles, including Piet Zwart letters received; Bauhaus typography collection; and Walter Dexel letters received.

114. The full list of contributors to *Gefesselter Blick* is as follows: Otto Baumberger, Willi Baumeister, Max Bill, Max Burchartz, Johannes Canis, Walter Cyliax, Walter Dexel, César Domela-Nieuwenhuis, Hermann Elias, Werner Graeff, John Heartfield, Franz Krause, Hans and Grete Leistikow, El Lissitzky, Robert Michel, László Moholy-Nagy, Heinz and Bodo Rasch, Hans Richter, Paul Schuitema, Kurt Schwitters, Mart Stam, Karel Teige, Georg Trump, Jan Tschichold, Friedrich Vordemberge-Gildewart, and Piet Zwart. Heinz Rasch and Bodo Rasch, eds., *Gefesselter Blick* (Stuttgart: Wissenschaftlicher Verlag Dr. Zaugg and Co., 1930), 4.

115. "Das Buch ist so aufgebaut, das jeder darin vertretenen Künstler 2–4 Seiten für seine Beispiele bekommt und eine rechte Titelseite, auf der sein Name, darunter klein seine Daten und ferner die Beantworten der Rundfrage: 'Welchen Prinzipen verfolgen Sie bei der Gestaltung Ihrer Typografien bezw. haben Sie überhaupt Prinzipen dabei?' steht." This form letter was sent to Dutch designer Piet Zwart and is likely a

good indicator of the initial solicitation sent to each contributor. Heinz Rasch, letter to Piet Zwart, January 29, 1930, box 1, folder 2, Piet Zwart letters received, 1928–46, Getty Research Institute, Los Angeles.

116. "Bei der Verschiedenartigkeit des zusammenkommen Materials hat sich als wichtig für die schnellere Erfassung durch den Leser herausgestellt, zu wissen, ob der Künstler Maler, Architekt, Drucker oder Buchgewerber ist und welcher Generation er angehört." (Due to the diversity of the assembled materials, it is important that the reader can quickly apprehend whether each artist is a painter, architect, printer, or book maker, and to which generation he belongs.) Rasch, n.p.

117. "Die Mittel, um über das Sehorgan des Menschen etwas mitzuteilen, sind Bild und Schrift." Rasch and Rasch, *Gefesselter Blick,* 4.

118. The Rasch brothers drew from Lessing's *Laocoön: An Essay on the Limits of Painting and Poetry,* originally published in 1766 as *Laokoön oder Über die Grenzen der Malerei und Poesie,* which posed the anticlassical argument that poetry and painting were distinct modes of representation and thus could not be modeled after each other. They summarized Lessing's argument as follows: "Lessing bereits hat dem Sinn nach schon erfaßt, daß demnach es sich bei der Schrift rein um Wiedergabe von Funktionen bei dem Bild rein um Wiedergabe von Objekten dreht." (Lessing already understood that, in essence, writing is purely about the reproduction of functions, while images are purely about the reproduction of objects.) Rasch and Rasch, 4.

119. "Werbegraphik ist eine ganz besondere Form der Mitteilung, nämlich eine Verschmelzung von Bild und Wort." Promotional brochure for *Gefesselter Blick,* circa 1930, box 4, folder 13, Bauhaus typography collection, 1919–37, Getty Research Institute, Los Angeles.

120. In the caption for this reproduction, they wrote, "Einerseits: den Text für den Kunden, die Bekanntmachung. Anderseits: das Bild, die Sache. Beide: Text und Bild berühren sich in dem roten Kreis, dem Blickfang." (On the one hand: the text for the customer, the announcement. On the other hand: the image, the object. Both: text and image touch each other in the red circle, the eye-catcher.) Rasch and Rasch, *Gefesselter Blick,* 57.

121. "Ein Objekt also löst im Beschauer eine Funktion aus." Rasch and Rasch, 4.

122. "Das engste Raster, die engste Auflösung der Handlung im Bild ist der Film. Der Film ist bildinterpretierte Funktion. Der Schrift nahe verwandt: Die Schrift ist eigentlich nu rein Film aus Symbolzeichen." Rasch and Rasch, 4.

123. In a short text originally published in the Dutch avant-garde journal *i10,* Moholy-Nagy wrote, "The fanatical zeal with which photography is pursued in all circles today indicates that those with no knowledge of it will be the illiterates of the future." Phillips, *Photography in the Modern Era,* 102.

124. "Der Fotoapparat nimmt natürlich auch vieles auf, was zufällig in der Umgebung des Blickzieles liegt, was man in Wirklichkeit gar nicht oder nur nebenbei gesehen hat, was nicht zur Sache gehört. Das kann man aber wegschneiden. Es kommt bei einem Bild auf nichts anderes an, als den Beschauer in nahe persönliche Beziehung zum Objekt zu bringen." (The camera naturally captures many things that happen to be around the focal point, things that one would not have noticed or only seen peripherally in reality, things that do not belong. But these can be cut out. What matters in an image is nothing but bringing the viewer into a close personal relationship with an object.) Rasch and Rasch, *Gefesselter Blick,* 7.
125. Rasch and Rasch, 8.
126. "Das Bildausschnitt ist durch den Sehrahmen der Augen bedingt. Dieser ist (wie die Iris einer Kamera) größer oder kleiner, je nachdem, ob wir den Gegenstand mehr oder weniger 'aufs Korn nehmen.'" (The image fragment is determined by the visual frame of the eyes. This frame, like the iris of a camera, is larger or smaller depending on how much we take aim at the object.) Rasch and Rasch, 7.
127. "In der Idee muß die Kamera identisch sein mit dem Auge des Beschauers." Rasch and Rasch, 7.
128. This photomontage is labeled "Ohler Photos Stuttgart Tübingerstr. 20.T.20081," suggesting that it was composed using fragments of photographs by the Stuttgart-based photographer Arthur Ohler, whose work was also represented in the exhibition *Film und Foto* (1929–31) and reproduced in a 1933 issue of *Das Neue Frankfurt* (no. 11) featuring art and architecture in Stuttgart. In a brochure advertising *Gefesselter Blick,* this photomontage is attributed to "Rasch" (likely referring to Heinz Rasch). Promotional brochure, n.d., box 4, folder 13, Bauhaus typography collection, 1919–37, Getty Research Institute, Los Angeles.
129. Rotogravure—a high-speed, rotary printing technology using intaglio cylinders to print long runs of newspaper, magazine, and book pages—facilitated the manipulation of letterforms and halftones beyond the confines of the layout grid, and its effects were evident in the visually striking layouts of magazines like French *VU* (1928–40) and the German newspaper *Arbeiter-Illustrierte Zeitung* (1921–38). For more on rotogravure, see Andrés Mario Zervigón, "Rotogravure and the Modern Aesthetic of News Reporting," in *Getting the Picture: The Visual Culture of the News,* ed. Jason E. Hill and Vanessa R. Schwartz (London: Bloomsbury, 2015), 197–205; and Michel Frizot and Cédric de Veigy, "*VU*": *The Story of a Magazine* (London: Thames and Hudson, 2009).
130. Tschichold, *Fotomontage* outline, 2.
131. "heitere fotozeichnung. zusammenfassung vonhandener bildelemente. sie warden zur ironie ihrer selbst. der maler arbeitet hier wie der architect, der für gegebenheiten (bauplatz und bauprogramm) eine form suchen muß." Rasch and Rasch, *Gefesselter Blick,* 19.

132. Roland Nachtigäller has cited a letter from Heinz Rasch to Willi Baumeister, indicating that Rasch had authored the captions for Baumeister's images in *Gefesselter Blick*. Nachtigäller, "Mit Scharfem Auge zum Gefesselter Blick," 96–97n35. This is confirmed by a number of letters now housed in the Archiv Baumeister, dated between January and February 1930, from Heinz and Bodo Rasch to Baumeister, in which they proposed descriptions of each image as the three negotiated which images would appear in the book and in what order. These confirm that only the biographical information and short statement on typography printed at the top of page 19 of *Gefesselter Blick* were authored by Baumeister. Archiv Baumeister, Kunstmuseum Stuttgart.

133. "die einbildungskraft un fantasie sind der nährboden alles spekulativ-künstlerischen schaffens." Rasch and Rasch, *Gefesselter Blick,* 19.

134. See, for example, Richard Hollis, *Swiss Graphic Design: The Origin and Growth of an International Style, 1920–1965* (New Haven, Conn.: Yale University Press, 2006), 29–30; and Martijn F. Le Coultre, *Jan Tschichold: Posters of the Avantgarde* (Laren: VK Projects, 2007), 61.

135. "fotozeichnung. eine fotografie wie viele andere auch . . . . . . das konstruktive gefüge ist so streng, daß der fremdkörper der fotografie vollständig verschmolzen wird. die rhythmischen versetzungen ergeben eine durchgehende bewegung, der das auge des beschauers ständig folgen muß.—resultat: kinetik." Rasch and Rasch, *Gefesselter Blick,* 21.

136. In the context of the Russian Revolution, artists, designers, and writers, including Osip Brik, Naum Gabo, Aleksei Gan, El Lissitzky, Lyobov Popova, Aleksandr Rodchenko, and Varvara Stepanova, promoted the construction of objects—as opposed to the composition of mimetic images—by rendering the facture of industrial materials and the labor of production visually evident, thereby implicating the beholder as coproducer. See Maria Gough, *The Artist as Producer: Russian Constructivism in Revolution* (Berkeley: University of California Press, 2005); Christina Kiaer, *Imagine No Possessions: The Socialist Objects of Russian Constructivism* (Cambridge, Mass.: MIT Press, 2005); and Kristin Romberg, *Gan's Constructivism: Aesthetic Theory for an Embedded Modernism* (Berkeley: University of California Press, 2019). For primary texts by Russian constructivists and discussion of their influence on the Central European avant-garde, see Stephen Bann, *The Tradition of Constructivism* (New York: Da Capo Press, 1974).

137. Tschichold, unpublished notes, page 67, box 74, Nachlass Jan Tschichold, Deutsches Buch- und Schriftmuseum der Deutschen Nationalbibliothek, Leipzig.

138. "Beispiel für die räumliche Erfassung von Schrift." Rasch and Rasch, *Gefesselter Blick,* 10.

4 TOO MUCH AND TOO LITTLE

1. Eric N. Simons, "The Art of Illustrating Engineering Products," *Commercial Art,* February 1924, 408.
2. Simons, 408.
3. Simons, 408.
4. I am grateful to Dina Murokh for her keen observations about the peculiar layout of this page of illustrations and for her incisive feedback on an early draft of this chapter.
5. Estelle Jussim, *Visual Communication and the Graphic Arts* (New York: R. R. Bowker, 1974), 12. Jussim proposed these terms in response to William Ivins's claim that photomechanical reproduction enables images without "syntax." See Ivins, *Prints and Visual Communication* (1953; repr., New York: Da Capo Press, 1969). See also Sarah Mirseyedi, "Side by Side: The Halftone's Visual Culture of Pragmatism," *History of Photography* 41, no. 3 (2017): 286–310.
6. For a concise summary of retouching practices in this period, see Lee Ann Daffner, "Retouching Revealed: Finishing Practices Observed in the Thomas Walther Collection," in *Object:Photo. Modern Photographs: The Thomas Walther Collection, 1909–1949—an Online Project of the Museum of Modern Art,* ed. Mitra Abbaspour, Lee Ann Daffner, and Maria Morris Hambourg (New York: Museum of Modern Art, 2014), https://www.moma.org/interactives/objectphoto/assets/essays/Daffner.pdf.
7. Retouching included the addition or removal of material from photographic negatives and prints (done before an image was translated into a halftone) as well as the alteration of the halftone block through etching and engraving. Thorough descriptions of halftone retouching as practiced in the 1920s are found in manuals such as Charles W. Hackleman, *Commercial Engraving and Printing: A Manual of Practical Instruction Covering Commercial Illustrating and Printing by All Processes* (Indianapolis: Commercial Engraving Publishing Company, 1921); R. Russ and L. Englich, *Handbuch der Modernen Reproduktionstechnik: Band I, Reproduktionsphotographie und Retusche* (Frankfurt am Main: Verlag von Klimsch and Co., 1927); and International Correspondence Schools, *Retouching for Halftones, Part 1* (Scranton, Pa.: International Textbook Company, 1921). See also Gerry Beegan, *The Mass Image: A Social History of Photomechanical Reproduction in Victorian London* (London: Palgrave Macmillan, 2008).
8. Manuals on halftone reproduction published in the 1920s included substantial sections on airbrushing techniques and the proper use and maintenance of airbrushing machines. See, for example, International Correspondence Schools, *Retouching for Halftones,* 20–43.
9. For studies of the halftone's early development and public reception, see Beegan, *Mass Image*; Neil Harris, "Iconography and Intellectual History: The Halftone

Effect," in *Cultural Excursions: Marketing Appetites and Cultural Tastes in Modern America* (Chicago: University of Chicago Press 1990), 304–17; Thierry Gervais, "La similigravure: Le récit d'une invention (1878–1893)," *Nouvelles de l'estampe,* no. 229 (March 2010): 8–25; Mirseyedi, "Side by Side"; David Clayton Phillips, "Halftone Technology, Mass Photography and the Social Transformation of American Print Culture, 1880–1920" (PhD diss., Yale University, 1996); and Robert Taft, "Photography and the Pictorial Press," in *Photography and the American Scene* (New York: Macmillan, 1938), 419–50.

10. Chapter 2, above, offers a thorough discussion of perceptual psychology as a source for graphic designers' understanding of how visual form affects memory, attention, and cognition.
11. W. G. Raffé's *Graphic Design* (London: Chapman and Hall, 1927) was among the first attempts at a comprehensive treatise on the practice of graphic design, and it may have been the first book to include the term "graphic design" in its title. It is the source of most of Raffé's many contributions to *Commercial Art.* His published books also include *Art and Labour: Six Essays* (London: C. W. Daniel Co., 1927).
12. W. G. Raffé, "The Elements of the Poster II: Representation and Suggestion," *Commercial Art,* May 1928, 221–22.
13. Raffé, 216.
14. Walter F. Schubert, "Advertising German Machinery," *Commercial Art,* February 1927, 185.
15. Studies of pictorialism include Annette Kicken and Rudolf Kicken, *Pictorialism: Hidden Modernism: Photography, 1896–1916* (Vienna: Georg Kargl Fine Arts; Berlin: Galerie Kicken, 2008); Beaumont Newhall, *The History of Photography: From 1839 to the Present Day* (1937; repr., New York: Museum of Modern Art, 1949), 119–38; and Thomas Padon, ed., *Truth Beauty: Pictorialism and the Photograph as Art, 1845–1945* (Vancouver: Douglas and McIntyre, 2008).
16. American critic Sadakichi Hartmann popularized the term "straight photography" in his 1904 essay "A Plea for Straight Photography," which leveled a critique of pictorialism. See Hartmann, "A Plea for Straight Photography," *American Amateur Photographer* 16 (March 1904): 101–9.
17. Nina Klöpper, *Fotografische Objekte in Schwarzweiß: Neusachliche Bildtraditionen 1920 bis heute* (Berlin: Dietrich Reimer Verlag, Berlin, 2014), 17–19.
18. Albert Renger-Patzsch, "Photography and Art," in *Photography in the Modern Era: European Documents and Critical Writings, 1913 40,* ed. and trans. Christopher Phillips (New York: Metropolitan Museum of Art, 1989), 143. Originally published as "Photographie und Kunst," *Das Deutsche Lichtbild,* 1929.
19. Klöpper, *Fotografische Objekte in Schwarzweiss,* 80–87.

20. See, for example, Hermann Behrmann's description of the work of Walter Cyliax, a German designer associated with New Typography. Specifically, Behrmann praised Cyliax's prospectus designs for the Swiss press Fretz Brothers, which featured photography heavily. See Behrmann, "Der Graphiker Cyliax und Gebr. Fretz A.G. Zürich," *Gebrauchsgraphik* 7, no. 5 (May 1930): 24–32.
21. Klöpper, *Fotografische Objekte in Schwarzweiss*, 108. See also, International Correspondence Schools, *Retouching for Halftones*, 43; Julius Verfasser, *The Half-Tone Process: A Practical Manual of Photo-Engraving in Half-Tone on Zinc, Copper, and Brass* (London: Iliffe and Sons, 1904), 263–64; and W. Livingston Larned, "Techniques of Advertising Illustration: II. Combination Line and Half-Tone," *Printing Art* 37, no. 1 (March 1921): 25–34.
22. Stephen Horgan, *Horgan's Half-Tone and Photomechanical Processes* (Chicago: Inland Printer, 1913), 107–8; Verfasser, *Half-Tone Process*, 261–66.
23. In some manuals on photomechanical reproduction, these techniques were not even referred to as "retouching." See, for example, Horgan, *Horgan's Half-Tone and Photomechanical Processes*.
24. W. G. Raffé, "The Elements of the Poster III: Composition: The Fundamental Factors in Design," *Commercial Art*, June 1928, 255.
25. "Die Werbemittel der Schwerindustrie dürfen einer gewissen Würde nicht entraten; sie müssen durch Wucht und Kraft in Fläche und Farbe sich Beachten erzwingen." Walter F. Schubert, *Das Deutsche Werbe-Graphik* (Berlin: Francken and Lang, 1927), 106.
26. "The Art of Retouching the Photograph," *Commercial Art*, December 1923, 343.
27. For histories of the advertising poster, see Bradford Collins, "The Poster as Art: Chéret and the Struggle for Equality of the Arts in Late 19th-Century France," *Design Issues* 2, no. 1 (1985): 41–50; Elizabeth Guffey, *Posters: A Global History* (London: Reaktion Books, 2015); Paul Jobling and David Crowley, *Graphic Design: Reproduction and Representation since 1800* (Manchester: Manchester University Press, 1996); Ruth Iskin, *The Poster: Art, Advertising, Design, and Collecting, 1860s to 1900s* (Hanover, NH: Dartmouth College Press, 2014); and Viktoria Schmidt-Linsenhoff, Kurt Wettengl, and Almut Junker, *Plakate, 1880–1914* (Frankfurt: Historisches Museum Frankfurt am Main, 1986).
28. For further discussion of the *Sachplakat* in the context of interwar advertising, see chapter 1, above.
29. *Die Reklame: Fachblatt für das gesamte Werbewesen*, a German trade journal that concentrated on advertising as a new science, was founded in 1925 as the official organ of the Verband Deutscher Reklamefachleute (VDR), replacing *Mitteilungen des Vereins Deutscher Reklamefachleute*, which had been published since the VDR's founding in

1908. See Julia Meer, *Neuer Blick auf die Neue Typographie: Die Rezeption der Avantgarde in der Fachwelt der 1920er Jahre* (Bielefeld: transcript Verlag, 2015), 300, 315–16.

30. "Das Ziel, eine Ware nicht nur naturgetreu, sondern auch ansprechend, interessant und werbend darzustellen, kann jedenfalls durchaus auf photographischem Wege erreicht werden." Heinz Giebelhausen, "Der Photograph als Werbehelfer," *Die Reklame,* September 1925, 1003.
31. Gilbert Russell, "Help from the Camera," *Commercial Art,* November 1923, 310.
32. Russell, 310, 314.
33. Russell, 314.
34. Zervigón describes this phenomenon as a politically persuasive tool used by German photomonteur and graphic designer John Heartfield, who "prized [photography's] subjective capacity to link the somatic and the psychic in deeply moving combinations." See Zervigón, *John Heartfield and the Agitated Image: Photography, Persuasion, and the Rise of Avant-Garde Photomontage* (Chicago: University of Chicago Press, 2012), 6.
35. R. L. Dupuy, "Advertising Photo in France," *Gebrauchsgraphik* 6, no. 11 (November 1929): 17–21.
36. As discussed in chapter 2, applied psychologists in this period frequently referred to "suggestion-value" as key to the effectiveness of advertising. This term was coined by Hugo Münsterberg in *Psychology and Industrial Efficiency* (Boston: Houghton Mifflin, 1913).
37. "Der Mensch produziert ständig Wunschphantasien, denn er ist niemals wunschlos glücklich. Diese Illusionen zu erkennen, ist die erste Aufgabe des Werbefachmannes. Dann hat er tausend Anknüpfungspunkte und seine Aufgabe besteht darin. Wunsche und Waren miteinander zu verknüpfen." Edmund Heilpern, "Nützt uns die Psychoanalyse?," *Die Reklame,* April 1932, 253.
38. Roland Barthes, *Camera Lucida: Reflections on Photography,* trans. Richard Howard (1980; trans., New York: Hill and Wang, 1981), 96.
39. "aber diese eindrücke haben nichts oder nur sehr wenig mit jener dame zu tun, die vor dem maler saß, als er zeichnete." Max Burchartz, "handscrift–type, zeichnung–foto," *Gebrauchsgraphik* 3, no. 8 (August 1926): 42.
40. "die fotografie vermittelt uns eine deutliche vorstellung von der erscheinung der dargestellten person; wir erkennen sie wieder, wenn sie uns auf der straße begegnet. die weichheit der lichtverhältnisse und der reichtum der zwischentöne entspricht dem eindruck, den wir haben, wenn wir den gegenstand in der realität von uns zu sehen." Burchartz, 41.
41. Marcus Adams, "Tone versus Line," *Commercial Art,* November 1922, 33.
42. Charles Wormald, "Camera Craft in Advertising," *Commercial Art,* September–October 1925, 209.

43. Adams, "Tone versus Line," 33.
44. "so sieht man doch hinreichend, welche Möglichkeiten und Reize selbst—oder gerade—bei einfachstem Aufbau und ungekünstelter Beleuchtung, in der photographischen Platte schlummern." (One can clearly see what possibilities and stimuli lie slumbering in the photographic plate, even with the simplest structure and natural lighting.) Giebelhausen, "Der Photograph als Werbehelfer," 1003.
45. This advertising campaign was backed by the Deutsches Hygiene-Museum in Dresden, of which Chlorodont was a major sponsor. See "Chlorodont-Schaubild, um 1950," Technisches Museum Wien, accessed November 20, 2019, https://www.technischesmuseum.at/object/chlorodont-schaubild-um-1950 (page discontinued).
46. Sapiens, "Anzeigen-Kritik," *Die Reklame,* November 1932, 612.
47. Sabine T. Kriebel, *Revolutionary Beauty: The Radical Photomontages of John Heartfield* (Berkeley: University of California Press, 2014); Sabine T. Kriebel, "Touch, Absorption, and Radical Politics in the Magazine: The Case of John Heartfield," *Kritische Berichte* 40, no. 4 (2012): 21–31.
48. The Weimar era saw the publication of numerous books and popular articles on hands and physiognomy. See, for example, Adolf Koelsch, *Die Hände und was sie sagen* (Zurich: O. Füssli, 1929); and Walter Tritsch, "Die Seele der Hände," *die neue linie,* February 1930, 18–19, 46. Stephanie D'Alessandro has noted that ideas about the hand as a reliable sign of character, and as an active agent, were promoted through tropes of popular culture as well as graphology, psychotechnics, and chirology. See Stephanie D'Alessandro, "Through the Eye and the Hand: Constructing Space, Constructing Vision in the Work of Moholy-Nagy," in *Moholy-Nagy: Future Present,* ed. Matthew S. Witkovsky, Carol S. Eliel, and Karole P. B. Vail (Chicago: Art Institute of Chicago, 2016), 66.
49. This trope was used to stand in for the hands of a seller as well, but according to my own observations, it was increasingly used to suggest the hands of a consumer as photographic illustrations became more commonplace in advertising.
50. Here I am indebted to Jennifer Greenhill's analysis of the activation of magazine design through handling and motion. See especially Jennifer A. Greenhill, "Flip, Linger, Glide: Coles Phillips and the Movements of Magazine Pictures," *Art History* 40, no. 3 (2017): 582–611.
51. Kriebel, "Touch, Absorption, and Radical Politics in the Magazine."
52. Terry Smith, *Making the Modern: Industry, Art, and Design in America* (Chicago: University of Chicago Press, 1993), 183.
53. Smith, 183.
54. Traugott Schalcher, "Advertising and Naturalism," *Gebrauchsgraphik* 6, no. 4 (April 1929): 49–57.

55. Schalcher, 52.
56. Schalcher, 52–53.
57. Schalcher, 53.
58. Siegfried Kracauer, *The Mass Ornament: Weimar Essays,* trans. Thomas Y. Levin (1963; trans., Cambridge, Mass.: Harvard University Press, 1995), 54–55.
59. Kracauer, 54–55. His language here invokes the idea of showing archetypes in German advertising in accordance with the ethos of *Typisierung.* This popular strategy, promoted by a faction of the Deutscher Werkbund, favored the design of objects as ideal "types" that reflected collective taste, as opposed to objects as expressions of the individual taste of their makers. See Frederic J. Schwartz, *The Werkbund: Design Theory and Mass Culture before the First World War* (New Haven, Conn.: Yale University Press, 1996).
60. Schalcher, "Advertising and Naturalism," 57.
61. David Charles, "Photographic Stunts in Advertising," *Commercial Art,* July 1931, 17–22.
62. Wood engraving had been the dominant medium of illustration since the beginning of the illustrated press. Rather than being replaced wholesale by halftone reproduction, wood engraving continued after the halftone came into popular use. Moreover, some halftone retouching included reengraving on the block, keeping the high-contrast aesthetic of wood engraving in fashion even as photography assimilated to the conventions of print illustration. See Beegan, *Mass Image,* 160–85.
63. Beegan, 177.
64. Beegan, 175.
65. Peter Behrens's comprehensive work for AEG—including the company's logo, stationary, product design, advertising, and architectural design of the AEG Turbine Factory in Berlin—was an important precedent for interwar corporate design commissions by New Typographers including Willi Baumeister, César Domela-Nieuwenhuis, Franz Krause, Robert Michel, Paul Schuitema, and Piet Zwart. For a thorough study of Behrens's work for AEG, see Tilmann Buddensieg and Henning Rogge, *"Industriekultur": Peter Behrens and the AEG,* trans. Iain Boyd Whyte (Cambridge, Mass.: MIT Press, 1984).
66. "The Art of Retouching the Photograph," *Commercial Art,* December 1923, 340–41, 343.
67. "Art of Retouching the Photograph," 341.
68. "Art of Retouching the Photograph," 341.
69. "Art of Retouching the Photograph," 341.
70. "Art of Retouching the Photograph," 343.
71. Eric N. Simons, "Retouching and Retouching," *Commercial Art,* November 1925, 230.

72. László Moholy-Nagy, "Photography in Advertising," in Phillips, *Photography in the Modern Era,* 87. Originally published as "Die Photographie in der Reklame," *Photographische Korrespondenz,* 1927.
73. Moholy-Nagy, "Photography in Advertising," 86.
74. Moholy-Nagy, 86.
75. Paul Renner, "The Photograph," in Phillips, *Photography in the Modern Era,* 165. Originally published as "Das Lichtbild," *Die Form,* 1930.
76. Paul Renner, *Mechanisierte Grafik* (Berlin: Verlag Hermann Reckendorf, 1930), 96.
77. Franz Roh, *Nach-Expressionismus: Magischer Realismus, Probleme der neuesten europäischen Malerei* (Leipzig: Klinkhardt and Biermann, 1925), 46. For a brief discussion of Roh's commentary on Citroen's photocollage, reproduced in *Nach-Expressionismus,* see chapter 3, above.
78. Jan Tschichold borrowed this phrase from Roh in his notes for the unrealized book *Fotomontage,* written circa 1930–31. For a thorough discussion of this planned publication, and the influence of Roh on New Typography, see chapter 3, above.
79. "Die Reize eines Fantasiegebildes verbinden sich mit der Anziehungskraft von Darstellungen, die den Akzent der Wahrheit tragen. Den Fotobildern wird geglaubt, weil sie die Welt wiedergeben, wie wir sie kennen. Die Montage ändert an ihnen nicht prinzipiell, sondern fügt sie nur in einem neuen Sinne, Wesentliches heraushebend, aneinander." Otto Bettmann, "Aufbaugesetze der Fotomontage," *Archiv für Buchgewerbe und Gebrauchsgraphik* 68, no. 6 (1931): 228.
80. "Einheitliche Struktur der Fotomontage ist schließlich auch in der Farbtönung erforderlich. Durch Auswägung der Gegensätze oder Nivellierung der Tonwerte kann diesem Gebot Genüge getan werden. Farblich überbetonte Teile, die kein Gegengewicht haben, vermögen die Einheit des Ganzen zu zerstören. Lau wirkende Partien nehmen der Fläche den Halt. Das klare Hervortreten der Grundidee, das ja alle kompositionelle Arbeit bestimmt, scheint damit in Frage gestellt. Auch hier kann durch Einbeziehung von zeichnerischen Elementen, durch Verwendung von Tonplatten und mit Hilfe der Spritztechnik ein Ausgleich geschaffen werden." (A consistent structure in photomontage is also necessary in terms of color tones. This requirement can be met by balancing contrasts or leveling tonal values. Overemphasized color parts without a counterbalance can destroy the unity of the whole. Dull areas undermine the stability of the surface. This calls into question the clear presentation of the central idea that guides all compositional work. Here, too, a balance can be achieved by incorporating drawing, underpainting, and airbrushing.) Bettmann, 230.
81. "Alle Prozesse aber sind zwecklos, wenn sie nicht von vornherein durch die Intention auf ein klarerfaßtes künstlerisches Ganzes bestimmt und geeint werden." Bettmann, 231.

82. "Bildrichtung und Typenrichtung scheinen ausgeglichen. Tonlich fügt sich die Schrift dem Schwartz-Weiß von Bild und Hintergrund ein, so daß sie nicht mehr als Fremdkörper erscheint, sondern als Stütze der Gesamtstruktur." Bettmann, 231.
83. I am grateful to Megan Luke for her observation that *Photoplastik* best translates to "photo-plasticity" in this instance.
84. Moholy-Nagy, "Photography in Advertising," 92.
85. *die neue linie* was published in Leipzig by Beyer-Verlag, the imprint of Otto Beyer. It began as a relaunch of the women's magazine *Frauen-Mode*. Its 1929 incarnation as *die neue linie* was modeled in part after the American women's fashion and lifestyle magazine *Vanity Fair*. See Patrick Rössler, *Das Bauhaus am Kiosk: "die neue linie," 1929–1943* (Bielefeld: Kerber Art; New York: Distributed Art Publishers, 2009).

5 *TYPOPHOTO* AND THE PROFESSIONALIZATION OF GRAPHIC DESIGN

1. Existing scholarship in English has tended to sideline *Kunstgewerbeschules* in Germany, which were primary sites where modernist designers introduced modernist theory and technique into design curricula. Schools that have received the most scholarly attention, namely the Reimann Schule in Berlin and the Dessau Bauhaus, offered graphic design training among many other subjects and assimilated many of the innovations of the *Kunstgewerbeschules*. At the Reimann Schule, Julius Klinger offered the first poster design course in 1911, and Max Hertwig began teaching a course on *Gebrauchsgraphik* in 1913. Carl Gadau taught courses on calligraphy, poster design, and advertising design at the Reimann Schule beginning in 1920. See Albert Reimann, ed., *25 Jahre Schule Reimann, 1902–1927: Ausstellung Kunst-Gewerbe-Museum, Prinz Albrecht-Str., 1.–14. April 1927* (Berlin: Verlag Schule Reimann, 1927), 11. See also Jeremy Aynsley, *Graphic Design in Germany, 1890–1945* (Berkeley: University of California Press, 2000), 102–14. By 1925, a graphic design curriculum was under development at the Dessau Bauhaus, formalized by 1929 as the printing and publicity workshop. For histories of the Reimann Schule, see Swantje Kuhfuss-Wickenheiser, *Die Reimann-Schule in Berlin und London, 1902–1943: Ein jüdisches Unternehmen zur Kunst- und Designausbildung internationaler Prägung bis zur Vernichtung durch das Hitlerregime* (Aachen: Shaker Media, 2009); Albert Reimann, *Die Reimann-Schule in Berlin* (Berlin: Verlag Bruno Hessling, 1966); and Hans M. Wingler, ed., *Kunstschulreform, 1900–1933: Bauhaus Weimar, Dessau, Berlin, Kunstschule Debschitz, München, Frankfurter Kunstschule, Akademie Breslau, Reimann-Schule Berlin* (Berlin: Mann Verlag and Bauhaus-Archiv, 1977). For studies of the Bauhaus, see Barry Bergdoll and Leah Dickerman, *Bauhaus, 1919–1933: Workshops for Modernity* (New York: Museum of Modern Art, 2009); Ute Brüning, ed., *Das A und O des Bauhauses. Bauhauswerbung: Schriftbilder, Drucksachen, Ausstellungsdesign* (Berlin: Bauhaus-Archiv, 1995); Ute

Brüning, "Joost Schmidt: Ein Curriculum für Werbegrafiker," in *Bauhauskommunikation: Innovative Strategien im Umgang mit Medien, interner und externer Öffentlichkeit,* ed. Patrick Rössler (Berlin: Mann Verlag and Bauhaus-Archiv, 2009), 257–64; Magdalena Droste, *Bauhaus: Reform and Avant-Garde, 1919–1933* (Cologne: Taschen, 1993); and Rainer K. Wick, *Teaching at the Bauhaus* (Stuttgart: Hatje Cantz, 2000).

2. Examples include the Frankfurter Kunstschule, Akademie für Kunst und Kunstgewerbe Breslau, and the Leipzig Meisterschule für das Buchdruckgewerbe.
3. The full name of the school was Meisterschule für Deutschlands Buchdrucker, Schule der Stadt München und des Deutschen Buchdrucker-Vereins (Master School for German Printers, School of the City of Munich, and the German Printers Association).
4. Christopher Burke, *Paul Renner: The Art of Typography* (London: Hyphen, 1998), 59.
5. Burke, 59.
6. "Die Absicht, die der Deutsche Buchdrucker-Verein bei der Gründung der Schule hatte, ist damit erreicht: den Söhnen seiner Mitglieder und anderen strebsamen jungen Kräften des deutschen Buchgewerbes ist heute in München Gelegenheit geboten, sich **systematisch und methodisch** auf ihren Beruf vorbereiten zu lassen." Pamphlet, "Der Ausbau der Meisterschule ist jetzt vollendet!," circa 1932, box 23, Nachlass Jan Tschichold, Deutsches Buch- und Schriftmuseum der Deutschen Nationalbibliothek, Leipzig. Emphasis in bold is original to the pamphlet text.
7. For a history of offset printing, see Richard Benson, *The Printed Picture* (New York: Museum of Modern Art, 2008); and Michael Twyman, *Printing, 1770–1970: An Illustrated History of its Development and Uses in England* (London: British Library; Reading: Reading University Press, 1998).
8. Though Renner only stayed in Frankfurt from July 1925 until early 1926, Christopher Burke notes that the reorganization of the school in tandem with Ernst May's plans for urban housing in Frankfurt seem to have had a major impact on Renner's approach to design education in Munich. See Burke, *Paul Renner,* 54–58.
9. Renner founded the school in conjunction with an overhaul of the faculty and curriculum of the Graphische Berufsschule. When the Meisterschule opened on February 1, 1927, it shared a building, teaching staff, and other resources with the Graphische Berufsschule. Burke, 59–63.
10. Tschichold also taught courses at the adjoining Graphische Berufschule. Before fleeing Germany, Tschichold was briefly imprisoned after a gestapo raid of his apartment turned up Russian children's books. Jeffrey Ladd, "Making *60 Fotos,*" in *László Moholy-Nagy: 60 Fotos,* by László Moholy-Nagy, essays by David Evans, Franz Roh, and Jeffrey Ladd (New York: Errata Editions, 2011), n.p. First English-language edition of Moholy-Nagy's 1930 work.

11. Burke, *Paul Renner,* 57.
12. Georg Trump's address in the Borstei Wohnsiedlung on Hildebrandtstrasse is confirmed on documents found in Box TRUM.5, Typographische Vorbildsammlung von Jan Tschichold, Bibliothek für Gestaltung Basel. For references to Roh's residence at Borstei, see Inka Graeve Ingelmann, "Mechanics and Expression: Franz Roh and the New Vision—a Historical Sketch," in *Object:Photo. Modern Photographs: The Thomas Walther Collection, 1909–1949. An Online Project of the Museum of Modern Art,* ed. Mitra Abbaspour, Lee Ann Daffner, and Maria Morris Hambourg (New York: Museum of Modern Art, 2014), https://www.moma.org/interactives/objectphoto/assets/essays/GraeveIngelmann.pdf.
13. Borstei was among a number of German and Austrian housing projects built in this period—including Karl Marx-Hof in Vienna, Weißenhofsiedlung in Stuttgart, Hufeisensiedlung in Berlin, and Das Neue Frankfurt—which offered new models for living collectively, economically, and with access to green space in fast-growing urban centers.
14. Gewidmet Bernhard and Erna Borst, *Die Kunstwerke der Borstei* (Munich: Borstei-Museum, 2010), 127; Jakob Wetzel, "Designer erforschen eigene Geschichte," *Süddeutsche Zeitung München,* July 17, 2017, https://www.sueddeutsche.de/muenchen/blick-zurueck-designer-erforschen-eigene-geschichte-1.3551159.
15. A number of unpublished lecture notes and printed flyers promoting Tschichold's public lectures on New Typography in Munich, from 1927 and 1928, are found in box 74, Nachlass Jan Tschichold, Deutsches Buch- und Schriftmuseum der Deutschen Nationalbibliothek, Leipzig.
16. Franz Roh and Jan Tschichold, *foto-auge: 76 fotos der zeit* (Stuttgart: Fritz Wedekind, 1929); László Moholy Nagy, *László Moholy-Nagy: 60 Fotos* (Berlin: Klinkhardt and Biermann, 1930); Aenne Biermann, *Aenne Biermann: 60 Fotos* (Berlin: Klinkhardt and Biermann, 1930).
17. See chapter 3, above, for a thorough discussion of Roh's influence on Tschichold's concept of New Typography and *Typophoto,* especially in relation to the unwritten book *Fotomontage.*
18. The inclusion of anonymous student designers in the history of New Typography is especially important given that many of their designs have been erroneously attributed to Tschichold. See, for example, Cees W. de Jong, ed., *Jan Tschichold, Master Typographer: His Life, Work and Legacy* (London: Thames & Hudson, 2008), 72, 74–75.
19. László Moholy-Nagy, *Malerei Photographie Film* (Munich: Albert Langen Verlag, 1925), 38–40.
20. See, for example, Charles W. Hackleman, *Commercial Engraving and Printing: A Manual of Practical Instruction Covering Commercial Illustrating and Printing by All Processes*

(Indianapolis: Commercial Engraving Publishing Company, 1921); R. Russ and L. Englich, *Handbuch der Modernen Reproduktionstechnik: Band I, Reproduktionsphotographie und Retusche* (Frankfurt am Main: Verlag von Klimsch and Co., 1927); and International Correspondence Schools, *Retouching for Halftones, Part 1* (Scranton, Pa.: International Textbook Company, 1921).

21. The Berufliches Schulzentrum (BSZ) Alois Senefelder is located in the central Maxvorstadt district of Munich. In 1956, the Meisterschule was renamed the Akademie für das Graphische Gewerbe, and again in 1973 as the Berufsbildungszentrum für Druck, Grafik und Fotografie. In 1999, the school was given its current name. The BSZ Alois Senefelder is a consortium of technical programs, which include training in bookbinding, paper processing, advertising design, printing, and photography. See "Schulgeschichte des BSZ Alois Senefelder," Berufliches Schulzentrum Alois Senefelder München, accessed November 12, 2019, http://www.senefelder.musin.de/index.php?id=schulgeschichte.
22. The original school building was partially destroyed by Allied bombing in the Second World War, and the present-day building was completed in 1952. Heinz Kal Schmid and Klaus Buchegger, eds., *Broschüre zur 100-Jahr-Feier des BSZ Alois Senefelder* (Munich: Berufliches Schulzentrum Alois Senefelder, 2006), 14.
23. "Sie will den Schüler theoretisch und praktisch zum Leiter einer Druckerei ausbilden." Josef Käufer, "Der Unterricht im Satz und Druck an der Meisterschule für Deutschlands Buchdrucker in München," *Archiv für Buchgewerbe und Gebrauchsgraphik* 68, no. 3 (1931): 486.
24. "Die Schule vermeidet es deshalb bewußt, zum Spezialistentum in irgendeiner Sparte zu erziehen. Der intensive und energisch betriebene, von Meistern auf diesem Gebiet betreute künstlerisch-typographische Unterricht sieht sein Ziel weniger darin, zum versierten ersten Akzidenzsetzer zu erziehen, als vielmehr den Leiter der modernen Setzerei heranzubilden und ihm wie dem künftigen Betriebsleiter oder Buchdruckereibesitzer jene Unterlagen zu vermitteln, die ihm helfen, die geistige Haltung seines Betriebes zu bestimmen." Käufer, 486.
25. "Es entsteht, wie sich dies in den letzten Jahren deutlich herausgestellt hat, sehr bald eine Werkgemeinschaft, eine Werkgesinnung, die wesentlich dazu beiträgt, daß der Betrieb das gebrauchsfähige Werkzeug bleibt, das er in geordnetem Zustand darstellen soll, und daß damit ein angenehmes, befriedigendes Arbeiten für jeden Schüler gewährleistet ist." Käufer, 487.
26. "Er wird damit zwangsläufig ein brauchbares Mitglied unsers Berufes werden, gleichgültig, an welche Stelle ihn seine besondere Befähigung oder der ihm vorgezeichnete Weg führen sollte." Käufer, 488.
27. Frederic Schwartz notes that the idea of the German *Werkstatt* (namely the Vereinigte Werkstätten and Dresdener Werkstätten) came from William Morris's novel

News from Nowhere (1890), which described "banded-workshops" as collective workspaces for the production of handcrafted objects. See Schwartz, *Blind Spots: Critical Theory and the History of Art in Twentieth-Century Germany* (New Haven, Conn.: Yale University Press, 2005), 159–60. See also John Heskett, *German Design, 1870–1918* (New York: Taplinger, 1986), 93. In 1891, Morris founded Kelmscott Press, which was an important model for preserving techniques of making, printing, and binding books by hand as an alternative to the industrial press. See William S. Peterson, *The Kelmscott Press: A History of William Morris's Typographical Adventure* (Berkeley: University of California Press, 1991).

28. David Jury, *Reinventing Print: Technology and Craft in Typography* (London: Bloomsbury, 2018), 38–39.
29. Jury, 39. For more on the Debschitz-Schule, see Wingler, *Kunstschulreform.*
30. Christopher Burke, *Active Literature: Jan Tschichold and New Typography* (London: Hyphen, 2007), 54.
31. Mechanized typesetting included the casting, composing, and line justifying of type. These processes were still relatively new in the late 1920s and early 1930s. See Lucien Alphonse Legros, *Typographical Printing-Surfaces: The Technology and Mechanism of their Production* (London: Longmans, Green, 1916), 279–452. Linotype machines, used to mechanically set lines of type, were introduced commercially in 1886. See S. H. Steinberg, *Five Hundred Years of Printing,* new ed. (London: British Library; New Castle, Del.: Oak Knoll Press, 2001), 170–72.
32. The images featured in the school's printed promotional materials are the only extant photographic evidence of its activities that I have found.
33. Burke, *Active Literature,* 57–59; Schmid and Buchegger, *Broschüre zur 100-Jahr-Feier des BSZ Alois Senefelder,* 15–24.
34. Jury, *Reinventing Print,* 38–39.
35. Meisterschule für Deutschlands Buchdrucker, München, "Typographische Beilagen und Schulprospekt," *Archiv für Buchgewerbe und Gebrauchsgraphik* 69, no. 8 (1932): 375. See also Burke, *Active Literature,* 56–57.
36. Meisterschule für Deutschlands Buchdrucker, München, "Typographische Beilagen und Schulprospekt," 5–6.
37. "Vorrechte für die Meisterschule?," *Typographische Mitteilungen* 29, no. 5 (May 1932): 101.
38. "Vorrechte für die Meisterschule?," 101.
39. This article noted that the evaluation of printers by vocational schoolteachers was opposed by some business organizations, but did not specify further. "Vorrechte für die Meisterschule?," 101.
40. Julia Meer, *Neuer Blick auf die Neue Typographie: Die Rezeption der Avantgarde in der Fachwelt der 1920er Jahre* (Bielefeld: transcript Verlag, 2015), 329.

41. Burke, *Active Literature,* 57–59. This tenure was interrupted when Georg Trump was drafted into the German Army in 1939 and discharged in 1945. He subsequently continued to serve as director of the Meisterschule until he retired from teaching in 1953. See Neil Macmillan, *An A–Z of Type Designers* (London: Laurence King, 2006), 174; and Schmid and Buchegger, *Broschüre zur 100-Jahr-Feier des BSZ Alois Senefelder,* 20.
42. Gerry Beegan, "Staring at the Screen: The Halftone Comes to Light," AIGA, July 31, 2007, accessed November 26, 2019, https://aigaaixom5kinte.dxcloud.episerver.net/staring-at-the-screen-the-halftone-comes-to-light (site discontinued).
43. Bettmann, "Georg Trump," 425–26. See Bettmann, "Georg Trump," *Archiv für Buchgewerbe und Gebrauchsgraphik* 68, no. 3 (1931): 425. For further information on *Pressa,* see Jeremy Aynsley, "Pressa Cologne, 1928: Exhibitions and Publication Design in the Weimar Period," *Design Issues* 10, no. 3 (1994): 52–76; and *Die Pressa: Katalog des Sowjets Pavillon auf der Internationale Presse-Ausstellung,* exhibition catalogue (Cologne: Dumont Verlag, 1928).
44. Georg Trump trained as a typographer at the Staatliche Kunstgewerbeschule in Stuttgart under German typographer Friedrich Hermann Ernst Schneidler, but his studies were interrupted by his first tour in the German Army during World War I. From 1923 to 1926, he lived in Italy, where he practiced ceramics, painting, and drawing. See Bettmann, 425.
45. "trump selbst betrachtet diese arbeiten als seine wesentlicheren leistungen. er will ungern sich nur reinen typographen stempeln lassen." Bettmann, 426.
46. "als freier künstler, der nicht setze übernimmt, sondern für jede arbeit ganz original ein neues gesetz schafft, hat er die typographie der letzten jahre massgeblich beeinflusst . . . trump will nicht künstlerische, ästhetisierende formen schaffen, in denen das material vergewaltigt wird. er ist handwerklich orientiert und von solchem boden aus erreichen seine schöpfungen das niveau der kunst." Bettmann, 426.
47. "er lässt die schüler sich nicht festlegen auf dogmatische formen. er zwingt sie vielmehr, jede arbeit von grund auf neu zu durchdenken—aber er zwingt sie auch, streng auf dem boden der technischen gegebenheiten zu verbleiben." Bettmann, 426.
48. A. G., "Die Bielefelder 'Richtung,'" *Typographische Mitteilungen* 29, no. 1 (January 1932), 5–6.
49. A. G., 5.
50. A. G., 6.
51. André Reuze, *Giganten der Landstraße* (Berlin: Büchergilde Gutenberg, 1928).
52. "an diese aufgabe ist trump kühn herangegangen. jedem bild gibt er eine besondere stellung auf der seite, eine besondere grösse, je nach gehalt und bedeutung, so das seine wirkliche einheit von type und photo entsteht." Bettmann, "Georg Trump," 426.

53. Otto Mente, "Autotypie nach Autotypie," *Deutscher Drucker* 37, no. 1 (October 1930): 20–23.
54. A copy of Paul Renner's *Zur Farbenlehre* is located in box 24, Nachlass Jan Tschichold, Deutsches Buch- und Schriftmuseum der Deutschen Nationalbibliothek, Leipzig. As far as I am aware, this brochure was only printed at the Meisterschule and not published elsewhere.
55. Paul Renner, *Ordnung und Harmonie der Farben. Eine Farbenlehre für Künstler und Handwerker* (Ravensburg: Otto Maier Verlag, 1947). An English translation was later published as *Color: Order and Harmony; a Color Theory for Artists and Craftsmen,* trans. Alexander Nesbitt (New York: Reinhold, 1964).
56. Renner, *Zur Farbenlehre,* 25–31.
57. A proof copy of this design is located in box 23, Nachlass Jan Tschichold, Deutsches Buch- und Schriftmuseum der Deutschen Nationalbibliothek, Leipzig. There is no evidence that this design was ever submitted to *Gebrauchsgraphik* for publication.
58. *Gebrauchsgraphik* (formerly *Das Plakat*) was founded in 1924 and became the official organ of the Association of German Graphic Designers (Bund Deutscher Graphiker) in 1928. It also circulated widely outside Germany, and its feature articles were printed in both German and English. The journal was edited by Hermann K. Frenzel until it ceased publication in 1937. See Jeremy Aynsley, "*Gebrauchsgraphik* as an Early Design Journal, 1924–38," *Journal of Design History* 5, no. 1 (1992): 53–72; and Patrick Rössler, *Eine Zeitschrift als gedrucktes Schaufenster zur Werbewelt: "Gebrauchsgraphik" 1924–1944* (Munich: Stiebner, 2014).
59. City was released in 1931 by the Berlin-based Berthold Type Foundry. "Slab serif" refers to the block-like thickness of serifs in this type family. While slab serif typefaces were popularized in the nineteenth century, City is a good example of New Typography's relevance not only to the design of sans serif typefaces like Paul Renner's Futura, but to the modulation of serif typefaces as well. See *Vita Activa: Georg Trump. Bilder, Schriften und Schriftbilder* (Munich: Typographische Gesellschaft, 1967); and Alexander Lawson, *Anatomy of a Typeface* (Boston: David R. Godine, 1990).
60. *Vita Activa,* 60–61.
61. The Polish-German commercial artist Valentin Zietara was a member of the New Association of Munich Poster Artists (Neue Vereinigung Münchner Plakatkünstler), a group that included Ludwig Hohlwein and established in 1931 with the intent to preserve artistry in commercial design. An article on the association was included in the August 1931 issue of *Gebrauchsgraphik* that featured Zietara's cover design, and a short feature was published in the April 1932 issue of *Die Reklame.* See also Rössler, *Eine Zeitschrift als gedrucktes Schaufenster zur Werbewelt,* 146. The aesthetic championed by this group stood in stark contrast to the speculative cover made at the

Meisterschule, which was clearly aligned with the so-called *Bielefelder Richtung* associated with Georg Trump.

62. Renner, *Zur Farbenlehre.* Renner further aligned himself with Goethe by critiquing the controversial remarks on color theory made by German chemist Wilhelm Ostwald at the 1919 meeting of the Deutscher Werkbund, held in Stuttgart. Renner rejected Ostwald's claim that artists could perfect their work by applying an objective, scientifically based understanding of color, which Renner regarded as too narrow regarding subjective experiences of color. See Joan Campbell, *The German Werkbund: The Politics of Reform in the Applied Arts* (Princeton, N.J.: Princeton University Press, 1978), 138–39.
63. This argument aligned with the findings of contemporary applied psychology research on perception discussed in chapter 2, above.
64. Friedrich Kittler, *Optical Media: Berlin Lectures, 1999,* trans. Anthony Enns (Cambridge: Polity Press, 2010), 124.
65. Goethe's discussions of creating harmonious totality through color combinations were part of his broader, holistic approach to nature that was particularly influential in the field of natural science as it developed in the early twentieth century in Germany. See Anne Harrington, *Reenchanted Science: Holism in German Culture from Wilhelm II to Hitler* (Princeton, N.J.: Princeton University Press, 1996).
66. Renner, *Zur Farbenlehre,* 45. Here, Renner quotes Goethe directly.
67. Renner, 45.
68. Renner, 55–62.
69. Renner, 53.
70. Cameraless photographs, commonly known as photograms, are created by placing objects on light-sensitive photographic paper or cloth and exposing the material to light. This technique served diverse purposes in the nineteenth century, from marketing intricate lace patterns to imaging botanical specimens. For histories of the photogram, see Martin Barnes, *Cameraless Photography* (London: Thames and Hudson and V and A Publishing, 2019); and Geoffrey Batchen, *Emanations: The Art of the Cameraless Photograph* (Munich: Prestel, 2016).
71. Larry J. Schaaf, *Sun Gardens: Victorian Photograms by Anna Atkins* (New York: Aperture, 1985), 8–9.
72. Borrowing from theories by Jeff Wall and Walter Benjamin, Silverman has drawn a stark distinction between what she sees as two distinct ways of understanding photography: as an analogical medium, a conduit for the "unstoppable development" of unfixed images received from nature, on the one hand; and as an industrial medium used to control nature through the production (and reproduction) of fixed, mechanical images, on the other. See Kaja Silverman, *The Miracle of Analogy or The History of*

Photography, Part 1 (Stanford, Calif.: Stanford University Press, 2015). See also Jeff Wall, "Liquid Intelligence," in *Works and Collected Writings* (Barcelona: Poligrafa, 2007), n.p.; and Walter Benjamin, "Little History of Photography" (1931), in *Walter Benjamin: Selected Writings*, vol. 2, ed. Michael W. Jennings, Howard Eiland and Gary Smith (Cambridge, Mass.: Harvard University Press, 1999), 507–30.

73. Bertrand Russell, "Vagueness," *Australian Journal of Psychology and Philosophy* 1, no. 2 (1923): 89.
74. Russell, 89.
75. Michelle Chang, "Something Vague," *Log*, no. 44 (Fall 2018): 103–13.
76. Lev Manovich, *The Language of New Media* (Cambridge, Mass.: MIT Press, 2001), 28.
77. Chang, "Something Vague," 111.
78. Manovich, *Language of New Media*, 28.
79. Manovich, 28.
80. László Moholy-Nagy, "Photography in Advertising," in *Photography in the Modern Era: European Documents and Critical Writings, 1913–40*, ed. and trans. Christopher Phillips (New York: Metropolitan Museum of Art, 1989), 88. Originally published as "Die Photographie in der Reklame," *Photographische Korrespondenz*, 1927.
81. Burke, *Active Literature*, 55.
82. In 1927, Futura was issued by the Bauerische Gießerei in Frankfurt. While working on it, Renner sent early sketches to Tschichold. See Alston W. Purvis, "Tschichold and the New Typography," in de Jong, *Jan Tschichold, Master Typographer*, 44.

EPILOGUE

1. *Gebrauchsgraphik* 18, no. 11 (November 1941).
2. In this early moment of digital graphic design, Greiman and others used Macintosh computers and PageMaker composition software in combination with digital printing, screen printing, and traditional offset printing. See April Greiman, *Hybrid Imagery: The Fusion of Technology and Graphic Design*, ed. Eric Martin (New York: Watson–Guptill, 1990).
3. Greiman.
4. Marshall McLuhan, *Understanding Media: The Extensions of Man* (New York: McGraw Hill, 1965), 7.
5. McLuhan, 22.
6. Francesco Casetti and Antonio Somaini, "Resolution: Digital Materialities, Thresholds of Visibility," NECSUS *European Journal of Media Studies* 7, no. 1 (2018): 88.
7. Casetti and Somaini, 88.

INDEX

JESSICA D. BRIER, PhD, serves as curator of photography at the Frances Lehman Loeb Art Center, Vassar College. She is coeditor of *Making a Life in Photography: Rollie McKenna* and editor of *On the Grid: Ways of Seeing in Print*.